WERNER RINGS

Life with the Enemy

Collaboration and Resistance
in Hitler's Europe
1939–1945

TRANSLATED BY
J. MAXWELL BROWNJOHN

WEIDENFELD AND NICOLSON
LONDON

For Ruth

CONTENTS

ILLUSTRATIONS

Fernand de Brinon and Yves Bouthillier at Salle Wagram, Paris (Archiv für Kunst & Geschichte, Berlin).
Hitler and Pétain at Montoire (Archiv Kindler, Zurich).
Attack on Gestapo Headquarters, Copenhagen (Nationalmuseet, Copenhagen).
Copenhagen street barricades (Nationalmuseet, Copenhagen).
Tito, May 1943 (Keystone, Hamburg).
Italian partisan unit (Archiv Kindler, Zurich).
Soviet partisan army (Archiv Kindler, Zurich).
Soviet partisans with radioed orders (Bundesarchiv, Koblenz).
Norwegian resistance training (Ullstein Bilderdienst, Berlin).
Danish railroad crew (Archiv für Kunst & Geschichte, Berlin).
Witold Pilecki (by courtesy of Józef Garliński, London).
Auschwitz barracks (Archiv Kindler, Zurich).
Lysander courier plane (Archiv Kindler, Zurich).
The "Kattegat Bridge" to England (Archiv Kindler, Zurich).
Churchill with Sikorski and General de Gaulle (Keystone, Hamburg).
SS troops in the Warsaw ghetto (Süddeutscher Verlag, Munich).
Generals Zervas and Scobie, and Colonel Sarafis (Bundesarchiv, Koblenz).
British forces in Athens under General Scobie (Archiv Zentner, Munich).
Warsaw uprising: the prisoners (Süddeutscher Verlag, Munich).
Warsaw uprising: the capitulation (Süddeutscher Verlag, Munich).
Warsaw after evacuation (Ullstein Bilderdienst, Berlin).
Randolph Churchill with Yugoslav partisans (Archiv Kindler, Zurich).
Tito and partisan commanders (Süddeutscher Verlag, Munich).
Draža Mihailović, a group of Tito's partisans (Archiv Kindler, Zurich).
Allied airdrop of small arms, France (Archiv Kindler, Zurich).
Partisans awaiting weapons drop (Imperial War Museum, London).
Executions in Yugoslavia (courtesy of Gerhard Gronefeld, Munich).
Special units of French Resistance (Archiv Kindler, Zurich).
Jean Moulin (Belgian Research Center on the History of the Second World War).
King Christian X, of Denmark (Royal Danish Ministry for Foreign Affairs, Copenhagen).
Werner Best (Ullstein Bilderdienst, Berlin).
Jewish Council workers (Archiv Kindler, Zurich).
The Dutch Jewish Council (courtesy of Joh. de Haas, Alkmaar).
Dutch Jewish police auxiliaries (Archiv Kindler, Zurich).
Knit caps in RAF colors, Denmark (Museet for Danmarks Frihedskamp, Copenhagen).
Forest *maquis* camp (Archiv Kindler, Zurich).
Dutch "Underground" residents (Archiv Kindler, Zurich).
Escape route map, Andrée Dejongh, forging documents (Archiv Kindler, Zurich).
Underground printing press (Archiv Kindler, Zurich).
Louis Aragon and Elsa Triolet (Bildarchiv Preussischer Kulturbesitz, Berlin).
Albert Camus and Paul Éluard (Ullstein Bilderdienst, Berlin).
Poster from De Gaulle (Süddeutscher Verlag, Munich).
Henri Frenay (Keystone, Hamburg).
General Delestraint (Studio X, Paris).
General Koenig (Süddeutscher Verlag, Munich).
Structure of the Combat organization (Archiv Kindler, Zurich).
Jan Kubis and Josef Gabčik (Bildarchiv Preussischer Kulturbesitz, Berlin).
SS officers find assassins in Prague (Süddeutscher Verlag, Munich).
Bombed trains on German supply lines (Museum voor het Onderwijs, 's Gravenhage).
Heavy-water plant in Rjukan (Süddeutscher Verlag, Munich).

PART ONE

The Grand Challenge

Hitler's Double Game

or

The Fruits of a Fruitless War

Hitler launched his war with a crime. On the evening of August 31, 1939, nine hours before his armies invaded Poland, armed SS men in Polish uniforms stormed a German forestry station on the borders of Upper Silesia. Simultaneously, other SS men posing as Poles attacked the German radio station at Gleiwitz. Having overpowered the staff and tied them up, they took over the broadcasting studio.

One of them went to the microphone and read out a proclamation which had been drafted by Reinhard Heydrich, chief of the German Security Police, and translated into Polish. A tirade against the Third Reich, it stated that Poland's patience was exhausted, and that her people had finally taken up arms.

The SS men withdrew, pistols blazing. To render their mock attack more credible, they left a wounded civilian at the entrance to the building. He was later identified as a prisoner named Franz Honiok, who had been arrested for the purpose and dumped there. The unfortunate man had been deliberately shot and fatally wounded in time to die at the scene as material evidence of Polish perfidy.[1]

At dawn, sixty more SS men disguised as Polish soldiers attacked the German customs post at Hochlinden, destroying the building and all the stores inside. This time, six dead "Poles" were left behind—in reality, selected prisoners from the Sachsenhausen concentration camp who had been murdered to serve as photographic models for the benefit of Hitler's press and propaganda machine.[2]

Hitler cited these "border incidents" the same day—"three extremely serious ones," he called them—when informing the Reichstag that fighting had broken out. Regular troops of the Polish Army had opened fire on German territory during the night, he declared, and German forces had been returning their fire since 5:45 A.M.[3]

Widely disseminated by domestic and international press agencies and heavily exploited for propaganda purposes by the German Foreign Office, Hitler's allegations and reports of the "border incidents" provoked by Poland were duly printed by the New York *Times* and other newspapers of international repute.[4]

Not just to drain the dregs of infamy, but in the hope of concealing the truth forever, the SS men involved in this successful charade were reputedly put to death.[5]

War. How had it come about?

Foremost among the factors that conduced to the disastrous outbreak of World War II was Hitler's cool and calculating duplicity—a double game which consisted in disguising his true intentions from the world at large.

That he wanted war was no secret to the observant eye. Everything, but everything, indicated that he was systematically preparing for it. But while swiftly rearming Germany and single-mindedly working toward the day when military conquest would bend the whole of Europe to his will, he contrived to attain his objective by stages. He outwitted his opponents again and again, presenting them with a rapid succession of accomplished facts but blinding them to his perilous grand design with fervent assurances of his pacific intentions. The more often this double game succeeded, the bigger and cheaper the dividends it paid while peace endured.

As late as the end of October 1938, Hitler instructed his Foreign Minister, Joachim von Ribbentrop, to offer the Polish ambassador in Berlin a whole quarter century of peace by proposing that the German-Polish non-aggression pact be extended to twenty-five years. His troops invaded Poland less than twelve months later.

This pact had been concluded on Hitler's initiative at the end of January 1934, one year after he assumed the chancellorship. It amounted to a joint disclaimer. The Polish and German Governments renounced the use of force and pledged themselves to resolve any future disputes by peaceful means. The treaty's original term had been ten years. To lend it due weight, both governments expressly subscribed to the principles of the 1928 Briand-Kellogg Pact, which outlawed war as a means of settling international differences.

Shortly after the treaty was signed, Hitler revealed its ulterior purpose to his closest associates. He told Hermann Rauschning, the then National Socialist president of the Danzig Senate, that the validity of any agreements with Poland was only temporary. He had no intention of building up a genuine German-Polish entente.

"I can reach an understanding with Soviet Russia any time I like," he added. "I can partition Poland whenever and however it suits me." The date of this cynical revelation? Early 1934.[6]

So Hitler's double game, which was not as transparent then as it subsequently became, dated from very early on. It shaped the prewar policies pursued by his European neighbors, who—for reasons to be explored below—persisted in basing them on a belief in his good intentions.

Taken at face value, Hitler's nonaggression pact with Poland seemed a cogent demonstration of his desire for peace. European governments soon warmed to the idea that the Reich Chancellor, whose earlier speeches and writings had often taken a bellicose line, should not be equated with the pugnacious party leader of yore. Had the most powerful man in Germany become reasonable, sociable, and—above all—predictable?

The development of German-Polish relations after the signing of the pact appeared to confirm this impression. Awkward disputes that might have led to friction between the treaty partners seemed to have been forgotten. As time went by, it was also noted with interest that Reich Minister Hermann Göring seized every opportunity, during the annual elk hunts in the Bielowiezer Heide, to make it clear to his Polish friends and hosts that a strong Poland was Hitler's dearest wish.

To the Poles, what happened in the crisis-ridden days that followed the Munich "peace" conference of September 1938 seemed to indicate that Hitler's word could be trusted to the hilt. He proved himself their friend, patron, and ally by permitting them to share in his seizure of the Czech Sudetenland. But for him, the Polish Army would never have ventured to invade Czech territory on the east bank of the Olsa and occupy nearly four hundred square miles of foreign soil with a population of 230,000. The Poles annexed this area, halting their troops on a demarcation line previously agreed to with Berlin.[7] They also received, as a mark of friendship, a sixty-million-reichsmark loan for the purchase of German machinery.

And so it went on. Early in January 1939, Hitler welcomed the Polish Foreign Minister, Colonel Józef Beck, to Berchtesgaden and showered him with tokens of the highest esteem. Three weeks later, and only seven months before the outbreak of war, a German Foreign Minister graced Warsaw with his presence for the first time in the history of the Polish Republic.

Much pomp and circumstance awaited the exalted visitor on his arrival in the Polish capital, which was awash with swastika flags and photographs of Hitler. Foreign Minister Ribbentrop attended celebrations marking the fifth anniversary of the nonaggression pact, a glittering state occasion, while Hitler himself paid tribute to German-Polish friendship in a speech delivered at the Berlin end.

Concurrently, the Chancellery and Foreign Office did their utmost to play down the gradual intensification of disputes over frontiers and ethnic minorities and the growing frequency of border incidents. Hitler's plan to absorb the Free Hanseatic City of Danzig and the Polish Corridor, which had been under diplomatic discussion since October 1938, was still represented as a mere wish—tentative, restrained, and uninsistent—not as a demand, far less an ultimatum.

This situation did not change until Hitler discarded his peacemaker's mask.

Many accounts have been written of the spectacle with which Germany's dictator confronted his startled neighbors and an uncomprehending world on March 15, 1939. For all his peaceful protestations, he tore up the Munich Agreement less than six months after signing it. He threatened the Czech President, Emil Hácha, with the imminent destruction of Prague by the Luftwaffe and made the older man grovel before him. German troops occupied "rump Czechia" pursuant to a secret directive issued five months earlier, and Bohemia and Moravia were declared a German protectorate.

A week later, when the Prague shock wave had barely subsided, Hitler sailed into the Lithuanian port of Memel aboard the pocket battleship *Deutschland*, escorted by fifty-nine naval units and a thousand German Navy personnel. Though strategically vital to Poland, the seaport itself was occupied and the surrounding territory wrested from the defenseless Lithuanians by means of an ultimatum and incorporated in the German Reich.

This came as a cruel disappointment and blatant challenge to the Poles, who responded with surprising vigor. The number of Polish troops under arms was promptly increased to four hundred thousand, and ten thousand of them were ordered into Gdynia, little more than ten miles from Danzig.

Politically, too, Warsaw's reaction was swift and unequivocal. Three days after Hitler's ominous appearance in Memel, the Polish Government conveyed its first flat rejection of Germany's demands for the reintegration of Danzig and the Polish Corridor, which by now had assumed a harsh and hectoring tone.

On April 28, Hitler countered with an unmistakable warning: he abrogated the nonaggression pact. Unbeknown to the outside world, he had already issued secret deployment orders for a Polish campaign weeks earlier, on April 3. The invasion was provisionally set for September 1, 1939.[8]

At this critical juncture, Hitler again changed tack and resumed his double game while the others continued, with the best of intentions, to act out the remainder of his peacemaker's farce. Apprehensive European, American, and Russian diplomats hastened to appease the German dictator with well-meant offers of mediation.

Moscow had proposed the convening of a six-power conference in March, President Roosevelt addressed a personal message to Hitler and Mussolini in April, and Mussolini himself intervened by letter on August 25. Hitler gained precious time while the German war machine continued to warm up. He must have been gratified by these almost daily reminders that the world's most powerful men still considered him a worthy recipient of their peace proposals. Despite the conclusion of an Anglo-Polish mutual assistance pact and the renewal of France's guarantees to Poland, the leaders of the Western Powers clung to their belief that they would ultimately reach an accommodation with the man who was rattling his saber in an easterly direction.

This seems doubly surprising because no such belief was warranted by practical experience of Hitler's conduct during six and a half years of brutal tyranny. The German dictator, who proclaimed the legitimacy of his exorbitant demands and harped on his love of peace at every available opportunity, had shown only too clearly what he thought of international agreements and undertakings. In 1936 he had given orders for the military occupation of the Rhineland, a flagrant breach of the Locarno Pact, having previously decreed rearmament and—in 1935—reintroduced universal conscription. He had incorporated Austria into the Third Reich in 1938 and the Sudetenland six months later. In 1939 he had sent his soldiers marching into Bohemia and Moravia. Finally, he had occupied and annexed Memel. This made him guilty of no less than seven blatant treaty violations.

But Hitler had done something more. Now that the Western Powers no longer contested Germany's claims to equal status, he had proceeded, step by step, to replace them as guarantors of European security in the Balkans and Eastern Europe. The system of states that had been erected after World War I as a wall to contain German expansionism was on the verge of collapse. Austria, the Sudetenland, Slovakia, Bohemia, and Moravia. . . . Now that these important bricks had been dislodged, Poland was the only eastern buffer state left intact.

Despite everything, Hitler's protestations of peace were still taken seriously. His last-minute restatement of his readiness to settle German-Polish differences by negotiation was noted and greeted with relief.

Hopes revived, even though the Third Reich's mass media had launched an inflammatory anti-Polish campaign which spoke of a "bleeding frontier" in the east, of "the ethnic Germans' right to self-determination," of Polish war fever and chaos, of Polish arsonists and the wanton destruction of German farmsteads. It was also alleged that German passenger aircraft had been fired on in Polish airspace.[9]

War? The possibility was dismissed. In the firm belief that an all-out policy of détente was bound to succeed, each little glimmer of hope was accepted as a hard fact.

"Peace is now being patched together," reported the *Neue Zürcher Zeitung,* a paper renowned for its Swiss restraint. "One can almost hear the sound of hammering coming from government offices in Berlin and London." This off-the-record remark, which its correspondent had just picked up in the German capital, was printed on August 30.[10]

Nobody could guess, of course, what Hitler had confided to the commander in chief of the Wehrmacht precisely a week before. His one fear, he said, was that "some *Schweinehund*" would submit a mediation proposal at the very last minute.[11]

What mattered was to get in first. On the penultimate day of peace, Hitler instructed the German Foreign Office to draft a sixteen-point "Offer to Poland." This document—a peace proposal of startling generosity—was on his desk next morning, as requested, after a night of concentrated endeavor.

The handsome concessions it embodied were broadcast on the evening of August 31 and relayed round the world.

No one knew better than Hitler himself that he had already, at noon that day, given orders that Poland be invaded at 4:45 the next morning.[12]

That Hitler should have succeeded in such a policy of systematic deception was due most of all to the gullibility of his contemporaries. For this, however, there was an important reason.

No one seriously believed that a prominent European political leader, even one of Hitler's stamp, could be genuinely intent on picking a fight. War, as everyone knew, had become pointless—the holocaust of 1914–18 had proved that beyond a doubt. Since then, Europe's politicians and the vast majority of its inhabitants had been imbued with the unshakable conviction that all threats of war were merely exercises in rhetoric. To *want* war seemed preposterous. The bloodletting and devastation of the Great War had been in vain. Neither victors nor vanquished had derived any tangible benefit or enduring advantage from the slaughter and mutilation of nearly thirty million people.

Hitler came to power early in 1933, less than fifteen years after the final act of the 1914–18 tragedy. Men who had survived the war in their twenties and thirties were now at the zenith of their creative powers. They belonged to the generation that now called the tune in parliaments and corridors of power, in industry and public life, and their judgment had been molded by their wartime and postwar experiences.

Hadn't the first war been fought to destroy, once and for all, the industrial and military threat posed by Imperial Germany? If so, it had done the opposite. One continental power, the Austro-Hungarian dual monarchy, had been abolished and its territory dismembered. Another great power, Imperial Russia, had been exhausted by revolutionary strife and indefinitely eliminated as a codeterminant of European politics. But Germany had weathered the storm. She was Europe's hard central core—a compact country with a population of sixty million.

Never had geopolitical conditions been more favorable to the expansion of German influence than they were after this fruitless struggle. Not a single problem, national or continental, had been resolved or disposed of by the armies of World War I. The conflict had bred unrest and internal tension, created new frontier and minority problems, unearthed new bones of contention, promoted the establishment of dictatorships, and deprived Europe of its predominant worldwide influence. Nor had any European nation succeeded in enriching itself as a result of the war. The victors' war debts were quite as horrendous as those of the vanquished. There was a universal failure to stem inflation and unemployment, a slump in commercial and industrial activity. No nation had remained exempt from these long-term repercussions of a war that no ordinary person had wanted or expected.

Thus the duplicity with which Hitler camouflaged his martial preparations paralyzed his opponents as effectively as it did because no European outside Germany was prepared, for the sake of anything or anyone, to wage a war whose futility could be predicted on the strength of recent experience. Although standing armies were maintained and new weapons forged, they were subordinated to one overriding aim: their function was to keep the peace, not wage war. Significantly enough, over 74 percent of Britons questioned during an extensive opinion poll conducted in the spring of 1935 voted in favor of peacekeeping by military means if necessary. Before Italy's invasion of Abyssinia could furnish immediate grounds for such action, 94 percent of the more than ten million ballot papers in another British poll endorsed the view that the great powers of Europe had a duty to bring aggressors to heel by exerting economic pressure.[13]

No such declarations of intent could impress a man like Hitler. For as long as the possibility of another war was discounted, his territorial encroachments and treaty violations were inevitably regarded as political maneuvers. In the same way, full credence was attached to his promises of future moderation and ready store of pacific utterances. It seemed to him as good as certain that his opponents' preoccupation with peace would always prompt them to back down when it came to the pinch.

A crisis of this kind arose in September 1938, when Hitler presented the Czechs with an ultimatum demanding the cession of the Sudetenland and its incorporation into the Reich. The true significance of "peacekeeping by military means" was now revealed.

The Czech Government decreed general mobilization. French reservists were recalled to the colors and a million men placed under arms. The Royal Navy was also alerted.

But Hitler had only to threaten general mobilization himself to clinch this trial of strength in his favor. The Western Powers yielded to extortion and ordained the surrender of Czechoslovakia without so much as consulting the Prague authorities: they concluded the Munich Agreement, which delivered up the Sudetenland to Hitler in exchange for further customary assurances of his peaceful intentions. Pushed to the limit, they had sacrificed a dependable ally on the altar of peace.

Many Europeans felt ashamed of this act, but few thought it too high a price to pay in the cause of peace. Chamberlain and Daladier, the bilked and humiliated Premiers of Britain and France, were rapturously acclaimed on their return from Munich—so much so that they became temporarily transformed from Hitler's stooges into venerable and heroic peacemakers. French parliamentarians ratified the Munich Agreement by an unusually hefty majority of 585 to 75. *Le Temps,* the leading Paris daily, still contended that there were no grounds for doubting Hitler's sincerity.[14] Jean Giraudoux poked fun at the French "obsession" with a war that would never take place, and Jean Cocteau sardonically proclaimed, "Long live shameful peace!"[15]

What a prodigious readiness to advance an enemy's cause—to collaborate with a man like Hitler, whether in Munich or elsewhere—in the blind and adamantine belief that anything was preferable to war! Many shared this belief, and the irresistible compulsion to swallow almost any rebuff, as long as it promised to avert or curtail the miseries of a fruitless conflict, dominated the hearts and minds of most Europeans long after World War II broke out. Hitler established his dominion over a continent that continued to seek peace in the midst of war.

Far from being quenched by the first tide of blood, this ubiquitous readiness to conform and collaborate seemed reinforced in most countries by the trauma of military defeat. Another universal factor was the attitude of the national Communist parties, which had enjoyed a prewar reputation for being the best-organized and most implacable anti-fascists of all, and had suffered grievously in their internal and external campaign against the Nazi regime. The German-Soviet nonaggression pact, signed only days before the outbreak of war, abruptly precluded them from membership in what could have been or become a united European front. They now openly sanctioned and defended the Soviet Union's partnership with Nazi Germany and regarded it as their duty to collaborate with the occupying forces until further notice, to a greater or lesser extent. The Resistance, whose beginnings were few and far between, originally resembled a scattering of forlorn and defenseless little islands in a mighty ocean of conformism and collaboration.

Such was the situation when war broke out. This fact, which had a fundamental bearing on all that followed, posed some disturbing questions.

Who, for instance, was a "conformist" and who a "collaborator"?

Although one thinks first of the homegrown fascists and National Socialists in the occupied countries, they always remained a minority and never came to power unaided. They did not constitute the bulk of those who conformed and collaborated longest with the Third Reich's despotic regime. That was made up of the vast majority of the population—men and women who were neither fascists nor National Socialists and as little in sympathy with Hitler and his New Order as the politicians who had signed the Munich Agreement under duress.

Were they committing treason?

Did whole nations defect to the enemy, as it were, or is a better explanation of this remarkable and widespread phenomenon that several quite different types of collaboration existed side by side? Under certain circumstances, could not collaboration itself be a form of resistance, as for example when it camouflaged the illegal organizations without which no fight for freedom could have been mounted?

Did not resistance, too, take many different forms, some of them quite compatible with simultaneous collaboration and others categorically opposed to any compromise with the enemy?

Finally, what drove Hitler's ill-starred contemporaries in occupied Europe to fight back and sacrifice their lives in the Resistance movements, or—at the opposite extreme—to sell their services to the invader?

These and other key questions occupy the forefront of this book. In tackling them, we shall not present a chronological account of resistance and collaboration, country by country, but systematically compare similar developments throughout occupied Europe. Examining these important and often dramatic occurrences in parallel, rather than separately and in chronological order, will enable us to define our subject with far greater precision. We shall also be able to keep an eye on all the occupied territories at once.

This method of arrangement is based on the simple notion that collaboration and resistance are closely related. Why? Because the mendacity and violence emanating from National Socialism posed a challenge which always admitted of the same two responses: submission or opposition—in other words, collaboration or resistance. The first three parts of this book follow a corresponding pattern, which ranges from THE GRAND CHALLENGE, via collaboration as a tempting but unrewarding form of LIFE WITH THE ENEMY, to RESISTANCE IN EUROPE. The fourth and last part deals with lesser challenges posed, in the East and the West alike, by the Allies themselves and by other PRICKLY PARTNERS whose strengths, weaknesses, and political antagonisms gave rise to tragic subsidiary wars and shifts of alignment. The extent to which the belligerent powers benefited from collaboration and resistance is discussed at the end of the book.

A False Sense of Security

The Polish Army collapsed within days, though Western experts had credited it with sufficient strength to hold out for a full year.

Less than seven months after the defeat of Poland, the Wehrmacht invaded Norway and Denmark. Four weeks later it attacked Holland, Belgium, and Luxembourg. This move heralded the campaign against France, with which Germany was already at war.

Denmark surrendered after a few hours, Luxembourg was overrun in a day, the Dutch Army beaten in five days, the Belgian in nineteen. After another seventeen days, Paris fell. Meantime, the Norwegian Army had also laid down its arms.

Shaken and bewildered, the world took stock of what had happened in the first nine months of hostilities, six of which—the so-called phony war—had passed without incident. By June 1940 the Wehrmacht had gained control of the entire European seaboard from North Cape to the Bay of Biscay.

But Hitler did not stop there. On July 16, three and a half weeks after the signing of the Franco-German armistice at Compiègne, he issued "Directive No. 16 on the Mounting of a Landing Operation against England."[16] Five days later he instructed his military advisers to "tackle the Russian problem."[17] Before the month was out, he requested them to prepare for an invasion of the Soviet Union.[18] Directive No. 21, which stipulated that the proposed attack on Russia should be carefully concealed, was dated December 18, 1940.[19]

Only another four months were to pass before Hitler launched his campaign against Yugoslavia and Greece. Then, a few weeks later, came the surprise attack on the Russian-occupied Baltic States—Lithuania, Latvia, and Estonia. Simultaneously, the Wehrmacht attacked the Soviet Union itself.

Hitler's technique had proved effective in every case. He prefaced each attack with a barrage of conciliatory speeches and solemn avowals of peaceful intent. He dealt out guarantees of territorial integrity. He concluded nonaggression pacts and treaties of friendship or offered them uninvited. He also voluntarily undertook to respect the neutrality of every minor European country, expressly reiterating and reaffirming his pledges as often as he thought it expedient—and all the time he was preparing to crush the recipients of his promises.

The Danish Government was offered a nonaggression pact in the spring of 1939. This treaty was signed at the end of May. Five weeks after war broke out, Hitler referred to it in a Reichstag speech and again assured little Denmark of his unalterable good faith. Less than ten weeks later, he decreed the mounting of a Scandinavian campaign code-named "Weserübung" [Weser Exercise].[20]

The Norwegians were reassured in the same Reichstag speech by a statement to the effect that neutral Norway had declined Germany's offer of a nonaggression pact solely because she "did not feel threatened in any way."[21] Six months later the Wehrmacht struck.

Where Holland, Belgium, and Luxembourg were concerned, Hitler's guarantees and professions of good faith were of such long standing that he deemed it expedient to mention and renew them on every suitable occasion. Three such assurances were given in 1939, the first late in April, the second four days after the outbreak of war, and the third—delivered with suspicious haste only six weeks later—early in October, after the conquest of Poland.[22]

Yet as early as the end of May 1939, or a year before he struck in the West, Hitler had informed his generals that no importance should be attached to declarations of neutrality, and that Holland and Belgium must be occupied at lightning speed.[23] His order to prepare for a campaign "traversing the area of Luxembourg, Belgium, and Holland" almost coincided with his final guarantee to both the last-named countries.[24]

In one classic case, German assurances were actually given "for all time." This pledge, which held good for only forty-eight hours, was addressed to Yugoslavia.

Hitler had assigned this kingdom a role of pro-German neutrality. As he saw it, a neutral Yugoslavia would fit nicely into the southern-flank defense essential to his projected campaign against the Soviet Union. Although he considered military intervention in Greece unavoidable—the British had been compelled to undertake some threatening countermeasures there by Mussolini's ill-fated Albanian foray—he believed that, where Yugoslavia was concerned, a straightforward "diplomatic siege" would suffice to lay the groundwork for his Russian campaign.

These calculations were upset by an unforeseen development which occurred after Hitler's diplomatic siege had rendered the Yugoslav Government tractable enough to join the Tripartite Pact, to which four neighboring countries (Hungary, Romania, Slovakia, and Bulgaria) had already subscribed. By the time the treaty was signed in Vienna by Yugoslav Premier Dragisha Cvetković and Foreign Minister Aleksander Cincar-Marković on March 25, 1941, Germany's southern flank seemed secure.

This was the occasion on which Ribbentrop handed his Yugoslav treaty partners two letters conveying the German Government's promise "to respect the sovereignty and territorial integrity of Yugoslavia for all time." Germany further expressed her determination not to request military transit rights from Yugoslavia "during the present war."[25]

Both ministers were arrested on their return to Belgrade. In an overnight coup, rebel officers had overthrown the Yugoslav Government, deposed the Prince Regent, and replaced him as head of state with young Prince Peter, the heir to the throne.

The new government headed by an air force general, Dušan Simović, hastened to give the German Government an unmistakable token of its good will by offering to conclude a nonaggression pact without delay.

This time, however, Hitler was totally uninterested in such a pact and had a fair idea of what it would be worth. Beside himself with rage—he reportedly threw one of his worst tantrums ever—he summoned his generals to the Chancellery.

According to the extant record of this meeting on March 27, he informed them that he wanted all requisite preparations made, "without waiting for possible declarations of loyalty by the new government, to smash Yugoslavia militarily and as a political structure." There would be no question of making diplomatic inquiries or presenting an ultimatum.[26]

The relevant directive was issued the same day,[27] and operational plans were drafted in the course of the following night.[28] Described as a "punitive operation," the invasion of Yugoslavia began at dawn on April 6, 1941.

So one gross breach of good faith followed hard on the heels of the last. Yet however frequent and unmistakable these danger signals, no European capital chose to take them seriously.

The Danish authorities had received timely warnings from more than one source. Although they could or should have known that a military onslaught was impending, no one showed the least alarm when, on the evening of April 8, 1940, a few hours before the German invasion, unidentified ships were sighted heading north along the Danish coast. King Christian X had dinner and repaired to the theater in a cheerful mood.[29]

A false sense of security was one of Hitler's most effective weapons. Even the German minister in Copenhagen found it hard to believe his eyes when handed a dispatch from Berlin during the night. He read to his dismay that he was expected to present an ultimatum from the German Government early the next morning, about an hour before sunrise. By that time, German forces would already have crossed the Danish border. The Danish Government was to be advised that every sizable city and town in Denmark would be bombed from the air if the country's "peaceful occupation" were opposed.[30]

The same purblind confidence reigned in Norway. Here too, warnings reaching Oslo from various sources on April 8 were cast to the winds. Similar information had often been received in the past, but the predicted catastrophe had never materialized. All the authorities did, tentatively and reluctantly, was secure Oslo Fjord by mobilizing a handful of military units. General mobilization, which would have taken three days, was never seriously considered.

Shortly after midnight the Norwegian capital was plunged into darkness. Air-raid sirens wailed in the gloom. The King, government, and civilian population assumed that an air defense exercise was in progress. The sirens continued to wail.

Halvdan Koht, the Norwegian Foreign Minister, happened to be walking home through the darkened streets at this hour. Hurrying to a phone booth, he called his ministry and asked what all the noise was about. He soon learned the truth: foreign warships were just entering the approaches to Oslo Fjord, and shore batteries had opened fire on them.[31]

While the city slept on, Koht groped his way to the Foreign Ministry. The Cabinet met at 1:30 A.M. Toward 4 A.M., before dawn had broken, the German envoy in Oslo requested an interview with the Foreign Minister.

At this early hour, by the light of two candles, Halvdan Koht was handed a document consisting of nineteen typewritten sheets. It was Hitler's ultimatum.[32]

The German invasion was "justified" on the grounds that Britain and France had declared war on Germany without due cause and embarked on naval hostilities against the neutrals.[33] The Wehrmacht was entering Norway as a friend, anxious to protect her from the Western Powers. The German Government therefore expected Norway to view its action with understanding and offer no resistance. Any opposition would have to be crushed by all available means.[34]

The German demands amounted to unconditional surrender.

Even while the Norwegian Cabinet was examining this lengthy memorandum, a distant rumble of guns could be heard. Military operations were already under way. . . .

The governments of Holland and Belgium had received several warnings of an even more cogent nature. On January 10, 1940, four months to the day before Hitler launched his general offensive in the West, the Wehrmacht's operational plans dropped into their lap. A German aircraft carrying copies of them had force-landed on Belgian soil.[35]

In view of the casual way in which these invasion plans had been ferried around, it was reasonable to suspect that their loss might be merely a feint. But anyone, however open to this belief, should have paid serious attention to the accurate reports which The Hague and Brussels had regularly been receiving from Colonel J. G. Sas, Holland's sharp-eared military attaché in Berlin. Sas gleaned his information from the best of sources. His informant was none other than Colonel Hans Oster, head of the Central Section of Amt Ausland-Abwehr [German Military Intelligence], whose opposition to Hitler was later to cost him his life.[36]

On May 9, 1940, Oster informed his Dutch friend that the Western offensive was definitely scheduled for the next day, and that it would open with the invasion of Holland, Belgium, and Luxembourg. The date was correct.[37]

Despite everything, Brussels and The Hague persisted in believing that they had nothing to fear from Hitler as long as they faithfully adhered to the rules governing their neutral status, which he had personally, expressly, and repeatedly guaranteed.

No one could fault them in that respect. The Dutch and Belgian Governments had already, back in September 1939, declined a Franco-British invitation to discuss the possibility of military cooperation in the event of a German attack. The two smaller countries' response to their friendly neighboring powers was a flat refusal.

Early in November 1939, shortly after Germany's lightning conquest of Poland, they had thought it expedient to stage a second display of good behavior. Wilhelmina, Queen of the Netherlands, and Leopold, King of the Belgians, publicly volunteered to mediate between Berlin, Paris, and London. Could anything have suited Hitler better at that particular juncture than a peace settlement on the lines of a second "Munich," this time at Poland's expense? He himself had broached the idea at the end of September.[38]

Four European kings, a president, and Pope Pius XII associated themselves with the Belgo-Dutch peace initiative, but the Western Powers firmly rejected it. For them, there was now no alternative left. Hitler, who had been carefully watching the European climate of opinion, wasted no time. On November 9, the morrow of an unsuccessful attempt on his life, he himself declined this invitation from eight European heads of state.[39]

Now that the situation was becoming grave, the Dutch and Belgian Governments found themselves seriously weakened by their past misjudgment of Hitler. Only inadequate precautions had been taken to repel a German attack. On May 7 and 8, the Dutch authorities recalled men from furlough, alerted unit commanders, and laid demolition charges under important bridges. Streets and buildings in the government quarter were placed under guard and expressway bridges and other key points occupied, but the Dutch High Command dared go no further because nobody wanted to furnish Hitler with the slightest pretext for a military riposte. The Belgians were just as hesitant. They did not start calling up their 250,000 reservists until German troops had actually opened hostilities.[40]

In Holland, Belgium, and Luxembourg, invasion was followed—after a carefully gauged delay—by the presentation of formal ultimatums. Count Zech, the German minister in The Hague, was received at dawn on May 10 by Eelco van Kleffens, the Dutch Foreign Minister, at his own urgent request. Even as the two men met, four thousand German paratroops were landing near the airports of The Hague and Rotterdam and other strategic points, and antiaircraft fire was rattling the windows—"sinister background music," as Van Kleffens described it in after years.

Count Zech, a diplomat of the old school and one who had represented German interests in Holland for the past seventeen years, had been cabled during the night and directed to hand the Dutch Foreign Minister the German ultimatum in person. His instructions from the Foreign Office ran as follows:

"Announce deployment of vast military forces. Resistance utterly futile.

"Germany will guarantee European and overseas possessions, also the dynasty, if no resistance offered. Otherwise, country and body politic risk total destruction.

"Therefore, urgently appeal to population and armed forces and invite them to establish contact with German military headquarters.

"Justification: we have incontestable proof of an imminent Franco-British attack on Holland, Belgium, and Luxembourg, long prepared with the knowledge of Holland and Belgium.

"Its objective: a thrust to the Ruhr."

Zech was incapable of presenting a statement or even of reading his instructions aloud. "He couldn't speak," Van Kleffens later testified, "he simply wept."

Van Kleffens took the sheet of paper out of the German envoy's hand and read Berlin's instructions himself. Then he penciled Holland's declaration of war on another sheet and gave it to the "still sobbing" German.

This interview, during which hardly a word was exchanged, lasted only a few minutes.[41]

The same specious arguments were used in an attempt to justify the German offensive in Brussels and Luxembourg, but false accusations of connivance with the Allies, not to mention simulated concern for friendly countries alleged to need protection but currently being struck down by their "protecting" power, were now seen—at least by those directly affected —as stark and brutal provocation.

Others, the statesmen and governments to whom Hitler had granted a short reprieve, saw things differently. Even a man like Stalin clung till the very last moment, and with a negligence surpassing belief, to Hitler's carefully nurtured illusion that peace was secure.

In April 1941, two months before the German attack on Russia, Churchill had tried to open Stalin's eyes by sending him a personal message.[42] Since then, 153 German divisions had deployed along the Russian frontier. Not only was it impossible to disguise such a huge concentration of strength—three million men—but Stalin had received pointed warnings from a number of other sources.

One of them was the Soviet military attaché in Berlin, who had seen through the diversionary maneuvers of German Intelligence and drawn the Kremlin's attention to the inescapable implications of the Wehrmacht's large-scale military buildup.[43] His opposite number in London had likewise transmitted some very alarming reports.

In Russia itself, the commander of Kiev Military District was so perturbed by German preparations that he called for the prompt and vigorous reorganization and reinforcement of his area's defenses. The civilian population, he said, was ready to evacuate the threatened sector without delay. The incomprehensible fact that Stalin misjudged and ignored these and other definite danger signals has been confirmed by modern Soviet historians.[44]

It is clear that Stalin grossly overestimated the value Hitler attached to tangible tokens of Russian good faith, and to the mutual advantages of the German-Soviet friendship treaty. The Soviet Union was not only supplying Germany's war machine with vital raw materials but was making itself useful in other respects. In the spring of 1940, when German forces battling for the Norwegian harbor and railhead of Narvik came under severe pressure, a German "Northern Base" supply ship fitted out in the Soviet Union was the only vessel to bring them the assistance without which their hold on this important strategic point might well have been broken.[45] It was hard to see why Hitler, whom Stalin believed to be preparing for a massive invasion of the British Isles, should sacrifice such benefits.

Stalin was right, on the face of things, and remained so until the moment of Germany's surprise attack on the Soviet Union. As Major General Georg Thomas, head of the Economics and Armaments Branch of the Wehrmacht High Command, subsequently stated in an official report, "[Russian] deliveries of rubber were being made by express freight trains from the Far East, even in the last few days."[46]

On the other hand, the German-Soviet entente had also paid dividends from Stalin's point of view. By the end of 1939, the Soviet Union had acquired bigger slices of eastern Poland than Imperial Russia had been awarded under the Third Partition of 1795. It had further contrived to swallow up the three Baltic States, Lithuania, Latvia, and Estonia, in the early summer of 1940 without incurring Hitler's veto. It was understandable, in the light of recent experience, that Stalin should—to quote the German naval attaché in Moscow—have become "the pivot of German-Soviet collaboration."[47]

But Stalin, whom Hitler had personally helped to delude, was only blind in one eye. A few weeks before the German attack he addressed an almost pathetic plea to Count Schulenburg, the German ambassador in Moscow, to do all in his power to reinforce the bonds of German-Soviet friendship.[48] On the very eve of hostilities, he instructed his Foreign Minister, Vyacheslav Molotov, to ask the German ambassador if Germany had any grounds for dissatisfaction with the Soviet Union, and, if so, what the Russians could do to remedy them. Count Schulenburg undertook to transmit this inquiry to his Foreign Office.

On returning to the German Embassy, he found his staff busy decoding a telegram from Berlin. To his own astonishment, Schulenburg was curtly directed to apprise the Soviet Government that Germany had declared war.[49]

Everyone was asleep, Stalin in the Kremlin and his soldiers in their barracks, when massed German artillery opened fire at three-fifteen the next morning. The formal declaration of war was delivered an hour later.

It took Moscow completely by surprise. Molotov's attitude was that of a friend who has been deeply disillusioned and basely betrayed. His utter dismay was summarized in a single question to the German ambassador: "You think we've deserved this?"[50]

The Soviet High Command's initial military response confirmed how disconcerted everyone was by the new situation: orders were given that German artillery fire should not be returned.

"We are being fired on. What shall we do?" ran a Russian radio message monitored by German signalers. "You must be mad," headquarters signaled back, and followed this up with a reprimand: "Why is your signal not in code?"[51]

One Red Army colonel went so far as to hazard the fanciful theory that Hitler had put Stalin into a hypnotic trance.[52]

In general, therefore, Hitler's diplomatic wizardry and unbridled mendacity succeeded in paralyzing his opponents before they could defend themselves against his invading troops. And even when they did so, what proved even more disastrous than unheeded warnings was lack of military preparedness in all the countries that had refused to believe in the possibility of war until they were attacked with lightning speed.

Even in Poland, mobilization was far from complete when the Germans invaded. The Polish Air Force was knocked out on the ground by a single surprise attack, almost in its entirety, and the command centers responsible for frontier defense were overrun before they could go into action.

The battlefields of the Polish interior became a demonstration of what was bound to happen when an army composed of peasant farmers and dashing cavalrymen—relics of a bygone age—hurled itself at the motorized units of a technologically supercharged, twentieth-century fighting force. The Poles fought and bled to death in vain. Riders and their mounts were literally pulped by advancing German tanks. . . .

Norway had next to nothing to pit against the dynamic German Wehrmacht. Only thirteen thousand men were under arms on the first day of hostilities, and they were an ill-trained, ill-equipped internal security force. Apart from nine old bombers and another forty obsolete machines, the Norwegian Air Force possessed a total of seven modern fighters.[53]

What was more, a firm belief in the futility of armed combat had ensured that only 90,000 out of 360,000 able-bodied Norwegians had received any military training at all. Of these, to repeat, none had been mobilized by the time the Germans invaded.

Denmark's armed forces were in an extremely awkward position on April 8, 1940. Her available military strength—two divisions numbering thirty thousand men—was at the mercy of German tanks for which the Danish flatlands provided an ideal and swiftly penetrable area of operations. There was no fortified line to hold, no effective tactical recon-naissance, and no resolute military leadership.[54]

Denmark could muster only two dozen obsolete and a dozen more mod-ern aircraft, plus two antiaircraft batteries, to oppose the 890 German combat, transport, and reconnaissance planes that dominated Norwegian and Danish airspace.[55] It was too late to make up for lost time. The Danes' only possible recourse was to surrender without a fight, the more so because no help could be expected from Britain. Churchill had taken the precaution of making this abundantly clear.[56]

Holland and Belgium tackled the Wehrmacht at a military disadvantage whose extent has already been described. In Yugoslavia, too, the armed forces were overwhelmed and beaten before general mobilization had been completed.

Even the Soviet Union, which was generally regarded as an alert and combat-ready military power, surprised the world by proving wholly un-prepared for a defensive war.[57] It only now became clear that the non-aggression pact and the German-Soviet friendship treaty, signed shortly af-terward, had deluded Stalin into making a number of grave mistakes. The Red Army frontier forces had previously possessed enough fuel, ammuni-tion, and food for at least three months. After the treaties were signed, these stocks were gradually run down until they covered only three days' requirements. Meanwhile, motorized units were withdrawn from their for-ward positions and transferred to the interior.[58]

We now know that Stalin and his generals had wasted twenty months. They were no shrewder than their counterparts in the West. Neither in the Baltic nor in eastern Poland, areas of immense strategic value, had they used their respite to organize an effective defense. The scanty fortifications in White Russia and the Ukraine were similarly neglected. Even the Stalin Line, which comprised a series of concrete pillboxes and fieldworks, re-mained little more than "semi-mythical."[59]

The Russians had no contingency plans when Hitler attacked, neither for a counteroffensive nor for a systematic withdrawal. Their military dis-positions were inappropriate and their air defenses inadequate. They also lacked tanks, artillery, and aircraft. These deficiencies have long been ad-mitted by official Soviet war historians.[60]

As for the now legendary partisan war, no serious consideration, far less preparation, had been devoted to it.[61]

The consequences are a matter of record. The Germans took only three weeks to clinch the "frontier battle" in their favor. After breaching the southern and northern sectors of the Stalin Line—the Soviet 20th Armored Division's bunkers in the central sector were simply bypassed—they went on to fight huge battles of encirclement at Minsk, Smolensk, Kiev, Vyazma, and Bryansk. These resulted in the capture of well over three million Russian soldiers.[62]

Hitler in the Ascendant
or
Power Without Plan or Purpose

Why war? Why all the duplicity, destruction, and bloodshed? What was Hitler after? What was it about his plans, intentions, and political objectives that prompted some Europeans to collaborate and others to resist?

First, though, two questions relating to Hitler himself.

Is it permissible to talk of "Hitler's Europe," "Hitler's war," "Hitler's provocations"?[1] Is it possible to contend that one man succeeded in molding the continent of Europe, like clay, to fit his own ideas and standards?

That Hitler's role in history must be viewed in relation to the circumstances which he encountered and by which he himself was molded—that economic and social conditions, the power of tradition and the class struggle, the status of knowledge and belief, and a complex web of other factors must be studied and taken into account by anyone seeking to discover how he acquired such epoch-making influence—none of this negates the fact that he was, in the most terrible sense of the phrase, his own master. He alone wielded the ultimate right and power of decision, often against the advice of his generals and industrialists, diplomats and party strategists. None of them was capable of successfully opposing his commands.

To this extent, the Third Reich was *his* domain, the war *his* war, occupied Europe *his* continent.

The second question concerns his marked predilection for political methods of the most despicable kind.

Hitler made a practice of systematically deceiving his opponents—"a trickster who succeeded for as long as people let themselves be tricked," to quote Golo Mann's description of him. From the very first, one of his techniques was to break his word in a gross and premeditated manner.

Conventional right-wing politicians and diplomats tended to be restrained in their use of the fifth ace, whereas Hitler unscrupulously disregarded all the rules and, far more so, all the ethical standards and moral principles of the civilized world. By ordaining every conceivable atrocity, he imposed a burden of personal guilt on all concerned, not only on himself. Crime, war, and politics eventually became a single process.

To understand this, we need only identify the products of his superficial education and vulgar mind. One was an irrational belief in the Germans' racial superiority and natural claim to supremacy, and the other an obsession with the omnipresence of war.

War was ubiquitous and unending, he used to say. War was life—the primordial human condition. War was the most natural and everyday phenomenon. "There is no beginning," he added, "and no peace."[2]

When he cited Heraclitus, whom he ignorantly regarded as a "great military philosopher," he did so by compressing a literary fragment into the single phrase—"war is the father of all things"—that suited his purposes best.[3]

Hitler must have been as ill acquainted with the writings of Karl von Clausewitz, the classical military theorist, as he was with those of the "dark" Greek.[4] He misunderstood Clausewitz so thoroughly that he transformed his most celebrated and often misconstrued maxim (that war is the continuation of politics by other means) into its diametrical opposite. To him, Hitler, politics was the continuation of war by other means.[5]

Viewed in this light, the custom of declaring war *before* launching it was senseless. War and peace differed, if at all, in their direct or indirect use of armed force. It followed that political murder in peacetime could be equated with a combat soldier's performance of his duty. Anything permissible in war was equally permissible in times of so-called peace.

This cardinal precept of the Hitlerian *Weltanschauung,* which was tricked out with all the appurtenances of a political religion, went hand in hand with two more. One stipulated a duty to preserve the purity of race and blood, and the other asserted the right of the Aryan "master and warrior race" to conquer a befitting *Lebensraum* at the expense of all "coolie and fellah races" and similar "parasites."[6]

Could this be called a program, philosophy, or political objective? Joachim Fest prefers to speak of Hitler's vague and dangerous "historical visions." One cannot, in fact, discern anything more. Hitler never defined the boundaries of the German *Lebensraum,* nor did he ever specify whom he included in, or excluded from, the "master race."

The practical inferences to be drawn from such "visions" were bound to be equally vague. Their main purpose was to justify Hitler's unbounded claims to supremacy, his policy of conquest in the West and the Balkans, his Eastern campaign and the enslavement or extermination of "worthless" races in Poland and Russia, and, finally, his anti-Semitism and "Final Solution." For the rest, they were confined to romantic dreams of a "Germanic" empire under German and National Socialist leadership in which "Aryan" Norwegians, Danes, Dutch, and Flemings would enjoy certain privileges dependent on their conversion to National Socialism.

Nothing more definite emerged. That Hitler never devoted any serious consideration to the internal structure of his dream empire, or to the political objectives underlying his wars of conquest, is an instructive fact that has seldom been brought to public notice.

Hitler was uninterested in the crucial problem of economic structure, let alone in the much-discussed plans for a European macroeconomic zone. Blueprints did exist, but they were not of his devising—in fact there is no proof that he ever saw or studied them. First drawn up at the end of May 1940 in papers drafted by Ambassador Karl Ritter, head of the Economic Policy Section of the Foreign Office, and by his deputy Karl Clodius, they were anyway limited to mere statements of principle and devoid of practical significance.[7]

It was not unnatural, though doubtless unintentional, that these hazy plans should have fostered a widespread delusion. Quite simply, they were accepted as the official German blueprint for a European New Order and macroeconomic system embracing the entire continent. Many well-meaning intellectuals, politicians, and entrepreneurs seized on them, took them seriously, and debated their merits. Accepted at far more than face value, they encouraged optimistic speculation in certain business circles and served to justify lucrative transactions with the seemingly invincible Germans. The higher hopes rose, the greater the disillusionment that set in when it became clear that the new Europe was virtually undefined, even on paper.

Hitler, who allowed his ministers and leading industrialists some scope for harmless and profitable sand-table exercises in economic policy, did not intervene. He said nothing, but his silence was not so much tactical as utterly indifferent.

It is very probable that Hitler's attitude took the form summarized by Arnold Toynbee in the introduction to his now classic collection of studies on aspects of German-occupied Europe: that he "indulged in the Prussian pleasure of offensively asserting his domination over satellite states and conquered peoples" but was uninterested in creating a new political and economic system. "His inspiration," Toynbee goes on, "seems to have been limited to two ideas that were both narrow-minded and narrow-hearted. He would annex to the German Reich the maximum amount of conquered territory that there was any prospect of his being able to assimilate. The rest of Europe—allies, satellites, and conquered peoples alike—he would reduce to a servile, and in the lowest categories to a sub-human, status in a swollen German Reich's European colonial empire." The inevitable outcome was that, with an empire in his grasp, Hitler had no conception of what to do with it.[8]

It is worth comparing his silence and lack of interest with the little that he himself had to say on the subject.

For some time, every word he uttered to his closest associates at meals in his headquarters, noon and night, was recorded in writing and preserved for posterity. There was no subject on which he failed to expatiate during these "table talks"—no subject, be it noted, save the economic structure of Europe. Only once in the space of twelve months, early in the third year of the war, did he even vaguely refer to it.

"I envisage," he said on September 10, 1941, "the development of an all-German and European economic system—a fine and wonderful thought. Imagine, for example, how much would be gained if we succeeded in using the steam that is now given off during gas production, but lost to thermal engineering, to heat greenhouses whose function would be to keep our cities supplied with fresh vegetables and fruit throughout the winter. There's nothing finer than horticulture. . . . Adding up all the creative energy now dormant in the European area—in Germany, Britain, the Scandinavian countries, France, Italy—one can only say, what is America's potential by comparison?"[9]

Visionary, nebulous effusions. They are reminiscent of earlier remarks made late in 1932, just before he came to power, which described how he would have preferred to begin and end the war of his dreams.

"When I wage war . . . troops will suddenly appear in the midst of peace—in Paris, let's say. They will be wearing French uniforms. They will march through the streets in broad daylight. No one will stop them. Everything has been thought out and rehearsed, down to the last detail. They march to the headquarters of the General Staff. They occupy the ministries, the Chamber of Deputies. Within a few minutes, France, Poland, Austria, Czechoslovakia, are deprived of their leading men. An army without a general staff! All political leaders disposed of! The confusion is beyond belief. . . . Peace is concluded before the war has begun. I promise you, gentlemen, the impossible is always successful."[10]

Adolescent fancies? An imaginary game of cowboys and Indians played by a forty-three-year-old who was about to assume political leadership of the German Reich?

His pronouncements on the use of force, a subject that never ceased to enthrall him, were neither visionary nor nebulous. They were crisp, concise, and explicit.

In answer to the question what he actually meant when he called for the removal of all "alien races" from the territories claimed by Germany,[11] he replied in the spring of 1934 that "a depopulation technique" had yet to be evolved. "If you ask me what I mean by depopulation, I mean the removal of entire racial units. And that," he went on, "is what I mean to do —that, more or less, is what it boils down to."[12] The Germans would have to shake off all sentimentality and become hard—they would have to learn to be cruel.[13]

"Cruelty impresses people," he explained. "The ordinary man in the street is only impressed by brute force and ruthlessness."

Intimidation? By all means. "Terror is the most effective political instrument. I shall not permit myself to be robbed of it simply because a bunch of naive middle-class milksops take offense at it."[14]

"Yes," he once declared, "we're barbarians. We choose to be barbarians. It's an honorable title."[15]

That was an avowal which both called for and transfigured every conceivable form of provocation, however bloodthirsty.

Hitler waged his war with grandiose visions, empty slogans, and sadistic daydreams, not with clearly defined military objectives and a political program.

"If anyone asks today how we imagine the new Europe, we must say we don't know." This startlingly candid pronouncement was made by Hitler's Propaganda Minister six months after the occupation of Poland. As for the shopworn catchword *Lebensraum,* all he could tell the German newspapermen who had been summoned to hear his remarks was that everyone was at liberty to construe it as he chose.[16]

Hitler himself interpreted it in various ways. He said more than once, before launching his attack on the Soviet Union, that the whole of the Eastern territories must be "split up into states, each with its own government," and that Germany would then be able to make *peace* with these governments. On other occasions, once at about the same time and again two and a half months later, he contradicted himself by stating that Germany was waging a *war of annihilation* in the East. The Third Reich must not, he said, be content to smash enemy armies which might reorganize and return to the fray in thirty years' time. The present war was not being fought "to preserve the enemy." Utter severity today implied future leniency, and no one should shrink from using "extreme brute force"—a view to which he adhered from then on.[17]

This eliminated the last remaining obstacles to unbridled despotism. German troops had barely reached the suburbs of Moscow and the Donets Basin in the south when maps of Russia were redrawn to show the Reich Commissariats that would extend from the Arctic Ocean to the Caspian and from Poland to the western marches of Siberia.[18]

Meanwhile, no indigenous central authority survived the German invasion. Economic and administrative functions were strictly supervised by the occupying power or, except at the lowest level, completely usurped.[19] The slogan "saving Europe from Bolshevism" shriveled into an empty cliché. Now, the Germans' sole concern was to gain possession of limitless tracts of territory, exploit them, and entrench German rule so firmly by means of "Germanic" colonization that it would endure, as Hitler once declared, for a thousand years. His own response to talk of an "anti-Bolshevik crusade" was that all that mattered was to "cut the gigantic cake into manageable slices so that we can (a) control it, (b) govern it, and (c) exploit it."[20]

What this would mean to the Russians was described by Reichsführer-SS Heinrich Himmler as "supremely unimportant." Whether they prospered or died of starvation was of interest only insofar as they could serve as "slaves for our civilization." The practical effect of measures taken in this spirit was that surplus or unwanted native inhabitants would be killed or deported and replaced by *Germanen* [a racist application of the term for ancient Germans] and "auxiliary peoples" such as "Norwegians, Swedes, Danes, and Netherlanders." A "resettlement policy" was drawn up, and promptly introduced, under which roughly three quarters of the (surviving) Slav population would in due course be deported to Siberia. The *Generalplan Ost* [Master Plan for the East] drafted in 1941–42 envisaged that the Germanization of the Government General [Poland] alone would entail "resettlements" of the order of ninety million people.[21]

So Poland, too, was covered by this *Ostpolitik*—indeed, she served as its preliminary proving ground. This was where the techniques of Germanization, including systematic economic exploitation and the "biological enfeeblement" of the native population, were first evolved and put into practice: forced labor, measures to curb the birthrate, "removal" of the Jews, abolition of all centers of higher education and academic facilities open to Poles, and elimination of the Polish intelligentsia. Far from being a policy of the moment, this was long-term planning. Addressing a police conference at the end of May 1940, Governor General Hans Frank transmitted the following personal directive from Hitler: "Whatever we have already identified in the way of a Polish upper crust is to be liquidated. Whatever grows back we must secure and dispose of in due course." Here too, the aim of the "master plan" was colonial rule founded on straightforward slavery.[22]

The same technique of exploitation and repression was later employed, not only in the Soviet Union but throughout occupied Europe, albeit in a milder form and often camouflaged—in deference to world opinion—as an anonymous crime. What could not be concealed, however, was the mass exploitation of conscripted workers, euphemistically known as "obligatory labor service."

In Poland this method was practiced from late October 1939, or only a few weeks after the country had been militarily occupied, and in the other Eastern territories from mid-December 1941, or roughly six months after the German invasion. In France, Belgium, and the rest of occupied Europe, on the other hand, twenty to twenty-two months elapsed before this stage was reached.[23]

Hitler's war machine was so insatiable that between eight and ten million men and women—workers from all over Europe—found wartime employment in the Reich itself, most of them brought there under duress.[24]

Over half, or 56.7 percent, came from the East, nearly a third from the Soviet Union and nearly a quarter from Poland.[25]

Methods of recruitment in the East and West differed as little as the reactions of those affected and their response to German provocation. The
following three examples, taken from German documents and relating to
incidents in Russia, might have occurred in any other occupied country.

"At Rovno, many people were picked up in the street and carted off.
They included mothers with children left alone at home and husbands out
at work. In one village in the Kiev area, the recruiting officer called all the
inhabitants together and filled his quota by picking out one in every three,"
stated a Security Service report dated June 12, 1942, and entitled "Compulsory Recruitment of Labor."[26]

Commenting on the situation three weeks later, Alfred Rosenberg,
Reich Minister for the Occupied Eastern Territories, called the unimagina-
ble hardships prevailing in the villages of Russia "excessive" even by Russian standards. In many cases, he said, people had taken to the woods as a
last resort.[27]

Finally, to cite a third case which bears out Rosenberg's statement, the
German Commissioner General at Lutsk decreed that those who evaded or
resisted compulsory labor should have their homes burned down and their
families taken hostage.[28]

More will be said about the excesses of this policy and its unprecedented life-or-death challenge to the Polish and Russian peoples.

First, however, reference must be made to a startling contrast. This was
provided by Germany's occupation policy in Denmark, which differed so
markedly from the one described above—and differed in every respect for
almost three and a half years—that its connection with the same dictator
and his panoply of power seems quite preposterous.

The Danish Experiment

In Denmark, where German troops were admitted in April 1940 with no
appreciable resistance and the government capitulated after a four-hour
debate, the occupying power waived most of the claims it enforced with
such uncompromising brutality and bloodshed in the East. The administrative and judicial systems remained in Danish hands. So did the police
force, whose arsenal was actually increased, and the Army, though its permanent strength was cut from 7,000 to 2,000 men.

Even the government remained in office and was recognized by the occupying power, regardless of the fact that it was led by a Socialist, Thor-
vald Stauning. Formerly a cigar sorter and union organizer, Stauning was
"a bluff, bearded Viking, vigorous, forceful and shrewd," who had not

only headed the Danish Cabinet since 1929 but had held the premiership still earlier, from 1924 to 1926.[29]

Stauning's ministerial team, which continued to wield the reins of government with a firm hand, was exclusively composed of Social Democrats and Radicals—in other words, representatives of two political parties noted for their opposition to National Socialism.[30]

The Danish Government remained what it had been hitherto: an administration formed and supported by democratic parties. Its complexion did not change two and a half years later, even when Erik Scavenius, a strongly pro-German politician, assumed the premiership after Stauning's death.

Parliament likewise continued to exercise its rights of control, and the King, who developed into a figure symbolic of well-gauged resistance, remained the undisputed head of state.[31]

The German authorities began by dealing so indulgently with this government of an anti-fascist monarchy that it would have been reasonable to talk of collaboration in reverse. National Socialist Germany did, in fact, "collaborate" for years with an intact Danish parliamentary democracy led by Social Democrats. This policy tolerated all political parties and their press organs, the Communists included. It also recognized the results of free and secret parliamentary elections held under German aegis, even as late in the war as March 1943. On that occasion the Social Democrats re-emerged as the country's strongest single party, with 44.6 percent of the poll and 66 parliamentary seats. The Danish National Socialists, who had gained only 2 percent and 3 seats, were quietly dropped by Berlin.[32] Meanwhile, over the eastern horizon, hundreds of thousands of Polish and Russian civilians were being murdered in accordance with Germany's extermination policy, whose methods were likened by leading Nazis to the extermination of vermin.

Officially, this remarkable state of affairs was founded on a sort of gentlemen's agreement which the Danish Government had concluded with the occupying power early on the morning of April 9, 1940, the date of Denmark's surrender. The Cabinet spent four hours examining the text of the German ultimatum for any points that might form a basis, however tenuous, for the preservation of national independence and sovereignty.

The Reich Government stated in its ultimatum that German troops had come to Denmark as friends, that there was no intention of violating the country's territorial integrity, and that the Wehrmacht did not propose to meddle in her internal affairs. Finally, Denmark's neutrality would remain intact.[33]

The Danes took these dubious assurances at their face value. They proceeded on the principle that their renunciation of military defense could not be equated with defeat. Denmark was not at war with Germany, so the question of a formal surrender did not arise either. What was involved was a voluntary accommodation with the Third Reich—an agreement which, among other things, permitted the Wehrmacht to guarantee Denmark's military security while respecting her neutral status.

The Danish Government was shrewd enough to accept the German concessions as more than mere promises. Rather, it construed them as integral parts of a "voluntary" agreement.

Although it was naturally debatable whether anything could be accomplished by such legalistic tricks when Denmark was up against a man like Hitler, whose forces were armed to the teeth and already on Danish soil, events followed a surprising course. Chance, that unpredictable spoilsport or fairy godmother, took an unexpected hand.

For reasons that at first seemed obscure, the fiction of Danish neutrality was nurtured and respected by both sides. Formal relations between the Danish Government and the occupying power were maintained through diplomatic channels, and German requests had to be submitted in the form of *aides-mémoire* and *notes verbales* addressed to the Danish Government, which in turn conveyed its agreement, objections, counterproposals, or conditions to the German minister in Copenhagen.

Though complicated, this procedure sometimes made it possible—as long as both parties observed the rules of the game—to resist pressure based on superior strength. The Reich Plenipotentiary in Denmark could not, at all events, afford to ride roughshod over the Danes. If the German authorities wanted something done, they were dependent on diplomacy: they had to sway the sovereign Danish Government in their favor and await its decision. This was how a totalitarian great power found itself negotiating and compromising with representatives of a parliamentary democracy on the soil of a minor European state—something which the National Socialists, in their habitual arrogance, found highly distasteful.[34]

Further German concessions made it plain that Berlin was prepared to pay a high price for peace in Denmark. The occupying power forbade its servicemen to buy up rationed foodstuffs and refrained from publishing a forces' newspaper. A circular addressed to German officials and members of the Wehrmacht warned them to avoid impugning Denmark's honor, treat Danish women and girls with respect, steer clear of political arguments, and constantly bear in mind that Denmark was not an enemy country. The Danes were *Germanen,* not Poles.[35] The Reich Plenipotentiary went so far as to intervene on behalf of some Danes who had been parachuted into Denmark by a British aircraft, detained, and taken to Berlin. He succeeded in preventing their execution.[36]

Berlin's kid-glove policy was not, as might have been supposed, based on the Danes' "Aryan" status. The Norwegians were likewise classified as Aryans, yet the German authorities in Norway maintained a regime which the Danes, and not the Danes alone, condemned with horrified disgust. The Germans' moderate line in Denmark was prompted by three other considerations, to which no public reference was made—understandably so.

In the first place, Berlin thought it expedient to create an idyllic antithesis to the reign of terror in the East—a species of model German protectorate that could safely be paraded before the eyes of the world, notably the United States and the European neutrals.[37] This was because the reputation of Hitler's Reich had been badly dented by reports of crimes and atrocities in Poland, which could not be suppressed and had spread with surprising speed.

A confidential situation report submitted by the Security Police early in 1940 had further pointed out that German servicemen at home on furlough were telling their families, friends, and acquaintances about the mass shootings in Poland.[38] The Reich Propaganda Ministry was compelled to deny such reports officially, dismiss them as mendacious "horror stories," and, as the minister himself put it, "do something definite about this atrocity-mongers' campaign."[39]

Tart criticism was also voiced in German diplomatic and military circles, though only sporadically and mostly in an undertone. Ulrich von Hassell, who regarded Hitler as a national disaster, spoke of "SS obscenities," Major General Helmuth Stieff referred to atrocities perpetrated by "organized bands of murderers, thieves, and criminals," and other dissidents began to parry or sabotage Hitler's orders as best they could.[40] Under these circumstances, it seemed that a Danish contrast might distract attention from the genuine horrors in the East.

Another motive—the most interesting of all—can be discerned in the bitter internal power struggles waged by various Reich agencies. Denmark was the only occupied country under the jurisdiction of the Foreign Office, and the loss of this unique sphere of authority would have dealt a severe blow to its status in the Third Reich hierarchy.

Late in October 1942, when the Danish situation became critical, the Foreign Office actually sought SS support against Hitler.

Fearful of losing its diplomatic preserve to another department, it assigned Copenhagen a "Reich Plenipotentiary" recruited from the SS dynasty. This was Werner Best, ex-head of Amt [Department] I at the Reichssicherheitshauptamt [Central State Security Bureau], a close associate of the powerful chief of the Security Police and Security Service, Reinhard Heydrich.

Best was one of a group of SS intellectuals who believed that the war must be won before any thought could be devoted to fulfilling Hitler's grandiose plans for world supremacy. He and his friends believed that, in the interim, every effort should be made to persuade the governments and inhabitants of the occupied territories to cooperate voluntarily with the Third Reich. Drastic measures would only spoil the game.[41]

From the Wilhelmstrasse's angle, Best was undoubtedly the man for the job. He did all he could to implement his ideas in Denmark. The lengths to which he went, notably his courageous but equivocal attitude toward the Jewish rescue operation in September 1943, will be examined in greater detail in Part Three of this book.

Yet another incentive to a conciliatory occupation policy was that the Third Reich's civil servants were much impressed by German achievements in Denmark. Like his predecessor Cecil von Renthe-Fink, Best got by with an exceptionally small staff numbering only two hundred officials and ancillary personnel. He could claim in Berlin that he and his two hundred subordinates "governed" four million Danes, whereas the ratio in neighboring Norway was three thousand to fewer than three million.[42] He also argued that his minimal outlay yielded maximal results. In fact, Danish agricultural exports in 1944 provided the food rations for 8.4 million of Germany's inhabitants.[43]

This unique experiment came to an end after three and a half years, when it was finally transformed into a fight for survival at Hitler's wish and behest. Until then the Danish Government had striven to hold its own against overwhelming odds by dint of a versatile policy which combined resistance with collaboration and was rich in subtle nuances. Until then, too, Germany's extermination policy in the East and her kid-glove approach to Denmark represented the opposite ends of the administrative pole in Hitler's Europe.

It is noteworthy that, including these two extremes, Germany employed no less than seven systems of control and administration to keep the inhabitants of the occupied territories docile—seven, not just one or two, and these seven were themselves embedded in an administrative and interdepartmental morass. In practice, the totalitarian system failed in just those areas where people granted it some chance of success. There could be no talk of consistency and a strict administrative framework, nor of a clear-cut and uniform occupation policy.

In northern France, Belgium, Serbia, and Greece, as well as in the Russian territories east of the Reich Commissariats of Ostland and the Ukraine, the Wehrmacht held sway. In these strategically important areas it exercised the full military and civil authority of an occupying power. Form of administration: military government.

By contrast, Alsace, Lorraine, Luxembourg, southern Styria, and Yugoslav Carinthia, being territories whose "union with the Reich" was definitely in prospect, came under "special civil administration," a central government category that anticipated their constitutional absorption.

Denmark, as we have already seen, started out as the only occupied country under Foreign Office control, to be joined in 1944 by Hungary. Form of administration: supervisory or allied.

Holland and Norway were superintended by Reich Commissioners directly responsible to Hitler. They exercised general control over government but reserved the right to take certain administrative measures. Form of administration: commissarial supervision.

The occupied territories comprising the Government General of Poland were ruled by a Governor General directly responsible to Hitler, like the Reich Commissioners. Any self-governing functions retained by the Polish authorities were exercised at the lowest possible level and strictly supervised by the occupying power. Form of administration: direct rule.

The occupied Eastern territories—the Reich Commissariats of Ostland and Ukraine—came under a colonial administrative setup headed by Commissioners General who were also directly responsible to Hitler. The colonial authorities had full charge of the civil administration at all levels.[44]

But the list did not end there.

The government of unoccupied France, for example, retained subsidiary sovereignty over occupied areas as well, down to and including the Departments of Nord and Pas de Calais, which were under German military control.

Nor were specific occupation policies, once introduced, always adhered to. Sudden changes of tack occurred, generally as a result of some unpredictable decision on Hitler's part.

One such change took place in Poland at the end of 1939, when plans for that area were amended.[45] Others affected Holland and Luxembourg in May and July 1940 and Belgium in July 1944, countries where the military government—carefully organized in the first two cases and armed with four years' practical experience in the third—was abolished overnight and superseded by a civil administration.[46] The wholesale revision of Germany's *Ostpolitik,* which began at the end of 1941, may be included in the same context.[47]

Last but not least, lurking in this jungle of seven ill-defined and oft-amended systems of control were the rival Berlin ministries. Whether operating within or adjacent to their own spheres of jurisdiction, whether infiltrating other agencies or establishing independent outposts, they all constituted highly antagonistic and conflict-laden agglomerations of power which frequently resorted to underhand methods in pursuit of their sectional interests.[48]

Fundamentally, therefore, German occupation policy was sustained by constant improvisation. One or another administrative system was selected and tailored to fit each given set of circumstances—and how could it have been otherwise? Hitler and his senior subordinates never got to grips with the knotty problems of organized government in occupied territory. At most, these were handled by individual departments, teams of junior civil servants, or men like the SS administrative expert who was later appointed Reich Plenipotentiary in Denmark, Werner Best, and not even he committed his ideas to paper until the war was in its second year.[49]

The public remained generally unaware of this administrative and jurisdictional chaos. All else apart, a makeshift policy would not have accorded with the popular image of the occupying power. Intensive German propaganda had long ago ensured that most Europeans looked upon the Third Reich as a tightly organized and centrally controlled colossus which always acted in response to orders from the highest quarter. Any seeming contradictions and anomalies were therefore assumed to be intentional.

This had a contaminating effect on morale, because day-to-day experience of German rule was so inconsistent with the Third Reich's granite image that the occupying power acquired a diabolical reputation. The victims of all these official and personal conflicts of interest, all these contradictory orders and directives, suspected that they were inspired by a deliberate and malevolent sadism forming part of some mysterious master plan—and this when the occupying power had no plan whatever.

Thus the German authorities became an omnipresent challenge to those living under the jackboot, not only because of what their policy *was,* but also—and in equal measure—because of what it was *not.*

Blood and Tears
or
The Rape of a Continent

The earliest European air raids of World War II not only reduced city centers to rubble but stunned the civilized world.

This is worth remembering, for we are now inured to many things that have ceased to offend our moral sensibilities. Indiscriminate bombing, which public opinion has come to accept as an inevitable and almost natural concomitant of "total war," was once considered an outrageous and unpardonable affront to human decency and military ethics. The ruthless waging of war on civilians was, in fact, regarded as a criminal act.

Military resistance had already been crushed and Poland occupied by German and Russian armies when, at the end of September 1939, the German High Command was faced with the problem of what to do about Warsaw and Modlin. The garrisons of the beleaguered capital and the encircled fortress refused to surrender.

Germany's generals wanted to bide their time. With victory assured, there seemed no point in launching an attack that was bound to result in heavy military and civilian casualties. Despite this, Hitler ordained that the Polish capital should be saturated with shellfire and bombed from the air.[1]

Warsaw's martyrdom dragged on for four days. Based on eyewitness accounts, an entry in Ulrich von Hassell's diary refers to the "terrible impression" made on those who had seen it by "the state of Warsaw, with its devastated city quarters" and "many thousands of bodies strewn around."[2]

Rotterdam's turn came next. The city was summoned to surrender or be destroyed from the air. Just what that meant, people had known ever since the destruction of Warsaw seven and a half months earlier.

Issued on the day fighting ceased, the German ultimatum was due to expire in three hours. Only twenty minutes after its submission to Dutch negotiators, when the city's surrender was already being discussed, German bombers struck. The old quarter of the city was completely destroyed.

Eight hundred and fourteen people were killed, several thousand injured, and seventy-eight thousand rendered homeless.[3]

"I shall spread terror by employing all my resources without warning," Hitler had told his cronies years before. "The sudden, dreadful shock of mortal terror—that's what counts."[4]

There followed fifty-seven night raids on London (September to early November 1940). The first two raids alone inflicted more fatal casualties on the civilian population than the bombing of Rotterdam. In mid-November, the English city of Coventry was reduced to an expanse of rubble.

Then came Belgrade.

Having decreed the military and political destruction of Yugoslavia at the end of March 1941, Hitler ordered Reich Marshal Göring to send in the Luftwaffe and destroy the Yugoslav capital "by attacking in successive waves."[5]

Although Belgrade had been declared an open city and possessed no antiaircraft defenses, 440 tons of bombs were unloaded on it in a series of low-level attacks.[6]

The result was carnage. More people lost their lives in Belgrade on April 6 and 7 than in Warsaw, Rotterdam, and Coventry put together.[7]

Colonel Rudolf Toussaint, the German military attaché in Belgrade, reported to Army High Command that, as he saw it, the air raids were less an adjunct to military operations than a way of bringing "strong psychological pressure" to bear on the inhabitants and, thus, an attempt to influence the course of the war by indirect means. He went on:

"Surprise constituted the most important and effective element in the aerial attack on Belgrade. Its success was complete. Although an air-raid warning was sounded shortly beforehand, the inhabitants mistook it for a practice alert and ignored it. The attack was highly concentrated and caught the inhabitants in their homes or on the streets. Many people were still asleep, and farmers were in the process of driving from the city's outskirts to the markets in the center. For that reason, the commencement of the attack inflicted particularly heavy casualties and the psychological impact was enormous. . . .

"The psychological effect of the raid was considerably heightened by the wail and whistle of Stukas and bombs, which fill the inexperienced with a sense of imminent danger even when the actual effect is more remote. Menfolk were unnerved by the presence of women and children and the feeling that they had no practical means of protecting or assisting them. People whose homes had been destroyed added to the mood of panic by running distractedly through the streets."[8]

Colonel Toussaint put the number of dead at four thousand, roughly half of whom were buried in the ruins.[9]

It was this utter lack of military restraint, this absence of legal and moral scruple, which later prompted Hitler's enemies to reply in kind. The

Allies' saturation raids—the "strategic bombardments" whose mass devastation and senseless expenditure of effort ultimately killed more people in Hamburg and Dresden than the first atomic bomb on Hiroshima—were an expedient that bore Hitler's hallmark.

Just six weeks after the shelling and bombing of Warsaw, a challenge of another kind occurred in Poland's former capital and coronation city, Cracow, where the Academy of Sciences was based. Cracow University, an institution that had been in existence for well over five hundred years, was about to reopen for the winter semester. Professors, lecturers, and assistants from every faculty had been summoned to the aula to hear an inaugural address delivered by an Obersturmbannführer [lieutenant colonel] in the SS. His scheduled subject was "The Relationship of the German Reich and National Socialism to Scholarship and Universities."

The anonymous German speaker dispensed with the usual *captatio benevolentiae*. He bluntly announced that the university had neglected to obtain express permission to inaugurate the academic year from the relevant German authorities. This was a sign of latent ill will. In any case, Polish professors and lecturers were notoriously hostile to "German scholarship." Everyone present, with the exception of three women, would therefore be removed forthwith to a concentration camp, and all discussion and comment was forbidden. His parting words: "Anyone resisting the execution of my order will be shot."

The grounds, entrances, and corridors had meanwhile been occupied by SS troopers. Out of 183 members of the teaching staff present in the assembly hall, they arrested 171 professors, lecturers, and assistants and deported them to the Sachsenhausen concentration camp in Germany.

Cracow's university buildings were closed and its precious libraries and items of equipment shipped off to the Reich. Only ten of the hundred and thirty research institutes affiliated to the university survived the war unscathed.[10]

Ten days later the German authorities turned their attention to Prague University, where three thousand students had filed silently past the coffin of a fellow student in the chapel of the Institute of Pathology. According to rumor, he had died after being tortured by the Gestapo.

What was known for certain was that he had been wounded and arrested at the end of October, when police clashed with demonstrators celebrating Czech Independence Day.

Twenty-four hours later, the government of the Czech Protectorate received notice that Hitler was determined not to tolerate such demonstrations. Any attempt to hold another would be ruthlessly crushed. If necessary, Prague would be cleared of German nationals and then shot to pieces.

When night fell, units of the German Security Police surrounded the five

largest students' hostels in Prague and another two at Brno. They stormed
the premises, arrested 1,850 students, and carted them away in buses.
Twelve hundred of them were sent to the German concentration camp at
Oranienburg.

Nine students were branded as ringleaders and summarily executed. In
their case, no judicial inquiry was held and no formal sentence passed, not
even by court-martial.

On the following day, the German authorities decreed that all other
Czech universities, including some technical high schools, should be closed
for a period of three years. They did not reopen until the end of the war.[11]

Brussels University was closed in February 1942.[12] A year later, the
police arrested six hundred students at various universities in Holland.[13]
At the end of November 1943, SS men forced their way into the lecture
rooms of Oslo University and herded three thousand students together.
Some fifteen hundred of them were interned and about seven hundred
deported to Germany. Here as elsewhere, all teaching and research activity
was suspended.[14]

The victor has a right to the spoils of war. Hitler abused that right, extend-
ing it to cover unlimited plunder and the almost total despoliation of occupied Europe. This policy yielded an immense harvest of raw materials and
machinery, foodstuffs and rolling stock, economic assets of all kinds, works
of art, bullion, and foreign currency.

The Third Reich seized 135,000 tons of copper in the first sixteen
months of the war alone. Copper being indispensable and in short supply,
this haul sufficed to keep Hitler's war machine ticking over for some time
to come.[15]

Expropriations in France were valued at a staggering 154 billion francs
(at the 1938 rate of exchange). More than half of them consisted of military equipment and rolling stock.[16]

Nearly a quarter of Germany's imports of raw materials from France
were "spoils of war" for which she paid nothing. The same applied to
nearly 14 percent of all imported processed raw materials and over 10 percent of imported foodstuffs and agricultural products.[17]

In Bohemia and Moravia the Wehrmacht took over all Czech War Department property, including 1,582 aircraft and over 2,000 pieces of artillery. This matériel, valued at 35 billion korunas, was sufficient to arm and
equip twenty divisions.[18] Nearly a third of the modern tanks deployed by
Germany against Holland, Belgium, and France in May 1940 came from
this store of "acquisitions."[19]

Figures, percentages, and statistics can mean everything and nothing,
but the spectacle that confronted the ordinary citizen in the occupied territories required no financial or economico-military price tag.

Freight trains and columns of trucks converged on Germany day and night, week after week and year after year, laden with all the things that were becoming scarcer and more expensive at home—laden with foodstuffs produced by countries forced to go hungry themselves.[20]

The knowledge that this spate of goods and commodities was benefiting a foreign power which persisted in attacking its peaceful neighbors steadily widened the gulf between victors and vanquished.

But that was not all.

At the beginning of August 1940, a few weeks after the fall of France, the French Government was informed how much it would have to pay toward Germany's occupation costs. The annual demand was for 146 billion francs (7.3 billion reichsmarks)—in other words, 400 million francs a day or 1.6 million an hour.[21]

As General Charles Huntziger, head of the French delegation to the Armistice Commission at Wiesbaden, submitted to his fellow negotiators on the German side, this sum would have sufficed to maintain a modern army of eighteen million men.[22]

Even those prominent French industrialists who had not been unattracted by the notion of a European New Order became antagonistic to the occupying power when the Reich Government, discounting a temporary reduction in occupation charges, stuck to its diktat. During 1943, France had to shell out 6,755 francs for every man, woman, and child in the country.[23]

To the occupying power, the impoverished Continent represented an inexhaustible gold mine. The Third Reich milked its occupied territories of approximately 60 billion reichsmarks under the heading of "occupation costs" alone.[24]

The significance of this hair-raising figure becomes fully apparent when we learn what proportion of the sums paid in "occupation costs" was surplus to Germany's actual requirements. In France, for example, the ratio of expenditure to income was one to six.[25]

What happened to these "surpluses"?

Johannes Hemmen, chairman of the economic subcommittee of the German Armistice Commission, explained it to his French partners in simple terms: "With that money the Germans will be able to buy up the whole of France."[26]

This was no mere figure of speech. In time, the procedure that came to be accepted as the principle governing Germany's foreign trade policy was that she should settle her debts with assets previously abstracted from her creditors.

The same method was sometimes used to advantage in the large-scale financial transactions whereby—not always to the unalloyed delight of the financial circles involved—Europe's foremost banking, raw materials, and haulage concerns were brought under German control.

In March 1941, for example, the Deutsche Bank and the Preussische

Staatsbank used French arms debentures found and confiscated by German forces invading Holland to cover part of the cost of taking over France's interest in the Bor copper mines of Yugoslavia (purchase price 1.8 billion francs) and in the Romanian oil industry. To put it baldly, loot was employed as a medium of payment.[27]

Hitler's policy of despoliation became more drastic the farther east he went—so much so that, even before invading Russia, he carried it to indescribable lengths in the Government General of occupied Poland.

To quote Hans Frank, his local viceroy, Hitler had ordained that Poland "be fully utilized by dint of ruthless exploitation" and that "Poland's entire economy be cut back to the minimum required to keep the population at the barest level of subsistence."[28]

This policy was duly enforced. Two years later, Frank himself answered the question whether and where it drew a line prescribed by common humanity. An informative entry in his diary makes it plain what was meant by "the barest level of subsistence." According to medical reports, he wrote, the Poles' malnutrition and poor state of health were attributable to an average daily food intake of only six hundred calories.[29]

It had fallen to one quarter of the normal adult diet, a starvation level which was bound to kill by slow degrees.

Organized Brutality

As for the acts of violence which subjected the inhabitants of the occupied territories to such extreme provocation, the few examples given below are horribly consistent with the foregoing picture. Mass arrests, the taking and shooting of hostages, arbitrary death sentences, secret executions, countless organized disappearances, the hunting down of innocent people, and the starving or lethal gassing of millions of prisoners of war and Jewish men, women, and children—all these developed into the grand challenge which every European had sometime to meet, either by conforming and collaborating, or by offering resistance.

Mass arrests: Whenever people were "taken away," their families and friends were doomed to sleepless nights of dread expectation—of fearing the worst. Thirty-five thousand families in the Protectorate and forty thousand in Norway waited—in vain, for all they knew. How many did likewise in Europe as a whole?[30]

The taking of hostages: This terrible instrument of political intimidation was coolly and calculatingly wielded against the civilian inhabitants of the occupied territories. How many innocent people must have gone in fear of their lives when all political prisoners were summarily reclassified as hostages by a stroke of the pen?[31]

The shooting of hostages: Poland witnessed 170 such executions in a

single day at the end of December 1939, Kiev 800 on another day in November 1941.[32] In France, German firing squads disposed of 471 French
citizens in nine months.[33] In Holland, 250 Dutch civilians were executed
as hostages because the German SS and police chief, Hanns Albin Rauter,
almost lost his life during a surprise attack by members of a Resistance
group.[34]

A distinction was drawn between secret and public measures. Where the
latter were concerned, the occupying power did its best to establish their
legitimacy and represent them as a reluctant but inevitable response to
outrages perpetrated by incorrigible fanatics who had banded together into
Resistance groups for the purpose, so it was said, of engineering a revolutionary upheaval.

In the case of certain occupied countries, we possess something akin to
a neat bookkeeper's record of court-martial executions for which the
highest degree of legitimacy was claimed.

The figure for Norway was 366, for Denmark 113,[35] for the Protectorate of Bohemia and Moravia in excess of 3,800, for France—according
to German statistics—approximately 3,000.[36]

The shooting of hostages, which the Germans likewise endeavored to
justify as an extreme form of self-defense practiced by troops on active
service, was authorized by a decree dated September 16, 1941. Originally
designed for the Eastern Front but later applied to all the occupied territories, this stated that "in general, the execution of fifty to a hundred Communists" was to be regarded as "proper reparation for the death of one
German serviceman." Furthermore, the manner of their execution should
"enhance the deterrent effect."[37]

The "Senior SS and Police Commander" responsible for the area under
the jurisdiction of the German military commander in France strove to
achieve this "deterrent effect" by means of posters affixed to the walls of
buildings in Paris. He announced that "runaway saboteurs or assassins"
would render their families liable to the gravest penalties unless they voluntarily surrendered to the German authorities within ten days. The penalties were listed as follows:

"1. All male relatives in direct line of ascent or descent, as well as
brothers-in-law and cousins, will be shot if aged eighteen or over.

"2. All women bearing the same degree of affinity will be sentenced to
forced labor.

"3. All children belonging to the male and female persons affected by
the foregoing measures, aged one to seventeen inclusive, will be committed
to an educational institution."

This announcement had been personally drafted by Reich Marshal
Göring.[38]

Another example, this time from Belgium: Here the German authorities
announced at the end of April 1943 that 832 "terrorists and Communist

officials" had been detained, shot, or handed over to military tribunals during the first four months of the year. To ram the point home, twenty Belgians were publicly hanged late in February 1944.[39]

In France at the beginning of June 1944, in reprisal for a partisan raid, ninety-nine Frenchmen were publicly hanged from balconies, window grilles, and lampposts in the main street of Tulle.

In Italy three weeks later, Field Marshal Albert Kesselring gave orders that villages from which shots were fired at German servicemen should be burned down and the "culprits and ringleaders" publicly hanged.[40]

But the Germans had recourse to secret as well as public measures.

"And they press on relentlessly; only now their executions are performed in secret so that there is no means of knowing . . . the names of the victims," stated an ecclesiastical report from Poland on conditions in the archdioceses of Gniezno and Poznań in April 1940. This document, which reached the Vatican by a clandestine route, went on, "The lives of the Poles are protected by no law, nor by any human feeling."[41]

The proportions assumed by the slaughter of Polish civilians in German-controlled territory can be inferred from a strict statistical survey which takes no account of those killed in action or during the Warsaw uprising. It is limited to members of the Polish intelligentsia, whom events at Cracow University prove to have been a special object of Hitlerian detestation. The dead numbered 22,400.

They included nearly 2,500 university professors, lecturers, and assistants, over 17,000 schoolteachers, roughly 300 actors and producers, 56.9 percent of all lawyers, 38.7 percent of all doctors, 27.2 percent of all priests, and so on.[42]

Estimates of the total number of Polish lives claimed by Hitler's war vary between four and six million, or 15 and 22 percent of the population.[43]

That secrecy should become the supreme principle governing his invisible reign of terror was one of Hitler's most loathsome ideas. For this, the macabre lyricism of inhumanity devised the weird appellation *Nacht und Nebel* [Night and Fog]. Issued by Hitler late in September 1941, the so-called Night and Fog Decree was quickly transmitted by the Wehrmacht High Command and furnished with executory and security provisions in the spring of 1942.

It was an order whose memory lives on. Persons suspected of resistance to the occupying power vanished without trace into the "night and fog" of the unknown. Spirited across the frontier into Germany, they were confined in concentration camps under the anonymous heading of "detainees for the duration of the war." No news of their whereabouts or eventual fate could be communicated to their families, friends, or national authorities.

Some five thousand people from France are said to have taken this dark road, and approximately seven thousand "N.N." detainees were consigned to official oblivion in German concentration camps.[44]

The same principle was observed, when Denmark finally rebelled, by squads of civilian terrorists recruited there under German auspices. Their identity was deliberately concealed, and their acts of violence, which claimed the lives of many fellow Danes, were disguised as ordinary crimes. Organized at a relatively late stage (January 1944) by specialist members of Otto Skorzeny's team, these groups operated under orders from the chief of the German Security Police. They blew up movie theaters, placed bombs in hotels and other public buildings, and murdered prominent figures—academics, lawyers, doctors, journalists—in their homes or on the street.[45]

The terrorist squads took only sixteen months to murder seven times as many Danes as were condemned to death by military courts and executed by firing squads throughout the war. No less than 899 men and women, all of them civilians, are reported to have died at their hands.[46]

Another official German report listed the "achievements" scored in Poland and Russia by the so-called Einsatzgruppen and Einsatzkommandos [operational groups or task forces] of the SS. Only three weeks after war broke out, they detained 800 Jews in the Polish township of Wloclawek and shot them "while trying to escape."[47] At Utena and Moletai in Lithuania they disposed of 3,782 Jews in a single day, among them "1,469 Jewish children."[48]

Orders for "the shooting of all Jews" could be issued and passed on by word of mouth alone. It was Hitler who dictated them, not the war.[49]

"Thus the number of shootings has been increased to 75,000 by a Sonderkommando [special detachment] and by Einsatzkommandos in Rokishkis to 85,000," stated a progress and situation report submitted by one Einsatzgruppe. And again: "According to the findings of a German physician, scabies had broken out in the ghetto at Nevel. To prevent the spread of infection, 640 Jews were shot. . . . In the ghetto at Minsk, 2,278 Jews were executed as saboteurs and activists."

Another official report, this time from the Ukraine: "In reprisal for acts of incendiarism in Kiev, all Jews were detained and a total of 33,771 executed on September 29–30."[50]

Four hundred shootings had been reported by the beginning of December 1941 and over a million by November 1942.[51] As everyone now knows, the "Final Solution" ultimately claimed between four and six million Jewish lives.[52]

Less well known is the fate suffered by Russian prisoners of war. Of these, 3,222,000 died in camps, were executed, or went missing. This figure appears in a table dated May 1, 1944, and compiled by the Organization Section of the German High Command's Prisoner of War Department.[53]

Men died in droves, both in Poland and in Russia, wherever prisoners not earmarked for transfer to Germany—they exceeded three and a half million by the end of 1941—were callously left in the open to die of cold and hunger.

Reich Marshal Göring gave Count Ciano, the Italian Foreign Minister, a sidelight on the Russians' life in captivity. Having eaten everything possible, he said, even the soles of their boots, they had taken to eating each other. Worse still, they had already devoured one of their German guards. Ciano found Göring's conversational tidbit sufficiently memorable to preserve it for posterity in his diary.[54]

Bubbling together in the cauldron of events were challenges of a physical and mental, economic and political nature, but they in turn were mingled with national, ideological, moral, and religious ingredients. To analyze and classify them at this late stage would be pointless because it was rare for one provocative act alone to trigger submission or intransigence, collaboration or resistance. Before these innumerable traumatic experiences could elicit a mass reaction, they first had somehow to coalesce and develop a common focus. That they did so was doubtless a function of processes occurring in the deeper levels of individual and collective consciousness.

Any psychologist and student of human nature knows that irrational challenges—humiliation, dishonor, degradation—will often make a stronger and deeper impact than rational ones. To say that nothing, absolutely nothing, can make amends for hurt pride, loss of reputation, and wounded self-esteem is to state the obvious. *"La raison prend à la longue le pli que le coeur lui donne* [Reason ultimately takes on the shape given it by the heart]," as Jean-Jacques Rousseau once wrote to Franquières—and it was just this propensity for crudely assailing the pride, honor, and self-esteem of his weaker brethren that represented one of the most salient features of Hitler's policy.

Military defeat and the realization that defeat connoted betrayal were enough in themselves to make the vanquished feel that their world had been shattered and their honor gravely tarnished.

During the shifts of power that took place in the first two years of the war, Hitler ousted the royal houses of five occupied countries. The king of a sixth was taken prisoner and that of a seventh provisionally tolerated. Institutions rooted deep in history, in national traditions and ideas, were overthrown from one day to the next.

Parliaments were dissolved or neutralized, constitutions abolished, professional associations and trade unions bullied into line or suppressed, and political parties—with the obvious exception of those tailored to the German pattern—sooner or later banned and smashed.

Generally speaking, moreover, national governments were brought under German tutelage or control, newspapers and radio networks "purged" and "coordinated," judicial systems distorted, and systems of public education remodeled or realigned to accord with Hitler's basic principles. The occupying power laid its heavy hand on the nerve centers of national existence.[55]

Quite in keeping with the above, this provoked intense feeling and a state of emotional turmoil into which all other provocations, including those of a purely material nature, could flow like poisoned streams converging on a boundless reservoir.

We need only think of the intolerable blows to national pride dealt by Hitler's Germanization policy. Tracts or strips of Polish, Belgian, and French territory, together with the whole of Luxembourg, were incorporated into the Greater German Reich by simple decree.

Picture a situation in which American, British, French, German, and Italian citizens were forbidden to marry fellow nationals. All Polish inhabitants of the "incorporated" Polish territories, male and female, were subject to just such a ban in the first seven months of the so-called New Era.[56]

Imagine how it would be if our mother tongue were downgraded into a mere auxiliary dialect, and if we were compelled to accept a foreign language—that of an occupying power—as our first and only official medium of communication. Such was the case in the Protectorate of Bohemia and Moravia and the Grand Duchy of Luxembourg.[57]

Assume that our ministers of religion, insofar as their places of worship had not been closed down, were only permitted to preach in a foreign language, and that the singing of hymns in our mother tongue was a penal offense. This state of affairs prevailed in the Polish territories annexed by Germany.[58]

Assume, finally, that unpleasant consequences would ensue if we dared cling to our own nationality instead of exchanging it, on demand, for that of an occupying enemy power. Purely because they had expressed a desire to remain French, one hundred thousand natives of Alsace and Lorraine were detained in November 1940, loaded into trains against their will, and deported to unoccupied Vichy France.[59]

Taken together, the swift succession of traumatic experiences undergone by the peoples of Europe became distilled into a noxious brew of shame and humiliation, guilt and hatred, injured national pride and shattered self-confidence—into a somber prevailing mood that enveloped the whole continent and expanded with the same rapidity as Hitler's domains. No European could take comfort from what lay strewn among the wreckage of his illusions: subjugated nations whose hopes had been dashed; corpses, cripples, and prisoners of war whose one desire had been to live in peace; and, last but not least, a stifling sense of impotence that could even prompt a few of Hitler's enthusiasts—people who had once been rabid National Socialists—to suspect that their German idol might, after all, have feet of clay.

Nourished by countless acts of inhumanity and arrogance, there sprang from this fertile soil the grand challenge which forms an essential and inseparable part of the history of collaboration and resistance.

The First Confrontation
or
The Choice Between Collaboration and Resistance

Twelve governments, five presidents, and seven monarchs were the first to have to debate their proper course of action on the brink of military defeat. In practical terms, they were faced with two alternatives: either to remain at their posts, or to quit and resume the fight against Hitler elsewhere. Most of them opted for exile and fled to London, where they proclaimed the metropolis of the British Empire the provisional capital of their respective countries.

There were three exceptions. The King of the Belgians chose to become a German prisoner of war and broke with his Cabinet. The Danish king and his government accepted Germany's assurance that their country's sovereignty and neutrality would be respected. The French government headed by Marshal Pétain banked on being able to come to terms with Hitler.

No matter what choice or decision they made, all these monarchs, presidents, and governments were open to a charge of betrayal.

If they fled to join Britain in the continuing fight against Hitler, they were deserting the people—people by whose consent they ruled—in their direst hour of need. If they stayed put, they were abandoning themselves and their countries to the enemy and betraying their foreign friends and allies.

So the history of collaboration and resistance opens on an oddly contradictory note. Those who stayed put and faced up to the victorious Germans, even at the expense of submitting to them, serving them, and probably collaborating with them, seemed steadfast and courageous. Those who took to their heels, even with a view to fighting on under foreign military aegis, gave an initial impression of disloyalty and cowardice. The resisters fled, the collaborators staunchly remained at their people's side.

Moral scruples had thus to be overcome before thought could be given to the consequences of either course. Was it possible to weigh the odds accurately with everything in a state of flux and Europe on the verge of collapse? What argued in favor of swift surrender and an accommodation with the enemy was his awesome military strength, the disclosure of one's own weakness, and, last but not least, the Allies' failure in the field. Could Hitler still be beaten? Wasn't Europe destined to become a German fief and remain so for an indefinite period?

Opponents of surrender and advocates of continued resistance argued that any government tolerated by the victor could just as well be abolished by him, together with the legitimacy of the state, the state itself, and possibly, even, the nation. When the state was personified by men who alone could salvage it from defeat, wasn't it their sacred duty to escape with all speed?

What was more, those who opted for flight and resistance could call on the still intact resources of their overseas possessions—on the French colonial empire, for example, which was twenty times the size of the motherland, or on the colonial territories of Belgium and Holland, which were vast enough to accommodate Europe twice over. They could also take advantage of worldwide lines of communication and sources of raw materials far beyond Hitler's reach, of colonial troops and a manpower reserve exceeding 150 million which could be mobilized in possessions scattered across four continents.

Sound and cogent arguments, all of them, but they bobbed like paper boats on a stormy sea while the battle raged outside and defeat loomed larger by the hour, with the irresistible momentum of a tidal wave. Now would have been the time for a cool and sober appraisal of the situation, but who was there left to consult? The men at the helm were dependent on their own judgment, on last-minute decisions which in turn were based on rapid fluctuations of mood, on false reports and rumors, on the uncontrollable workings of chance.

Such were the circumstances under which King Leopold III of Belgium held a final meeting with four members of his Cabinet on the evening of May 24, 1940. Only two weeks had elapsed since fighting began, but Belgian troops had been thrown back on their last defensive line and compressed into an area equivalent to little more than one twentieth of the entire country. It was the most densely populated region in Europe.[1] Over two million people were now sandwiched between the front line and the North Sea, including 450,000 soldiers and 800,000 refugees.[2]

The King and his ministers were agreed on one point: militarily, the situation was hopeless. In every other respect, their opinions differed widely.

The King argued that the war was lost, but not just for Belgium. The

French were near the end of their tether and the British would be lucky if they succeeded in extricating even part of their expeditionary force from the Continent. Could Britain still muster enough strength to repel a German invasion? Everything suggested that the Germans, having once gained continental supremacy, would be impossible to dislodge. Consequently, Belgium's only course was to lay down her arms and come to terms with the victorious enemy as soon as she could.

Premier Hubert Pierlot and Foreign Minister Paul-Henri Spaak informed the King that his cabinet unanimously opposed this view. No one could be certain that the war was already lost, they said, and no political decision of such scope and magnitude should be based on pure conjecture. Furthermore, the government had certain inalienable commitments to fulfill. By soliciting French and British assistance, Belgium had assumed partial responsibility for the disaster that had overtaken the Allied forces. The idea that she should repay her friends for their help by deserting them was so intolerable as to be out of the question. Nothing in the world could absolve the monarch and government of their duty to show solidarity. The Cabinet therefore recommended that Leopold follow the example of the Queen of the Netherlands and the Grand Duchess of Luxembourg, who were already in London. Both had called for the continuation of the war against Hitler and the liberation of their countries.

Leopold countered by pleading that, whatever happened, he had a royal duty to share the sufferings of his fellow countrymen. He then produced an argument which his ministers found hard to rebut.

It could only be a matter of days or hours before German tanks pushed on into what remained of Belgian territory, overcrowded as it was with hundreds of thousands of frightened and demoralized refugees who were capable of any desperate act. The result might well be bloodshed on a calamitous and unparalleled scale.

To avert such a disaster, said the King, he proposed to order an immediate cessation of hostilities. He further told his ministers that they could never justify the deliberate exposure of their compatriots to a massacre that would still be remembered a hundred years hence.

It later transpired that Foreign Minister Spaak fainted at this point. So heated was the debate, so irreconcilable and unyielding the stand adopted by both sides, that the stresses and strains of the occasion had become almost unendurable.

When discussion was resumed, Premier Pierlot took the floor. Although the monarch was the supreme national authority, he said, no order to capitulate was legally valid unless endorsed by his cabinet. The sovereign himself was the first to be bound by this constitutional provision, and nothing could shake it. Pierlot and his colleagues then announced that they refused to sign the royal decree.

Leopold was prepared for this refusal. As head of state, he said, he had always observed the constitution. As supreme commander of the armed forces, however, he was entitled to decide on his own authority what orders were appropriate to any given military situation.

The Premier then asked if His Majesty intended to appoint a Belgian Government under German occupation. The only word that occurred to Finance Minister Camille Gutt when he heard Leopold's monosyllabic affirmative was "treason." Since the King declined to follow his Cabinet to London, they had to take leave of him. The breach between them was complete and irreparable.

Accompanied by their personal aides, the ministers set off on a hazardous journey to France under cover of darkness.[3]

But the situation was far from resolved even then. Both parties, the King in Brussels and his government abroad, continued to debate the merits of their case. Could the government-in-exile claim to be the country's sole legal representative? If so, was the King entitled to order a surrender on his own authority, over its head and in its absence?

Hitler's tanks, which had skirted the pocket crowded with refugees, were already pushing along the Channel coast toward Dunkirk when Leopold hurriedly summoned three eminent lawyers to examine the question of legitimacy. This they did while the battle for Belgium neared its climax.

Their written opinion, which was submitted without delay, stated that the commander in chief of the Belgian armed forces was naturally entitled to order his men to stop fighting. If he made use of this prerogative, however, he himself would be taken prisoner in company with the army to which, after all, he belonged.

What followed was of supreme importance, for no prisoner of war was in a position to govern a country. Under Article 82 of the Belgian Constitution, executive power would automatically pass to the legally elected government—in other words, to Pierlot's cabinet, which, unlike the captive King, would still be at liberty.[4]

This expert opinion prompted Leopold to send a courier to France with a message for the government-in-exile. In it, he asked the ministers for blanket powers to deal with some ostensibly urgent legislative matters.

Did Leopold propose to use these signatures to dismiss his exiled Cabinet? Should the ministers approve their own dismissal sight unseen, as it were? If they signed, their dismissal would be legally incontestable. Rather than accede to the King's request, they sent his courier back to Brussels empty-handed.

Leopold's readiness to negotiate an armistice with Germany was ill requited. Hitler informed him that he had no intention of parleying and demanded his country's unconditional surrender. His forces would be taken prisoner and the main roads of Belgium must be kept clear for the benefit of German troop movements.

The King was now compelled to do what he had hoped to do of his own accord: he conceded defeat and accepted a form of detention appropriate to his rank. The Germans imprisoned him in Laeken Castle, on the outskirts of Brussels, with a retinue of twenty courtiers and officers and a hundred or so servants.[5]

Meantime, the government-in-exile continued its not unhazardous flight from the Germans. It had scarcely established a temporary base in Paris when it had to move on for fear of falling into enemy hands.

Pierlot's cabinet met at Limoges on May 31 and at Poitiers six days later. A royal courier who had managed to get through via Switzerland brought word that Leopold no longer proposed to form a new government.

That the fourteen ministers in Poitiers should have needed any such warrant of legitimacy is symptomatic of the hopeless mental confusion from which they were seeking to escape. They eventually decided to transfer the seat of government to London, whither the six hundred civil servants, public employees, and parliamentarians who had followed them to France were to be conveyed as quickly as possible.

But another week of grave developments put everything in doubt again. No attempt was made to defend Paris, and the German tanks continued their irresistible advance. The Belgian Government-in-exile left Poitiers and hurried south to Bordeaux, where it cast around for a bolt-hole somewhere in unoccupied territory. France was beaten.

Confronted by the sight of a country, an army—a world—in the throes of dissolution, the Belgian ministers debated where to go after leaving their temporary quarters in Bordeaux. The Belgian Congo, perhaps?

Turmoil reigned at a hastily assembled cabinet meeting. "It was hot, and everyone smoked a good deal. We debated in an atmosphere that was psychologically stifling as well," recalled Camille Gutt. "It is inconceivable, the speed with which despondency can take hold of an entire city, penetrating buildings and even men's heads like a poisonous fog. There was no more talk of war—not a word about leaving for London."[6]

Should they resist? Should they persevere with a war which, after all that had happened, seemed definitely lost? Should they continue their flight in the face of insurmountable problems of transportation? As for the public servants who had accompanied the Cabinet thus far, wouldn't it be wiser to send them back to Belgium? The latter question, too, was broached and discussed.

The Belgians were at a loss—incapable of decision and thoroughly disheartened. Early in July they moved to Vichy. Only one cabinet minister, Camille Gutt, headed for London.

When Gutt called on Churchill and assured him that the Belgian Government's fighting spirit remained unbroken, he must have done so with mixed feelings. His ministerial colleagues in Vichy showed no signs of budging.

Gutt bombarded Premier Pierlot with letters and telegrams whose contents were not published until over thirty years later. The Cabinet must act before it was too late, he urged. From what he had heard, there was talk at Vichy of resigning—even of returning to Belgium rather than endure the sensation that they were caught in Vichy like rats in a trap. "I assume this SOS to be the very last," he wrote to Pierlot in mid-August. It was no longer the eleventh hour; the clock was about to strike twelve.[7]

"Your response to all our telegrams in the past sixteen days has been silence," he cabled. "We fear that you have abandoned your original intention and are either unwilling or unable to come here, and that attempts are being made to coerce you into resigning your post. If this goes on much longer, we shall have no government at all."[8] He added that London believed the Belgian Government to be in the custody of the French Government and the latter in the hands of the Germans.[9]

The situation was not resolved until the end of October. After well-nigh three months of burning indecision, the Belgian Cabinet finally arrived in London.

Resistance is customarily thought of as a swift, spontaneous, or preconceived decision, just as a readiness to collaborate is dismissed as straightforward weakness or treachery. The attitudes adopted by King Leopold and his ministers reveal how wide of the mark this simplification is. By remaining in Belgium because he wanted to avert a bloodbath, Leopold may have committed a political blunder but did not betray his country. Despite their prompt decision to soldier on, his ministers took months to prevail over their fears, misgivings, and moral dilemmas sufficiently to seek exile in London.

What made up their minds for them?

Conjecture, perhaps, but not certain knowledge; tanks, planes, and guns, to be sure, but also the written provisions of constitutional law; subtle argument and moral constraint, by all means, but also the imponderables of mood and emotion.

Meanwhile, faced with similar problems and the very same choice, the French Government had opted for surrender. Hopefully—more hopefully than any other—it sought refuge in overt collaboration with the enemy.

The comparison is inescapable. Two nations and two governments at the scene of the same drama, presented almost simultaneously with comparable alternatives, had formed different judgments, drawn different conclusions, and steered in diametrically opposite directions.

Was it that here more than elsewhere, in the metropolis of an empire prone to Gallic self-acclaim, the sudden and totally unexpected shock of military defeat seemed like an all-destroying, all-uprooting natural cataclysm?

In London on the morning of May 15, 1940, Winston Churchill received a telephone call from Paul Reynaud, the French Premier. "We have been defeated," Reynaud began without preamble. Churchill made no comment. "We are beaten," Reynaud insisted. "We have lost the battle." The German offensive had been in progress for only six days.

Reynaud again: "The front is broken at Sedan; they are pouring through in great numbers with tanks and armoured cars. . . ."[10]

Just how chaotic the situation was, Churchill discovered for himself in Paris the next day. General Maurice Gamelin, the French commander in chief, informed him that France had no strategic reserve. The Seventh Army, which had been ordered to Holland, was done for. All sectors of the front were undermanned, even the Maginot Line.[11]

While Gamelin was speaking, Churchill stared out of the window and saw senior officials busy burning secret archives in the garden of the Quai d'Orsay, France's Foreign Ministry.[12]

Many detailed accounts have been written of the fall of France. What interests us here is the attitude of the government and the role of Marshal Pétain, then eighty-three years old.

After telephoning Churchill on the morning of May 15, Reynaud apparently expressed a desire to enlist the venerable Marshal's "wisdom and calm." Pétain was recalled to Paris from his ambassadorial post in Madrid the same day and appointed Vice-Premier in Reynaud's government on May 18.

To the French people, who had yet to grasp the full gravity of the situation, Pétain's return seemed an auspicious sign—a good omen. Headlines like "The Victor of Verdun Joins the Government," which were splashed by leading Paris newspapers the next day, reinforced their firm belief in France's invincibility. A similar effect was produced by the replacement of Gamelin as commander in chief with another hero of World War I, General Maxime Weygand, who had once been chief of staff to the victorious commander of the Allied armies in France, Ferdinand Foch. With such men in charge, it was thought, any foreign invader would ultimately shatter on the French nation and its armies like glass on rock. According to the press, Marshal Pétain owed his exalted reputation and unique store of experience to "the flame of his extraordinarily lucid mind."[13]

This picture did not accord with what was going on behind the scenes. It is said that Pétain and Weygand privately expressed themselves in favor of an armistice on May 18, though neither of them came out with it at a War Cabinet meeting the following day.

President Albert Lebrun, too, confined himself to saying that peace with Germany might be preferable to the total destruction of the glorious French Army. As for Generalissimo Weygand, he declared with diplomatic caution that he would not engage in a sanguinary fight to the death without first consulting the British.

This set the ball rolling. Premier Reynaud stated that he was expecting a

German peace offer, and that the government must consult London on how to reply. The sooner the better, urged Weygand.

During the next few days, France's military leaders were chiefly preoccupied with "saving the Army." An intact Army would be needed to cope with the possibility of internal disorder. No honorable peace with Germany could be attained without one, and military forces of a respectable size were essential to the country's future reconstruction.

What attitude did the Cabinet take?

Marshal Pétain made his first open and unequivocal plea for an armistice on the evening of June 13.

If the government left French soil, he stated in Cabinet, it would be guilty of desertion and could no longer claim to be the country's legitimate executive authority. In this dark hour, anyone who deprived France of the men appointed to lead her would be abandoning his homeland to the enemy.

It was clear that the Marshal had drafted his statement with care. He read it aloud from a sheet of paper. "I declare, so far as I am concerned, that, if need be outside the government, I shall refuse to leave home soil. I shall remain with the French people, to share their sorrows and tribulations."[14]

Familiar words, familiar circumstances, familiar questions of conscience. First the Belgians, now the French. At this stage, there was little to choose between them because far from all Pétain's fellow ministers shared his views. Many would have preferred to quit Paris and fight on.

But they, too, were sucked into the vortex of defeat and swept from one extreme to the other.

The following afternoon, Premier Reynaud advised his cabinet to follow the Dutch example. They should order a cease-fire but then leave Paris and join the Allied line of battle.

Marshal Pétain said nothing—made no demur. To all appearances, he was at one with Reynaud.

Fifteen minutes later he changed tack completely. After a brief conversation with Generalissimo Weygand, who had been waiting in an adjoining room, he firmly opposed the surrender he had so far advocated. No self-respecting army commander could be asked to order his men to lay down their arms, and no self-respecting government could expect it of him.

Admiral Jean Darlan, commander in chief of the French Navy, was another who underwent a swift and unexpected change of heart. Having stated, only the night before, that he would put to sea with his fleet in the event of an armistice, he now disclaimed any such intention.

In that case, should they resist at all? This seemed to be the prevailing view. Only ten cabinet ministers now favored an armistice, with the Premier and fourteen others against.

If a cabinet crisis was to be avoided, a compromise had to be found.

Ex-Premier Camille Chautemps put forward a proposal calculated to appeal to a majority: first make discreet inquiries about Germany's terms for an armistice, then request the British Government's comments, and finally settle on one course or the other.

Everyone seemed unaware that this compromise anticipated the final decision because it made the idea of a cease-fire respectable. If it was worth noting and exploring, it was as good as accepted.

No wonder the hard-liners crumbled the next day, when Pétain persuaded the Cabinet to appoint him head of government and resign.

Two days later, without consulting his ministers, he delivered his historic proclamation to the French people. "With a heavy heart," he announced that the fight must be abandoned. The government of the German Reich had already been invited to state its terms for an armistice.

This did not, however, put an end to debate, soul-searching, or political speculation. The Marshal's announcement was prefaced by pealing bells. But, even as French ears rang with their promise of peace, most leading Frenchmen were still resolved to withdraw to their country's nearby African base and continue the war from there. Apart from President Albert Lebrun and Pétain's Vice-Premier, they included the presidents of both parliamentary chambers. Bowing to their insistence, Pétain prepared to appoint Vice-Premier Chautemps his deputy in Africa.[15]

Matters were now resolved by a swift succession of events. The Cabinet and the presidents of the two chambers formally determined to transfer the seat of government to Algeria, but they reckoned without Pétain. The elderly Marshal and victor of Verdun, who had already become a remote national figurehead towering above a turbulent sea, nursed a devout belief in his patriotic mission. Grimly swallowing any scruples he may have felt, he reportedly considered arresting President Lebrun as he boarded the *Massilia,* which was ready to sail.

But it never came to that. The political scene was so befogged by false reports, delaying tactics, and the machinations of ambitious second-string politicians who scented opportunities for self-advancement in the general turmoil, that essentials were well-nigh swamped by irrelevancies. After all, no one knew from personal experience that national collapse resembles the most commonplace of processes: it occurs by degrees, not at one particular juncture. The men who had decided on resistance failed to act on their decision in good time.

The same drama was enacted almost simultaneously by two casts, one French and one Belgian, but with two different endings. The *Massilia* set sail for Africa with only thirty deputies and one senator on board—no head of state, no president of either chamber, and not one minister out of twenty-four.[16]

Presented with the choice between resistance in voluntary exile and an attempt to compromise and collaborate with the enemy, government leaders in every country save Denmark, Belgium, and France opted for exile, though not under universally similar circumstances.

In Poland, the mere idea of conciliation and compromise was precluded by the brutality with which the country had been invaded and occupied, not to mention the Russian presence there.

The President of the Republic, Ignacy Mościcki, together with his cabinet ministers and service chiefs, sought refuge in neighboring Romania. Here, despite the Polish-Romanian alliance, they were detained and interned for fear of military intervention by the great powers who were fraternally sharing the Polish cake.

How legitimate was a government incarcerated in a foreign country, albeit an allied one, and powerless to exercise its functions? Could its claim to represent the state and nation be upheld?

To extricate themselves from this grotesque and awkward predicament, the Poles resorted to a legal artifice. President Mościcki resigned from office so that his presidential powers could be transferred to a still undesignated successor.

The next move took place in Paris at the end of the month, when Marshal Wladyslaw Raczkiewicz was sworn in on the Polish Constitution and a government-in-exile formed under General Wladyslaw Sikorski, whose administration took up its duties forthwith.

Though not beyond criticism in terms of international law, this proceeding was accepted by Poland's allies, the Western Powers. As we shall see later, an important role was played by this government whose membership had been switched to salvage a country's national identity. By early 1940 it had set up a delegatory authority in occupied Poland to coordinate resistance there and finance it with funds provided by the government-in-exile.

The kings and governments of Yugoslavia and Greece were as little in a position to compromise with the victor as Poland had been. They, too, were confronted by a pair of hostile powers—in their case, Nazi Germany and Fascist Italy—so the exodus of their government representatives was not a question open to debate. In both instances, however, their flight abroad was purposely delayed.

Churchill urged Yugoslavia's young King Peter II and his ministers to stay put for as long as possible, pointing out that their country's mountainous terrain, being inaccessible to tanks, would lend itself to the organization of armed resistance.[17] He likewise encouraged King George II of Greece and his government to stand firm, initially on the mainland and later on the island of Crete. The kings and governments of both countries were not evacuated by the British until the military situation left them no choice. They, too, set up their military and political headquarters in London.[18]

Holland's position was crystal clear. Having undertaken a prewar study of the problems that would arise from the military occupation of their country, the Dutch authorities had issued directives covering such an eventuality. Everything went more or less as planned. On the morning of the fourth day after Germany invaded, Queen Wilhelmina boarded a British destroyer. The Cabinet followed her a few hours later, but not before the last two ministers to quit Dutch soil had, on the Queen's behalf, transferred supreme executive power to the commander in chief, General Henri Gerard Winkelman. The general was simultaneously authorized to order a cease-fire if circumstances required it.

Government ministries were taken over, again as planned, by the undersecretaries who had stayed behind. The fact that this was done by government decree was of constitutional importance. When the Queen and her ministers went into exile and General Winkelman signed the German-Dutch armistice on May 15, no doubt attached to the legitimacy of the government-in-exile or to that of the Dutch administration in occupied territory. The departure of the Queen and her government had left it fully intact, so any infringements by the occupying power could henceforth be judged in accordance with the laws of war to which the Germans themselves subscribed.[19]

In Norway, matters followed a more dramatic course. The King, royal family, Cabinet, and Parliament quit the capital only a few hours after the outbreak of hostilities and moved to Hamar, a railroad junction north of Oslo. At the same time, trucks transported the Bank of Norway's gold reserves and the Foreign Ministry's most secret documents to a place of safety. This foiled the German plan to capture the King and his government by surprise.

The Norwegians acted with remarkable speed and precision. Parliament convened at Hamar on the afternoon of the first day. Johan Nygaardsvold, the Socialist Premier, promptly submitted his cabinet's resignation on the grounds that the emergency called for an all-party government. The deputies unanimously voted to keep the ministerial lineup unchanged but agreed that it should be augmented by three ministers without portfolio drawn from the conservative opposition.

As nightfall approached, the session had to be adjourned because enemy troops were nearing Hamar. The deputies reconvened the next day at Elverum, on the Swedish frontier, where they invested the government with unlimited powers—even in the event that King and Cabinet be compelled to leave Norwegian soil. This ensured that any future government-in-exile could claim to be the country's sole legitimate representative.

Meanwhile, the Foreign Office in Berlin had instructed Curt Bräuer, the German minister, to maintain diplomatic contact with the Royal Norwegian Government despite the fact that Germany was already at war with Norway. Bräuer followed the government and deputies to the Swedish border and urgently requested an audience with the King.

King Haakon consented to receive Bräuer, after much hesitation, but flatly rejected Germany's demand that he sanction the formation of a government acceptable to the Third Reich and headed by Vidkun Quisling, the Norwegian National Socialist. The German minister was curtly dismissed and returned to Oslo empty-handed.

The King thereupon empowered his government to decide for itself whether or not the Army should fight on, though he made his own position abundantly clear. "Should the government decide to accept the German demands," he added, ". . . I see no alternative but to abdicate. I have reached this decision after rigorous self-examination and inner conflict."

There was no argument: the war went on. The first British troops landed at Narvik, Namsos, and Andalsnes in mid-April, and French units disembarked a few days later. Meanwhile, the Luftwaffe harried King Haakon and his ministers as they retreated northward. Berlin would have preferred it if the entire Norwegian Government had succumbed to an air raid like those that devastated Nybergsund and Molde in Romsdal Fjord. Both places went up in flames, but the King and Cabinet fled to the nearby woods. They were eventually rescued by a British cruiser and taken to the northern port of Tromsö, which was proclaimed the provisional capital of Norway on May 1, 1940.

Although it was now clear that nothing but resistance could be expected from Norway, the Germans did their best to make political capital out of a fairly predictable military victory. What they needed was a puppet administration which would meet all their requirements but could also claim international recognition as the country's legal government.

They made a crude attempt to achieve this during the latter half of June 1940. On June 9, after Allied troops urgently needed in France had been withdrawn from Norway, King Haakon was compelled to order a ceasefire. The next day, he and his government departed for London and five long years of exile.

Of the country's 150 parliamentary representatives, 130 had been obliged to remain in Norway, so they could be convened under German occupation and made to pass resolutions whose legitimacy was inarguable.

This was where Berlin applied pressure. Four days after Haakon's departure, Reich Commissioner Josef Terboven requested Parliament to meet, depose the King, withdraw the powers that had been transferred to the government-in-exile, and set up a Council of State invested with full executive authority.

For five days on end, the deputies wrangled over the extent of the concessions that were warranted in the national interest and tried to determine where the inviolable line should be drawn.

It proved impossible to reconcile the views of all 130 deputies. One group was prepared to yield, another rejected compromise in any form. At last, under extreme pressure, a majority took shape. The Reich Commissioner had publicly threatened that all able-bodied Norwegian males would be sent to German concentration camps if Parliament opposed the wishes of the Reich Government.

It was probably because this threat coincided with the grim news of France's collapse and Pétain's depressing proclamation to the French people that a majority brought itself to accept the German demands and come to terms with the occupying power, though the modus operandi was left undefined.

The agreement which the majority eventually reached with the German authorities was not legally binding upon Parliament. Perhaps in order to preserve this advantageous state of suspense for as long as possible, the parliamentary secretariat dragged its feet. It was not until the end of June that it dispatched a letter to Haakon suggesting that he abdicate.

The King's response was an unequivocal negative. He would bow to a majority decision of the people, but not to an unconstitutional proposal that had clearly been made under duress. Parliament had no constitutional right to depose the King or summarily dismiss his government.

BBC London broadcast this statement the same day.

The 130 deputies were subjected to steadily increasing pressure in the three months that followed. At the end of September, the parliamentary secretariat invited them to ratify the agreement reached between the majority group and the occupying power.

This proposal, too, was fiercely resisted at first. But in a weak moment, and in the erroneous belief that a shrewd proviso would somehow enable it to wriggle off the hook later on, Parliament reluctantly approved the new scheme of things demanded by the occupying power. Reich Commissioner Terboven was now able to announce that the King had been deposed, Parliament dissolved, and all political parties—with the exception of the National Socialists—banned. He complacently informed Berlin that Norway could at last be treated like a "conquered province."[20]

One monarch, the most powerful in Europe, was spared such ordeals. This was George VI, titular ruler of Great Britain and the British Empire. How would he have acted if the worst had happened?

Few people seem to have posed this awkward question while Hitler's hordes were flooding across the Continent, but the King once answered it himself. Speaking in confidence to William Stephenson, an intelligence chief conversant with all the best-kept state secrets, he declared in the spring of 1940 that he would never leave the United Kingdom if German forces invaded it. There would be no question of his going into exile in America or collaborating with the enemy in any way. His personal example must convey to every Briton what was expected of him: steadfast resistance to the occupying power and its accomplices.[21]

On the same occasion, King George referred to the "Auxiliary Units," a name that masked the preparations already under way for a guerrilla campaign in the British Isles. Though habitually uncommunicative, Stephenson later disclosed to his biographer that, by July 1940, every little hamlet in Great Britain had its own guerrilla detachment complete with subterranean tunnels and stores of equipment.[22]

Was the example set by kings, presidents, and governments universally and spontaneously embraced by their peoples? How did the ordinary citizen react when first confronted by Hitler's soldiers, by war and defeat?

When the Belgian Government-in-exile, rent by indecision, was still at Bordeaux, its members learned from Belgian refugees arriving there that the King, who had surrendered three days earlier and become a German prisoner of war, was being acclaimed as a hero by his people, whereas they themselves, who had preached resistance to the enemy, were targets for abuse.

"We heard the same tale for two whole years," Camille Gutt resignedly noted in his memoirs, "or as long as the fortunes of war remained against us."[23]

In Holland, too, the Queen's departure for London with her ministers met with little understanding. There was talk of "flight," of "indignation, resentment, and resignation."[24]

In Denmark, the agreements granting Germany's armed forces the right of "peaceful occupation" were generally welcomed. The vast majority of Danes approved of their government's decision to remain in office and go about its business as though it alone were master in its own house. It was clear that most Danes had come to terms with the new situation and entertained no thought of resistance.[25]

In Norway, when the Lysaker Bridge was blown up on the fourth day of the invasion, thereby depriving the Germans of an important road link with the airfield at Fornebu, many of the capital's leading citizens backed the German military commander, General Nikolaus von Falkenhorst, who threatened reprisals—summary executions and the destruction of the city center—should the saboteurs' example be followed elsewhere. No less than two hundred prominent Norwegians supported the German general by publishing an appeal to the population to refrain from all acts of violence likely to provoke the occupying power. This renunciation of active resistance by the leaders of Oslo society was universally imitated, and no popular unrest declared itself for the remainder of the year.[26]

In France, a French tank officer was murdered by local inhabitants—fellow Frenchmen—for refusing to abandon the defense of a bridge over the Cher at Vierzon.[27] On June 20, five days before the still unsigned armistice came into effect, a French colonel who ordered his unit to break through encircling German forces was shot by his own men.[28]

The Franco-German armistice was "no minority plot," as the U.S. historian Robert O. Paxton so aptly points out.[29] The whole of France, both in and out of uniform, not only wanted peace but made peace without waiting to see what would emerge from the armistice negotiations. Anyone who continued to resist was endangering everyone else's chances of survival. Wherever resistance still smoldered, it was the vanquished who quenched it.

Yet the initial shock of defeat was nowhere more intense than in France. Ex-Premier Léon Blum likened it to the trauma inflicted by a serious accident. Never, in the words of Anatole de Menzie, had the French people experienced "so long a period of anesthesia."[30] "In the space of a few days," Paul Valéry wrote in June, "we have lost all certainty. We are on a terrifying and irresistible slope. Nothing we could fear is impossible; we can fear and imagine absolutely anything."[31]

When Hitler's armored divisions thrust deep into the French interior, a nation took flight. The towns and villages of France emptied. At Evreux, a town with a population of twenty thousand, only 218 adults and children remained. The refugees on the roads—yesterday's peaceful citizens who had been convulsed overnight by a national disaster of unknown dimensions—were estimated at ten million.[32]

Intense as the sudden shock may have been, however, it was swiftly surmounted. Although emotional turmoil lingered beneath the surface for a long time, it was submerged by the strong desire for peace that had become as natural since the "futile war" of 1914–18 as the passage of the seasons. Hadn't everyone learned, yet again and from personal experience, that anything was preferable to war?

Manès Sperber, then a Polish volunteer in the French Army, describes the ambivalent mood of those days in his memoirs:

"Whenever possible, we steered clear of the roads and marched through woods and across country. Often, however, we had to regain the highway to obtain food in villages and small towns. Whenever we entered a town we marched in close order and sang marching songs at the top of our voices, as though ready for anything, and never more loudly than when passing café terraces where the locals were leisurely sipping their aperitifs. It was as if the people, countryfolk and townsfolk alike, had come to terms with their disastrous defeat; they found consolation in the certainty that their sons would come home unscathed. Only a few more days—weeks at most—and all would be as before. Solid ground remained beneath their feet, the grain was ripening in their fields like the fruit on their trees, and well-husbanded wine was maturing in their cellars. All this was still intact and proof against loss."[33]

French intellectuals who later joined the Resistance felt just the same. Simone de Beauvoir recalls how all that animated her then, in July 1940, was the prospect of returning to teach at her Paris lycée. If her salary were paid, she told herself, she would stay on. Jean Guéhenno, who later became a Resistance writer and editor of *Cahiers de Libération,* voluntarily returned to occupied Paris with the same unconcern, happy to be able to resume teaching. The idea of moving to unoccupied France seems rarely if ever to have been entertained.[34]

Did the yearning for peace and the desire for a return to paradise lost become a European obsession? In neutral Switzerland, Denis de Rougemont gave his daughter, who was born in the seventh month of the war, a name that symbolized peace and would always remind him of a sleepy French village in 1938.[35] To Aage Bertelsen, the future Danish Resistance fighter, the welfare of his family and friends at first meant more than the freedom of his native land. "We were all in favor," he later admitted, "my wife included, of the so-called collaboration policy."[36] As for André Gide, who had spent the early days of the war learning pages of Racine, Cyril Tourneur, and Eichendorff by heart, he noted in his diary on July 9, 1940: "If German rule were to bring us affluence, nine out of ten Frenchmen would accept it, three or four of them with a smile."[37]

Even in default of affluence and despite a severe shortage of food, this attitude remained temporarily unaltered. Henri Frenay, who founded one of the major French Resistance movements, characterized the situation in August 1940 by saying that his compatriots' sole and overriding concern was food, but that they were adapting themselves to defeat just as they had to victory.[38] A year later he recorded how hard he found it to remain sanguine when he heard people talking on streetcars. "Ninety percent of all Frenchmen," he wrote, "take the view that this war isn't their war."[39]

In Western Europe—unlike the East, where the brutality of German military methods and occupation policy precluded any peaceful compromise with the enemy—the initial prospects for collaboration were far from bleak. The grand challenge had yet to take shape here, and its beginnings were either suppressed or explained away. On the other hand, everyone was face to face with two basic facts: Europe was condemned to live with the enemy; and, as far as could be seen, the enemy seemed quite well behaved.

It had, for example, to be conceded that the armistice enforced on France, though harsh, embodied no provisions that were beyond fulfillment. Germany lodged no claim to a single square mile of French soil. The defeated country retained its colonial empire and an army of 100,000 men. Hitler even refrained from insisting that the French fleet be handed over to him. The warships had to be laid up and mothballed, but they rode at anchor under French supervision in a port in unoccupied territory. The Wehrmacht occupied three fifths of the country, but the administration of the whole of France remained in the hands of an autonomous French Government which, in the unoccupied zone, represented the interests of an outwardly sovereign state and maintained diplomatic relations with foreign countries.

Where Holland and Belgium were concerned, not to mention the privileged Kingdom of Denmark, the wording of Germany's declared aims seemed readily acceptable. The Reich Government expressly stated that it would not encroach on the countries' sovereignty or colonial possessions, and that it had just as little intention of meddling in their internal affairs.

But apart from this, and for all the mistrust that greeted such assurances, it was an undeniable fact that the occupying forces did not behave as people had expected or feared. Here in the West, they were conspicuous for their almost exaggerated correctitude. Everyone had been expecting "Huns," but the newcomers proved to be courteous, well disciplined, and helpful.

All these factors combined to produce some initial contradictions which were not without danger. On the one hand, most monarchs, heads of state, and governments had opted for exile and resistance at the first confrontation; on the other, the vast majority of ordinary people began by showing little sympathy for this radical step and preferred to wait and see. This was why, notwithstanding all the provocative acts which Hitler had previously committed, the Third Reich's soldiers and civil servants encountered an almost miraculous tolerance and readiness for peaceful cooperation in the occupied territories of Western Europe—and this despite the basic mood of sullen hostility and the resentment, contempt, and underlying hatred of the vast majority of their inhabitants. The irreconcilable antagonisms between victor and vanquished were a positive spur to underground resistance in the East, whereas the broad masses in the West could see no immediate or sufficient grounds for rebelling against their National Socialist overlords.

With or without the enemy, life had to go on.

PART TWO

Life with the Enemy

Hitler's Europe
A Brief Survey, Country by Country

National Socialist domination of all or part of seventeen European states inhabited by 260 million people is a story whose beginnings antedate the outbreak of war.

On March 15, 1939, the Wehrmacht moved into what remained of the former Czechoslovak Republic. The Czech President was already in exile. Eduard Beneš, co-founder of the Republic, had announced his resignation and quit the country early in October 1938, a few days after the signing of the Munich Agreement. The terms of that extortionate document had been imposed on him, and he refused to legitimize them by remaining in office.

Czechoslovakia had then been dismembered. She not only lost the Sudetenland and the territories occupied by Poland, but was compelled to grant internal autonomy to Slovakia and the Carpatho-Ukraine. These areas, comprising 24,000 square miles with a population of four and a half million, were ceded to Czechoslovakia's neighbors when Germany marched into Prague six months later. Slovakia itself became "independent" and was placed under German protection. President Beneš's successor, Emil Hácha, now presided over the German-occupied rump state known as the Protectorate of Bohemia and Moravia.

The occupying power's interest in this area centered on its exceptionally efficient armaments industry. The Protectorate would be able to supply the German war machine with artillery, rifles and ammunition, trucks and aircraft. That was temporarily more important than any rather vague future plans to "Germanize" a substantial part of the Czech population. For the present, it was decided to tolerate a species of sham autonomy and government in the occupied Czech Protectorate in the hope of maintaining industrial morale at a high level and keeping the natives work-happy.

Once the police had arrested some two thousand Communists and German émigrés in the first few days, therefore, the Germans adopted a relatively moderate occupation policy because it was not to their advantage—in this case—to confiscate or dismantle factories and other economic assets. On the contrary, new plants were built with an eye to augmenting arms production still further.

This did not, of course, prevent the occupying power from taking over the nerve centers of the Czech economy, though it exercised extreme care and discretion. Well-justified resentment was averted by enlisting the help of leading German banks and acquiring joint-stock corporations or setting up German-controlled concerns.

Generally speaking, the Czechs remained quiescent until long after war broke out. They were almost as well fed as the Germans, and it was not until the winter of 1939 that the occupying power was driven to take action by one or two incidents. At about the same time, it also proceeded against a handful of Resistance groups that had formed in the interim. These it succeeded in smashing, together with some combat groups belonging to the banned Czech Communist Party—the only one in Europe that had not complied with Comintern instructions arising out of the German-Soviet nonaggression pact and treaty of friendship.

The political climate changed radically with the opening of hostilities on the Eastern Front in June 1941. The Czechs prayed for Germany's defeat while German occupation policy hardened. The head of the Central State Security Bureau, SS-Obergruppenführer [General] Reinhard Heydrich, who personally assumed the functions of Reich Protector at the end of September 1941, ordained a series of drastic measures designed to cow the population. His assassination at the end of May 1942 unleashed a spate of the most brutal persecution and repression. On Hitler's orders, Security Service personnel razed the village of Lidice to the ground and shot all its male inhabitants.

Repeatedly crippled by heavy losses, the national Resistance movement failed to muster enough strength for any major disruptive operations until the war's end. Neighboring Slovakia became the scene of a Soviet-backed, Communist-led revolt and fierce guerrilla fighting in July 1944, whereas the Protectorate of Bohemia and Moravia remained wrapped in the graveyard hush of successful subjugation. It was not until May 5, 1945, that a party of Czech officers struck the blow that heralded the fight for freedom—five days after Hitler's suicide and five days before the Red Army entered the Czech capital.

In Poland, as all the world knows, the victorious Germans instituted an appalling reign of terror. When the territories that had not been incorporated into the Reich were placed under German civil administration in mid-October 1939, contrary to the original plan to amalgamate them into a Polish rump state, Poland ceased to be a political entity in its own right. From now on, it was nothing more nor less than a German "Government

General." Only the most junior civil service posts were retained by Poles, who acted as mere errand boys and instruments of an occupying power with unlimited authority.

In the belief that the war would soon be won forever, Berlin promptly subjected these territories—unlike the Protectorate—to the policy of despoliation and extermination to which reference has already been made. Anything of value to the German war economy was confiscated and carried off, and any Polish men and women capable of rebuilding their country at some future date were killed or deported. Hundreds of thousands were condemned to utter slavery and perished in concentration camps.[1]

Under these circumstances, organized resistance seemed the sole alternative to national extinction. Although the first military Resistance groups were formed very early on, they took some time to become operative against *two* occupying powers, German and Russian, which jointly and separately strove to quell any stirrings of national opposition. Until Germany attacked the Soviet Union in June 1941, "illegal Poland"—secretly in constant touch with its London-based government-in-exile—waged an unequal two-front war against the great powers on either flank.

Russia's enforced change of alignment was a turning point for the Poles, too, but its effects were short-lived. Although diplomatic relations were restored at the end of July 1941, the Russians severed them again late in April 1943 because the Poles had infuriated them by demanding a neutral investigation of the mass graves found near Katyn, which contained the bodies of thousands of executed Polish officers. Meanwhile, innumerable small Resistance groups had merged by mid-February 1942 to form the illegal Polish "Home Army" (Armia Krajowa, or AK for short). This was formally subordinated to the Polish commander in chief in London.

As time went by, the political conflicts that underlie our present international power structure became more and more apparent. In the summer of 1942, even before diplomatic relations were severed, an army corps recruited in Russia from released Polish prisoners of war and commanded by General Wladyslaw Anders left the Soviet Union and linked up with the Western Allies by way of Iran. In the spring of 1943, on the other hand, Moscow proceeded to form a Soviet-Polish division which later expanded to become General Zygmunt Berling's Red Polish Army. Friction was further aggravated, early in 1944, by the formation of a "Polish National Committee" in Moscow and an anti-Communist counterpart set up by the Home Army. Then, during August and September 1944, the Home Army bled to death in a dramatic but unsuccessful attempt to liberate Warsaw under General Tadeusz Bor-Komorowski—a politically pregnant tragedy described in detail in Part Four of this book. Poland's frontiers and her future were eventually determined by Moscow's recognition of the Communist "Lublin Committee" as the provisional Polish Government in January 1945, and by the Yalta Conference decisions of the following month.

In Norway, on the periphery of the European theater, the Germans' main concern was to guard a long coastline against Allied invaders with a minimum of defense and internal security forces, while simultaneously exploiting the Norwegian economy to the full. One major precondition of this policy was an ability to keep the country docile. It was never fulfilled.

Having courted voluntary cooperation for the first four months, the German authorities could not resist combining a policy of friendship with one designed to deter and intimidate all potential enemies. After five months, they dismissed the Norwegian "Administrative Committee" to which they had originally entrusted government business and replaced it with a Provisional Council of State whose composition all too clearly betrayed their intention of converting the Norwegians to National Socialism. The opposition they encountered drove them to enforce their policy by issuing "coordinative" decrees and ordering mass arrests, confiscating all radio sets, introducing SS jurisdiction, and similar measures. It was their extensive reliance on members of Vidkun Quisling's hated National Socialist Party that set the seal on public hostility toward them and their Norwegian henchmen.

In January 1942, when the occupying power appointed Quisling head of a puppet government which promptly and overzealously tried to dragoon its citizens into the role of docile Nazi schoolchildren by bombarding them with regulations and decrees, national resistance became organized. A secret army named MILORG (an acronym for Military Organization) was formed, and deliberate acts of sabotage carried out in close consultation with the government-in-exile in London and the British High Command more than once gave the Germans genuine cause for concern.

The resulting process was one that could be observed in every occupied country at almost every stage: each act of defiance evoked a response which was, in its turn, construed as a challenge. Just as the measures taken by the occupying power excited public fury, so this reaction proved a red rag to the occupying power. When German forces in Norway were increased during the first half of 1942 from 100,000 to 250,000 men—in the mistaken expectation of an Allied invasion attempt—MILORG units scattered throughout the country were hurriedly brought under unified command. It could now be fairly said that a state of war existed between the Norwegian Resistance and the forces of occupation. By the time Norway suffered its own Lidice in the spring of 1942—the village of Televaag was totally destroyed in the course of a punitive operation and its male inhabitants were deported—the Germans' original bid for voluntary cooperation had finally failed.

In the case of Denmark, which was invaded at the same time as Norway, three and a half years went by before Hitler's "model protectorate" likewise began to feel the effects of unbridled German violence. The Danish

Government had thus far striven, as best it could, to exploit the fiction of neutrality for its own purposes. No open breach occurred until it denied the occupying power the right to use German personnel to hunt down Danish saboteurs. Then, on August 29, 1943, the Germans proclaimed a state of emergency, seized power, dismissed the government and dissolved Parliament, disarmed the Danish forces, and brought the country's administration under their direct control. Already considerably disrupted by the growth of clandestine resistance, the "negotiation policy" that had endured for three and a half years was succeeded by something close to a state of war. On the very first day of the crisis, Copenhagen witnessed the formation of a Danish "Resistance Council" which functioned as the central organ of all Resistance groups.

As elsewhere, so in Denmark, the German authorities were now faced with strikes and raids on arms depots, as well as with deliberate acts of sabotage carried out by an organized Resistance movement. Ultimately financed by the Danish Government itself, this operated to such good effect that it appreciably delayed the transfer of German forces from Scandinavia to the Reich during the last winter of the war.

The pattern of events in Holland was not dissimilar. Here too, the occupying power had hoped to find friends or even allies. Hitler permitted Dutch prisoners of war to return to civilian life. What was more, the German supervisory authorities trod gingerly at first and avoided any clashes with the undersecretaries who were running government departments on behalf of ministers in exile. Hostages taken in the first few days because of the alleged maltreatment of German citizens in the Dutch East Indies were handled with kid gloves and in some cases released. Discounting the curfew and food rationing, life for the bulk of the population went on much as usual. The occupying power also saw to it that German troops and police personnel remained as inconspicuous as possible.

This picture changed when the German authorities began to impose National Socialist views on the country by streamlining its press and political life. The more Dutch Nazis ensconced themselves in important posts, and the more anti-Semitism became manifest in the persecution and deportation of Dutch Jews, the greater the hostility toward the occupying power.

Until Stalingrad marked a turning point in the war, Dutch factories worked almost uninterruptedly for the German war machine and Dutch administrators made no attempt to impede large-scale exports of raw materials and foodstuffs to Germany. The population remained adequately nourished and there was a satisfactory flow of Dutch volunteers for employment in the Reich. The disruptive activities of illegal Resistance groups had so far been suppressed with relative ease.

Now, however, Holland was rapidly transformed into a hostile land. Economic mobilization for total war, the introduction of forced labor, the reinternment of Dutch servicemen in April 1943, and similar drastic measures, most of which entailed police raids, mass arrests, reprisals, and other resorts to violence, prompted the clandestine Resistance movement to mobilize in turn. It not only stepped up attacks on German installations and personnel, as well as on Dutch collaborators, but in September 1944 called a railroad strike which lasted until the end of the war. The German authorities hit back with a wholesale ban on goods traffic which ultimately caused a severe famine and claimed fifteen thousand lives.

For their part, Belgium and Luxembourg underwent mere variations of the occupation policy pursued in Holland. Here too, the Germans at first enjoyed a surprising measure of public cooperation. In relative terms, no country condemned to death and executed more of its citizens for collaboration with the enemy than Belgium, where in the summer of 1945 over fifty thousand prisoners awaited trial in jails designed to house a tenth of that number.[2]

Like Luxembourg, where compulsory military service was introduced at the end of August 1942, Belgium witnessed a duplication of the developments that were simultaneously goading the Dutch into active resistance. These included attempts at conversion to National Socialism with the aid of indigenous fascists, drastic coordinative measures, and the mass conscription of labor.

Thus in Holland and Belgium—areas of great strategic importance—the Germans provoked the creation of armed and organized Resistance movements which girded themselves for the final showdown in close consultation with their governments-in-exile across the Channel.

For at least three reasons, events in France followed a different course. In the first place, the Wehrmacht left part of her territory unoccupied for two and a half years. Secondly, the unoccupied zone was the seat of a sovereign government which at first retained the allegiance of France's colonial empire. Thirdly, the administration headed by Marshal Pétain established an authoritarian regime of conservative character which bore more resemblance to the Third Reich than to the parliamentary republic of the Popular Front years, whose surviving representatives were ruthlessly eliminated.

The moderate terms of the armistice strengthened Pétain in his belief that genuine collaboration with the victorious Germans would enable France to gain their trust and develop, in time, into an equal partner and co-founder of a "New European Order." He and his cabinet—notably Pierre Laval, who was appointed Vice-Premier on the day the armistice was signed—at once began to demonstrate their collaboration-mindedness by making substantial concessions which the Germans themselves had never demanded or expected. When Pétain conferred with Hitler at Montoire late in October 1940, he came away convinced that he had provided his policy with a firm foundation.

Laval, who took over the Foreign Ministry soon afterward, carried this policy of voluntary submission to extremes in the belief that Germany's triumphant domination of Europe was an irreversible fact. Although he quit the Cabinet in December 1940—for reasons then obscure—and did not rejoin it for over a year, collaboration continued unabated. After resuming office in August 1942, he openly affirmed his hopes for a German victory and France's desire to play her part in it by engaging in limited military cooperation. In November of the same year, German forces occupied the rest of the country.

What contributed to the utter failure of this policy was the steady growth of the Resistance, which gathered itself into a number of large clandestine organizations and was gradually coordinated by Pétain's arch-enemy, General de Gaulle, who had installed himself in London at the head of a French National Committee. The various elements of the Resistance movement were amalgamated into a National Resistance Council in May 1943 and eventually subordinated to the Provisional Government of the French Republic formed in June of the same year. The fighting that now broke out—in defiance of Pétain, the occupying power, and organizations composed of French Nazi extremists—was conducted with unsurpassed ferocity by both sides. The ultimate effect of the Germans' repressive measures and their inhuman manhunts for young workers who evaded forced labor by taking refuge in the mountains and forests was to swell the ranks of the partisan units and of France's secret army-in-the-making. By the time Pétain's government was forced to concede that its policy had failed, Vichy was on its last legs. The dawn of liberation was at hand.

Yet another situation developed in Southeastern Europe—in Yugoslavia, Albania, and Greece. Here the occupying power established new regimes which could serve as useful instruments of political and military cooperation, namely, puppet governments in Greece and Serbia and an enlarged and autonomous Croatian state under fascist leadership. Parcels of Yugoslav, Albanian, and Greek territory were awarded to the Third Reich, neighboring allied countries, and Mussolini's Italy, and the military defense and policing of the remainder undertaken by the beneficiaries of German victory.

But the very multiplicity of these power centers and occupation forces, coupled with the rugged, mountainous terrain, conduced to an outbreak of suicidal guerrilla warfare between armed bands and partisans of the most varied political complexion. In Greece, regardless of their common German foe, Communist and non-Communist partisan units fought each other under the command of rival Greek generals. In Yugoslavia, a similar struggle raged between supporters of Draža Mihailović, the Serbian royalist, and those of the Communist leader Josip Broz Tito. In spite of the heavy losses inflicted on his forces by the Wehrmacht, the latter not only proved a match for his political opponent but outclassed him. Tito, who founded a sort of provisional parliament known as the Anti-fascist Council for the National Liberation of Yugoslavia (Avno) late in November 1942, and was intent on creating a socialist Yugoslav state, impressed everyone with his toughness and qualities of leadership. In March 1943, British Headquarters Middle East decided to contact him from Cairo. Before long, the Western Powers began to arm his partisans, who had waited in vain for Russian aid, and incorporate them in their strategic plans. In Greece, by contrast, the Germans' withdrawal in December 1944 was followed by an outbreak of hostilities between British forces and Communist partisans. Even then, therefore, the future polarization of the great powers cast its shadow across the Balkans.

The Russians recovered from the grave military reverses inflicted on them in 1941. Their desperate defensive battles and powerful counteroffensives won heartfelt and worldwide admiration, but they also surprised the world by drawing a political inference from what they had undergone. The leaders of the only existing state to have been spawned by Bolshevik revolution became convinced that national survival was a reflex far more potent in its effect on the masses than any revolutionary ideals or objectives. Stalin proclaimed a "national war" in the name of Russia, not of revolution, dissolved the Comintern, and carefully refrained from involvement in all parts of occupied Europe where national and revolutionary interests conflicted. The Communist parties, which suffered themselves to be used as instruments of Russian foreign policy, obeyed his instructions, and their revolutionary hopes were often badly dashed. Even in Hungary and Romania, neighboring countries allied with Germany, Stalin did not come to the aid of hard-pressed Communist Resistance groups until it was tactically or strategically beneficial to the Red Army's advance to do so.

Inside the Soviet Union itself, large sections of the population in German-occupied territory showed a spontaneous readiness to collaborate. However, this good will was so thoroughly squandered by Hitler's manic ideas and his policy of deliberate extermination that Moscow was very soon able to mount a centrally directed guerrilla campaign behind the German lines. This was where Hitler, with paranoid persistence, engineered his own destruction and that of the Third Reich.

Neutral Collaboration
or
I Conform

The neutral collaborator says: I accept that life must go on. Knowingly and from self-interest, I directly or indirectly work for the occupying power without professing the political and ideological principles of National Socialism. My attitude is dictated by circumstances beyond my control. The sole alternative appears to be bankruptcy, unemployment, starvation, chaos, and destruction. I am determined to survive the war and my country's defeat as best I can.

National and local government officers were the first to recognize the need for neutral collaboration. Public services had to be maintained in the interests of the community at large and of each individual citizen. Roads and railroads, public utilities and food supplies, fire brigades and hospitals all had to function as before. Like it or not, therefore, some form of arrangement with the occupying power was essential. Administrative cooperation was an automatic process—unless, of course, it had been studied and rehearsed before the war.

This was so in Holland and Belgium.

As early as 1937, Belgian railroad officials and power station personnel exempt from military service had been issued with a "civil mobilization" booklet. This reproduced a 1935 law defining the duties of civil servants in wartime and contained the text of the relevant Hague Convention of 1907.

It was stated that public employees should offer no resistance in the event of invasion by external forces. On the contrary, they would be expected to perform their duties loyally and conscientiously, even under foreign occupation. They were further enjoined to do nothing that might harm the occupying power in any way, and were authorized to give its representatives a written undertaking to that effect. They could resign their posts only if the occupying power requested them to do something that conflicted with their duty of national allegiance.[1]

Thus the Belgians were acting quite legally when, in June 1940, they made an agreement with the occupying power which guaranteed administrative continuity, even in the absence of the government. Called into being for this purpose by Belgian politicians, a so-called Committee of the Legislative Council invested the undersecretaries of the various ministries not only with ministerial authority but also with certain legislative powers.[2]

A similar state of affairs prevailed in Holland, where every public servant's desk contained a sealed envelope to be opened in the event of invasion. This in turn contained government directives, also dating from 1937, on the procedures to be observed in collaborating with the enemy.

Here too, the transition to official collaboration passed off with surprising ease. Before leaving the country, government ministers had instructed their number twos to stay put and establish contact with the occupying power. Fundamentally, therefore, all that had occurred was a change of personnel. The ministers' functions were now exercised by their undersecretaries, and the latter were initially responsible to the commander in chief of the Dutch Army, General Winkelman, who had—as we have already mentioned—been invested with supreme executive powers.

So there was no need whatever for an administrative shutdown. In consultation with the German authorities, the undersecretaries declared their readiness to form a sort of "civil servants' cabinet" which would keep the administrative machine running just as smoothly as a properly constituted government. Their sole proviso was that the Germans should refrain from installing a National Socialist government, and that Dutch public servants should not be required to harm their national interests.

At first, therefore, all went fully in accordance with the confidential injunction "to strive, in the public interest, to ensure that the administration . . . performs its function as well as may be." Both sides, the undersecretaries and the German authorities, were interested in keeping relations as unstrained as possible, so collaboration began in a thoroughly decorous manner.

Two weeks after Holland surrendered, the German Reich Commissioner, Arthur Seyss-Inquart, formally invited the undersecretaries to join him for a ceremonial transfer of "supreme executive power." They accepted the invitation even though General Winkelman, who was to be stripped of all his powers at the same "state ceremony," had been ignored by the German authorities.

Though naturally reluctant to offend the Reich Commissioner, they let him know in advance that they would leave the Rittersaal if any criticism were leveled at the conduct of their Queen.

"In view of their Fatherland's grave predicament," reported General von Falkenhorst, they also courteously declined Seyss-Inquart's invitation to a "communal meal" at the conclusion of the ceremony. The Reich

Commissioner gallantly and considerately informed them that he had taken "sympathetic note" of their decision.[3]

After a mild inaugural address which any Dutchman might have approved of, Seyss-Inquart received the undersecretaries at his official residence for a preliminary exchange of views. As representative of the supreme government authority, he asked if they were prepared to give their loyal cooperation and explained what he meant by this. Should they ever disagree with him, he expected them to say so frankly and, if need be, quit their posts. They had a perfect right to resign if ever they felt unable to endorse any measure taken by the occupying power. He would make no trouble for anyone who openly and honestly said him nay, but those who chose to remain in office must be loyal collaborators.[4]

The undersecretaries promptly consulted General Winkelman, who, under these circumstances, raised no objection to their working with the enemy.[5]

But that was not the end of the matter. Hardly had the country's administrators resumed their duties under different auspices, and hardly was collaboration under way, when the economy claimed its pound of flesh.

A complete shutdown? Nobody wanted that. The Dutch people had to be fed, clothed, and employed. They were dependent on receiving their economic due—work, an adequate income, and the necessities of life—but Holland's warehouses were empty.

It did not take long to grasp the meaning of economic subjection to the occupying power. Every worker and manufacturer, every employee and employer, every wage earner and capitalist was dependent on the victor's good will.

So all eyes turned to the Third Reich, which was gradually tightening its grip on the Continent by seizing and monopolizing every available source of raw materials. Berlin had become the headquarters and control center of the European economy—the place where decisions were taken as to who should receive raw materials and who should not. And that, in turn, determined whether any firm based anywhere in Europe could continue to employ its work force or would have to shut down for an indefinite period.

Given that only those with something to offer the victor could hope for raw materials, doing business with the enemy became a matter of life and death.

Dependence was not, however, entirely one-sided. The occupying power, too, was interested in keeping the wheels of industry turning. If it wanted to hold the occupied territories without undue expense, it had to ensure that their inhabitants remained tractable and that order was, wherever possible, maintained by their national authorities.

Thus the imperative of survival and the strategic and political interests of the occupying power coincided in a way that created an involuntary relationship between victor and vanquished—a singular and exceptionally precarious relationship.

The victor, of course, wielded absolute control over the vanquished. His decisions and decrees were unchallengeable. He could obtain whatever he needed, if necessary by force. But it was also no secret that peaceful and compliant nations were easier to manage and economically more productive than a continent in revolt. Tact and consideration were therefore the order of the day, if only because they promised to pay off. Such, at least, was Berlin's ulterior reason for tolerating quasi sovereign governments in France and Denmark and formally recognizing their neutral status.

At the headquarters of the Franco-German Armistice Commission in Wiesbaden, both sides engaged in years of agile, dogged negotiation. The official minutes of these meetings, which survived and were published after the war, are a shattering documentary record.

Shortly after the fall of France, for example, supplies of Algerian iron ore and French bauxite came up for discussion. Once Berlin had shown interest in these, the French delegates not unnaturally sought to get their country the best deal possible, their aim being to offset some of the heavy financial burdens that had just been imposed by the armistice terms. They offered bauxite for sale at the high price of 195 francs per ton. Negotiations dragged on.

The French industrialists earmarked as prospective bauxite suppliers soon lost patience. Eager to do business with the Germans and unable to see why they should have to await the outcome of discussions at government level when they could approach Germany's Vereinigte Aluminiumwerke direct, they pressed on regardless. Their tenders were submitted at prices far below those quoted by the government representatives at Wiesbaden.

Before August was out, French and German businessmen swiftly clinched a purchasing agreement for 250,000 tons of bauxite at a price per ton of only 75 francs. The French delegates at Wiesbaden, who were still arguing their case for a higher price, had been neatly bypassed.[6]

This marked the start of a collaboration contest between government and industry whose chief beneficiary was the Third Reich, which neglected no opportunity to profit in every conceivable way from the rivalry between private and public economic interests.

Both sides were quite content. It mattered little whether deals were concluded by government negotiators or businessmen. What counted was the feasibility of politically neutral economic collaboration between victor and vanquished, and it was this divide between business and politics which French industrialists cited in rebuttal of hostile criticism.

They soon scored some dazzling successes. By April 1941, French industry had secured German contracts to the value of 1.5 billion reichsmarks. By April 1942, the value of these transactions amounted to 2.36

billion reichsmarks, and in the autumn of the same year it crossed the 4-billion threshold.[7]

To France, therefore, economic cooperation represented an extremely lucrative process that offset at least a small part of what she had forfeited as spoils of war. Although this form of collaboration was primarily, though not exclusively, inspired by the profit motive and kept clear of political commitments as far as possible, it quickly assumed such dimensions that even the Vichy Government, which had nailed its colors to a policy of outright collaboration, was obliged to restrain French businessmen eager to supply the Germans with even more than they had demanded.[8] In this instance, neutral collaboration took a direction unacceptable to the government of a country recently at war with Nazi Germany on Britain's side.

Vichy's original intention was to impose certain limits on cooperation with Germany. It would not go to the lengths of rendering Hitler military assistance or supplying him with guns and ammunition, though the bauxite shipments were debatable in themselves because, once in Germany, they were converted into aluminum for the Junkers aircraft and aero-engine factories and thus became part of Germany's arsenal. Setting aside the precise definition of matériel, however, the interests of the French aircraft industry weighed heavily from the outset.

This industry had greatly expanded in the space of a few years. Its output had multiplied twenty or thirty times since 1938. By the time the Western offensive was launched, it was producing eight hundred planes a month instead of thirty, and substantial increases in output had since been achieved.[9]

The industry's leading executives, most of whom had moved to unoccupied France, were itching to do business with their only really promising customer, Nazi Germany. They were among the first to place themselves wholeheartedly at the service of the German war economy.

In July 1940, a mere four weeks after the armistice was signed, the Caudron-Renault Works applied to the French Ministry of Aviation for permission to build several hundred trainers for the German Air Force. In August, the managing director of France's largest aero-engine manufacturers, Gnome & Rhône, offered to supply the Germans with engines and spare parts. Meanwhile, with even greater business initiative, the Schneider-Creusot Works obtained firm German orders for bomb components.[10]

Under pressure from powerful industrial and financial interests, the French authorities caved in. They approved the manufacture for Germany, first of transport and training aircraft, then of aero engines and spare parts, and ultimately of combat aircraft. One last stipulation was upheld: the warplanes must not be equipped with weapons of destruction.

Thus, little more than three months after the military collapse of France, her leaders had already gone far beyond the self-imposed limits on economic cooperation laid down in the armistice agreement.[11] They could, of course, argue that they were acting under force of circumstance. Many industrial concerns had been compelled to close down and others had cut their labor force to about half the prewar level.[12] Although nearly two million Frenchmen had been killed or taken prisoner, a million unemployed were still on the street.[13]

To obtain the raw materials essential to a resumption of industrial production, Vichy was reluctantly prepared to make almost any concession. In view of the countless problems looming over them, the French leaders would secretly have preferred to harness the whole of their industry to the German war effort. The economic policy enforced on them developed a growing identity with that of the Germans, whose aim—to employ one of their euphemistic turns of phrase—was "the total economic and financial integration of France into the European area."[14] Thus, moves toward economic cooperation emanated more from the vanquished than the victor. Putting it still more strongly, one would have to say that the French flung themselves at the Germans.

Incredible as it may seem, there was actually a superabundance of economic cooperation on the part of the vanquished—and not in France alone.

To take one example, roughly 80 percent of Belgium's coal production went to the Third Reich after initially being restarted for the benefit of her own industries.[15] To take another, Denmark exported more foodstuffs and agricultural products to Germany than were stipulated by the quota agreements between the two countries.[16] Danish commercial interests expected big business—colonial-style business, even—to flow from cooperation with Germany. At the beginning of December 1941, they set up a Copenhagen-based "Working Committee for the Promotion of Danish Initiatives in Eastern and Southeastern Europe," toured the occupied Eastern territories, and volunteered to help the Germans exploit the area with Danish capital and labor. These endeavors proved ultimately abortive because the Germans never extracted anything from European offers of cooperation that was not in perfect harmony with their plans. Denmark's participation in looting the East did not interest them.[17]

In fact, Hitler viewed all offers of collaboration with the gravest suspicion. Speaking of collaborators, he once said that "if they act against the interests of their own people, they are dishonorable; if they try to help their people, they become dangerous."[18] His verdict on the zealously collaborating French, those "hereditary foes of Germany," was particularly venomous. He said of them that they put him in mind of bourgeois who had "risen in the world by a series of accidents." In dealing with them, he went on, one should take the view that it would be a sin ever to give back what had been captured with so much effort.[19] "Talk of collaboration" was intended "only for the moment," Reich Minister Goebbels noted in his diary.[20] On another occasion, he remarked that France's military and political power would have to be eliminated, once and for all, from the future interplay of forces in Europe.[21] "If the French knew what demands the Führer will one day make on them, their eyes would probably pop. That's why it's better to keep mum about such things for the present."[22]

So Berlin looked on calmly while occupied Europe, which had already been bled white, voluntarily offered its last drop of blood for sale.

It should at the same time be said that, of the businessmen who took Franco-German cooperation seriously in their own way, the French undoubtedly recovered their costs. German contracts placed with them by the end of 1942 included orders for 3,620 aircraft and 11,783 aero engines. Significantly enough, almost half these contracts were negotiated with German industrialists, though the single most important customer was the Reich Air Ministry in Berlin.[23]

What of working-class attitudes in occupied Europe?

Some Resistance historians and labor journalists return a largely dogmatic answer to this question. According to them, the class consciousness of the European industrial proletariat precluded any form of collaboration with Fascism or National Socialism. The very fact that Hitler's and Mussolini's police forces brutally suppressed all labor parties and trade unions and crushed all attempts to uphold their interests left the workers with no choice but to wage war on their natural class enemies. It is then implied, with rhetorical vehemence, that collaboration was a beastly capitalist business, whereas resistance was a natural working-class cause. What is more, upper-class ruling circles had been the backers and beneficiaries of Fascism and National Socialism even before the war, whereas the working class had merely been their victims.

What is true is that the labor parties were stronger than others in their prewar opposition to Italian Fascism and German National Socialism—and with good reason. Where the war itself is concerned, however, the widespread view that European labor's resistance to the occupying power was instinctive and class-based is one of those pious myths that fail to withstand serious scrutiny.

A hundred thousand Frenchmen had been killed and nearly two million taken prisoner by the Germans, yet 59,000 French workers voluntarily left to take up jobs in the Third Reich during the first sixteen months after the fall of France.[24]

Long before the introduction of forced labor, 403,000 Belgian workers volunteered their services to German industry or the German armed forces. Of these, 321,000 were found jobs in Germany at their own request and 82,000 employed by the Todt Organization to construct the fortifications, airfields, and other military installations that were planted on Belgian soil in furtherance of Hitler's war against the Allies.[25] Undeterred by any stirrings of class consciousness, over 120,000 Belgian workers left for Germany in the first fourteen months.[26]

Workers from Denmark also volunteered. There, 103,000 hurried off to Germany in the first fourteen months,[27] though the trade unions made genuine attempts to dissuade them.[28]

Workers from all the occupied territories left for Germany of their own free will. By the end of August 1941, a grand total of over two million European workers, male and female, had voluntarily gone to the Third Reich to work for Hitler's war machine.[29] They included 93,000 Dutchmen, 109,000 Serbs and Croats, and 140,000 Czechs.[30]

What of the workers who stuck it out at home under German occupation? Did they flock to join the Resistance with similar alacrity and in similar numbers? Holland furnishes us with an example which not only holds good for other countries but does, to say the least, give food for thought.

More than 30,000 Dutch railroad workers and salaried employees, who were at that time organized in five different trade unions, permitted their representatives on the staff council to endorse a managerial declaration of loyalty to the German authorities shortly after the invasion of May 1940. This volunteered administrative and technical cooperation provided the railroad network remained under Dutch management. The German authorities accepted the offer and its provisos without more ado.

What did this cooperation entail? What followed from the fact that 30,000 Dutch railroadmen and salaried staff had opted for a collaborative policy which involved no political commitment and was, in other words, as neutral as the millions of workers who felt impelled to migrate to Germany?

They repaired German rolling stock from the very outset. They manned Dutch trains in German frontier areas. They handled the transportation of German loot and German strategic supplies. They did not balk at consigning political prisoners to concentration camps or, later on, Dutch labor conscripts to Germany—410,000 of them, according to official Dutch figures. With disciplined alacrity, they also dispatched ninety-eight freight trains laden with 112,000 Dutch Jews destined for German extermination camps. Their loyalty to the occupying power was almost unbounded.[31]

Their conduct was just as well disciplined when they rather belatedly launched a strike on the evening of September 17, 1944, after British airborne troops had landed at Arnhem and Nijmegen. The strike, which had been arranged with the Dutch Government-in-exile and Allied Supreme Headquarters, was intended to assist military operations by paralyzing railroad traffic throughout Holland. Historians of the Dutch Resistance rightly record that the railroad workers and staff performed their task with remarkable efficiency.

By this time, barely nine months before the Third Reich collapsed, the outcome of the war had long been decided. Resistance now assumed spe-

cial importance because it could accelerate the course of military operations already in progress and hasten the end of the fighting. The railroadmen were fully alive to the value of their role in the final battle against
Nazi Germany, which they had served so well, but they were equally alive
to the dictates of self-interest. They demanded full pay for the entire duration of the strike, plus overtime and the usual Christmas bonus—and they
got it.

The National Assistance Fund maintained by the government-in-exile
paid them 37 million gulden. Of all the financial aid received throughout
the war years by the Dutch Resistance, over 44 percent ended up in the
strikers' pockets.[32]

This flagrant case does not in any way detract from the efforts and
sacrifices made by other Dutch workers who joined the organized Resistance. Like the migration of millions of European workers to Germany,
however, it symptomizes the general tendency and readiness of the inhabitants of the occupied territories to compromise with the enemy for as long
as humanly possible.

It should in fairness be pointed out that workers were quite as hard hit
as their employers by the consequences of war and defeat, by devastation
and universal economic chaos, by the dismantling of factories and the seizure of assets, by shortages of raw materials, and, last but not least, by a
disastrous level of unemployment which seemed unlikely to fall for a long
time to come.

Even in the miniature paradise known as Denmark, which had seen no
fighting at all, 200,000 unemployed and approximately 100,000 short-time
workers were recorded in all but a few summer months.[33] In France, Belgium, and Holland, however, over two million workers remained jobless
for weeks and months after their countries' defeat.

This surplus of unemployed labor in the occupied territories coincided
with a shortage of manpower in Germany, where nearly four million
workers were withdrawn from industry during the first three years of the
war.

There were three ways of meeting this demand. Under international law,
prisoners could be put to work. Attempts could also be made to recruit as
many volunteer workers as possible. Finally, if even this proved insufficient, consideration could be given to the establishment of a compulsory
labor service. The ultimate solution, in other words, was forced labor for
millions.[34]

The German authorities launched an intensive propaganda campaign for
the recruitment of volunteer labor in which they painted a glowing picture
of the benefits accruing to willing workers and their dependents. Attractive
brochures, public meetings, radio broadcasts, and press advertisements all
disseminated the palatable idea that it was no disgrace to provide for oneself and one's family.

In fact, the occupying power had much to offer its workers: high wages, facilities for sending money home, regular vacations with pay, and the right to call on a social security system which was undeniably more advanced in Nazi Germany than in many of the occupied countries.[35]

Promising results were obtained from the Third Reich's earliest recruiting drive, which it launched only a week after marching into Czechoslovakia. Thirty thousand workers volunteered during the first three weeks of the campaign and seventy thousand during the first six months. According to a subsequent poll conducted in Germany among the seventy thousand Czech volunteers employed there, only two thousand odd would have preferred to return home rather than stay on for a lengthy period.[36]

It was consistent with this policy that in the Protectorate of Bohemia and Moravia, where workers were required for industries of strategic importance, the occupying power should have introduced a generous new pay and conditions structure, as well as successive wage increases. Czech workers were forced to concede that they owed their improved living and working conditions to the occupying power, not to their own authorities or trade unions. They would have had absolutely no objection to the replacement of their own administration by the Germans. As a German Security Service report from the Protectorate noted in the spring of 1940, there were plenty of people "who described the National Socialist regime as the most pro-labor of all."[37]

The German authorities in Poland proceeded even more briskly. Just three days after war broke out, the first labor recruitment offices opened in areas captured by the Wehrmacht only hours before.

Thirty such offices came into operation during the first two weeks. By the end of October, 110,000 Polish workers had been signed up. By the end of May 1940, 210,000 had left for Germany.

These surprisingly high figures are attributable to the fact that unemployment in Poland became greatly aggravated when a million refugees from Upper Silesia and East and West Poznań poured into the already overpopulated Government General. To many of the unemployed, the tempting German offer seemed like manna from heaven.[38]

So employers were certainly not alone in their high degree of readiness to engage in politically neutral collaboration. Apart from the workers who went to Germany of their own free will, any accurate survey of neutral collaboration should include those who stayed at home but knowingly produced goods vital to the German war effort. The executives and directors of the French aircraft industry would never have been able to supply Germany with airplanes and spare parts had they not been assured of their workers' wholehearted support.

It is no exaggeration, therefore, to say that the whole of occupied Europe worked primarily for Hitler's war machine. Ardent National Socialists were not the only ones to exert themselves in furtherance of a German victory; industrialists and businessmen of all kinds and a majority of workers did likewise, irrespective of the trade union or political party to which they belonged.

Stark confirmation of this fact may be seen in some official German figures dated spring 1942. According to these, no less than 845,000 French workers were then employed exclusively on behalf of the Third Reich, either in French munitions plants and factories or in constructing airfields and fortifications on French soil. French locomotive builders and machine tools manufacturers allocated, respectively, 100 and 95 percent of their output to Nazi Germany.[39]

Even in the occupied territories of the East, neutral collaboration attained a surprising level. Hundreds of thousands of "Hiwis" [*Hilfswillige*, or volunteer auxiliaries]—a popular term that underlined the voluntary nature of their collaboration—worked for the German armed forces. Largely agricultural laborers born and bred in the Soviet Union, they were, to Western eyes, a Soviet rural proletariat devoid of political awareness and incapable of forming personal judgments. Their employment by the Wehrmacht as bootblacks, cooks, and drivers, stable boys, ammunition toters, and performers of a thousand menial tasks, enabled German auxiliaries to be released for other forms of war service.[40]

These Russians were far from being National Socialists and devotees of Hitler. They served the Wehrmacht, but not for political reasons. They did so because they were hungry or afraid, or both. It was hardship, coupled with the fear that they might one day be numbered among the countless victims of the manhunt and firing squad, that drove these men into the arms of the Germans. Others, who felt less immediately threatened, collaborated for material reasons. Like the European middle and working classes, they wanted to go on living—if possible, more comfortably than before.

The recruitment of these "Hiwis" began during the first few months of the Eastern campaign. By the spring of 1942, they were estimated at 200,000, and by summer of the same year at nearly 500,000. In July 1943, the Reich Commissioners of Ostland and the Ukraine, Lohse and Koch, put them at somewhere between 600,000 and 1.2 million.

Also recruited from this vast reservoir of "Hiwis" were the Ukrainian and White Russian volunteers who served in engineer units and SS task forces, as concentration camp guards and auxiliary policemen under German command.[41]

Painstaking research has disclosed that the occupied areas of the Soviet Union produced more collaborators than partisans. According to German and Allied figures, a million Soviet citizens were in Germany's service during the closing stages of the war.[42]

We therefore find ourselves at odds with the widespread view that, compared to the Resistance movements of World War II, collaboration played only a minor role. It is known that collaborators existed. They were tried and sentenced for their actions: there is little more to be said on the subject, or so we are told. Although books, newspapers, and public speakers expend much time on the Resistance, they seldom refer to those who aided and abetted the occupying power.

Resistance writers have, it is true, produced thousands upon thousands of works.[43] After the war, research centers almost entirely devoted to the history of the Resistance were set up in capitals and large provincial cities all over liberated Europe.[44] Survivors of the Resistance formed clubs and associations to commemorate their heroic dead and their own wartime prowess. Over the years, Resistance became a banner and a myth—a term synonymous with selfless courage and patriotism.

It is also true that there has been a tendency to avoid collaboration as a theme for writing or research. With few exceptions, modern historians only skirt the subject. Books on collaboration are completely swamped by the flood of chronicles, memoirs, personal accounts, and scholarly studies devoted to the Resistance.[45]

The self-evident reasons for this unequal treatment are mainly of a moral and aesthetic nature. Collaboration is regarded as shameful and obnoxious on principle. It is unappealing, and bears the stigma of treason. If mentioned at all, it is thrust aside or used as a blurred backcloth designed to show off Resistance in an even more dramatic and favorable light. Unlike collaboration, Resistance testifies to the lionhearted courage and adamantine faith of free men and women.

There is an element of truth here—one that nourishes the fervent devotion and understandable hatred of Resistance veterans who cannot forget the past—and no one would seek to deny it.

Yet the time has come to examine certain thought patterns, however popular and convenient, not in order to devalue the Resistance, its achievements and sacrifices, and least of all to rehabilitate or justify collaboration, many instances of which are rightly condemned. Either course would be equally foolish, but there is an urgent need for a better and more accurate knowledge of the events that still cast a shadow over Europe to this day.

This much is certain: the outset of the occupation period was in general marked more by a readiness to collaborate than by the spirit of resistance. As though numbed by the trauma of national defeat, government and industry, civil servants and employers, shop-floor and white-collar workers instinctively, self-defensively, trimmed their sails to the prevailing wind.

Many other factors were involved, of course. There was, for example, the strong and primarily middle-class penchant for bowing to authority rather than openly opposing it, though it was allied with a wary and mistrustful approach to anything novel and unforeseen. There was also, particularly in France but also in other countries, a genuine belief that collaboration with the occupying power was essential to the preservation of internal order from attack by social-revolutionary forces. Such tendencies and ideas had an appreciable effect on relations between "occupied" peoples and the occupying power. Mute detestation and mute collaboration were quite compatible.[46]

It was different with the business-minded French industrialists and financiers who arranged lucrative deals with their German counterparts behind Vichy's back. Reporting to the State Department early in January 1942, the then U.S. ambassador in London, A. J. Drexel Biddle, wrote: "This group should be regarded not as Frenchmen, any more than their corresponding members in Germany should be regarded as Germans, for the interests of both groups are so intermingled as to be indistinguishable; their whole interest is focussed upon furtherance of their industrial and financial stakes."[47]

To the U.S. historian William L. Langer, a leading expert in this field, such men were good fascists like many others of their kind in Europe. In his view, they feared the Popular Front and its possible consequences, and were satisfied that, even under Hitler, business could flourish. Langer writes that many of them had long maintained close contacts with leading German industrialists and had always dreamed of a new "synarchic" system—a European order founded on fascist principles and controlled by an international brotherhood of financiers and industrialists.[48]

This certainly applied to some business circles in France, though not to all. They collaborated not only for profit's sake but also in keeping with their political views. Although this did not make them National Socialists, it is doubtful whether one can speak, in their case, of "neutral" collaboration.

One question leads to another. What, for instance, of the Fascist and National Socialist movements and parties which ranged themselves on Hitler's side, openly and unreservedly, in the occupied territories? Though hardly mentioned so far, it is they and their aggressive, ideologically inspired activities that first spring to mind when collaboration comes up for debate—they and the man who has become their epitome: Vidkun Quisling.

Unconditional Collaboration
or
Our Enemy Is My Friend

The unconditional collaborator says: I join forces with the occupying power because I endorse its principles and ideals. My attitude is dictated, not by circumstances, but by allegiance to National Socialism. I am prepared to do anything and make any sacrifice for the occupying power as long as I can thereby serve our common cause.

Vidkun Quisling, the man who has gone down in history as the embodiment of treason and collaboration with Nazism, shares the fate of Nicolas Chauvin and the Marquis de Sade. Just as one was not the supreme chauvinist nor the other the supreme sadist of his age, so Quisling failed to live up to his posthumous reputation. That he was the first European to be called traitor in World War II and has left posterity with the image of a would-be hero who abjectly crawled to Hitler are just two facets of a legend whose basis in real life was not as straightforward as many choose to think.

An intellectual with a self-assured manner, not a strongman. A cultured person, not a crude exponent of violence. A self-professed Christian; charming, often pensive, neither cruel nor bent on revenge. Reluctant to introduce and enforce the death penalty. A man who never sought to enrich himself in the political jungle and cared as little for orders and decorations as he did for a luxurious life style. Not a vain man, not a perfidious schemer, but no great statesman either. Such are the verdicts handed down to us by contemporary observers of the man in question.

However true or false they may be, Quisling was certainly not someone who aspired to soar from the depths of insignificance to a pinnacle of power from which to take revenge on a world that had finally learned to admire him. He quickly embarked on a brilliant career that might well have been envied by Adolf Hitler, who was two years his junior.

By the time Corporal Hitler was demobilized at the end of World War I and could find nothing better to do than guard a camp full of French and Russian prisoners of war in the shabby uniform of a defeated army, thirty-year-old Quisling was a captain on the Norwegian General Staff and had completed his studies at military academy with outstandingly good examination results. By the time Hitler was practicing his oratory on a couple of dozen listeners in a Munich beer cellar, Quisling had won his spurs as the Norwegian military attaché in Petrograd and become a legation secretary with the diplomatic corps in Helsinki.

In the years that followed, one of which was spent in jail by Hitler, now a rampaging demagogue and amateur revolutionary, Quisling worked in Soviet Russia for the League of Nations. As personal assistant and secretary to the celebrated polar explorer and diplomat Fridtjof Nansen, he organized League of Nations relief operations for famine-stricken Russians. And while Hitler, the sectarian bigot, was busy mapping out the future of Europe in his bizarre and baneful magnum opus, Mein Kampf, Quisling had become secretary of the Norwegian Legation in Moscow, headed the "Foreign Services" section, and was decorated by the British for representing their interests.

By the time Hitler was finally appointed Chancellor, Quisling had been a minister of the Royal Norwegian Government for eighteen months.[1]

Just why Quisling's career came to a standstill is not known, but his years in the foreign service as secretary and assistant to Nansen in Russia failed to get him any further. He had married a Russian woman in 1923 and intended to remain in Russia for good, but in December 1929 he returned to Norway, a major with a promising past but no discernible future, devoid of prospects and out of a job. Margret Boveri writes: "No longer was he the brilliant young General Staff officer, the prominent philanthropist and well-known figure in Moscow's international set. He was just a captain on half pay, embittered and forgotten."[2]

Deeply preoccupied with the question of how to refloat his stranded career, he decided to enter politics.

We are told that he was attracted to the Communists and the Socialists in turn, but that both groups took exception to his "authoritarian manner." Having finally settled on the Farmers' Party, he joined the conservative Kolstad cabinet and took over the Defense Ministry. He seemed to be back on course and favored by fortune once more.

But this was an illusion. Shortly before, in March 1931, he had founded a party organized on authoritarian lines and given it the programmatic name "Nordic Awakening." Quisling had fallen prey to the idea that his fellow countrymen must be persuaded of the superiority of the Nordic race. Strangely confused and suddenly adrift, he became more and more given to wild philosophical speculation and made himself extremely unpopular as a minister. He delivered violent public tirades, flung charges of treason in all directions, panicked for no good reason and turned soldiers loose on strikers, accused the Socialists of treacherously siding with the Communists, and squandered his energies in a senseless manner. Before long, everyone ceased to take him seriously. When the Kolstad cabinet resigned in March 1933, he was back to square one—high and dry.

But by now his course was set. Quisling amalgamated his infant party with a "Nationalist Club" composed of pro-fascist businessmen, and from this merger there sprang the "Nasjonal Samling" (National Assembly), which he faithfully modeled on Hitler's NSDAP (National Socialist German Labor Party).

In Quisling's estimation, this new party was destined to become his springboard to political success. As a former staff officer and diplomat, Russian expert and ex-minister, champion of the Nordic race and Norwegian party leader, he reckoned that Berlin, at least, would take him seriously.

Nor was he mistaken. In January 1938, the head of the NSDAP's Foreign Policy Bureau and leading racial theorist of the Third Reich, Alfred Rosenberg, rewarded his political ideas by subsidizing the Nasjonal Samling to the tune of 6.5 million reichsmarks.[3]

That was a start, but more important to him than foreign cash and recognition was the support and good will of an up-and-coming continental power which might one day help him back to a position of political power in his own country. He patiently nursed this hope for years until, in December 1939, when World War II was already under way, he finally obtained an audience with Hitler.

No minutes of this interview have survived, so we are dependent on secondhand accounts and statements made long afterward by Admiral Erich Raeder, then commander in chief of the German Navy, who arranged and attended the meeting.

According to Raeder, Quisling presented Hitler with a plan for a coup d'état which would bring him to power in Oslo.

To this end, he had apparently held preliminary discussions with Rosenberg and Raeder in which he put forward various ideas calculated to appeal to Berlin, notably that an Allied landing on the Norwegian seaboard was imminent and that it would be in Germany's interest to forestall it. He, Quisling, who stood foursquare behind Germany, would "place the necessary bases at the disposal of the German armed forces" as soon as the coup d'état had succeeded. As to the latter, he could place absolute reliance on the Norwegian officers who were loyal to him. The German Navy would naturally have to remain on call.[4]

Why should Hitler have entrusted Norway to a failed politician with little more to offer than an insignificant and ill-organized party which owed its survival to Germany's example and German money? Quisling's native cunning failed to work, and Hitler turned him down. For the present, he said, he had no wish to take on any new commitments and would prefer Scandinavia to remain neutral.

The very same day, Hitler ordered plans to be drafted for the invasion of Norway and Denmark—no coincidence, one presumes. He could seize Norway without any help from a man like Quisling.

When the Wehrmacht struck on April 9, 1940, Quisling acted on his own initiative: he appointed himself head of government.

Here, chance came to his aid. The German landing party assigned to capture Oslo met with unexpected resistance. Norwegian shore batteries in the ancient fortress of Oskarsborg sank the German flagship, the heavy cruiser *Blücher,* with the loss of sixteen hundred men. The Gestapo and administrative officers whose job it was to arrest the King and his ministers and take control of the capital were either killed or disabled, and those survivors who managed to swim ashore, like the squadron commander, Rear Admiral Oskar Kummetz, and divisional commander General Erwin Engelbrecht, were temporarily detained in custody. The German squadron was compelled to turn back. Troops were flown in to occupy Oslo and hold it until the fleet could show up, which it did the next day. Meanwhile, King Haakon and the government had escaped and Vidkun Quisling had resolved to fill the resulting political vacuum with himself and his party members.[5]

In an address to the Norwegian people broadcast that night, he announced that a new "national government" had assumed power under his premiership and that his cabinet would comprise eight members of his own party. He then appealed to all ranks in the armed forces to obey his call. Anyone who opposed the instructions of the new government would be severely punished.[6]

His actual words were: "Under present circumstances, it is the duty of the Nasjonal Samling to take over the business of government in order to defend the vital interests of the Norwegian people and preserve Norway's independence."[7]

It was a coup d'état worthy of Don Quixote. Quisling's political associates, whom he had transformed into ministers with a wave of the wand, only learned of their "appointment" through the radio or at third hand. No one had been consulted or notified in advance. Five of the eight appointees could not be found and were not even in Oslo at the time, and none of them was overjoyed by his unexpected inclusion in Quisling's homemade cabinet.

Quisling's "seizure of power" came as a complete surprise to Berlin, too, and Goebbels's Propaganda Ministry began by directing the German press to avoid all mention of him. Significantly enough, its editorial circular stated that the would-be dictator's "sham government" was merely an attempt to dissuade the Norwegians from further resistance.[8]

In Oslo itself, the German minister, Curt Bräuer, presented Quisling with a formal protest against his usurpation of executive power. He also put a guard on the Norwegian Foreign Ministry with instructions to prevent Quisling from entering the building, but canceled this order when Berlin directed him to seek out the King and persuade him, if possible, to recognize Quisling's cabinet. Germany did, after all, need some kind of legal government.[9]

As we already know, the King rejected Bräuer's proposal. Not even this lame German démarche, which anyone might have known would find no favor with Haakon, could extricate Quisling from his political isolation.

Nobody budged—nobody wanted to join his cabinet. The head of a non-existent government, he took over first the Ministry of Justice, then the Ministry of Defense, and finally the Foreign Ministry. He hastily summoned the staff of all three ministries, intending to swear them in. No one turned up. All the offices were locked. The Permanent Secretary of the Ministry of Justice, who eventually put in an appearance, refused to hand over the keys. Fuming, Quisling stormed into the Ministry of Defense, escorted by German soldiers. More deserted desks met his eye. As in every other ministry, the staff had followed the government and quit the capital, almost to a man.[10]

Quisling's interregnum lasted all of six days. On April 16, 1940, he was removed from office by the German authorities and transferred from his Oslo headquarters, complete with storm troopers, to the Hotel Continental. As a sop to his pride—and on the principle that he might someday come in handy after all—he was appointed "Commissioner for Demobilization." His so-called government was replaced by a provisional administrative council.[11]

In the next few days, Propaganda Minister Goebbels twice instructed German news editors to handle "the Quisling question" very gingerly or, better still, avoid it altogether. The Norwegian people might yet come to see that Quisling would have been the right man for them after all, and it was not beyond the bounds of possibility that he would be "reinstated on a new basis in a few weeks' time."[12]

Years were to pass, not weeks, before Quisling was reinstated as head of government, and they were years of ungentle treatment at the hands of the Germans, who denied him their protection. They permitted one Norwegian newspaper to remark, in connection with a forthcoming broadcast by Quisling, that every Norwegian would have to decide for himself whether or not to listen, and their press censors refrained from intervening even when another newspaper wrote that the people's verdict on Quisling and his party took the form of mute contempt. Even when it was stated, in black and white, that Quisling's political exploits had aroused "disgust" in Norway, the occupying power took no steps to defend the man whom it later resurrected.[13]

The German authorities did, however, show some interest in his party, being at pains to convert it into a serviceable and compliant ally. They not only allotted the Nasjonal Samling ten out of thirteen seats when setting up the Provisional Council of State in September 1940 but assigned it a dominant and monopolistic role in domestic politics by banning all other parties. Any Norwegian who aspired to be or become a somebody had to belong to Quisling's party or join it in double-quick time.

But Quisling himself, who led it by Germany's kind permission, continued to be excluded from government.

There were two sound reasons for this. Quisling had exhausted his political credit inside Norway by putting all his eggs in the German basket. He never at any time managed to command the allegiance of more than a dwindling minority of Norwegians. Even at its peak in April 1942, despite its dominant status and Germany's patronage, the Nasjonal Samling boasted fewer than 43,000 members, or barely 1.5 percent of the population. Quisling and his party by themselves were no match for the resistance they encountered, at first spontaneous and later organized.[14]

Weightier still, perhaps, was the second reason. Broadcasting on the day of the German invasion, Quisling had referred to national independence and stressed the importance of preserving it. An empty form of words, or did he believe what he was saying?

The question would be pointless had he himself not reverted to the subject time and again. He left no doubt that what he had in mind was an independent Norway forming part of a "Greater Germanic" league—or, more concretely, a peace treaty that would guarantee Norwegian sovereignty.

Hitler parried Quisling's repeated inquiries about his country's future quite as evasively as he had in December 1939, when the Norwegian sought German backing for his projected coup d'état: no discussion, far less negotiation, could be devoted to postwar problems of this kind while the war was still in progress.

Reports from the "Reich Commissariat of Norway" reveal that the German authorities grew increasingly suspicious of the way in which Quisling's nationalistic ideas, which ran counter to German interests, became rife within his party. According to one such report, the Nasjonal Samling was attracting more and more people with markedly anti-German views. The party's secret slogan was: "With our help, the Germans will be bowed out of Norway." It was also alleged that a party spokesman had uttered the following remarks in November 1940: "What do you think happens inside a German protectorate? . . . it means conditions like those in Poland and Czechoslovakia—it means coercion, concentration camps, and a lot of other things. . . ."[15]

After Quisling paid a state visit to Berlin in February 1942, Goebbels noted in his diary that the Norwegian visitor, whose appointment to the premiership was two weeks old, had voiced "naive ideas" in conversation with the Führer. He not only wanted to create a "free Norway" and build up a new Norwegian Army but requested that the military defense of Norway's ports and territorial waters be re-entrusted to the Norwegians themselves. In June 1942, the German Wire Agency drew attention to an article by Quisling which took the same line: because Norway's existence "as a free and independent nation" must be secured, he had written, there was a need for "sincere and sympathetic cooperation" between the Germanic peoples.[16]

In Goebbels's view, these "naive ideas" weighed heavily against Quisling, whom he regarded as a "dogmatist and theoretician"—twin terms of abuse in National Socialist jargon. One could not, he said, expect such a man to develop any great statesmanlike qualities.[17]

So Quisling was a write-off even before Berlin granted him the premiership—perhaps for that very reason—in 1942. People knew pretty well what to make of him in Berlin and Oslo alike. While Minister of Defense before the war, for example, he had publicly accused some unidentified assailants of trying to throw pepper in his eyes. This ludicrous allegation, for which no evidence was ever produced, had been charitably explained away as a hallucination induced by malaria contracted in Russia years before. Paranoid traits were just another aspect of his makeup.[18]

As for the nature of his collaboration, it may be summarized in a single paragraph.

After returning from Russia, he spent years on the lookout for a political force that could revive his dormant career. This long and fruitless quest eventually took him to Berlin. Having come thus far, he was thwarted by his own ingrained ideas. As a former professional soldier, he could not stomach national self-destruction. He collaborated for the sake of a career —yes, but his collaboration was not unreserved.

Thus the man who lives on in the popular imagination as a supreme collaborator who rendered faithful and fanatical assistance to National Socialism cannot be reduced to so simple a formula. Even when he decreed inhuman measures or implemented them under irresistible pressure from the German authorities and the death-defying Norwegian Resistance—even when compelled to lend his name to atrocities committed by his merciless Minister of Justice, Jonas Lie, a blindly subservient Nazi stooge—he persisted in clinging to the concept of an independent homeland.

On February 1, 1942, his ceremonial appointment as Premier was attended by several senior Third Reich dignitaries: Martin Bormann, deputizing for the Führer; Heinrich Müller, head of the Gestapo; and Admiral Hermann Böhm, representing the German armed forces. Quisling delivered his inaugural address in German.

We are told that he later remarked to a journalist, beaming with delight, that all the power once shared by the King, the head of government, and Parliament, now repose in a single pair of hands: his own.[19]

It would have been truer to say that Quisling was the weakest head of government in Europe, and totally devoid of political authority. The

Germans retained their executive and decision-making powers to the bitter end.

Quisling's activities were largely confined to enacting the legislation required to "Nazify" his country. He founded a movement modeled on the Hitler Youth, created a National Socialist educational association which all teachers had to join, and made it obligatory for youngsters between the ages of ten and eighteen to attend rallies designed to imprint them with National Socialist ideas. In doing these things, he seemed to be acting under some kind of inner compulsion. With extraordinary perseverance, he destroyed what he had really undertaken, but ultimately lacked the strength, to preserve. By abolishing Norway's internal freedoms, he inevitably sacrificed her national independence.[20]

Quisling may, with some justification, be likened to a character in a comedy of errors. The part assigned him by history was played, not by him, but by the Minister of Justice mentioned above. Twelve years younger, Jonas Lie behaved precisely as Quisling is commonly supposed to have done. He was a rabid but cynical Nazi and a pugnacious, unscrupulous collaborator.

A professional policeman-cum-crime writer who lived out on paper what was denied him in real life, Lie could not have been better fitted for his role.

Back in 1934, when heading a League of Nations team appointed to supervise the plebiscite that was to decide the Saar's political status, he had become friendly with the Gauleiter of Essen, Josef Terboven, "an energetic, purposeful, brutal and dangerous fellow." The same Terboven was now Reich Commissioner of Norway and, thus, the most powerful man in the land.[21]

Although Lie supported Quisling's party without belonging to it, Terboven had no difficulty in playing him off against Quisling because it still rankled with him that the leader of the Nasjonal Samling had once kept him waiting five hours for an interview.

At the end of January 1941, the Reichsführer-SS and chief of the German Police, Heinrich Himmler, signed up the promising young Norwegian and sent him to the Balkans for further training and experience. Having there been decorated with the Iron Cross, Lie returned to Oslo, where—behind Quisling's back but with secret encouragement from his friend Terboven—he founded the Norwegian SS and was appointed Standartenführer [colonel] by Himmler. In the summer of 1942 he was given police command of the "Norwegian Legion," an organization subordinate to the Waffen-SS [armed or military SS], and was rewarded for his faithful service with promotion.[22]

Lie possessed all the drive and initiative which his nominal superior, Quisling, was so rapidly losing, and he exercised it ruthlessly. In August 1943, when one lone Norwegian police officer opposed his authority, he summarily arrested 470 fellow officers and surrendered them to the Germans, who interned them in a concentration camp near Danzig.[23]

A man like Lie could not but welcome it that, as head of government, Quisling had to lend his name to, and take responsibility for, everything his Minister of Justice perpetrated in an excess of collaborative zeal. Unlike Quisling, who was tried and executed for high treason after the war, Jonas Lie cheated the gallows by committing suicide.

Miniature Hitlers

In common with Quisling, the son of a Lutheran pastor, two other National Socialist leaders, Anton Adriaan Mussert of Holland and Fritz Clausen of Denmark, came from solid middle-class families. Mussert, a schoolteacher's son, had been chief hydraulic engineer for the Province of Utrecht before entering politics. Fritz Clausen, a doctor of medicine who had trained at the University Clinic, Heidelberg, practiced in his own home town.

Neither Mussert nor Clausen had scored any public successes before going into politics, an aspect in which they differed from Quisling, but it is noteworthy that none of the trio turned to politics until he was the wrong side of thirty-five—in Quisling's case, forty-three.

It may have been fortuitous that Clausen and Quisling both tried their political wings in agrarian parties and took a tumble before switching to parties in the Nazi mold. Mussert, who had co-founded the Dutch National Socialist Movement, maintained an unswerving course for his political objective from the first.

As a historical figure, the Dutchman is undoubtedly more interesting than the Dane, who was a stereotyped imitator of Hitler. Like Quisling, he had two sides to his character.

Even before Mussert opened his mouth, his public appearances made it clear whom he emulated and where he was heading. Black-shirted and erect in a big open car, he took the salute at paramilitary parades with his right arm raised. He seemed to fancy himself in the role of an adored leader and genuinely believed that he was born to create and preside over a Greater Netherlands.

It had been his respect for a policy of direct action, as practiced by Mussolini and Hitler, that encouraged him to found an authoritarian party. While regarding himself as a friend of the Third Reich, he expressly dissociated himself from German National Socialism in two important respects: he preached religious toleration—was not, in other words, an anti-Semite—and firmly rejected the idea that Holland might someday be absorbed into the Third Reich.

Mussert's inaugural program, published in June 1932, had stated that his party must not be confused with the Nazi movement in Germany, and that it opposed anti-Semitism in any form. He continued to welcome Dutch Jewish members until the imposition of a ban in October 1938, by which time his party included 150 Jews in its ranks.[24]

As for the Third Reich's claims to sovereignty, no committed Dutch nationalist could have reacted more sharply than Mussert. All party members who had in any way assisted the German invasion of their country were expelled from the movement.[25]

When Gottlob Berger, head of the SS Operations Department, asked Mussert to release two thousand young party members for SS training in Germany only three weeks after the invasion, Mussert noted in his diary that he regarded the enrollment of Dutchmen in the SS as treason. He duly forbade his party members to join the organization.

Berger then submitted an order from Hitler relating to the establishment of a "Standarte Westland" under the auspices of the "Germanic SS." Mussert made another entry in his diary: ". . . felt like a slap in the face— does it mean incorporation? . . . seemed to me that the supreme command of the SS looked upon the Dutch people as a German people. That is terrible. How will it end? If I refuse, I shall be aiding those who wish to annex my people . . . God grant that I can get to the Führer and convince him. . . ."[26]

Addressing members of his National Socialist Movement (NSB) in July 1940, Mussert declared, "There are at present in Holland many people who say they would rather have the Germans rule us than the NSB, and that they call patriotism." The same message emerged even more clearly from a remark made by his party's propaganda chief to a meeting in November of the same year. This was to the effect that Mussert was the only Dutchman who could prevent the annexation of Holland.[27]

In September 1940, under pressure from Reich Commissioner Seyss-Inquart, Mussert signed a telegram to Hitler "placing the welfare of the Dutch people in your hands" ("in the knowledge that all your decisions and commands are ultimately for the good of the Dutch people. . . .") Almost on the same day, however, he concluded an agreement with the proprietor and publisher of De Telegraaf, a leading daily, for the defense of the Dutch press, on which the Nazi Party's publishing organization had designs.[28]

Seyss-Inquart summed up Mussert correctly when he reported to Hitler early in June 1940 that the Dutch party leader was "by nature a liberal nationalist" who made use of fascist methods. Mussert's attitude was "essentially nationalistic, not National Socialist," he stated in a special report dated September 1941.[29] Yet another year later, in mid-November 1942, Himmler received a memorandum from Hanns Albin Rauter, Senior SS and Police Commander and Commissioner General for Security in Holland, who wrote that consideration should be given to dissolving the NSB. Far from being a National Socialist, said Rauter, Mussert was at heart anti-German and would have to be removed.[30]

So mutual trust and friendship were lacking between Mussert and the German authorities—and had been, remarkably enough, even in the prewar years when Mussert represented a sizable political force that might have been nurtured and exploited by Berlin. His NSB had, after all, been Holland's fifth-strongest party in 1935.

But at no time was he treated like an ally, still less a fellow Nazi. He was not initiated into Berlin's military plans in 1939, nor was it even hinted to him that hostilities were imminent. Mussert was quite as surprised by the German onslaught as the majority of Dutchmen. On May 16, when he followed Quisling's example by proposing to broadcast to the Dutch people, the German military authorities strictly forbade him to do any such thing.[31]

This was not the only snub he had to swallow. He first learned of Reich Commissioner Seyss-Inquart's appointment from the newspapers. Resentfully, he noted, "The Reich Commissioner has begun to rule his 'Reich' as if the NSB did not exist."[32] He was not even invited to the big reception in The Hague's historic Rittersaal, where Seyss-Inquart introduced himself to his exalted guests, including the undersecretaries of all the ministries, in the most conciliatory language.[33]

Like Quisling, Mussert had naturally counted on being entrusted with the reins of government once the Germans were installed in his country. He must have been bitterly disappointed by their callous rejection, but what angered him still more was that they flatly excluded him from the national executive for years on end. He was even denied quasi ministerial status in a consultative shadow cabinet like the "Political Secretariat of State" formed in August 1943 and composed of ten prominent members of his own party. Mussert began and ended his career as the leader of a small political party which the occupying power entrusted with errand boy's duties alone.[34]

Just as Jonas Lie, a super-collaborator and protégé of Himmler's, was played off against Quisling in Norway, so Mussert had to contend with a keen rival described as "one of Himmler's earliest *hommes de confiance*." This man, who wanted to turn Holland into a German province, was Rost van Tonningen.[35]

German policy in Holland was quite similar to the one adopted in Norway. Party stalwarts were at least permitted to help Nazify their country. The NSB supplied the mayors of more than half of Holland's municipalities, and seven out of ten provincial commissioners were also NSB men. Himmler, too, made use of the party. Of the 50,600 Dutchmen who donned German uniform (17,000 served in the Waffen-SS and 12,000 in police and auxiliary police units), 20,000 were party members. In addition, several thousand of Mussert's supporters volunteered to work against their fellow countrymen as agents provocateurs and informers in the service of the Gestapo and Security Police.[36]

Like Quisling, Mussert was fobbed off by Hitler with placebos about the postwar period whenever he alluded to Holland's future role. Late in 1943, when he almost brusquely insisted that Hitler should make "a clear and unequivocal statement about the political future of the Netherlands," he was dismissed with a few vague hints and a benevolent pat on the shoulder.[37]

Compared to Mussert, Clausen was a model pupil. All the Danish Nazi said and did was inspired by Germany's example. Whole passages in his party program were translated almost word for word from Hitler's own. His "Storm-Afdelingr" wore brown uniforms like Hitler's SA, the party anthem was identical with the German *Horst-Wessel-Lied,* and the party's structure, its paramilitary and civilian organizations, were meticulously copied. In the same way, Clausen himself—with his bombast and intolerance—resembled the German "Führer" whom he so faithfully emulated.[38]

Clausen would gladly have been appointed Premier by the Germans— indeed, he would have been the happiest man in Denmark had they permitted him to wield power as their faithful satrap—but his wish to collaborate even more fully and intensively remained unfulfilled. Cecil von Renthe-Fink, the German minister and Reich Plenipotentiary, who was not enamored of the persistent collaborative zeal displayed by Clausen and his confederates, warned Berlin against becoming involved with them. What he needed most, to help him extract as much as possible from Denmark for the benefit of the German war economy, was internal peace and quiet.

Clausen did his level best to be recognized by Hitler as a fully qualified collaborator. He threatened the Reich Plenipotentiary with a coup d'état; he pestered the Danish Government for a share in the affairs of state; he mobilized profit-hungry industrialists and landowners who were interested in good relations with Germany; and he requested an audience with King Christian in the hope of gaining his support for the formation of a National Socialist government.

He also promoted a merger between his party and the agrarian movement headed by the landowner Knud Bach, hoping that this would lend greater weight to his plan for a Clausen government on the lines of Hitler's first cabinet and predispose the Germans in its favor. Finally, he tried to demonstrate his strength by sending his men into the streets and organizing Nazi rallies and brawls with the Danish police.

But it was not granted to him to labor on Hitler's behalf. The King refused to see him, the Danish Government rebuffed him, and Renthe-Fink continued to counsel patience until his last chance vanished. As early as December 1940, Clausen complained in a letter to the German Foreign Office that he was feeling more and more hemmed in.

Clausen's belief in his prospects—his "mission"—was somewhat restored by the receipt of German financial aid, which amounted by September 1941 to over 1.6 million reichsmarks. However, the extent of his self-delusion is apparent from a Foreign Office report to Hitler dated November 17, 1941. This stated that Clausen was opposed by the elderly King and the vast majority of the Danish people, so a legal assumption of power and a coup d'état were equally out of the question. Hitler promptly gave orders that Clausen be dropped.

From 1942 on, Clausen and his party were only a shadow of their former selves.[39]

Thus, German National Socialism did nothing—or less than nothing—to halt the steady decline of the National Socialist parties or movements in Holland and Denmark, which had set in during the mid-1930s after a relatively brief and deceptive heyday. What was more, Nazi Germany's occupation policy was hardly a good advertisement for the political tenets espoused by men like Mussert and Clausen.

Clausen's party, which had gained 31,032 votes and three parliamentary seats in the 1939 elections, numbered only 6,000 members in April 1940.[40] In the provincial elections of 1935, nearly 8 percent of the electorate had voted for Mussert's NSB. Only 4.2 percent cast their votes for it in the parliamentary elections of 1937. By the time Mussert "went underground" on the day the Germans invaded Holland (he spent four days hiding on a secluded farm), his party's membership had dwindled considerably. By May 1940, only 22,000 of the 52,000 members registered in 1935 were still on its books. Less than 1 percent of the adult population had remained loyal to him.[41]

The paucity and insignificance of the Danish Nazis who were prepared to engage in unconditional collaboration may be gauged from the fact that Clausen's party was the strongest of twenty similar movements and factions which had either disbanded or merged with it before the Germans marched into Denmark.

Some ten such parties had also existed in Holland, among them a "National Socialist Netherlands Labor Party" (NAP), which remained in being until the end of 1941. This was made up of rabid Nazi extremists who called for the complete absorption of Holland into the Third Reich. Its uniformed Brownshirts strutted through the streets with swastika banners and Hitler salutes, a group of fanatical anti-Semites dedicated to the dissemination of Greater German slogans.[42]

Clausen abandoned the struggle comparatively soon. On November 1, 1943, he gave up and volunteered for the Waffen-SS.

Three months later, having become an alcoholic, he was admitted on Himmler's orders to the Neurological Institute at Würzburg. Shortly afterward, at the beginning of May 1944, he resigned his leadership of the

DNSAP (Danish National Socialist Labor Party). He died in jail after the war, snuffed out by a heart attack while awaiting trial.[43]

Mussert found himself deserted by his supporters when the Allied armies launched their attack on Holland. Few of the men who had compromised themselves under his leadership wanted anything more to do with him. They took to their heels, and with their wives and children—some forty thousand of them—fled across the frontier and disappeared into the *Götterdämmerung* of the Third Reich.

Armed with an identity card forged by himself, as well as a memorandum which he hoped would gain him access to Hitler, Mussert set off on a hurried, aimless trek through Wehrmacht-held territory. He did not escape arrest. Brought to trial after the war, he was condemned to death and executed in May 1946.[44]

Other Collaborators in Chief

In Belgium, the parties and movements which unreservedly supported Hitler were so closely linked with the longstanding problems arising from Fleming-Walloon antagonism ever since Belgium's severance from the Netherlands in 1830 that their origins and political orientation preclude them from comparison with those of any other country.

On the one hand, the Flemish Nationalist Party (VNV) developed into a party of extreme collaboration under the leadership of an ex-teacher and parliamentarian named Staff de Clercq, whom German Military Intelligence listed as one of its agents. The VNV's declared aim was to create a Germanic Greater Netherlands which would, including French Flanders and the colonies, number fifty million inhabitants.

On the other, the Walloon Young Catholic Rexist Party headed by Léon Degrelle, a former Charles Maurras supporter, spawned an equally radical collaborationist party which pinned its hopes on a Hitler-dominated European New Order in which Belgium would be accorded her due place.

Both parties, which had achieved short-lived but substantial electoral successes during the 1930's and become increasingly fascist in complexion (Degrelle had received lavish financial backing from the Italian Government and Belgian industrialists during his "march into fascism"), regarded collaboration with Hitler as a patriotic duty whose fulfillment would determine whether Belgium managed to transform military defeat into political victory.

The German authorities were not interested in bringing either party to power. By order of the German military commander, General Alexander von Falkenhausen, who was anything but a Nazi himself (the Gestapo arrested him in the aftermath of July 20, 1944), they were compelled to divide Belgium between them and expressly undertake to refrain from political activity in each other's parish. This meant that the two largest collaborationist parties were, in a sense, cordoned off—a state of affairs that thoroughly suited Hitler, who wanted to see Flanders and Wallonia as separate components of the Third Reich and planned to annex them after the war.

De Clercq's VNV (led after his death by Hendrik Elias) was the only authorized party in Flanders, and its members were allotted senior administrative posts. However, the relative unimportance of the VNV and Degrelle's Rexists is apparent from their combined wartime membership, which barely exceeded 50,000, including 20,000 uniformed militiamen. The Germans regarded them primarily as a reservoir for supplying the Wehrmacht and military police with young blood for the Eastern Front. Degrelle himself joined the first group of Walloon volunteers and went to Poland for training as a private soldier in August 1941. Wounded five times, he later saw action as a Sturmbannführer [major] and brigade commander in the East.[45]

France presents yet another picture. The chief collaborators of the two large fascist parties, Marcel Déat and Jacques Doriot, who readily and wholeheartedly danced to Hitler's tune, came neither from the "Croix de Feu" nor from Charles Maurras's "Action Française"—in other words, they were neither extreme nationalists nor extreme conservatives. Both had been leading left-wingers, Déat a Socialist and Doriot a Communist.

Jacques Doriot, the metalworker who has been called France's "first fascist," was no run-of-the-mill Communist functionary. Trained at the Party School in Moscow in 1923, he worked his way up the Communist hierarchy at a fast and furious pace, and almost reached the top. In 1924, when general secretary of the French Communist youth movement, he was elected to the Chamber of Deputies and simultaneously appointed to the Executive Committee of the Comintern in Moscow. Acclaimed by the workers of Paris for his impassioned oratory and ruthless tactics, he was by 1925 reputed to be the most popular Party leader in France and spoken of as the "Red Crown Prince" who would probably succeed his rival, Maurice Thorez. In 1926, having opportunely plumped for Stalin rather than Trotsky, he was sent by the former to China. On his return in July 1927, he ventured to question the infallibility of the Moscow leadership and further stated that its authority within the Party was crumbling. To cap everything, this successful "Red mayor" of the Paris suburb of St.-Denis proceeded to violate the directives of the Party leadership and Comintern by arbitrarily supporting a Socialist-Communist united front. Outmaneuvered by Thorez in June 1934, he was expelled from the Party and, thus, from the Third International.

Cut to the quick, he developed a blind hatred of the Communist Party and in 1936 founded the Parti Populaire Française, which began to enroll disenchanted deserters from every political camp in a new-style mass movement.

The German-Soviet nonaggression pact turned Doriot's party into a genuine catchment area for disillusioned Communists. No less than 1,556 of the delegates attending its congress in November 1942 had belonged to the Communist Party. Doriot was joined even by such prominent ex-Communists as Marcel Gitton, the former Party Secretary; Fernand Soupé, a member of the Central Committee; Albert Clément, editor of the Communist trade union newspaper; Émile Nédélec, vice-president of the Communist veterans' association; and a senator and several deputies.[46]

The renegades' hatred and disillusionment imbued Doriot's party with great anti-Communist momentum. As for Doriot himself, the moderate anti-Semite became a rabid Jew-hater, and the anti-German who had stated that collaboration with Hitler was out of the question—and said so as recently as 1939—swiftly developed into an unscrupulous collaborator in chief.[47]

Like other fascist leaders in occupied Europe, Doriot had counted on active German support. But although many Third Reich luminaries held him in high esteem and thought his party the only one "capable of comparison with the NSDAP in Germany," Hitler decided against him. Doriot could not, he said, be considered as a future head of government.[48]

As the German ambassador in Paris, Otto Abetz, once candidly admitted, it was in the interests of German policy to prevent the founding of a French Nazi Party or any similar organization and leave only enough scope for the activities of "a few small fascist-oriented groups." Coping with Vichy's overzealous collaborationism was enough of a job in itself.

The Germans were so reluctant to become involved with Doriot that they declined to equip his party's paramilitary units with the small arms they had been trained to use—a fact which should have made him think twice.[49]

Doriot was nonetheless permitted to render the Third Reich certain limited services. Being a bitter opponent of Vichy's "reactionary" policy, he could sometimes be used as a lever when Berlin wanted to bully Marshal Pétain and his associates into line. In the fall of 1941, Doriot left for the Eastern Front, where he intermittently served for eighteen months, first as a noncommissioned officer and then as a lieutenant, in the "Anti-Bolshevist Volunteer Legion" which he himself had helped to raise. Betweentimes, he took part in operations against the French Resistance, which were conducted with the utmost ferocity.

Hitler waited until France was already lost to the Third Reich to offer the most fascist of all French fascists permission to seize power in an imaginary satellite state which could not now come into being.

Doriot was killed during a low-level air attack in February 1945.[50]

Marcel Déat, France's other leading collaborator, was not a proletarian strongman, not a daredevil, not a temperamental and obsessive political adventurer like Doriot, but an intellectual. A civil servant's son, Déat had joined the French Socialist Party at the age of twenty, been appointed professor of philosophy at the École Normale Supérieure in Paris at twenty-six, and become president of the Socialist students' association. In 1926 he was elected to the Chamber of Deputies, and two years later he took over the administrative secretariat of the Socialist parliamentary group under Léon Blum. In 1933, having become gradually estranged from the Socialist Party, he was expelled in company with twenty-eight deputies and seven senators. He then founded his own rival French Socialist Party, and in 1936 spent five months in the Sarraut cabinet as Minister of Aviation.

Déat's "march into fascism" was triggered by his prolonged theoretical analysis of socialist ideas in a swiftly changing society and by experience of the grave functional disorders besetting parliamentary democracy during the interwar years. He came to the conclusion that socialism could be achieved only if power were seized, not by one class alone, but by the broad mass of the middle classes. For this, he believed, a ruthless resort to totalitarian tactics would be needed. Concepts such as "authority" and "nationhood" began to loom large in his ideas—indeed, so closely did they approximate to fascist trains of thought that National Socialism, which tore down every existing structure, seemed to him a natural ally with whom it was not only expedient but, in the long term, politically prudent and imperative to collaborate. The unconditional collaboration preached by his "Rassemblement National Populaire," a party which was founded in 1941 and attracted 50,000 recruits in its first year, stemmed from an ideology whose origins entitle one to describe it as left-wing fascism.[51]

Déat, too, learned the hard way. His unqualified willingness to collaborate did not earn its due reward from the occupying power, although his firm support of Laval had put him in a stronger position than Doriot. In the summer of 1941, when he joined with Doriot and the leaders of other, less important, fascist parties in founding the Anti-Bolshevist Volunteer Legion with the concurrence of the German Embassy in Paris, Hitler and the occupation authorities reacted in a rather lukewarm way. Hitler, who wanted no more than a symbolic French contribution to the Eastern campaign, restricted the number of legionaries to ten or fifteen thousand at most.

The Wehrmacht was even less disposed to become involved with the all-out collaborators in Doriot's and Déat's ranks. Of the 13,400 who volunteered in the first few months, only 3,000 or so were accepted, and German figures indicate that only 6,400 volunteers had been enrolled by May 1943. Nor, incidentally, were the legionaries permitted to wear French uniform. They had to swear an oath of allegiance to Hitler, wear field gray, and serve as members of a German infantry regiment. Anonymous and unrecognizable, the would-be heroes of collaboration vanished into the maw of Hitler's millions-strong army.[52]

Marcel Déat escaped trial by a French court after the war and sought refuge in Italy.

None of the collaborators in chief—neither Déat nor Doriot, neither Quisling nor any of his Danish, Dutch, and Belgian counterparts—received a genuine hearing from Hitler, who exploited their self-sacrificial zeal by using them as mere auxiliaries. They may have been allowed to work off their power complexes by subjecting their compatriots to the most abominable acts of cruelty, but they were mistaken if they imagined that their German masters would reward them by trusting them or granting them some measure of influence on the course of events. In that they had no say.

When twenty-one strikers were condemned to death in Luxembourg in September 1942, even the Grand Duchy's "Quisling," Professor Damian Kratzenburg, found the sentences excessive. Though head of the "Volksdeutsche Bewegung" [VDB, or Ethnic German Movement], the only officially authorized party in Luxembourg, he failed to quell his uneasiness at such draconian punishment and requested the authorities to be lenient for once. Seven thousand Luxembourgers whom the Germans found "suspect" were thereupon detained and deported.[53]

General Rudolf Gajda, Czechoslovakia's foremost fascist and leader of the "National Fascist Community" (NOF), was the first in the Quisling-Mussert line. He planned to seize power by means of a coup d'état when the Germans invaded his country, but, like the well-disciplined soldier he was, thought he needed Berlin's prior consent. In March 1939, shortly before Prague was occupied, he approached the German Legation there and was curtly shown the door.[54]

A similar lack of success attended the fascist organizations formed by Russian émigrés who were prepared to cooperate wholeheartedly with the Germans. These included the White Russian Nazi Party (PBNS) and the well-organized Russian Solidarity Movement (NTS), neither of which got anywhere. Their leaders were arrested by the Gestapo in the summer of 1944.[55]

The sole exception worth recording is General Kaminsky, a Russian who enjoyed the full trust of the occupying power. He needed no consent or permission for the measures he decreed in his "Administrative District of Lokoty." Here on the eastern edge of the Bryanska forests, where the Soviet authorities had sentenced him to compulsory residence after a spell in a Siberian prison camp, he spontaneously offered his services to the Germans. Kaminsky could point to the fact that he had already risen to become a district mayor and proved his personal competence. The German authorities, who granted him full executive powers, appointed him chief regional administrator, brigadier general, and commander in chief of the forces he had raised.

Kaminsky diligently and energetically built up a sort of petty state. He abolished collective farms, organized the labor force, supervised public education and food distribution, and saw to it that his farmers and workers fulfilled their quotas on time.

His combat units, recruited from among the male inhabitants of his fief, were armed with a variety of weapons, heavy as well as light, including artillery and T-34 tanks abandoned by the retreating Red Army. They were far superior to the partisans who were trying to take control of the area.

The speed with which Kaminsky managed to gain the Germans' confidence was probably a function of his personal image, which combined the attributes of a resolute fascist general and a savage brigand chief. Hermann Teske, a German staff officer who once visited Kaminsky on official business, noticed four corpses dangling outside his headquarters. The general explained that they were his own chief of staff and three aides whose loyalty he had begun to doubt.[56]

Late in September 1943, when Kaminsky eluded the advancing Red Army by moving west in good time, he was accompanied by his soldiers and the entire population of his district—thirty thousand-odd civilians complete with vast herds of cattle. Some of his troops were loaded into trains while the remaining fifteen thousand or so, with Kaminsky and his officers at their head, marched in column. On reaching partisan-controlled territory in the neighborhood of Lepel, several of his regiments mutinied. Kaminsky reacted in his own inimitable way. Alone and unescorted, he visited each mutinous commander in turn, landed outside the culprit's headquarters in a light aircraft, and throttled him in front of his own men.

Not even Kaminsky, perhaps the Germans' doughtiest collaborator, rated a monument of any kind. He led his men, who were by then incorporated into the Waffen-SS, against the Warsaw insurgents. Then, having been tipped off that Himmler had signed a warrant for his arrest, he made a run for it.

South of Tarnów he was cornered by German Security Police and killed. To simulate an armed robbery devoid of political implications, his car was daubed with goose blood and his corpse arranged beside it.[57]

A strange and motley crew rallied beneath the banner of unconditional collaboration: Marcel Déat, the socialist professor of philosophy; Kaminsky, the Russian general; Fritz Clausen, the Danish doctor; Vidkun Quisling, the ex-staff officer and diplomat; Jacques Doriot, the ex-Comintern official; Léon Degrelle, the Catholic fascist; and numerous others—a bewildering assortment of characters, motives, ambitions, and political bankrupts. It is nonetheless possible to generalize.

1. In no occupied country were extreme collaborators granted the recognition and authority they had banked on.

2. Whether as supernumeraries, soldiers, aids to administration and repression, or political pawns in the hands of the occupying power, they were always in the minority and always on the sidelines.

3. Under German occupation, their average support amounted to no more than 2 percent of the indigenous population.

Conditional Collaboration
or
I Collaborate Up to a Point

The conditional collaborator says: I cooperate with the occupying power although I endorse only some, not all, of the National Socialist doctrines. Subject to that proviso, I am ready and eager to collaborate faithfully because I wish to change the circumstances that dictate my attitude.

It is not always easy to fathom the wartime role played by the sizable and politically significant group of collaborators who adopted the attitude summarized above.

They differed from self-seeking neutral collaborators in that their motives and objectives were political, and from all-out collaborators like Quisling in that their ranks contained no fascists or National Socialists. Nothing could have been further from their intentions than the establishment of a Hitlerian regime.

They, too, were collaborators—industrious, wholehearted, and in many cases shrewd. They, too, accepted that Hitler's dominion over Europe was irreversible. They, too, had written off the old international order and the liberal ideas of their age, but they coupled their collaboration with the proviso that it must never degenerate into total subjection, political emasculation, or national dissolution.

In some cases, this political proviso went hand in hand with others of an ideological, religious, or ethical nature, and—last but not least—with reservations stemming from a conservative mentality that was fundamentally at odds with National Socialist practices.

The importance attained by this group may be gauged from the fact that conditional collaboration became the official policy of the French Government and was practiced in part by the Danish Government as well. Elsewhere, it decisively conduced to the growth of national collaborationist blocs and mass movements, and even to essays in administrative cooperation which transgressed the bounds of political neutrality.

To begin with a brief allusion to the last point, this was what happened in Norway.

There, administrative chaos threatened to engulf the areas occupied during the first week of the invasion. The Norwegian Government was no longer in a position to act, and no legal transfer of power to junior ministers had been provided for as in Holland and Belgium. To avert a complete breakdown in public services, the Supreme Court appointed an "Administrative Committee" to govern the occupied territories.

The Committee was never, from the outset, conceived of as a politically neutral authority. Its aim was to ward off German tutelage by ensuring that the occupied territories were run by the Norwegians themselves. Although the Norwegians realized that they would have to cooperate with the occupying power, they aimed to do so in accordance with the principles of conditional collaboration, which left some scope for resistance.

This emerged clearly when the Administrative Committee, which could not start work without express permission from the occupying power, insisted to the German authorities that Quisling and his men should be excluded from all governmental and administrative activity—a condition to which the Germans raised no demur.

Significantly enough, apart from the conservative civil governor of Oslo, I. C. Christensen, the seven respected citizens who made up the Committee included two prominent figures who later distinguished themselves as leaders of the Norwegian Resistance: the president of the Supreme Court, Paal Berg, and Bishop Berggrav.

To the chagrin of the German authorities, the Committee further displayed its cool self-assurance by seeking formal accreditation from King Haakon, whom the Germans had been trying to capture or kill. The King's response was just what the Committee wanted. While confirming it in office, he clearly stated that it could not claim to be a government or represent the wishes of the Norwegian people.

A politicized administration of this type was highly distasteful to Reich Commissioner Josef Terboven, who did everything possible to bring the Norwegian civil authorities under his control.

Although the Administrative Committee collaborated with some flexibility whenever this seemed justified, it was quite unprepared to bow to every German demand, so the experiment failed. The Committee was removed from office after five months.[1]

A similar experiment was later tried under comparable circumstances in Luxembourg, where Undersecretary Wehrer headed an "Administrative Commission." This body, which likewise collaborated to a limited extent, was also dissolved after roughly five months.[2]

In Holland, surprising successes were scored by a mass movement pledged to the principles of conditional collaboration. This was the "Nederlandsche Unie," which enrolled four hundred thousand members in eight weeks and could boast twice that number after six months. Founded as a result of discussions between the chairmen and parliamentary leaders of Holland's six largest democratic parties, the movement drew its inspiration from a highly controversial pamphlet by Hendrik Colijn, seventy-four-year-old chairman of the right-wing Antirevolutionary Party.

As a prewar Premier, Colijn had issued restrictive decrees that were clearly aimed at Mussert's National Socialist Party. He now declared that since the Continent would henceforth be dominated by Germany—he likened her to the conductor of a symphony orchestra—everyone must be prepared to act accordingly.

At the same time, he publicly championed national independence and professed allegiance to the Queen of the Netherlands, who regularly broadcast to the Dutch people from London.

Together with other party leaders, Colijn agreed to form a "national bloc" for the preservation of Holland's "popular rights, liberty, and independence." A committee of three, to which he himself belonged, was coopted to draft a manifesto with this end in view.

Even before the Nederlandsche Unie was founded, however, unexpected problems cropped up.

The founding committee's draft contained a pledge of loyalty to the royal house. The Germans objected to this and forbade it. They also "coordinated" or banned the free trade unions and the Social Democratic Party, which had been represented on the committee, but Colijn and his associates refused to give up. They eventually founded the Nederlandsche Unie without the democratic parties' official participation and, in a manifesto approved by the occupying power, called upon the people to recognize "changed circumstances" and strive for a new "affiliation" by dint of their "own efforts" and in keeping with their "own Dutch character."

The party, which bore all the marks of a national revival movement, encouraged the occupying power to hope that it would evolve into a force of potential use to the German cause. The outcome was different. It soon became clear what had really prompted the masses to flock to the new party in their hundreds of thousands. It was their way of demonstrating against Mussert and his National Socialist Party, or, as a Dutch historian put it, of "advertising their repugnance in an organized manner." Their desire to keep Mussert's unpopular National Socialists out of power was compounded with the hope that loyal cooperation with the occupying power would enable them to preserve the autonomy and independence of their country—a textbook example of conditional collaboration.

The German authorities did not take long to grasp the truth. In January 1941, a report to the Foreign Office described the Nederlandsche Unie as a catchall for anti-German elements. By the end of the year, it was banned.[3]

The party was no more, but the spirit of conditional collaboration lived on. The question that now arose, more than once, was how far this concept permitted one to go.

The members of the Supreme Court had remained at their posts, ostensibly to prevent the Nazification of the Dutch legal system. In November 1940, when the Jewish president of the court and all Jewish law officers were removed from their posts by the occupying power and replaced with Dutch National Socialists or pro-Germans, none of the Supreme Court judges uttered a word of protest. In January 1942, they went so far as to validate some illegal German measures. Was this breach of humanitarian, ethical, and professional obligations defensible on the grounds that limited collaboration preserved more than it destroyed?[4]

No one could pretend that it was easy to find a satisfactory answer to this question.

Similar developments occurred in other occupied countries—surprisingly enough, even in the East. Preliminary steps along the same road were taken in the Protectorate of Bohemia and Moravia during the first two months of occupation, before anyone else had set the pattern.

The country's two largest political parties went into liquidation. The government party, the National Unity Party, and the major opposition party, the Working People's Party, voluntarily quit the political arena—only to join forces in a new, united movement entitled the National Community. Under a committee headed by an Agrarian and an ex-Social Democrat, this mammoth organization accumulated representatives of every political group in the country, homegrown fascists not excluded.

It irritated Berlin that this party should have come into being even though the occupation authorities had been expressly instructed not to encourage such endeavors. A united nationalist party was not to the Germans' taste.

They were nonetheless gratified to note that the party manifesto, which did not appear until April 1940, was entirely couched in Nazi propaganda jargon. It talked of overcoming liberalism and "class socialism," resisting Marxist, Jewish, and Masonic influences, and "excluding Jews from the national community." Not long afterward, a party proclamation stated that the Czechs were prepared to make any sacrifice and would conscientiously perform all the tasks imposed on them by war. No collaborator could have devised a more acceptable program.

What the Germans found suspicious, on the other hand, was the feverish haste with which the party had been organized from top to bottom. More suspicious still was the peculiar circumstance that its 18 regional and 220 district chairmen had to be personally appointed, not by its executive committee, but by the country's head of state, President Emil Hácha, the very man whom Hitler had some weeks earlier induced to sign away his country by hectoring him so unmercifully that he fainted and had to be revived with injections.

Quite clearly, the real reason for these peculiarities was that Hácha wanted the new party to buttress the authority of the Czech Government. He thus attached great importance to its becoming effective as soon as possible—in other words, while he still enjoyed a relatively free hand. In this he succeeded. Early in April 1939, when ex-Foreign Minister Konstantin von Neurath was appointed Reich Protector and took over the President's powers, the new party possessed at least the rudiments of an infrastructure.

Here we have a classic case of conditional collaboration. The party, which could count on the membership and support of Czech fascists, had made its readiness to collaborate contingent on an endeavor to salvage the remains of political autonomy with presidential consent. This was also apparent from the party program, which not only adopted National Socialist concepts but additionally sought to define Germany's obligations. It even accorded the party certain functions which the occupying power had reserved for itself.

The prerequisites for such a policy did not, however, exist in the Protectorate. Matters developed in such a way that the National Community was compelled to abandon its reservations one by one and ultimately drop them altogether—a process which condemned it to subside into complete political insignificance.[5]

"That France Should Remain France"

"Collaboration," in the specific sense attached to it since World War II, was first introduced into our political vocabulary by Marshal Pétain. In a speech delivered at the beginning of October 1940, he declared that Germany's defeat of France left her with the choice between a "traditional peace of oppression" and an "entirely novel peace of collaboration."

An official French communiqué released after Pétain's meeting with Hitler at Montoire stated that the two men had reached agreement on "the principle of collaboration." Shortly afterward, on October 30, the Marshal confirmed that consideration had been given to the possibility of "collaboration between our two countries," and that he had "accepted it in principle."[6]

These statements created a misleading impression. There could be no talk of "agreement" on the principle of collaboration, nor of the Marshal's having "accepted" the same. This would have implied that the idea had been floated by Hitler himself rather than raised by the French—and that, as Eberhard Jäckel has convincingly shown in his exhaustive study of Hitler's policy toward France, was genuinely not the case.[7]

The truth is that, quite unlike the French communiqué, the first German announcement of Hitler's meeting with Pétain at Montoire made no refer-

ence whatever to "cooperation" or "collaboration." This was not fortuitous. At the beginning of October, the Reich Propaganda Ministry had instructed the German press to blackout Pétain's first collaboration speech.[8]
Even after Montoire, care was taken to ensure that the Third Reich's press
and radio outlets confine themselves to issuing so-called "purely factual
reports" and refrain from commenting on French references to Franco-
German collaboration.[9] From then on—discounting the German Embassy
in Paris, which occasionally found it expedient to play off French illusions
against Vichy itself—no authoritative German source ever used the expression.

Two and a half years were to pass before Hitler adopted Vichy's pet
term, though not in Pétain's sense. In November 1942, when German
forces occupied the hitherto "free" zone of France, he wrote the Marshal a
letter reminding him that he had been anxious to discuss prospects for
Franco-German cooperation.

Vichy and Berlin conceived of these "prospects" in entirely different
ways. For his part, Hitler did not have the slightest intention of relaxing
the armistice regime. In his view, the French had first to prove themselves
"worthy" of better treatment by doing as German interests dictated and
defending "Europe's back door"—in other words, by preventing the British
and De Gaulle from setting foot in their African colonies.[10]

But what did Vichy have in mind?

Its oft-repeated aim was the earliest possible conclusion of an honorable
peace settlement with the victor, preferably before Britain bit the dust as
well.

But on what terms, and—more important still—to what purpose?

There was no doubt what Marshal Pétain and his government did *not*
want. That France should have to content herself with being little more
than a German province they found unthinkable and unacceptable. However, it was impossible to devise a simple formula for what they aspired to,
and what they hoped to accomplish, by collaborating, because Vichy's
ministers and senior civil servants used the same policy to pursue different
objectives.

One group collaborated in order to gain time. Being unconvinced that
Germany's victory was complete, they were determined to collaborate as
little as possible and do their utmost to pave the way for France's re-entry
into the war on Britain's side.

Three other groups took it for granted that Britain's ultimate military
defeat was inevitable. In their view, France had to collaborate with the
prospective victor so as to forestall a separate peace between Britain and
Germany. They also agreed that collaboration with the occupying power
was essential if internal order was to be protected from the menace of social revolution.[11]

But considerable differences of opinion existed, even among these last three groups.

Some people advocated a well-gauged policy of collaboration whose underlying aim must be to avoid excessive and gratuitous sacrifices. This would at least ensure that France made the best of her predicament.

Others were all for collaborating as actively as possible. In their belief, tangible evidence of France's cooperative attitude would convince the Germans that she was capable of playing a useful and constructive role in a new European system on equal terms with the Third Reich. Substantial concessions should, they thought, make it possible to convert military defeat into political victory.

What mattered mainly to the third group, which took no great interest in Vichy's foreign policy, was to seize the chance to set up an authoritarian regime and a political system in the traditional conservative mold. This aim would, it was thought, be furthered by a climate of active and positive collaboration.

That so many diverse views and schools of thought could coexist inside Pétain's government is one of the peculiarities of the French political scene. Vichy, that celebrated peacetime spa and notorious wartime pseudo-capital, became the seat of something which the American historian Stanley Hoffmann once christened, with elegant precision, a "pluralistic dictatorship."[12]

Vichy was certainly a dictatorship. It banned political parties, installed a new political and administrative Establishment, and substituted an authoritarian regime for the Republic's parliamentary democracy. In 1940, within the space of only four months, more than two thousand civil servants were dismissed and three thousand French Jews removed from public office and replaced with supporters of right-wing parties.[13] Liberal politicians, party leaders, trade unionists, and ex-ministers were either stripped of influence or detained and, if possible, brought to trial on some pretext or other.

The Vichy dictatorship was also pluralistic because it derived support, not from one internal pressure group, but from a variety of political forces, all of which could be described as right-wing. Their common cause was the suppression of parliamentary democracy, their common emotion hatred of its weaknesses and functional disorders. "Cagoule" terrorists, authoritarian Catholics, right-wing intellectuals, "Maurassiens" of the old conservative opposition and pro-fascist technocrats of the new—such were the elements that foregathered at Vichy to revenge themselves on the Popular Front and all the French Revolution had produced in the way of ideas and achievements. As Pétain's Foreign Minister, Paul Baudouin, told a *Journal de Genève* correspondent in June 1940, "twenty years of uncertainty, discontent, disgust, and latent insurrection" had paved the way for "total revolution" in France, and now this abscess had been burst by the war.[14]

It should nonetheless be borne in mind that Vichy was not National Socialist. Its sentiments were anti-liberal and anti-democratic, anti-Marxist and anti-Semitic, but it lacked the fascist party and power-obsessed dictator, the private armies, the National Socialist claim to racial superiority and profound contempt for conservatism, that would have put it on a par with Hitler's regime. None of Vichy's right-wing factions wanted to create a National Socialist France. They aspired after a society founded on the family and the Church, on the Army and tradition, on independent professional associations and an economy directed from above—and all of it shielded by the state and guided by a benevolent paternal hand.

For all its affinity and similarity to Italian Fascism and German National Socialism, it was only because the Vichy regime differed from them ideologically that it was able and compelled to decide on a collaborationist policy whose proviso was that France should remain France—albeit the sort of France envisaged by authoritarian conservatives and traditionalists.

Vichy's individual pressure groups and schools of thought were as undeniably agreed on fundamentals as they were opposed in their practical objectives. It was only natural, therefore, that the conflict inherent in Vichy's pluralistic dictatorship should become manifest in its official collaborationist policy, from which different groups expected different things. The resulting confusion was not only absurd but fraught with danger.

Collaboration's Double Agents

A marshal as head of state and generals in charge of four ministries. . . . France had not possessed such a highly militarized regime since 1832. Almost a third of the rump state's political executive was controlled by the military—by the men who had been hardest hit by defeat and were consequently the first to organize resistance in every occupied country.

At Vichy, the seat of power, any thought of resistance had to be shelved in favor of giving practical effect to the provisos that had been imposed on official collaborationist policy. This idea was self-evident, not a product of deliberation.

Immediately after the armistice agreement was signed, for example, an official Vichy department had been set up on the initiative of Colonel Rivet, former head of the intelligence and counterespionage service. This "Bureau for Antinational Machinations" (BMA) directed Vichy's secret intelligence service, as well as a counterespionage center in Marseille. To these, in October 1940, was added a Lyon-based front organization named "Firme Technica," which was really an independent counterespionage center operating against Germany and Italy.[15]

While Vichy was positively showering the Third Reich with offers of collaboration, as we shall see, the officers attached to these "special services" spent their time hunting German spies. Vichy's intelligence center dealt with five hundred cases of espionage in the first twelve months. Several hundred secret agents employed by Germany were handed over to military courts of which the public and the occupying power knew nothing, forty-two of them condemned to death and executed, others allegedly executed without trial, and a hundred-odd spirited off to Algeria.[16]

In July 1941, Vichy's secret intelligence service—"secret" in a twofold sense—employed no less than 429 agents. Resident French liaison officers in Lisbon, Marseille, and Tangier are recorded as having exchanged information with British Intelligence and the U. S. Office of Strategic Services (OSS). Contact with the Allies was also maintained through diplomatic channels in Canada and the United States. It goes without saying, too, that Allied agents operating in France and her African colonies could in general count on the assistance of Vichy's "special services" and their centers in occupied France and North Africa.[17]

The special service officers, who thoroughly approved of official collaborationist policy because they saw it as a means of gaining time, included the hundred-thousand-strong "armistice army" in their calculations. Where its equipment and command structure were concerned, this force was to be placed in readiness to join the Allies in their eventual assault on Hitler's Europe.

Soon after the armistice, the generals commanding the eight military districts in the South of France were duly instructed not to hand in all their weapons, but to conserve as much equipment as possible and establish secret arms dumps. The relevant organization, consisting mainly of officer reservists, was run by two colonels named Mollard and Du Vigier.[18]

In addition, senior officers from the intelligence and counterespionage services regularly met for planning sessions and situation reports. Against the possibility that the Wehrmacht might march into unoccupied France and invalidate the armistice terms, secret mobilization orders and operational plans had been drafted at the beginning of 1941. These provided for delaying actions that would enable French forces to establish a firm bridgehead for Allied troops landing on the Mediterranean coast. London and Washington are reported to have been informed of these and other plans by courier, even at this early stage.[19]

How many people were in the know?

There is evidence to suggest that preparations for armed resistance to an invasion of the "free" zone were made with the knowledge of some Vichy ministers. As Minister of Defense, General Maxime Weygand is said to have expressly approved the establishment of the Bureau for Antinational Machinations and the reconstruction of the secret intelligence and espionage services.[20]

Further evidence suggests that secret arms depots were inspired by Weygand himself and issued by General Colson, Vichy's Minister of War.[21]

General Charles Huntziger, who signed the armistice agreement on behalf of France and originally headed the French delegation to the Armistice Commission at Wiesbaden, was later appointed Minister of Defense. Despite the need for extreme caution, he is said to have distinguished himself on his second day in office by approving and actively supporting a secret plan of action devised by Colonel Georges A. Groussard, then Inspector General of the French Security Police and commander of Vichy's regular police force.[22] In January 1941, when tipped off about a large cache of arms near Marseille, Huntziger reprimanded the officer responsible but confined himself to remarking, meaningfully, that the government would be unable to protect him if it came to the pinch.[23]

The circumstances surrounding Colonel Groussard, a dare-devil character who eventually deserted Vichy for the Allies, are significant enough in themselves.

In June 1941, Groussard was instructed by Huntziger to fly to London, where he was received by Winston Churchill, Foreign Minister Eden, and some aides of General de Gaulle, who happened to be away.[24] He then returned to Vichy and reported to Huntziger on the outcome of his trip.

After consulting Marshal Pétain, Huntziger held out the prospect of a second trip to London. For this purpose, Groussard was issued by Dr. Bernard Ménétrel, Pétain's personal friend and physician, with a Vichy passport and a valid Spanish visa in the name of Georges Gilbert. He was arrested soon afterward, presumably on orders from Admiral Darlan, who had become one of Vichy's most powerful figures in his capacity as Vice-Premier and head of the Foreign and Interior ministries.

Darlan had for some time been trying to develop closer relations with Nazi Germany by stepping up his offers of collaboration, and Groussard's trips to London were liable to endanger such a policy.[25] Caught in the twilight zone between conspiracy and legality, between what they dared and were at liberty to do, individuals and pressure groups frequently clashed over the ways and means of collaboration. Things had gone so far, in fact, that few people knew for certain who was shielding whom, what Pétain thought and wanted, and how much latitude he would allow. Who ought to stand in fear of whom? Where were secret links being forged, either with the victorious Germans or with the Resistance that was only now developing into an appreciable counterforce?[26]

Pierre Pucheu, another of Vichy's Interior Ministers, who was sentenced to death for collaboration and executed in 1944, actually conferred with one of the most prominent members of the Resistance in January 1942. This was Henri Frenay, founder and leader of the "Combat" organization. Pucheu had previously released one of Frenay's men from jail, where he was being held by the Vichy police, instructed him to tell his chief that he wished to see him, and offered a guarantee of safe-conduct.

Once closeted with the Resistance leader, Pucheu tried to persuade him that Pétain's government was waging a constant battle against the Germans' overweening demands. For its part, the Resistance kept thwarting this policy by inflaming public opinion and destroying the calm and moderation on which the Marshal depended. Clearly, the Resistance was poorly informed about government policy and what lay behind it. He, Pucheu, did not propose to negotiate. He merely wanted to warn the illegal Resistance organizations before proceeding against them with merciless severity, and he urged Frenay to give the matter thought.

Frenay asked for time to consider, and Pucheu had him issued with a police pass.

Hurriedly convened by Frenay, the executive committee of his Resistance organization defined its attitude in a memorandum which he personally delivered to Pucheu early in February. This stated that no agreement or compromise was possible: the Resistance flatly rejected any form of collaboration with the enemy.

Frenay's executive committee did, however, approve the conclusion of a gentlemen's agreement with the Interior Minister under which the clandestine press would desist from personal attacks on Pétain in return for the release of Resistance fighters held in custody.

Both parties kept the pact at first. There were few army officers—Frenay included—who did not cherish a secret respect for Pétain. The Marshal and his cabinet further agreed, in consultation with Pucheu, that men and women of the Resistance should in the future be administratively interned rather than brought before a court. The new arrangement amounted to a truce, if only a temporary one.[27]

Neither side succumbed to the illusion that these hazardous maneuvers in the internal no-man's-land could be of long duration, and the diabolical urge to play a double game became almost irresistible as time went by.

Until the end of 1942, Frenay kept in regular touch with the Lyon-based "firm" that masked Vichy's espionage operations against the Wehrmacht. At the same time, the Bureau for Antinational Machinations was compelled to take action against him and his Underground organization because Berlin was becoming more and more insistent that Vichy should combat the Resistance. The Bureau had also to justify its existence by producing some results. The more active the Resistance became, and the more it obstructed Vichy's collaborationist policy, the greater the moral dilemma that afflicted Frenay's secret allies: sooner or later, whether they liked it or not, they would have to hunt him down.

Only a clear-cut decision could extricate them from this quandary. Like a number of senior officers serving in the treaty army, many officer members of the Bureau for Antinational Machinations and the intelligence and counterespionage services eventually joined the Underground. Meanwhile, Vichy was becoming more and more deeply involved with Hitler.[28]

Gratuitous Concessions

One searches in vain for a foreign policy doctrine into which Pétain's collaborationism can neatly be fitted. Little more comes to light than a scanty set of guidelines and, if one examines his personal attitude, the weak-willed vacillations of an elderly man.

On the one hand, he allowed his government to promulgate anti-Semitic laws unasked for by the Germans.[29] In the summer of 1940, Jews were debarred from public office, the teaching profession, and all spheres of cultural life. They were also forbidden, among other things, to set foot in the provisional capital and the Department of Allier.[30] Against this, Pétain later opposed the German request that unoccupied France, too, should introduce the yellow star which Jews were obliged to wear in the occupied zone, and he also refused to sanction the deportation of French Jews. But while his Foreign Minister, Laval, was glibly informing Carl-Albrecht Oberg, the SS and police chief, that Vichy was not a department store capable of supplying any number of Jews at a fixed price, seven thousand of the foreign Jews arrested by Vichy's police were, with the knowledge and assistance of Pétain's own government, being hauled off to Poland in sealed trains. Laval had meantime given his firm consent to the "delivery" of ten thousand Jews from the unoccupied zone.[31]

Pétain behaved just as diffidently in the case of two Resistance attacks which claimed the lives of the German area commander at Nantes and an administrative officer in Bordeaux. On Hitler's express orders, the German military commander in France, General Otto von Stülpnagel, had retaliated by shooting forty-eight French hostages. A further fifty were to be executed if the culprits were not arrested within seventy-two hours.[32]

Accounts of what went on in Vichy during these days have been left by some of the Marshal's closest associates. While differing on points of detail, they all agree that Pétain, after a sleepless night, resolved to oppose the executions with all the personal authority at his command. He even proposed to travel to Paris and offer himself to the German authorities as a hostage.[33]

Apparently, his cabinet talked him out of it. To square things with the Germans, Interior Minister Pucheu was sent to Paris instead, having meanwhile persuaded the German authorities to delete the names of "good Frenchmen" earmarked for mass execution on the second list of hostages and replace them with French Communists.[34]

The second batch of hostages, fifty strong, faced a firing squad on October 24, 1941.

Three days later, Pétain broadcast to the French people. He condemned the Resistance assassinations but uttered no word of protest—no word of regret for the Germans' ninety-eight innocent victims.[35]

The question that inevitably arises, in regard to Vichy's collaboration with the Third Reich, is what role was played by its three successive Foreign Ministers. Did they differ in the extent to which they toed the line?

Interestingly enough, there was little to choose between them. With or without Laval, who rates as the true representative of Pétain's collaborationism, the constancy of Vichy's foreign policy is as striking as the indecision of its head of state.

What form did that policy take?

On the one hand, French delegates to the Armistice Commission honestly strove to abide by the letter of the agreement and uphold their country's interests in a legalistic manner. On the other, they embarked on collaboration of their own accord—swiftly, unequivocally, and on a massive scale.

Only two weeks after it was signed, General Huntziger of the French delegation tried to persuade his German partners at Wiesbaden that the armistice agreement had already been "superseded" because France was, to all intents and purposes, in a state of war with her former ally and the Third Reich's principal foe. He was alluding to the fact that, four days earlier, over a thousand French sailors had lost their lives when the British Mediterranean Fleet fired on French warships at Mers-el-Kebir, whereupon French aircraft had bombed Gibraltar. Soon afterward, Foreign Minister Baudouin clarified General Huntziger's meaning by informing the Reich Government, in Marshal Pétain's name, that he wished to confer with Reich Foreign Minister Ribbentrop in Germany. He also intimated that Vichy was aiming at an early peace settlement—one that would enable France to become a *"puissance associée"* or associate power at Germany's side.

The same day, Huntziger left a document lying on his desk in Wiesbaden. When found and read within hours, as the French had foreseen, this proved to be a "Study of Petroleum Sources in the Near East"—alias a plan to use French forces in the eastern Mediterranean to capture the oil fields of Iraq. The project envisaged that these strategically vital and potentially lucrative sources of energy should be jointly exploited by Germany, France, and Italy. A week later, Huntziger openly proposed to his German fellow negotiators that the French should carry out sabotage attacks on oil-pumping installations in Transjordan.[36]

Thus, French offers of collaboration went a very long way from the outset. Vichy cannot be said to have wasted any time on feeling out or exploring the German attitude. Its moves were made so rapidly, and in such swift succession, that one would be justified in calling them a diplomatic bombardment.

Within days, Huntziger submitted a second memorandum embodying fresh concessions which far surpassed all the Germans' expectations. The Reich Government was given leave to install German commissioners, not only in the Finance Ministry at Vichy but also in the French Goods Control Office. Their expressly stated function would be to supervise the export controls introduced by the French Government and prevent all exports to "a power with which Germany is currently in a state of war." This meant nothing more nor less than the complete cessation of trade with Britain and the admission of German authorities to unoccupied France—in other words, a unilateral offer of economic cooperation beneficial to the German war effort.[37]

But these generous and gratuitous concessions bore no immediate fruit. On the same day, Hitler requested Vichy to recompense him militarily for the fact that the disarming of French forces had been left in abeyance after the British attack on French warships at Mers-el-Kebir. His price was a steep one: first, the use of airfields in the Casablanca area; second, the availability of French Mediterranean ports to the German Navy and of the Tunis–Rabat rail link to German land forces; and, third, the use of French merchantmen—operating under German control—to supply German "air bases" in the Mediterranean area.

Pétain firmly but politely rejected these demands, which far exceeded the terms of the armistice agreement, and stated that exhaustive discussions would be needed to clarify the situation arising from Germany's requirements.

It became evident that Vichy and Berlin had no real desire to fall in with each other's proposals. Hitler refrained from provoking the British into striking back at French-controlled territories in the Middle East— Syria, for example—to which German forces had no access, and Pétain declined to embark on any form of military cooperation that might embroil him in a war with Britain.

Once again, it was Vichy that hurriedly produced fresh tokens of its readiness to collaborate. Pétain's representatives in Wiesbaden and Berlin restated the proposals which the Germans had left unanswered. Shortly afterward, at the end of July, it was suggested to the chief of the German Security Police and Security Service in Paris that there might be "an agreement on all matters affecting our two countries." Meanwhile, Vice-Premier Laval had already told the Germans that he was in favor of "collaboration without ulterior motives for the benefit of Europe as a whole."[38]

Vichy, the Lamentable Failure

It was not fortuitous that Laval should actively have meddled in French policy toward Germany long before the end of October 1940, when he himself took over the Foreign Ministry.

Laval was Vichy's last surviving example of the French parliamentarians and political negotiators who inspired such repugnance in the
Marshal, his generals, and authoritarian conservatives in all his ministries.
Originally a Socialist, then an Independent, Laval had been mayor of a
working-class Paris suburb for decades, four times head of government,
and thirteen times a minister. An adept at party arithmetic and parliamentary horse trading, he had succeeded in persuading the National Assembly to step down on July 10, 1940, and invest Marshal Pétain with absolute power. Pétain had for some considerable time nursed the greatest
respect for the abilities of this shabby and hopelessly unmilitary little man
—a caricaturist's dream in his eternal white tie and ill-cut storekeeper's suit
—who disrespectfully chain-smoked in his presence and blew the smoke in
his face. It was Laval, that sliest of all French foxes, whom Pétain believed
most likely to reach an accommodation with the Germans and Italians.[30]

It was also Laval—not Paul Baudouin, Vichy's earliest Foreign Minister
—who first crossed the demarcation line and traveled to Paris on July 19,
1940. There he conferred with the American diplomat Robert Murphy and
senior representatives of the occupying power. Three weeks later he turned
up a second time, and late in August he was received at the German headquarters in Fontainebleau by Field Marshal Walther von Brauchitsch,
Commander in Chief France. On this occasion Laval is reputed to have
suggested that the French Air Force should cooperate in bombing Britain—
an offer which, as Foreign Minister Baudouin remarked, the Field Marshal
contemptuously declined. At about the same time, when France's possessions in Equatorial Africa went over to De Gaulle, Laval further recommended to his cabinet colleagues that war should be declared on Britain.

Prominent political refugees who had relied on the traditional French
right of asylum were unscrupulously handed over to the Third Reich,
among them the German industrialist Fritz Thyssen and leading Social
Democrats Rudolf Breitscheid and Rudolf Hilferding. Soon afterward,
Vichy legalized the manufacture of military equipment for the Germans
and, in the same month, approved the sale to them of French holdings in
Romanian oil companies. And while some Vichy officers were establishing
secret arms dumps, others were supplying the Germans with more rifles
than they thought the French possessed.[40]

Finally, late in October 1940, after months of persistent French over-
tures, Hitler condescended to meet, first with Laval and then with Pétain
at the little railroad station of Montoire.

In March 1941 Vichy went even further. Admiral Darlan, who wanted
to employ French warships to protect French merchant shipping, sought
the German Government's permission and got it. At the end of March,
French and British warships clashed off the Algerian coast.[41]

Four weeks later Vichy signed the so-called "Paris Protocols," which
embodied more military concessions. Pétain's government agreed, first,

aced with the threat that Prague would be bombed by the uftwaffe, and unequal to the burdens of his office, President Emil áche of Czechoslovakia put the fate of his country in Hitler's ands.

President Ignacy Mościcki of Poland sought asylum in Romania with the members of his government when all hope of stemming the German advance had gone. Fighting continued for about two weeks after his departure.

King Christian X of Denmark (left) did not put up a fight when German forces occupied his country, but his subtle blend of collaboration and esistance staved off an open clash for three and a half years. King Haakon VII of Norway (right) left his government free to collaborate or esist. He himself chose to fight on in exile.

Place, date, and occasion unknown. This scene of peaceful communion between victor and vanquished, German SS man and F
gendarme, leaves us wondering what the pair of them are doing or planning to do, and why Gendarme No. 10,922 is collaborating wi
occupying power. Is he a devotee of Hitler's—a French National Socialist—or just a public servant with a wife and children to sup

s he support Marshal Pétain because he believes that the old soldier may set France on the road to recovery, or is he a member of some
destine Resistance group who simply uses his policeman's job and uniform as camouflage? The whole problem of collaboration is
eyed by this photograph and its range of hidden meanings.

Queen Wilhelmina of the Netherlands left her country before it was invaded and occupied by the Wehrmacht. It had been agreed for years that Dutch forces would resist if attacked.

King Leopold III of Belgium, who was convinced that Germany would win the war, deemed it his "royal duty" to remain at his people's side and collaborate with the enemy.

President Albert Lebrun of France (left), a Resistance sympathizer, was outmaneuvered at the last moment by Marshal Pétain and the politicians who pinned their hopes on collaborating with Hitler. Like most European monarchs, King Peter II of Yugoslavia (right) refused to compromise with the Third Reich.

The sight of corpses dangling from trees, balconies, and lamposts was intended to convince the inhabitants of the occupied territories that resistance would be futile. Hitler expressly aimed at instilling "mortal terror."

Before the "Final Solution" became an accomplished fact and the technology of mass murder had been adequately developed, the German Security Police turned selected criminals loose on Polish Jews and ordered them to club their victims to death with iron bars (above). "Yes," Hitler once declared, "we *are* barbarians! We *choose* to be barbarians! Its's an honorable title."

Millions of European workers voluntarily migrated to Germany in the first two years of the war, before the introduction of forced labo[r]
They worked for the Third Reich's armaments industry of their own free will, while millions of others catered to the needs of Hitler's wa[r]
machine on home soil. Above, labor delegates representing nineteen nations visit Berlin.

Dutch National Socialists greet invading German troops with the Hitler salute. The rest of the Dutch people stood aloof, profoundly shocked by the occupation. During the initial phase, however, they too were prepared to come to terms with the occupying power.

Many Ukranians greeted the German invaders with misconceived delight, hoping that National Socialism would bring them greater freedom. Their expectations were quickly dashed. Hitler's scenario cast them in the role of a slave race.

Summary sentences of death were pure formality. Hitler had set his henchmen so immense and murderous a task that any means were justified. This photograph captures the penultimate moment—the speechlessness, the horror, the unfathomable banality of the condemned man's death. We can almost hear the noose tightening on his neck.

An SS firing squad "on duty" at the end of 1939. Hans Frank, Governor General of German-occupied Poland, put the achievements of the occupying forces into proper perspective. "If I had one notice posted for every seven Poles we have shot," he said, "the forests of Poland would be inadequate to produce the paper for them."

Homegrown National Socialists in the occupied countries never amounted to more than a small minority of the population, and Hitler's string of victories did them little good. Holland's "National Socialist Movement" lost over 40 percent of its members between 1935 and 1940. Above, all of five dozen Dutch SS men march through the streets of Amsterdam.

"Franciste" collaborators stage a rally at the Vélodrome d'Hiver in Paris, complete with color parade and Hitler salutes. Although right-wing extremists in every occupied country imitated the unmistakably National Socialist style of such demonstrations, they failed to command the support and enthusiasm characteristic of a spontaneous mass movement.

Pétain's first cabinet, enlarged on June 20, 1940, included General Weygand (right), Pierre Laval (left), who favored all-out collaboration, and Interior Minister Adrien Marquet (between Pétain and Laval), another collaborationist. Peering over Pétain's right shoulder is Finance Minister Yves Bouthillier, a shrewd and self-effacing wire-puller.

General Huntziger (center), head of the French delegation to the Armistice Commission at Wiesbaden (and later Minister of Defense), bombarded his German opposite numbers with generous offers of cooperation in a vain attempt to convey what Vichy expected the future to hold in store for France and Germany: a mutually profitable economic partnership of continental proportions.

sident Emil Hácha of Czechoslovakia (left) was the first European statesman to opt for a policy of "qualified collaboration." He enlisted
support of a "fascistoid" party to retain as much political independence as could still be salvaged. Abortive attempts at tactical
laboration were later to end in the abandonment of all resistance.

One group of Soviet prisoners, including a divisional commander and a Party secretary, evolved a clear-cut program of condition collaboration and joined forces with the Third Reich. Its key figure was General Andrei Andreevich Vlasov, here seen inspecting membe of his German-equipped "Russian Army of Liberation."

idkun Quisling, the Norwegian ollaborator whose name has unairly become synonymous with traitor."

Nazi extremist Jonas Lie, Quisling's Minister of Justice, was a former policemen and crime writer.

Fritz Clausen, country doctor and ill-starred "Führer" of a few thousand Danish National Socialists.

nton Adriaan Mussert, Holnd's leading Nazi, hydraulic gineer and man of principle.

Rost van Tonningen, Mussert's keenest rival, was a protégé and confidant of Himmler's.

Staff de Clercq, Flemish "Führer" and Belgian collaborator in chief, worked for German Military Intelligence.

Hitler's extremist Belgian collaborator, Léon Degrelle, a former Catholic activist.

oseph Darnand, Vichy's dread olice chief, was highly thought f in Berlin.

Philosopher Marcel Déat, erstwhile socialist theoretician and prominent Parisian collaborator.

Jacques Doriot, ex-member of the Comintern's Executive Committee and French collaborator in chief.

Failed Czech collaborator Rudolf Gajda, head of the "National Fascist Community" in Prague.

Fascist general Kaminsky, the Russian collaborator who made a habit of strangling his own officers.

French fascists, members of the "Anti-Bolshevist Volunteer Legion" (LVF) founded by extremist collaborators in July 1941, marching to the Tomb of the Unknown Soldier.

In Denmark, too, local National Socialists opened recruiting centers for the "Regiment Nordland" and "Freikorps Dänemark," but they attracted only one thousand volunteers by January 1942. These uniformed sentries are two of them.

French volunteers for the Russian Front. Appearances are deceptive, however. The "Anti-Bolshevist Volunteer Legion" was a flop, and only 3,600 men enrolled in the first eight months. They suffered from a double handicap: Hitler strictly limited France's contribution to his armed forces, and the first volunteers earned such public contempt that they had to ask for police protection.

A Norwegian (left) and a Dane (right) swear "loyalty unto death" on the sword of an SS officer—their oath of allegiance to the "Führer of the German Reich." Of the 860,000 Europeans who fought in the Waffen-SS, less than 10,000 were Norwegian and Danish volunteers.

French proponents of all-out collaboration attend the opening of an anti-Bolshevik exhibition in the Salle Wagram, Paris, dwarfed by a colossal painting entitled *Hitler and Pétain at Montoire*. Among them are Fernand Brinon (later president of the "Anti-Bolshevist Volunteer Legion") and Yves Bouthillier, Pétain's Minister of Finance.

Taken by Hitler's personal photographer, Heinrich Hoffmann, this picture of the historic Montoire meeting was not released at the time. Unlike the mural painting above, it conveys a frosty and uncongenial atmosphere. Marshal Pétain's resigned expression contrasts with the wary mistrust of Hitler, who clearly has no intention of forming a genuine Franco-German partnership.

that the Germans should avail themselves of French airfields and military installations in Syria; second, that they should supply the Afrika Korps with military equipment via the French port of Bizerta; and, third, that they should use the port of Dakar and French military installations in West Africa as bases for their warships, merchantmen, and military aircraft.

Apart from relinquishing a few torpedo boats and (temporarily) reducing occupation charges from 20 to 15 million reichsmarks a day, Berlin promised Vichy that between seventy and eighty thousand World War I veterans would be discharged from prison camps.[42]

In the economic sphere, the head of the German economic delegation at Wiesbaden, Johannes Hemmen, was able to announce with extreme satisfaction in his annual report for 1941 that France's huge consignments of goods and military equipment had not been surpassed during the year under review by any other country in Europe.[43]

The inescapable question was: How could this blatant imbalance between generous French concessions and the meager German response to them be justified in the long term? The conflict between Vichy's persistent readiness to negotiate and its relentless exploitation by the Germans was bound, in the end, to excite misgivings in more than one French leader. It eventually did so in Marshal Pétain and even, at long last, in Pierre Laval himself.

General Paul Doyen, who had succeeded Huntziger as chief of the French delegation to the Armistice Commission, resigned in mid-June 1941. In a memorandum to Marshal Pétain headed "Lessons of Ten Months at Wiesbaden," he summarized his experiences in one terse sentence: "France has given too much and received nothing." He went on: "The Germans are treating France like a warehouse to be cleared at will. The vast majority of Frenchmen have become liable to labor service since our defeat, yet they despise the victor and in general yearn for revenge. Under these circumstances, little progress will be made along the road to collaboration."[44]

Some time later, Pétain addressed a stern and unequivocal protest to Hermann Göring. In the presence of his deputy and Foreign Minister, Admiral Darlan, and of the French commander in chief in North Africa, General Alphonse Juin, he told the Reich Marshal at St.-Florent that Germany had failed to fulfill the undertakings given at Montoire. French prisoners of war had not been sent home, the demarcation line between the occupied and unoccupied zones, which was to have been abolished, still existed, and the economic burdens imposed on France had not diminished. Under present circumstances, the French people would never be persuaded of the advantages of a policy of collaboration—nor could there be any talk of collaboration as long as it amounted to coercion of the vanquished by the victor. Göring wound up a heated exchange between himself and his fellow marshal by asking, "Well, *Monsieur le Maréchal,* who *are* the victors, you or we?"

Pétain turned on his heel. He later said that he had never been made to feel more keenly that France was a defeated country.[45]

To anticipate the course of events, Laval returned to Vichy as Pétain's administrative chief at the beginning of April 1942, took over the Interior and Foreign ministries as well, and carried the policy of conditional collaboration to the verge of a total sellout. But not even he, after another nine months of lavish giveaways and futile angling for German concessions, could eventually restrain his anger. Early in January 1943, when the Third Reich's "Plenipotentiary for the Deployment of Labor," Gauleiter Fritz Sauckel, requested him to supply the German war economy with another quarter of a million Frenchmen, he cut in, "I represent a country which has no army, no navy, no empire, and no more gold. I represent a country which still has 1,200,000 prisoners of war in Germany, while 900,000 of its workers, whether in Germany or in France, in the last resort work for Germany." There could be no more talk of collaboration, he said. On the French side, it had become a policy of self-sacrifice; on the German, a policy of coercion.

Reporting this conversation to Hitler, Sauckel told him that Pétain's government saw itself in the role of an abandoned, well-meaning friend, and that it was now being compelled to withdraw to another position.[46]

It was in the nature of things that, whenever a crisis arose and discussion turned to what should be relinquished or retained, Vichy plumped for the collaboration it thought so essential. In most cases, this meant giving way. And the nearer Hitler drew to the acme of his power—until hardly a politician in Europe could withstand German pressure—the faster the original curbs on collaboration were dismantled, one by one.

In October 1942, or roughly the date which Eberhard Jäckel attaches to "the end of collaboration" in France, Laval was congratulated by the German military commander, General Karl-Heinrich von Stülpnagel (his cousin Otto's successor), on the grounds that his Vichy police had seized nearly 5,500 French Communists and 400 members of the Resistance, as well as 40 tons of hidden arms.[47]

At about the same time, Vichy's intelligence service, and, more particularly, the counterespionage service directed against Germany, got out of hand. Laval insisted on their disbandment and the release of 118 German agents. Numerous French intelligence and counterespionage officers proceeded to desert Vichy and offer their services to the Resistance.[48]

Meanwhile, Vichy had also been persuaded to allow three hundred members of the German Security Police to enter the unoccupied zone in plain clothes, provide them with identity cards bearing French-sounding names, and assist them in hunting down clandestine radio stations. The French authorities could soon pride themselves on the elimination of some twenty transmitters operated by the Resistance and the Allied intelligence services. The men and women detained in these raids were not taken to Vichy but spirited off to Germany by the quickest possible route.[49]

So it was already too late for a bold about-face when the Wehrmacht blatantly violated Germany's treaty obligations by occupying the South of France in November 1942. Marshal Pétain and his ministers could have resigned and quit France to join the Allies against their faithless partner, but they did not. Although plans for mobilization were complete, the officers of the treaty army and its clandestine general staff waited vainly for Pétain's order to resist. The Marshal's sole response was to lodge a solemn protest against the German move. Even so, his appeal to the people— ". . . have faith in your Marshal, whose sole concern is France"—was heeded and respected by the bulk of the French people.

On November 27, the Wehrmacht occupied all French barracks. The treaty army was disarmed and disbanded, and most of its secret arms dumps fell into German hands.[50]

In the following year, 1943, the Vichy police detained another nine thousand persons "for Gaullism, Marxism, and hostility to the regime," while the German Security Police in Vichy arrested all the French intelligence officers they could lay hands on, shipped them off to Germany, and interned them in concentration camps.[51]

Next, Vichy established a paramilitary force known as the "Milice" and placed it under the command of Émile Joseph Darnand, an ex-professional soldier and Obersturmführer [first lieutenant] in the French Waffen-SS. Forty-five thousand volunteers joined its ranks.

Darnand, whose subsequent appointment as chief of the French police was bitterly opposed by Pétain and Laval, spread fear and dismay. He and his men, with their love of bloodthirsty terrorist tactics, were responsible for many deaths. Touring the jails with his firing squads, Darnand set up summary courts which passed sentences of death in secret. His militiamen also proved their mettle in a ruthless campaign against the Resistance, fighting alongside German regular troops and police.[52]

Reverting to the officers of the "special" or intelligence and counterespionage services, it is interesting to speculate whether they genuinely collaborated in the same sense as the government they served.

That they did serve Vichy is beyond dispute. They were part of Pétain's regime and acted in the spirit of that regime, not against it. When they spied on the Wehrmacht, tracked down and executed German agents, swapped information with London and Washington, and helped them to establish secret arms dumps in the South of France, they did so—at least initially—on behalf of, with the knowledge of, and sometimes even with the express or tacit consent of Pétain and some of his ministers and senior civil servants.

The Vichy Government regarded this merely as one way of upholding
the main limitation it had placed on its collaborationist policy from the
first: that France's independence, sovereignty, and national identity be
preserved at all costs, so that she could later become a capital investment
in Hitler's grand European "business venture." Thus the "special services"
that watched over national security had likewise to be preserved at all
costs, not *despite* but *because* of France's collaboration. It was their task
to guard the institutions and secrets of the state against all comers, but especially against the insidious power of Nazi Germany.

Some Vichy officers took a different view of things. They started out in
the firm belief that their revered Marshal privately "didn't mean what he
said." They were convinced that he would resume the struggle against Germany at the first opportunity, and that it was their duty to prepare for a
military comeback. Even though they simultaneously took action against
Allied agents, Gaullists, dissidents, and members of the slowly burgeoning
Resistance, and even though they arrested resisters and handed them over
to the judicial authorities, their collaboration—however much it suited the
occupying power—differed from the government's in that they believed it
would gain time for the mounting of a military revolt or a war of liberation
alongside the Allies. Judged in the light of their basic attitude, their collaboration was more tactical than anything else. As soon as they felt that
Pétain and his associates were unequal to their difficult task, they joined
the Resistance.

General Vlasov and Others

Conditional collaboration occurred in the East as well. In some cases, senior Red Army officers and Communist Party officials who had been taken
prisoner by the Germans offered to collaborate with them. They did so for
a wide variety of reasons, one of them being that capture and imprisonment had presented them with a first-ever chance to exchange views freely
with other Russians. Once in camp, they met kindred spirits who had
hitherto been as chary as themselves of entertaining forbidden ideas and
putting them into words. They could not help wondering, at the very least,
how the Soviet Union, the Red Army, and Stalin's vast empire—an edifice
twenty years in the making—could have been brought to the verge of collapse by a capitalist army with hundreds of thousands of good German
workers in its ranks.

Having doubtless begun by indulging in discreet criticism of the regime
and voicing doubts about Stalinism and the Party's repressive leadership,
they came to the conclusion that Russia needed freedom.

They knew what they did not want: they wanted no revival of Tsarist
rule or return to a capitalist society, which Russia had in their view out-

grown for good, and no dictatorship by a single man or party.[53] They would rather have sought help from the Western Powers, but beggars could not be choosers.

The key figure in this group of Soviet military commanders was a Red Army general whose name has passed into the annals of World War II: Andrei Andreevich Vlasov.

A politically indoctrinated career officer and favorite of the Soviet regime—he had been a member of the Soviet Communist Party since 1930— Vlasov was regarded by Moscow as one of its most gifted generals. After distinguishing himself in the defense of Kiev, he had gone on to command the Twentieth Army and emerged from the fierce winter fighting as one of the "victors of Moscow." Thereafter, he was honored as a hero. In the spring of 1942, Stalin gave him command of the Second Assault Army, a crack formation which the Germans had encircled in the Volkhov area, but not even Vlasov could prevent its total destruction.

Hunted down by a German patrol and captured in the barn where he was hiding, Vlasov was congratulated on his military prowess by General Georg Lindemann, commanding the German Eighteenth Army, and taken to operational headquarters at Vinnitsa in the Ukraine.[54]

There he met other Russians of senior rank, including Colonel Vladimir Boiarskii, commander of the Red Army's 41st Guards Division, and Political Commissar Georgii Nikolaevich Zhilenkov, formerly Party Secretary of one of Moscow's most important urban districts.

Vlasov, Zhilenkov, and Boiarskii drafted a memorandum setting out their ideas and held discussions with German military commanders, among them Field Marshal Hans Günther von Kluge. They declared their willingness to form a "political center" and raise a Russian army—recruited from prisoners of war and inhabitants of the occupied territories—which would join with the Wehrmacht in ridding Russia of Stalinism, though only on certain conditions. Their main proviso was that Russia should not be colonized or enslaved by the Third Reich, and that this should be guaranteed and laid down at the highest level. There must be no recurrence of the "grave abuses" committed by the occupying power.[55]

It was a straightforward program of conditional collaboration, but one that ran counter to Hitler's *Ostpolitik* and could never have won his approval. Politically, the Vlasov movement was described in German quarters as "a dilute fusion of liberal and Bolshevik ideologies," and anything but National Socialist.[56]

For this reason, Vlasov's hopes were never fulfilled. All reports concerning him were withheld from Hitler, who never saw him or granted him a hearing. His sole backing came from a small group of German officers— one of them being Colonel von Stauffenberg, Hitler's would-be assassin— who were convinced that Germany could never win the war against Russia without Russian assistance.

Vlasov owed whatever he received in the way of facilities to these officers alone. In September 1942, German aircraft dropped leaflets bearing his signature behind the Russian lines. These called on the generals, officers, and soldiers of the Red Army, together with the civilian population, to support "an honorable peace with Germany" and the formation of an anti-Stalinist government. Vlasov was also appointed commander of a "Russian Army of Liberation" (ROA), at first on paper only. The "legions" later attached to it consisted of units of company or, at most, battalion strength.

It was not until after the Battle of Stalingrad that the German press began to take notice of Vlasov. He was now permitted to deliver a policy statement to captured officers and men of the Red Army. In every other respect, his hands remained tied. He continued to lend his name to German front-line propaganda and sign leaflets calling on Soviet soldiers to desert, and his "Army of Liberation," which formed the nucleus of the so-called *Ostgruppen,* attained a strength of 160 battalions. Despite this, however, he could not but realize that he was fighting a lost battle. He was never permitted to lead a Russian army against Stalin, nor were his hopes of a change in Germany's *Ostpolitik* fulfilled. In June 1943, he was completely shelved on Hitler's orders and spent his days in idleness at a villa in the Berlin suburb of Dahlem. The recruitment of volunteers was discontinued, and even Vlasov's front-line propaganda was reduced in volume and subjected to strict supervision.

This spelled the end of collaboration by Vlasov and his supporters. His men became demoralized and began to desert to the partisans, and the more they did so, the more exasperated Hitler became. "Unreliable" units were disbanded and the rest withdrawn from forward areas and transferred to France, Holland, Italy, and the Balkans, where they were used in mopping-up operations against the Resistance. In the end, Russian freedom fighters found themselves pitted against the liberation movements of Western Europe.[57]

Hitler's chances of winning the war had long evaporated when his minions in Berlin bethought themselves, not only of their luckless chief collaborators in France, but also of Vlasov. In mid-November 1944, he was permitted to assume the chairmanship of a makeshift "Committee for the Liberation of the Peoples of Russia" (KONR), based in Prague, and have himself appointed commander in chief of a "Liberation Army" whose two divisions were hurriedly cobbled together out of Russian prisoners of war and workers and soldiers from the Eastern territories.

During Germany's death throes, one of Vlasov's divisions deserted to the Allies under General Buniachenko, a Ukrainian. Withdrawing their allegiance from the German High Command, Buniachenko and his twenty thousand men fought their way into Czechoslovakia, where they joined the revolt against the SS in Prague. There, Vlasov's men did battle in the very same uniform as the Germans who had become their eleventh-hour enemies.[58]

Vlasov himself marched the men who had remained loyal to him and those who had joined him at the last moment—a force nearly one hundred thousand strong—into American prison camps. They were later handed over to the Soviet authorities.

The story of collaboration by senior Russian officers, and Vlasov and Zhilenkov in particular, ended in Moscow in the summer of 1946, when they were condemned to death and hanged.[59]

Tactical Collaboration
or
I Do but I Don't

The tactical collaborator says: I agree to collaborate despite my hostility to National Socialism and the Third Reich. I may do so for a variety of reasons: to throw off the foreign yoke and regain my freedom; to prevent the mass murder of innocent people whenever possible; or to consummate a political idea whose fulfillment is obstructed by National Socialism. In every case, collaboration disguises resistance and is part of the fight.

One can readily imagine what life must have been like for those who worked with and for the enemy, like millions of others, not out of ideological inclination or belief, not out of material self-interest, but for practical and altruistic reasons. They did so in order to rescue, hide, and feed refugees; to procure arms, ammunition, explosives, clothing, and food for organized Resistance groups; to pass on information of military value or distribute illegal publications; to plan acts of sabotage or assist in the gradual development of underground networks dedicated to armed insurrection. Few of these clandestine and potentially suicidal forms of resistance could have been carried on without tactical collaboration.

In everyday life, tactical collaboration was a hazardous and contradictory business. Consider, for example, the position of the anti-Nazi factory worker who could, within a short space of time, publicly demonstrate against the occupying power, place a time bomb on a railroad track used by German freight trains, and return to his lathe at a plant that turned out high-explosive shells for the people he had just attacked. So many inhabitants of occupied Europe behaved with like inconsistency that the Dutch historian Louis de Jong concluded that "almost everyone practiced resistance and collaboration at one and the same time."[1]

To reflect on this is to concede that collaboration and resistance, so far from being irreconcilable opposites, were as close as two sides of the same coin. It was quite fair in wartime to equate "Resistance fighter" with "pa-

triot" and "collaborator" with "traitor." Today this view is an anach-
ronism that understandably lives on in the dark recollections of those
who escaped slaughter at the Germans' hands, but also in the works of certain political writers with a continuing interest in basing the study of history on what Manès Sperber has, in a different context, called "the false alternative."[2]

Simultaneous collaboration and resistance was, in fact, the essential feature of all the policies open to national administrators in every occupied
country, provided that they themselves were not National Socialists. If
they spurned all contact with the occupying power, their days were numbered. But the longer they contrived to yield on the right point at the right
moment, the longer they could keep up the tug-of-war and the more they
could hope to accomplish. What counted was not political dexterity alone,
however, but the latent objective and political purpose of collaboration.
This was what distinguished the exponents of tactical collaboration from
the politicians who took their cue from Marshal Pétain and his conditional
collaborators.

In mid-January 1941, the German minister in Copenhagen, Cecil von
Renthe-Fink, presented the Danish Government with a diplomatic note
containing a request from the German Government that the Danish Navy
should temporarily place eight torpedo boats at the disposal of the German Navy. He discreetly intimated that Danish neutrality would in no way
be infringed by this friendly gesture, and pointed out that the United States
had leased Britain no less than fifty destroyers.

The Danish Government regretted that it was unable to accede to the
German request. Borrowing torpedo boats would be inconsistent with the
declarations made by the Reich Government on the day its forces peace-
fully occupied Danish territory. It had then guaranteed that the Danish
fleet would remain intact, and that it would never be employed in any kind
of warlike operation against a third power. The Danish reply was firm and
unequivocal.

The German minister retreated a step. He had been misunderstood, he
said. There was no intention of using the torpedo boats in a warlike role.
Berlin proposed to employ them merely as training vessels, or at most for
patrol duties in the Baltic. The Reich Government would be glad to lease
the Danish vessels for this purpose.

The Danish authorities saw no reason to change their view. They rein-
voked the German declaration of April 9, 1940, and stated that they
wished to abide by it.

The German minister's next move was to call on the King and convey
how much he was counting on His Majesty's consent. Otherwise, he said,
someone in Berlin might hit on the idea of stopping German coal deliveries to Denmark.

With unruffled courtesy, King Christian asked Renthe-Fink to recapitulate his remarks in writing. Berlin promptly confirmed that German coal supplies would be at risk.

To forestall a sudden swoop by the Germans, the Danish Defense Ministry had stripped the eight torpedo boats in short order and rendered them virtually unserviceable. Their guns and torpedo tubes had been dismantled, and every navigational instrument of value had been smuggled ashore and cached in the home of a Copenhagen optician.

Meantime, Berlin was subjecting the Danish authorities to intense pressure in another connection. The German minister had been urging them for months to remodel Stauning's cabinet in a way that would sever its party-political ties. He also insisted that the Danes should combat anti-German agitation with greater vigor and cooperate more closely and sympathetically with the Reich Government. Last but not least, Renthe-Fink demanded that Harald Petersen, the Minister of Justice, and Hans Hedtoft-Hansen, chairman of the Social Democratic Party, be forced to quit the Cabinet.

The Danish Government refused to give in and dump the two ministers. So did the King, and the labor organizations demanded that Stauning, the Socialist head of government, remain in office. Everyone felt sure that compliance with the German request would pave the way for a cabinet including Dr. Clausen and other National Socialists.

The ministers stood firm. In order to preserve their inflexibility on this major political issue, however, they decided to sacrifice the eight torpedo boats.

The hand-over took place on February 5, 1941. Shortly before, flags had been dipped on Copenhagen's Royal Dockyard and all buildings with shipping and maritime trade connections. When the German authorities telephoned to demand the immediate removal of these flags, they were told that the order to half-mast them had come from the King himself.

Not long afterward, the King made an unheralded appearance at the dockyard, where the torpedo boats' eight hundred officers and men were drawn up on parade. A royal order of the day was read out. Then the King spoke.

He had been forced to relinquish the boats, he said, but he looked forward with confidence to the day when they would once more sail under the Danish flag. . . .

There were two vital issues at stake: first, that the country continue to receive supplies of precious German coal; and, secondly, that the "home front" be strengthened against Nazi infiltration. The relinquishment of the torpedo boats could hardly fail to strike the outside world as an incomprehensible concession—as collaboration in the true sense. Collaboration it was, but the surrounding circumstances and the royal demonstration at the dockyard made it plain that it was also a well-weighed gambit.[3]

Unless the Danes wanted to risk everything, they could not afford to reject every last German demand. What mattered was to keep concessions to a minimum and offer purposeful resistance at the same time—not that this could always be accompanied, as it was in the case of the torpedo boats, by an impressive display of self-assertion. More often than not, events took their course without public knowledge.

Something of the kind occurred at the end of November 1941, when Denmark became the only ostensibly neutral and independent country under German occupation to join the Anti-Comintern Pact—a major political concession to Nazi Germany and a nasty surprise for the free world.

The Reich Government had demanded and stubbornly insisted on Denmark's accession to the pact. The Danish Cabinet had just as stubbornly refused. Four days of negotiations failed to produce any movement on either side. Berlin threatened that, if the Danes persisted in their refusal, the Reich Government would no longer feel bound by the agreements on which the sovereignty and neutrality of their country depended. A showdown seemed imminent.

The Danes stood their ground, and Foreign Minister Scavenius was summoned to Berlin. His German opposite number toyed with the idea of arresting him on arrival.

But Ribbentrop thought better of it. On the very eve of the Anti-Comintern Pact's renewal at a ceremony scheduled to be attended for the first time by politicians from Bulgaria, Croatia, Romania, Slovakia, Nanking China, and Denmark, negotiations were resumed. They dragged on far into the night, and it was not until the early hours of the morning that Berlin acceded to certain previously rejected Danish conditions. It agreed that the Danish Government should clarify its position in a rider to the treaty documents, and that the contents of this note should be embodied in the official press release.

The note stated that Denmark's accession to the pact imposed no obligations in regard to foreign policy, and that her nonbelligerent and neutral status remained inviolate.

The Danes had given in. By subscribing to the pact—a conspicuous token of their willingness to collaborate—they had to some extent pleased and appeased the Reich Government. Even now, however, they had collaborated within the narrowest possible limits. No change of any substance had been wrought by their submission to Germany's extortionate demand.[4]

On another occasion, both sides fought grimly over Danish judicial independence, one of the pillars of national sovereignty.

This came under fire at the end of December 1940, when the German authorities called upon the Danish Government to introduce the death penalty and enact laws that would permit the prosecution and punishment of Danes who impaired the security of the occupying power—in other words, members and supporters of the organized Resistance movement, Danish saboteurs, and agents of the Western Powers. Unless the Danes attended to this themselves, they were told, the German military commander would exercise his right to have Danish offenders court-martialed. Denmark was not only a sovereign neutral country but a Wehrmacht theater of operations, and it was the practice of German military courts to pass sentences of death and imprisonment when necessary.

While negotiating this matter, the Danish Government conveyed that, although it attached great importance to preserving the security of the occupying power, the measures it was prepared to take must not cause excessive public disquiet, and that this should be taken into account.

Underlying these negotiations was the case of a Danish lieutenant colonel named Ørum, who had been arrested on suspicion of having recruited Danish pilots for the Royal Air Force and was to be tried by a German military court on the ominous grounds that Danish laws were inadequate to punish him with due severity. In plain language, Ørum was in danger of the death penalty.

The Danes may fairly be said to have attained their objective by tactical collaboration. It was agreed that they would increase the maximum penalty for offenses against Danish neutrality to life imprisonment. This meant that captured members of the Danish Resistance could in the future be tried by Danish courts.

In return, the Germans dropped their original insistence on the introduction of the death penalty. The passing and implementation of sentences remained a Danish preserve. No Dane who had been legally convicted ran the risk of having to serve his sentence in a German jail or concentration camp.

Lieutenant Colonel Ørum was promptly handed over to the Danish legal authorities, as were the only two Danes to have been convicted by a German military court in 1941. They, too, were spared the worst.[5]

Danish Resistance organizations furiously condemned the government "collaborators" who had so far demeaned themselves as to jail Danish patriots for rebelling against foreign oppression. They regarded it as a sordid and unwarranted deal, even though it was to their own advantage—even if they themselves might someday owe their lives to government "treason."

On this point, the Danes were divided into two irreconcilably hostile camps: on the one hand, anonymous Resistance fighters drawn from every walk of life and prepared to make the supreme sacrifice; on the other, suave and subtle ministers, diplomats, and civil servants whose collaboration was often a mere pretense.

Insoluble as this conflict may have been, the three incidents cited above —the dismantling of the torpedo boats, the rejection of the death penalty, and qualified acceptance of a pact signed under extreme pressure—were examples of simultaneous resistance and collaboration. Resistance began where collaboration ended.

Sometimes, of course, concessions had to be made with no immediate prospect of repayment.

The Danish Government had, for instance, to surrender certain military equipment to the occupying power and was also compelled to sanction the formation of a "Danish Volunteer Corps." In the field of foreign policy, it was coerced into breaking off diplomatic relations with the Soviet Union.[6] Internally, too, its concessions included the banning of the Communist Party (though not until August 1941), the arrest of Danish Communists, the imposition of harsher penalties for serious political offenses, and the passing of a limited enabling act.[7]

Most important of all were the Danes' economic concessions. They had to promote the voluntary migration of Danish workers to Germany (103,000 of them by the end of 1942), step up industrial production for the Third Reich tenfold in the first two years and achieve a very considerable increase in agricultural exports, grant export credits to the tune of 1.1 billion reichsmarks, and pay a further 1.5 billion reichsmarks in occupation charges.[8]

These were substantial concessions, to be sure, but incomparably smaller than the French. Moreover, none of them was freely offered, still less forced on the Germans—merely extorted or granted in return for valuable concessions on the German side.

What makes this all the more surprising is that the Danish Cabinet contained various schools of thought on how to accommodate the occupying power.

Foreign Minister Erik Scavenius, a backward-looking politician of the old school who had molded Danish foreign policy to suit German interests and requirements during World War I, believed that final victory would go to the Third Reich. Like Pétain, he therefore esteemed it his patriotic duty to secure Denmark an honorable and independent place in Hitler's New Order. His position in Cabinet was that every effort should be made to ward off the Germans' threats and encroachments—or preferably forestall them—by granting as many of their requests as possible.

Interior Minister Knut Kristensen, who opposed Scavenius, represented the majority Cabinet view. He argued that the government must say and do nothing to convey that it was on Germany's side and expected or hoped for a German victory. It must not sanction, far less assist in, the fulfillment of any major German demand that exceeded the terms of the instrument of surrender. Finally, it must risk the possibility that the occupying power might take by force what the government was unable to grant.[9]

The Danish Government managed to keep important areas of national sovereignty intact for nearly three and a half years. The Germans continued to tolerate this partial independence until the summer of 1943, when strikes, acts of sabotage, and hostile demonstrations of all kinds multiplied to such an extent that the military authorities felt bound to intervene. The situation now became extremely critical.

On August 28, 1943, the Danish Government was requested to proclaim an immediate and nationwide state of emergency, impose a curfew and a ban on strikes and public gatherings, confiscate privately owned firearms, and set up summary courts. It was also to make sabotage and the possession of firearms subject to the death penalty which it had so vigorously resisted over the years. This time, the Germans presented their demands in the form of an ultimatum.

Fifteen minutes before the expiry of this ultimatum, which expired at 4 P.M., the government rejected its terms in toto—an unprecedented and unqualified refusal to collaborate in an area vital to German security.

Early the next morning, the Germans proclaimed martial law and assumed executive powers. They also occupied the palaces of Sorgenfri and Amalienborg, after a brief exchange of fire with members of the royal guard, and swooped on Danish Army units throughout the country.

Fighting was unexpectedly heavy. In Copenhagen, resistance had to be crushed with the aid of tanks. The Navy scuttled most of its ships, and the Army was disarmed within hours. Some ten thousand officers and men from both services were taken into custody, as were hundreds of civilians.

The Danish Government resigned.

A few days later, the Germans summarily passed and carried out their first-ever death sentences on Danish soil. Here as elsewhere, collaboration had now become utterly discredited and resistance a matter of life and death.[10]

Administrative functions were provisionally taken over by undersecretaries, as they had been in Holland and Belgium, but it was doubtful how long they would be able to withstand pressure from every quarter. Denmark was in turmoil—caught up in the frightful, self-perpetuating process of terror and counterterror.

Hitler's "model protectorate" was a thing of the past.

Prague: Camouflage, Not Compliance

Tactical collaboration was also practiced in Eastern Europe and, under very special circumstances, in the Protectorate of Bohemia and Moravia.

Hitler had abolished Czechoslovakia as a national entity and substituted the Protectorate, but he had tolerated the existence of a head of state and a Czech Government. For their part, the Allies had been quick to issue a formal statement to the effect that, since the German occupation of Czechoslovakia was illegal, Hitler's establishment of a protectorate was null and void. The Czechoslovak state continued to exist.

The resulting anomaly may be reduced to a brief formula which no one found more bewildering than the head of state and his government in Prague: in the German view, there was a Czech Government but no Czech state; as the Western Powers saw it, there was a Czech state but no Czech Government, neither in Prague nor anywhere else in the world.

President Emil Hácha and his ministers were impaled on the horns of an urgent moral dilemma. How could they decide on their own authority—which they really no longer possessed—what course of action to adopt? On the other hand, how could they ignore a set of problems on which their own survival depended? Should they collaborate or resist? Somehow, they would have to resolve this fateful question—they, whom Berlin and the outside world thought as insignificant as the "government" of a petty principality with half a dozen soldiers. Should they resign? Collaborate within limits? Quit office and stand up to the German colossus? All else apart, what decision would gain the acceptance and compliance of the people in whose name they proposed to act?

Perhaps they could call on outside aid and advice. At large in the free world were men who represented the Czech state with paramount authority, even though they held no office and had not been empowered to do so by any organ of government. Eduard Beneš, for example, the Republic's co-founder and its President from 1935 until he resigned as head of state and emigrated in September 1938, only a few days after the signing of the Munich Agreement; and Jan Masaryk, Czech minister in London and son of the founder of the Czechoslovak state, who had been elected President of "his" republic four times in seventeen years—Beneš and Masaryk, Jr., two fifty-year-olds in the prime of life.

In June 1939, three months after the Germans marched in, the Prague Premier, General Alois Elias, secretly contacted Jan Masaryk. Elias asked Masaryk to inform Beneš that, although he and his cabinet were temporarily conducting government business to save the Czech people from the clutches of the occupying power, they were solidly behind him. If Beneš thought it proper, they and President Hácha would be prepared to resign en bloc at any time.

Beneš's reply was firm enough to be construed as an order. Elias and his colleagues were urgently advised to remain in office, but they must allow for the possibility that the Germans would replace them with a prominent fascist like General Rudolf Gajda.[11]

The same question cropped up in November, after the occupying power had committed a number of gravely provocative acts, to which reference has been made in a previous chapter: nine students arbitrarily shot, nocturnal police raids on student hostels in Prague and Brno, 1,850 students arrested and 1,200 sent to German concentration camps, all Czech universities closed. It was in this very climate of hatred and humiliation that President Hácha and Interior Minister Jezek had to yield to German pressure and issue public statements pinning the blame for what had happened on foreign propaganda, which had allegedly called for a "revolutionary struggle" against German oppression.

In despair, the Prague Cabinet again consulted Beneš. A report dated early December 1939 and transmitted to London through underground channels declared that President Hácha and his ministers stood foursquare behind the Czech Resistance abroad and recognized it as their supreme authority. They firmly opposed the incorporation of Bohemia and Moravia into the Third Reich and would actively contend that Germany was not entitled to conscript Czechs for military service. If, apart from maintaining a firm stand on these points, they were expected to persevere in an "opportunist policy" designed to assist in averting "national and economic detriment," they again required express approval from the Czechs in London.

A few days earlier, Hácha had informed Beneš of the uttermost limits he had imposed on himself and on any collaborationist policy. Rather than affix his signature to any new constitutional instrument—for example, one that lent spurious validity to an act of territorial annexation—he would commit suicide.

The crisis worsened when the German-appointed Secretary of State, Karl Hermann Frank, delivered a speech containing the following unvarnished threat: "Anyone opposing us will be crushed . . . the present Czech Government and Czech leaders must desist from duplicity and deceit. Their current methods have been exposed and are leading to disaster."[12]

The Gestapo had, in fact, just discovered that Premier Elias was in touch with London, Paris, and Beneš, and that he was funding internal Resistance groups.[13]

At this point, after deliberate German threats had driven the Czech Minister of Agriculture to vanish overnight and seek refuge abroad, a reply arrived from Beneš. It was a reiterated plea to Elias and his cabinet colleagues to remain in office. The world sympathized with their plight and the fact that they were compelled to dissociate themselves publicly from their exiled compatriots.[14]

This was tactical collaboration of a purity unequaled in any other occupied country. What really set it apart, however, was its date. The first experiments in resistance-oriented collaboration took place before the outbreak of World War II. Developments in Europe as a whole were to some extent foreshadowed by what happened in Prague, a test bed for political behavior under rigorous foreign control.

What was the Prague experiment all about? Often about words, about everything and nothing—about mere acceptance of an unwanted and enforced status quo or an express admission of total surrender.

Berlin was anxious that every Czech public servant should swear an oath of allegiance to Hitler and the Greater German Reich. This possibility had already been broached in early summer 1939, or prior to the weeks of crisis described above.

"I swear to render obedience," ran the proposed oath, "to the Führer of the Greater German Reich, Adolf Hitler, in his capacity as custodian of the Protectorate of Bohemia and Moravia; to respect the laws; and to carry out my duties in accordance with the interests of the Greater German Reich and for the good of the Protectorate of Bohemia and Moravia."

Should the Prague authorities even discuss such a matter with the occupying power? Beneš, whose advice was sought, urged extreme caution. President Hácha acted accordingly. He made his attitude toward the question of the oath dependent on whether the Reich Government would guarantee Czech autonomy. This gave the Czech-German discussions a twist that enabled him to tread water, his object being to gain time by tactical means.[15]

But how long could the game go on, and at what price? This question reared its head on March 15, 1940, the first anniversary of the German invasion.

The tenseness of the situation called for a public statement by the Czech President. Berlin was expecting his final assent to the "oath of allegiance," but Hácha made no mention of it.

All he did was send Hitler a telegram reaffirming his cabinet's willingness to cooperate. That, of course, was not enough for the Germans. To make his recalcitrance even faintly palatable to them, he had to add a conciliatory remark—the price that must, he believed, be paid: he cabled his best wishes for a German victory.

Berlin did not react, but Beneš did. Hácha, he said, had overstepped the bounds of what was permissible in the way of "opportunist concessions," and any further declarations of loyalty to the Germans would be not only superfluous but dangerous. He stuck to this line even when the Wehrmacht launched its offensive in the West, arguing that Churchill's accession to the premiership was a commitment to the cause of resistance.

But the ministers in Prague were thrown off balance by what happened next.

Hitherto, their policy of tactical collaboration had been founded on a belief in Germany's imminent military collapse. Once Hitler's armies clashed with those of the major Western Powers, France and Britain, Hitler's downfall and the liberation of Czechoslovakia would—they thought—be only a matter of weeks or months.

Disaster in the West, Holland and Belgium laid low, the front ripped open, the British Expeditionary Force hemmed in at Dunkirk and desperately trying to escape by sea—Prague's illusions were shattered by a series of crushing blows. On June 2, 1940, Premier Elias sent Beneš a preliminary warning that "alarmists in the government" were already recommending far-reaching concessions to the Germans.

Hácha was not the man to withstand the tempest that was sweeping across Europe: he congratulated Hitler on his victory in the West. For the first time, Czech newspapers brought out special editions. The government not only offered the Germans a hospital train and specialist personnel but decreed that Czech towns be ceremonially decked with flags for a week.

According to the SD's monthly report for June, the Protectorate was pervaded by a mood of despondency comparable only to the one that had reigned in the aftermath of Munich.

President Hácha plumbed the depths of self-abasement. He belatedly agreed to swear the oath of allegiance, but Berlin spurned his offer. Having so recently vowed to commit suicide rather than overstep the bounds of justified collaboration, he now volunteered one concession after another. So far from opposing the establishment of a customs union between the Protectorate and the Third Reich, he actually urged his fellow countrymen to take out German citizenship.

Vainly, Beneš fired off a "final warning" and spoke of "treason" in an irate message addressed to Hácha and his government. Just as vainly, he warned his compatriots in a radio broadcast that any Czech who collaborated with the Germans would be held accountable for his actions.[16]

Then came September 29, 1941. Hácha, who had drafted his letter of resignation, did not send it.

This was the day on which the new Reich Protector, SS-Gruppenführer [Lieutenant General] Reinhard Heydrich, was scheduled to pay him a first formal visit. Hácha knew that the head of the Central State Security Bureau, who was honoring him with this courtesy call, could have had him and most of his cabinet ministers indicted for maintaining secret links with London and the internal Resistance movement. Although Heydrich's interview with Hácha betrayed no hint of any such intention, he had Premier Elias arrested the same day. Reduced to its simplest terms, collaboration was now synonymous with stark self-preservation.[17]

There was no turning back. Hácha consummated his self-abasement by broadcasting a speech in which he told the Czech people that Beneš was their "public enemy number one" and urged them to report all his agents to the police. Hácha's appeal did not go unanswered. After Heydrich had been assassinated at the end of May 1942, mass demonstrations were organized against Beneš and the exiled politicians in London. The government offered 10 million korunas for the apprehension of the killers, a reward which was later increased to 20 million.

And the result of all this bootlicking? On June 9, 1942, Hácha and his ministers were received by Hitler and compelled to listen to a torrent of naked threats. Nothing, he said, could prevent the expulsion of several million Czechs from Bohemia and Moravia. Hitler later recalled, with glee, that Hácha and his associates literally "crumpled" on being told this.[18]

Premier Elias had already been condemned to death by a People's Court on October 1, 1941. Now, in June 1942, he was executed. Hácha himself died at the age of sixty-three, six weeks after the liberation of Prague, while remanded in custody on a charge of collaboration.

The Jewish Councils

It is common knowledge that millions of Jews were killed during World War II. What is less widely known is that their route to destruction was lined by tens of thousands of fellow Jews who had been lured or coerced, for good or ill, into collaborating with the Nazi regime.

The only form of collaboration that could be expected of them, let alone accepted and practiced by them, was understandably tactical and opposed to the enemy's aims. It did, however, provide the basis for special collaborative agencies known as "Jewish Councils," the first of which was established in February 1941. These the Germans designed as exclusive channels of communication between themselves and the Jewish denizens of occupied territory in Holland, Greece, Poland, and the Soviet Union, of the ghettos in the East, the concentration camp at Theresienstadt (Terezín), and the secret death camps that represented the end of the road.

Such were the liaison committees through which all "dealings" between Germans and Jews had to pass. They transmitted the occupying power's decrees and directives and supervised their implementation. They also set up "police forces" of their own—Jewish auxiliary formations whose members wore special armbands, participated in raids, and rounded up coreligionists. Their commanders in the ghettos, notably the one at Łódź, were responsible for deciding which of their companions in misfortune should be hauled off or earmarked for the next "resettlement operation," an official euphemism for committal to an extermination camp.[19]

In Greece and Holland (and also, from 1944 on, in Hungary) the Jewish Councils administered frozen Jewish bank accounts, compiled lists of names and addresses for the German authorities, issued travel and resettlement permits, and handled all formalities connected with the wholesale deportation of Jews for forced labor or consignment to the death camps.[20]

To the Germans, the calculated advantage of this arrangement was that it obscured the source of their orders. German directives had to be conveyed to Jewish citizens or internees by the Jewish Councils. This made it seem that they emanated from a central Jewish authority—in other words, that their possible consequences had been explored and found acceptable by respected Jewish citizens. Human trust was the bait with which unsuspecting victims were lured to their doom by the German authorities and their well-meaning Jewish collaborators. The added advantage was that German propaganda could parade that miracle of magnanimity, Jewish "self-government," before the eyes of an astonished world.

Where Jewish Councils in ghettos and camps were concerned, very few people joined or acted for them of their own free will, and most were compelled to do so on pain of death. Outside the ghettos and camps, many decent Jews were prompted to collaborate with the Germans and assume positions of responsibility in the Councils by a moral and religious sense of duty—by the desire and expectation that they would be able to protect fellow Jews from persecution and preserve the existence of the Jewish community.

This gave rise, on the Jewish side, to the growth of what may be described as "collaborative shadow states"—scarcely an overstatement, when one learns that the Jewish Council of the Warsaw ghetto employed as many as 5,000 people,[21] and that the staff of the various administrative branches of the Dutch Jewish Council fluctuated between 9,000 and 17,500 during the fall and winter of 1942–43.[22]

Jewish Council officials in Holland ran employment agencies, schools and vocational training centers, social services for the old and sick, a provident fund, a free meals service, and charitable institutions of all kinds. They supplied Dutch Jews with information and advice and conveyed their requests to the German authorities. From April 1941, they also published a Jewish weekly which became an indispensable aid to collaboration.[23]

The Jewish Councils in the East performed similar functions. In the Warsaw ghetto, they supervised the accommodation of new arrivals in bomb-damaged buildings and cellars. They provided welfare services and schooling for many thousands of Jewish youngsters, collected taxes, and were responsible for the efficient running of the public services, water and power supplies, posts and telephones, medical treatment and the courts. To maintain order, they used—as we have already said—a police force of their own, and if they needed funds they raised loans on frozen Jewish assets held by German banks.[24]

But all this was, in a sense, a gigantic white lie. The Dutch Jewish newspaper naturally made no mention of police raids, wholesale arrests, or deportations, nor did it devote any column inches to the almost unbelievable reports of mass murder in the East and the true significance of the outwardly innocuous "resettlement operations." Thus the Jewish Council itself helped to shroud the truth in false hopes and a false sense of security. Those in charge—perhaps the only people in possession of the full facts—shouldered a crushing moral burden of complicity.

Complicity? Leo Baeck, a German rabbi who survived the holocaust, put it this way: "When the question arose whether Jewish orderlies should select Jews for deportation, I took the view that it would be better for them to do it because they would at least treat them more gently and be more likely to assist them and make their lot easier than the Gestapo. Effective resistance to the task was beyond our power."[25]

The commander of the Jewish police in the Łódź ghetto found himself in a similar predicament. Anxious to preserve the Jewish elite, he was guided by each individual's chances of survival when he selected the old and the sick for "resettlement," knowing that they would be gassed.[26]

In January 1943, the Jewish police in Holland were made responsible for the evacuation of mental defectives and mentally retarded children. In May, they took part in raids and mass arrests. In September came the turn of the Jewish Council itself.[27]

Not only in Holland but wherever Jewish Councils existed, Jewish community leaders and police chiefs shared the fate of their protégés and subordinates. Those in the know committed suicide or volunteered for deportation. Others let themselves be taken by force to the place where Hitler wanted them.[28]

Communist Collaboration

Tactical collaboration occurred on a large scale in the Communist world, though under various conflicting auspices.

A relatively small group of revolutionary Communists—those who considered Stalin's dictatorship a betrayal of the Revolution—joined forces with the Third Reich in the hope of eliminating Stalin with German help and establishing a democratic Soviet regime throughout Russia.

At the opposite end of the scale came the European Communist parties, which clung to Moscow's Stalinist line and invoked higher authority in support of their claim that collaboration with the Third Reich would ultimately benefit the Communist cause.

The most prominent leader of the first group, who was not a Russian nationalist like General Vlasov and dissociated himself from Vlasov politically, was the "left-wing Communist" Miletii Alexandrovich Zykov, who is reported to have been deputy editor of *Izvestia* from 1931 to 1935. When captured, Zykov himself told some German officers that he had been arrested for "deviationism" before the war and sentenced to a term of imprisonment.

Zykov sponsored the formation of a "Russian Committee for the Implementation of the Constitution of 1936." He naturally concealed the revolutionary ideas that were his real motive for collaborating with the Germans and relied on anti-Stalinism—the only acceptable reason. He also made a habit of quoting Sigismund III's dictum from Schiller's *Demetrius* to the effect that Russia could be defeated by Russia alone.

Soon after his capture, Zykov sent Goebbels a letter in which he put forward a plan that formed the basis of subsequent discussions in Berlin. He envisaged the creation of a Russian army and air force commanded by a Russian general. In his view, a purely Russian force of this kind would not only pack a substantial military punch but bring invaluable political advantages as well. Early in May 1942, he summarized his proposals in a paper entitled "Plan for the Practical Mobilization of the Russian People against the Stalin System."

He evidently failed to gain the confidence of the German officials appointed to deal with him. As soon as they detected his true political aims and discovered that he had Jewish blood—a fact which he had hitherto disguised—his fate was sealed. Zykov was secretly done to death by Gestapo officers, probably at the instigation of right-wing extremists in the Russian émigré camp.[29]

Far more important politically was the tactical collaboration of the national Communist parties, a not illogical consequence of the German-Soviet nonaggression pact of August 1939 and the treaty that set a contractual seal on Hitler's "friendship" with Stalin a month later. In company with the Soviet Union, the Comintern had become an ally of the Third Reich.

Once the initial shock had subsided, Communist Party members throughout the world were enjoined to practice tactical collaboration as a step on the road to Communist supremacy.

The first victims of this radical change of course were the Communist parties themselves.

The French Communist Party, the largest and most powerful in the world outside Russia, was officially banned in September 1939, the month war broke out. At the same time, all parallel organizations were dissolved, thousands of Party members and trade unionists arrested, and the editorial offices of the Party's newspapers closed down. Within weeks, the Party lost all the footholds in the press, in local government, Parliament, and the trade unions, which it had managed to gain during the Popular Front years.[30]

Widespread confusion reigned. One in every three Communist deputies (twenty-one out of seventy-two) broke with the Party. Numerous Communist mayors and local councillors, together with fifteen Communist members of the General Council of the Department of Seine, turned their backs on it too. Once more condemned to political outlawry, those Party members who had remained loyal to their leaders were laboriously regrouped into cells of three.

The Politburo had remained intact with the sole exception of Marcel Gitton, the Party's erstwhile general secretary. Gitton, who publicly defected to Doriot and, thus, to National Socialism, was murdered on the orders of a Resistance group in September 1941.[31]

Party Secretary Maurice Thorez deserted from his unit at the beginning of October 1939, took charge of the Party's antiwar propaganda in Brussels, and then, at the end of the year, moved to Moscow. Meanwhile, Communist collaboration in France had assumed alarming proportions. Most dangerous for France and of practical benefit to the German war effort were acts of sabotage skillfully carried out by Communist workers employed in the munitions industry.

In the Farman aircraft factories at Boulogne-Billancourt, for example, aero engines were doctored in such a way that they exploded after a few hours' flying time, destroying bombers or fighters in midair and killing their crews. Six Farman employees belonging to the now illegal Communist Party were arrested. One of them had built the destruction of a military aircraft and its crew into twenty engines a day. Four members of the group were sentenced to death by a court-martial in May 1940, and three were executed. At least two of the convicted men had demonstrably been members of a Communist Party sabotage team.[32]

Fifty issues of the banned Party newspaper, *Humanité,* were published during the first nine months of the war. Comparing them with those distributed after the fall of France, one cannot fail to be struck by the way in which Party slogans themselves were tailored to the needs of the Third Reich.

As long as French industry was working for the French armed forces and against Nazi Germany, the Party motto was that every hour of production lost was an hour gained for the Revolution. No sooner had France fallen and German arms contracts begun to roll in, however, than *Humanité* called upon the labor force to combat "the ill will of the capitalists" and resume work. This it did on July 24, 1940. Three days later, employers who refused to work for Hitler's war machine were branded as "saboteurs" who merited elimination.[33]

Only a few days after the armistice was signed, *Humanité* printed some remarks worthy of any fascist collaborator: "One is genuinely gratified in these difficult times to see so many Parisian workers cordially conversing with German soldiers in the street or in bars. Bravo, Comrades! Carry on, even if it does annoy a few stupid, ill-disposed bourgeois."[34]

"The French people want peace," *Humanité* had written a short time before, coming out openly against resistance. "They demand that vigorous measures be taken against all who try to drag France back into the war at the behest of British imperialism." The Vichy Government, it went on, was a puppet government; only the Germans were in a position to take the "vigorous measures" demanded by the people.[35]

Politburo directives issued to leading Party cadres during the second half of June 1940 were concerned with slogans—immediate demobilization of the French Army and antiwar propaganda—and designed to justify Moscow's Party line. To cite one such communication: "French imperialism has sustained the worst defeat in its history. The enemy who lurks inside the country in every war has been felled. For the French and the international working class, this event constitutes a victory. It has one enemy the less. What matters now is to make every effort to ensure that the downfall of French imperialism is permanent. Consequently, the French people are fighting the same enemy as German imperialism. It is therefore correct to regard German imperialism as a temporary ally. Anyone who fails to realize this is no revolutionary."[36]

People have wondered how, and to what extent, the Communists' tactical collaboration with Nazi Germany could have flourished in the face of such insuperable mistrust. In the German view, relations between the French Communists and the occupying power were "obscure."[37] Nevertheless, there is firm evidence of extensive cooperation.

Early in July 1940, the Politburo informed its leading cadres in a confidential circular that the Party had ceased to be completely illegal and become "semilegal." Comrades arrested by the French police while distributing leaflets had been promptly released at the request of the German military authorities. "With the exception of all deputies, political prisoners in the occupied zone were released at the same time as members of the Fifth Column."[38]

Subsequent Politburo circulars called upon Party members to behave with tact and moderation because "as far as our propaganda is concerned . . . the occupying power is turning a blind eye."[39]

This is not so surprising. According to as reliable a source as Angelo Rossi (pseudonym of the Italian writer Angelo Tasca), some of the Communist leaflets preaching opposition to the "imperialist war" and an immediate peace with Hitler, as well as several illegal issues of *Humanité* dating from the first nine months of the war, or before the German offensive, had been printed in Nazi Germany itself.[40]

Further confirmation of this remarkable fact was provided by Foreign Minister Ribbentrop in conversation with Mussolini on March 10, 1940, at a Rome meeting attended by Count Ciano and Hans Georg von Mackensen, the German ambassador.[41]

It is equally certain that, from February 1940 onward, the Germans ran two secret pseudo-French radio stations. One broadcast patriotic pronouncements on "love of peace," and the other, which styled itself Radio Humanité, after the banned Party newspaper, urged French Party members to tear up their draft papers or desert.[42]

One is nevertheless surprised at the speed with which the French Politburo got in touch with German military headquarters in Paris after the fall of France, anxious to make the most of its willingness to collaborate.

Paris fell on June 14, 1940. Four days later, General de Gaulle broadcast his appeal for continued resistance from London. On the same day, the Press Service offices at German headquarters in Paris became the scene of negotiations between Maurice Tréand, a Central Committee member who came accompanied by two women comrades, and an officer in the

German Propaganda Section. These talks concerned the publication of *Humanité* in the occupied zone. On June 19, after two further sessions, the Germans agreed to permit its distribution. A printing order was placed and the owner of the press handed fifty thousand francs in cash.

The Central Committee undertook to harness its newspaper to "a European pacification policy," "support the conclusion of a Franco-Soviet pact to supplement the German-Soviet Friendship Treaty, and thus lay the foundations of a lasting peace."

Before copy for the first issue could be submitted for German censorship, Tréand and his female companions were arrested during a French police raid. Because they were found to be carrying written matter relating to their discussions with the German authorities, they were taken off to jail and charged with violating the ban on the Communist Party.

Vichy and the Communist Party had clashed—paradoxically, since they were both steering hard for collaboration—but the German military authorities intervened and the detainees were released. Three days later, Tréand and a second member of the Central Committee, Deputy Jean Catelas, sent a letter to German headquarters confirming the agreements and undertakings they had made and requesting an interview with the relevant German official.

This time, however, Vichy and its efficient "special service" officers managed to thwart the plan. Once hostilities had broken out between Germany and the Soviet Union, Jean Catelas and three other fellow Communists were sentenced to death by a Vichy court and executed.[43]

France was not unique in this respect. Communist collaboration paid off in Belgium, where the Party had been banned several months before Hitler's offensive. The German authorities lifted this ban but prohibited all other political parties except the Flemish and Walloon fascists. The Communist Party newspaper, *Vie ouvrière,* was also permitted to resume publication under National Socialist aegis.

The Party was banned again in August 1940, but only because it had misjudged the situation and failed to observe its tacit agreement with the occupying power. Having gained political control of the municipal administration at Liège and other places while fighting was still in progress, and having extended that control to the coalfields of Charleroi, the Communists infuriated the German authorities by refusing to step down.[44]

The Communist Party was tolerated in Denmark, too, where the Germans sanctioned its existence for nearly eighteen months. It was not until the end of August 1941, or two months after the Russian campaign began, that they got the Danish Government to ban the Party and its newspaper, *Arbeijderbladet.* Of the 295 Communist Party officials whom the Germans had compelled the Danish police to arrest on the day they invaded Russia,

179 had been released in the interim. The occupying power had not insisted on their being handed over.[45]

Tactical collaboration was also practiced by the Norwegian Communists.

As soon as the Germans marched into Oslo, the Party secretaries and the editorial staff of their newspaper made contact with Wehrmacht headquarters. Apart from Quisling and his confederates, they were the sole representatives of a political party to have remained in the capital and awaited the entry of German troops. Their offices remained untouched and their newspaper, *Arbeideren,* continued to appear with German permission as if nothing had happened.

It need hardly be said that the Party and its newspaper condemned the Norwegian Army's defensive operations against Hitler's invading forces. Two weeks after the German invasion and seven weeks before fighting ceased, *Arbeideren* declared that Germany was really waging war on Britain, not Norway. The sooner the Norwegians surrendered, the better, because it was "in the interests of the Norwegian people to bring this resistance to an end."

Together with a Communist splinter group tolerated by the Gestapo, the Party approached the occupying power and suggested in all seriousness that it be given charge of the major labor organizations.

The Germans sanctioned this proposal. They made the trade unions and their central administrators responsible to a committee in which representatives of the Communist Party and its splinter group were to work closely with delegates from Quisling's fascist party.

Once again, however, things turned sour.

The Norwegian trade unions and every political party with the exception of Quisling's "National Assembly" declined to cooperate with the occupying power in any way. Completely isolated, the Communists eventually lost their credit with the Germans—which they owed to Moscow —because their usefulness was at an end.

The Norwegian Communist Party and its newspaper were banned in mid-August 1940.[46]

Temporary Truces

Probably the crudest form of tactical collaboration, and one from which, as a rule, both sides hoped to derive immediate benefit, was the temporary truce. It is worthwhile at least touching on the subject with the aid of two examples which may at first sight seem incredible—incredible because, remarkably enough, this species of collaboration occurred most often in places where war was waged with the greatest ferocity and fanaticism.

As, for instance, in Yugoslavia, where Tito reached an informal understanding with the Wehrmacht. Heavy fighting had left his partisans in a critical position. What with typhus, a central field hospital crowded with over four thousand wounded, and persistent harassment by Draža Mihailović's royalist partisans, who showed every sign of renewing their attacks in the near future, Tito decided to get in touch with his principal enemy, the Wehrmacht, on the pretext of a possible exchange of prisoners. This he did with the approval of the Central Committee of the Yugoslav Communist Party but in flat contravention of directives from Moscow, where the very suggestion had been greeted with sullen disfavor.

These ultrasecret negotiations, which could not be made public until long after the war, took place in March 1943. Conducted between officers from German headquarters and a delegation headed by Milovan Djilas, a Politburo member who was also Tito's closest friend and associate, they resulted in an unwritten agreement which both sides observed.

Tito's partisan high command undertook to discontinue acts of sabotage and attacks on the important Belgrade–Trieste railroad line carrying raw materials and strategic supplies to the Third Reich. In return, the Germans temporarily left the hard-pressed partisans in peace. As a token of good faith, the pact was sealed with an exchange of prisoners.[47]

Tactical agreements of a far more extensive kind had already been concluded in Yugoslavia by the Chetnik partisan commanders, not only with the Germans but, more especially, in July 1941, with the Italians. The latter undertook to station their troops in large towns and along major lines of communication. The interior they left to the partisans. In their turn, the Chetniks had to keep Italian-occupied areas clear of Tito's partisans, for which purpose the Italians supplied them with arms and ammunition.[48]

How much was sacrificed in such cases, and how much gained? What value should be placed on the psychological losses and material gains arising from these sudden spells of tactical collaboration? Even in as extreme a case as the one described below—an illustration from France—one would hesitate to answer off the cuff.

In 1944, the commander of the German Security Police in Bordeaux negotiated with the leaders of the OCM, a Resistance organization long regarded as one of the strongest in occupied France. This had been formed in December 1940 by the amalgamation of various Resistance groups with a membership largely recruited from influential circles in government, industry, and the armed forces. Tightly organized along military lines, it adopted a political stance which has been described as "right-wing bourgeois, technocratic, and anti-Semitic."

At the time when "OCM Bordeaux" entered into negotiations with the SD, it possessed numerous well-hidden caches containing some seventy-five tons of arms and ammunition. This had been airdropped by the British SOE (Special Operations Executive), whose task it was to coordinate operations by European Resistance movements and smuggle the requisite arms, explosives, radio sets, sabotage experts, and military equipment into occupied territory.

OCM Bordeaux was extremely well armed, therefore, but its fighting strength had been substantially diminished by the capture of three hundred of its best men.

Both sides sought agreement and duly came to terms. The Germans released their three hundred prisoners; the French turned over forty-five tons of London-supplied arms and explosives, including two thousand submachine guns and a million rounds of ammunition.

Three hundred lives saved, three hundred fighting men regained, thirty tons of arms and ammunition retained. . . . It seemed a fair enough bargain, except that any form of collaboration, tactical or not, was then regarded as "trafficking with the enemy," or treason. Those in charge of OCM Bordeaux paid for the deal with their lives. Their leader, together with his wife and leading associates, was ambushed by another Resistance organization and executed.[49]

Unconditional, neutral, conditional, and tactical collaboration. What conclusions may be drawn from our account of collaboration—the Cinderella of twentieth-century history—as a phenomenon in its own right?

First, that individuals, nations, and authorities in Hitler's Europe tended to behave in a highly erratic way. Some collaborated with varying degrees of reservation, others wholeheartedly, others for purely tactical reasons, and others while simultaneously offering active resistance. No basic attitude could develop until one particular behavior pattern predominated and became the norm. This it did most clearly among the collaborators in chief, the homegrown Nazi leaders, in the occupied territories.

Second, it is apparent that the various behavior patterns cannot be precisely differentiated. The intervening boundaries are blurred. In place of them we find broad, twilit, transitional zones where quite as much took place as in the bright light of firm commitment. Vichy's basic attitude, for example, seems to belong somewhere in the no-man's-land between conditional and unconditional collaboration.

Third, it is noticeable that these ill-defined transitional zones left plenty of scope for irrational behavior, which the stresses and strains of war rendered commonplace.

In April 1942, for example, General Henri-Honoré Giraud of the French Army escaped from imprisonment in Germany and took refuge in unoccupied France. The German authorities offered 100,000 reichsmarks for his recapture, but in vain. Hitler thereupon decreed that the general should be murdered, and his order was passed on by Field Marshal Wilhelm Keitel, chief of the Wehrmacht High Command.

Some days later, Giraud accepted a German invitation to meet with Otto Abetz, the German ambassador in Paris, on the border between occupied and unoccupied France. Abetz proposed that Giraud voluntarily return to captivity in Germany in return for an assurance that he would be given charge of all French prisoners of war. Giraud turned the offer down.

He was about to leave when a German divisional commander, who had been staying at the same frontier hotel, learned of his presence and was tempted to arrest him on the spot. Being a prudent man, he put through a top-priority call to Field Marshal Keitel. Although Keitel had transmitted Hitler's order in person, he blocked Giraud's arrest and allowed him to return to his hideout in the South of France.[50]

Fourth and last, there was a development which any common-sense person could readily have foreseen. Those condemned to live with such an unpredictable enemy allowed their attitude to be influenced by the fortunes of war and the growing brutality of the provocative acts committed by the occupying power. Everyone had to show his true colors sometime—at the latest when Stalingrad marked a turning point in the war. When that happened, volatile behavior gradually ceased.

This could be observed almost everywhere, in some cases at a relatively early stage. Pressure of events compelled the government of the Czech Protectorate, for example, to abandon its initial policy of tactical collaboration in favor of conditional and, as early as the summer of 1940, unconditional collaboration. The Vichy Government progressively dropped its provisos as time went by and likewise steered a course for almost unconditional cooperation with the enemy. By contrast, the outbreak of hostilities between Germany and Russia prompted national Communist parties to abandon tactical collaboration and commit themselves to its diametrical opposite. Even in peaceful little Denmark, the government's cautious collaborative policy collapsed within hours in August 1943. Here, too, there was a switch to resistance.

PART THREE

Resistance in Europe

Symbolic Resistance
or
I Remain What I Was

The symbolic resister says: I signalize my inviolate self-respect by means of personal gestures or actions expressing allegiance to my country, its individuality and right to exist. I do not shrink from conveying to the forces of occupation that they are dealing with a proud and confident people.

When the shattering news of France's collapse reached Denmark, a schoolteacher and a baker in two small Jutland townships hit on the idea of inviting their friends and neighbors to a communal songfest. So many people turned up that they overflowed into the street and had to sing outdoors. The idea caught on, and summer evenings in an otherwise depressing year were enlivened by the sound of voices raised in every Danish village.

It was a spontaneous outburst of symbolic resistance in the truest sense. One Sunday in September 1940, 150,000 Danes gathered to sing in Copenhagen's Faelled Park, another 20,000 at Esbjerg, and over 70 percent of the population at Hasle. Sten Gudme estimates that the public squares resounded that evening to the voices of two million Danes, or two thirds of the entire population above the age of fourteen. The German authorities did not intervene.[1]

Bohemia and Moravia were subject to a general ban on public gatherings, traditional pilgrimages excepted. On five separate occasions—once six weeks after the Germans marched in, again three months later, and again in January, May, and June 1940—these pilgrimages attracted up to a hundred thousand Czechs. They sang national songs, like the Danes, and were joined in summer 1940 by their Premier, General Elias, and other prominent figures. It also went without saying that the Czechs deliberately stayed away from Wehrmacht parades on Hitler's birthday and chose instead to lay wreaths on monuments to Tomáš Masaryk, the father of their country. Prague presented an eerie spectacle on the anniversary of the Munich

Agreement. Normally jam-packed, streetcars rattled empty through the streets of the capital. Two Resistance groups had passed the word that streetcars should be boycotted, simply to test the strength of public opposition to the Germans.[2]

Five sixths of the Norwegian merchant marine—the world's fourth-largest—were sailing the high seas or berthed in foreign ports when the Wehrmacht attacked Norway. One thousand and twenty-four vessels with a combined burden of four million tons failed to return home.

This fleet, which was almost the size of Germany's, headed for Allied ports. Formed in London, the "Norwegian Shipping and Trade Mission" (Notraship) took over the exiled fleet and became what experts have described as "the biggest single shipping company in the world."[3] Notraship administered and directed the thousand vessels, together with their thirty thousand crewmen, and maintained a wartime peak of more than fifty offices staffed by a thousand employees on five continents. It also supervised and ran the Norwegian tanker fleet, then the world's third-largest, which had likewise run for Allied ports and, until the United States entered the war, carried 40 percent of all the British Empire's petroleum requirements.[4]

Denmark's merchant marine seemed irretrievably lost to the Allied cause. The Danish Government had surrendered within hours and been compelled to order all vessels to head immediately for Danish, neutral, or German-controlled ports. It was hardly to be expected that shipmasters would disobey their King and legal government, and just as unlikely that a broadcast appeal from London to join the Allies would prove effective.

But the contrary happened. Nearly two thirds of the fleet—five thousand seamen and a million tons of cargo space—defied the royal command and ran for Allied ports. The captains sensed that King Christian and his government were no longer free to make their own decisions.[5]

Four weeks later, when the Wehrmacht invaded Holland, the same drama was repeated. Almost the entire fleet—three million tons of it, including 180 oceangoing ships and 200 coasters—succeeded in escaping to Allied ports.[6]

These were displays of spontaneous resistance fraught with great symbolic significance and equally momentous material consequences. Three small, neutral, maritime nations proudly acclaimed the sea captains who had landed in British or other Allied ports with eight out of their total of nine million tons of merchant shipping.

Other swift reactions to the German onslaught followed in each of the occupied countries. In Norway, Oslo's Lysaker Bridge went up three days after the German invasion. Its destruction was the work of two young men acting on their own initiative. The German military commander, General von Falkenhorst, threatened summary executions.[7]

In France, a German sentry was shot by an unidentified sniper in the

French township of Woincourt (Somme) four days after the armistice.[8]

Only four hours after the Germans walked into Denmark, the first leaflets appeared in Copenhagen—sixteen handwritten copies. Entitled "Ten Commandments for Passive Resistance," they were reportedly drafted and distributed by a group of seventeen-year-old students.[9]

In Holland, the first chain letter began to circulate on the very morrow of the invasion. The second appeared three days later, followed by a dozen more. Recipients of these letters were invited to make a number of copies in disguised handwriting and pass them on to trustworthy friends and acquaintances. "We know what lies in store for us," ran one such missive. "Our supplies, our foodstuffs, clothing, footwear . . . will be taken away from us. Our young men will be compelled to work abroad for the conqueror. . . . But the Gueux Campaign will organize us, and we shall regain our freedom as we did in the Eighty Years' War. Courage and confidence! Our country will never belong to Germany!" The author of this letter, a Haarlem tapestry restorer named Bernhard Ijzerdraat, had christened his campaign after the Netherlanders who fought for their freedom against Spain in the sixteenth century and styled themselves "Les Gueux" ["Beggars," a term originally applied in contempt but later adopted as a title of honor]. Arrested in November 1940, Ijzerdraat was subsequently condemned to death and executed with fourteen of his associates.[10]

Telephone wires were cut in Denmark on the day of the German invasion and in France during the days immediately following the armistice. Angry individuals engaged in countless uncoordinated acts of sabotage and displays of recalcitrance which persisted in France until the end of the year. When young people tore down German wall posters, their fathers were arrested and their local communities fined. Shots were sometimes fired from ambush at German soldiers or vehicles, as in Nancray at the end of July or in Surdon at the beginning of August. Those concerned were invariably rebels acting on their own initiative, either alone or in very small groups, so they could betray no one if captured. They belonged to no organization and had not conspired with anyone else. The Germans' punitive countermeasures—collective penalties, curfews, hostage-taking— fell on empty air.[11]

It therefore seemed in those early days that the Germans had already set in motion a potentially vast avalanche of resistance, and that the "shadow war" had already begun.[12]

But this was an illusion. Wherever armed and organized resistance occurred, it took several years to mature and was the end product of a laborious process hampered by many grave setbacks. The war had already been decided, and the Battle of Stalingrad was over, before it manifested itself at all. In May 1943, Commander in Chief West reported for the first time that "armed guerrilla bands" five hundred strong had formed in the

Department of Corrèze. These consisted of deserters from the labor service —parties of men who had evaded conscription by taking to the woods without military organization and equipment. It was not until the summer of 1943 that German situation reports from France spoke of Resistance groups run on quasi-military lines, "some wearing a variety of uniforms, others identified by armbands." And this was over three years after the fall of France.[13]

Until then, resistance had manifested itself in other ways.

What surfaced fairly quickly was the emotion psychologically inherent in the sad plight of any conquered people: a burning desire for the self-assertion without which their political straits would seem intolerable. "Yes, we have been defeated, humiliated by a foreign power and subjected to its dominion. We have lost our independence, our liberties, our rights, but . . ."

All depended on this "but," on the mobilization of their own kind, their own history and traditions, their national self-respect, and the latent superiority of the weaker to the malign power of the stronger. The Dutch discovered how much it boosted their self-confidence to wear a badge made out of a coin bearing the head of their exiled Queen. Norwegians hit on the idea of wearing a tiny Norwegian flag or a razor blade in their buttonholes, Danes the royal monogram in enamel and silver or the three initials SDU (short for *smid dem ut* or "chuck them out"). Mute displays of national self-assertion occurred everywhere: gardens and front yards ablaze with flower beds planted in the national colors, moviegoers ostentatiously waiting for German newsreels to finish before coming in off the street, passers-by demonstrating their nonchalance by staring straight through members of the occupying forces, people dressing up on Czechoslovakia's National Day, schools emptied of children, street vendors selling ribbons in the national colors. Or again, take the native cunning shown by the editor of *Politiken,* a leading Danish daily. Pinned to the wall of his office was a picture of Prime Minister Churchill at his best, jaw set and cigar in mouth. It was a front page from the *Berliner Illustrierte,* conveniently captioned "Winston Churchill in despair on hearing that France has fallen." Later on, when *Politiken* referred to Churchill as "a dangerous man," twenty thousand readers canceled their subscriptions.[14]

Purely individual reactions, these. Everyone thought and acted for himself, possibly in response to a whispered message or a neighbor's example. No secret organization or party was as yet at work behind the scenes. Even later on, when Resistance groups or the BBC issued slogans and called for public demonstrations, their success or failure was wholly dependent on individual decisions. Wherever tacit agreement came into being, individuals would alternately converge on a place and scatter like grains of sand. Having formed a compact but unorganized mass, if only for a few brief hours, they carried out their symbolic act of collective resistance and then dispersed.

In Holland, the first large-scale display of symbolic resistance occurred just seven weeks after the country's surrender. The occupying power had banned the flying of flags on June 29, 1940, the birthday of Prince Bernhard, who was by then an exile in London. The singing of the national anthem had likewise been prohibited. According to one German report, however, many people marked the day by either carrying a red, white, or pink carnation—the Prince's favorite flower—or wearing one in their buttonhole. Policemen at Wageningen adorned themselves with ribbons in the Dutch royal colors, and at The Hague thousands of "flower-wearing" Dutch citizens spectacularly demonstrated their loyalty to the royal family by queuing outside Nordeinde Palace and signing a register provided by the royal chamberlain.

When General Winkelman, ex-commander in chief of the Netherlands Army and the country's supreme executive until only a few days before, drove up to the palace and added his name to the declaration of allegiance, a stir ran through the silent crowd. They cheered and broke into the national anthem, which spread to the surrounding streets.

This violation of a definite ban imposed by the occupying power did not go unpunished. The mayor of The Hague was removed from office and General Winkelman arrested and sent to a concentration camp in Germany. He had already made himself unpopular with the occupying power by instructing the Dutch authorities not to undertake any work or dispatch any supplies that might prove useful to the German war effort.[15]

November 11, 1940, was the anniversary of Imperial Germany's surrender at the end of World War I. In France, where this thought could hardly have been more consoling in the circumstances, about a thousand Paris schoolchildren and students defied a strict German ban by marching down the Champs-Élysées waving flags, singing the "Marseillaise," and chanting anti-Hitler slogans composed on the spur of the moment. The German police cleared the streets and arrested ninety schoolchildren and fourteen students. The Sorbonne remained closed for a week. "Just rousing our self-confidence," replied one of the young people, when asked the purpose of the demonstration, "not rebelling against the *puissance occupante*."[16] Similar demonstrations took place on the same day in other parts of France.

People wearing flowers, deserted streetcars, crowds singing in public squares—such were the solemn, devout, and uplifting displays of national narcissism and self-esteem with which resistance began to manifest itself, here and there, as "the will of the people." Provided no rules were broken, the Germans tended to leave these quiet individuals and crowds in peace— and wisely so, because symbolic resistance was quite compatible with collaboration of all kinds. Middle-class citizens loyal to their sovereign or republic, singing factory workers, office clerks with flowers in their buttonholes—all these people returned with enhanced self-respect to the places of work where they obediently turned out ammunition for the German armies, dispatched strategic supplies to the Third Reich, and saw to it —grinding their teeth, perhaps, but efficiently and not without profit to themselves—that the occupying power lacked for nothing.

This ambivalent approach to a menacing environment is the key to many apparent mysteries. It accounts for the unruffled conscience of the reluctant daily collaborator and the charisma of a man like Pétain. It even provides an answer to the problem that perplexes any modern viewer of two French wartime newsreels, one showing a vast crowd of Parisians cheering Pétain in April 1944, and the other a similar throng applauding Charles de Gaulle on the same spot only four months later.

There is no point in speculating on the fickleness of people in the mass: this pair of newsreels speaks for itself. Pétain, a living symbol of bygone military might and imperial grandeur, offered his fellow countrymen a chance of recovering their self-esteem when they were smarting at the dishonor of defeat; De Gaulle, the haughty knight in shining armor, led them back into the victorious fold. Pétain, the willing collaborator, and De Gaulle, the stubborn champion of continued resistance, both symbolized the imperishable qualities of nationhood.

Nothing exemplifies this more clearly than an anecdote related by De Gaulle himself. Shortly after Allied troops landed in Normandy in June 1944, he was driving through one of the liberated towns in an open car. The streets were thronged with cheering, weeping people, one of whom—a peasant woman—came panting up and tossed a bunch of flowers into his lap with the heartfelt cry: *"Vive le Maréchal!"*

There was an element of truth in this comedy of errors. The woman had mistaken one man for the other, but not without reason. De Gaulle's comment: "A good Frenchwoman, to be sure!"[17]

The Miracle of Tacit Agreement

Early in 1941 the German authorities in Holland requested the central council of the Netherlands Medical Association to permit a leading member of the National Socialist "Medical Front" to bring professional practices into line with "the concepts of National Socialist medicine"—a blatant attempt at Nazification.

No storm of protest or spectacular rebellion ensued. During the next few months, most Dutch doctors resigned from the Medical Association of their own accord, quietly and without publicity. In September, likewise without any public announcement, the members of the central council resigned too.[18]

Early in March 1943, after six hundred Dutch students had been arrested in retaliation for the murder of a Dutch Nazi general, the occupying power insisted that all students who wished to continue their studies should pledge themselves in writing to obey the law and comply with the regulations imposed by the Wehrmacht and the German and Dutch authorities. The number of university places was simultaneously reduced, and every student was made liable to six months' voluntary labor service in Germany. It was further announced that all who refused to sign the oath of loyalty would rate as unemployed and be conscripted into the labor service forthwith. Time for consideration: four weeks, expiring on April 10, 1943.

A difficult decision, but one on which plenty of advice was forthcoming. A majority of the faculty members at Delft University recommended that the students sign the declaration, and most parents were scared enough of the consequences to follow suit. By contrast, the denominational universities advised their students not to sign and even refused to distribute the forms supplied by the German authorities. The government-in-exile in London also warned against signing a declaration of loyalty under any circumstances.

In the event, only 15 percent of students signed. Delft led the field with 26 percent, but the student body at the Catholic University of Nijmegen showed particular fortitude. Its score was a mere two.[19]

Much earlier, only three months after the occupation began, the German authorities had appointed so-called "standstill commissioners"—leading Dutch National Socialists belonging to Mussert's National Assembly. Rost van Tonningen, Mussert's keenest rival, provisionally administered and ran the Communist and Social Democratic parties while his colleague H. J. Woudenberg did the same for the Socialist Netherlands Association of Trade Unions, which had 319,000 members. Rost van Tonningen's task was to liquidate the Communist Party by slow degrees and transfer its assets to the Social Democratic Labor Party, which would in turn be purged —as the Germans put it—of "Marxist activity and ideology." The role assigned to the trade unions was that of "a broad platform on which to influence the Dutch people politically."

Trade union and labor party members reacted as the doctors were to do. Most editors of the labor press submitted their resignations, one by one. A Socialist press director, who had been hoping to keep his organization intact, sought refuge in suicide. The chairman of the Social Democratic Party, Koos Vorrink, refused to collaborate in any way. The Communists had destroyed or safely hidden their documents and membership lists in good time, and the Socialists quietly dissolved their party during the summer of 1940. Members resigned, lists of names and addresses were removed, and no more dues were collected. In June 1941, the German authorities banned a party that had long since ceased to exist.

Similar developments occurred in the Socialist, Roman Catholic, and Protestant trade unions, whose combined membership at the outbreak of war had been 800,000. The quiet mass exodus from the Socialist labor organization amounted to 25 percent by October 1941 and 66 percent by spring 1942. The Roman Catholic labor organization had virtually dissolved itself in summer 1941, after the episcopacy had announced that collaborators would in the future be denied the sacraments. Rost van Tonningen and Woudenberg were left empty-handed.[20]

Trade unions in Norway adopted a similar course, though at a relatively earlier stage. They went into dissolution at the end of September 1940, after the German authorities had appointed some National Socialists from Quisling's party to be provisional councillors of state.[21]

A solemn and momentous display of symbolic resistance occurred on February 1, 1942, when Quisling was appointed head of government and one of the few Norwegian clerics with Nazi leanings tried to celebrate the occasion by holding a special service in Trondheim Cathedral.

Nobody turned up. Everyone waited to attend the regular service, which had been postponed until that afternoon and was conducted, as usual, by the dean. The cathedral was filled to overflowing, and many thousands of people defied a police ban by standing shoulder to shoulder in the bitter cold outside. Stubborn silence reigned until they all broke into "A safe stronghold our God is still."

The dean was removed from his post, whereupon all the bishops resigned. A pastoral letter informing churchgoers of their decision was read aloud from every pulpit in the land.

At this, over 92 percent of ministers (645 out of 699) quit their posts in the established Church, among them almost all those who had been ordained (151 out of 155). Although they continued to perform their duties as preachers and pastors, the Church usurped by Quisling was almost destitute of clergy. The few replacements he appointed found themselves preaching to empty pews, whereas services conducted by ministers who defied him were heavily attended. From Easter 1942 until the end of the war, Norway possessed no established Church.[22]

Another interesting example of symbolic resistance occurred in the Grand Duchy of Luxembourg. Here, in the fall of 1941, Gauleiter Simon organized a census designed to be construed as a referendum on the proposed incorporation of Luxembourg into the German Reich. To guarantee the desired political result, he ensured that two rules were laid down in advance: *luxemburgisch* and *letzeburgisch* were declared impermissible and invalid replies to the questions concerning nationality and language.

When the questionnaires had been collected, it turned out that 96 percent of the urban and 99 percent of the rural population had described themselves as *letzeburgisch*-speaking Luxembourgers. At this, several thousand people were detained and thrown into jail or deported.[23]

Many more examples could be cited without adding to the substance of what has already been said. Symbolic resistance occasionally crystallized into mass demonstrations but created no real focal points of organized resistance. Generally speaking, it retained the character of a spontaneous individual reaction which could, under certain circumstances, find collective expression. Those who took part in such demonstrations did not run too great a risk unless, like the dean of Trondheim Cathedral, they aired their views in public.

One is therefore in danger of attaching too much importance to the spectacular symbolism of these acts and professions of faith. Many historians of the Resistance do this almost on principle, but the rational observer must put a damper on their involuntary apologias.

It is certainly no accident that the history of the Resistance should have begun with unplanned and unorganized opposition—with a form of individual recalcitrance that was purely symbolic. Organized resistance and the techniques of clandestine conspiracy had first to be learned and practiced at great personal cost.

The fact that symbolic resistance occurred less often during the latter part of the war was connected with the intervening turn of events. Liberation and the defeat of Germany had ceased to be a hope and become a certainty. The curtain had risen on the final act.

In 1944, the Danish playwright and clergyman Kaj Munk, an erstwhile admirer of Hitler and Mussolini, used his New Year's sermon to condemn the German reign of terror and urge his compatriots to commit sabotage. He was promptly dragged from his home by a terrorist squad and shot. The news spread like wildfire. That night, the actor Kjeld Abell stepped forward during a performance at the Theater Royal in Copenhagen and called on the audience to spare "a moment's thought for Denmark's greatest dramatist, who died today." A stirring silence fell. Then Abell picked up his coat and walked out. Despite a German ban, many ministers held memorial services in the next few days, and booksellers who had been expressly forbidden to stage commemorative displays of Munk's work dressed their windows in black paper.[24]

Polemic Resistance
or
I Tell the Truth

The polemic resister says: I oppose the occupying power by protesting or organizing protests, even at risk to myself. I say or do things calculated to persuade my fellow countrymen of the need to fight on.

When Dutch munitions factories were harnessed to the German war effort, one man protested with all the authority vested in him by his high office. C. Ringeling, Holland's Undersecretary for Defense, was duly dismissed for his pains by the Reich Commissioner.[1]

The director-general of the Belgian State Railroad declined to release Belgian railroadmen for employment in Germany, and the mayor of Brussels, J. F. van de Meulebroeck, refused to dismiss senior members of his staff and replace them with officials amenable to German requirements. He made himself still more unpopular by sternly criticizing certain decrees emanating from the Belgian Ministry of the Interior, whose undersecretary had issued them in keeping with the collaborationist line. In June 1941, after pronouncing them illegal and invalid, Van de Meulebroeck was also removed from office.

He thereupon issued a public statement proclaiming that he was the capital's only legitimate mayor, and that nothing the occupying power did could alter the fact. He was then arrested and his municipal exchequer fined five million francs.

John Christmas Moeller, leader of the Danish Conservative Party and an avowed opponent of the Third Reich, had been compelled to relinquish his post as Minister of Commerce in response to strong German pressure. He continued to criticize German occupation policy and agitate against it at mass meetings. Exasperated by Moeller's hostile pronouncements, the German minister in Copenhagen approached the Danish Government with a demand that Moeller be expelled from the executive body of the Conservative Party, deprived of his parliamentary seat, and forbidden to make anti-German speeches.

The Danish Government rejected this request, arguing that there were no legal grounds for granting it. Efforts would, however, be made to persuade Moeller that he might be better advised to desist from addressing mass meetings.

But Berlin wanted to wrap the case up quickly. Unhappily for the German minister, who was authorized to arrest the obdurate critic and have him brought to Germany, Moeller got wind of his intentions and escaped to London. No finer representative of the Danish Resistance could have been safely ensconced in the "capital of the Resistance."[2]

The attitude adopted by these courageous men was not a symbolic one. They were not impelled by an urge to assert themselves, nor did they need to prove, either to themselves or to others, that they were conscious of their own individuality and their nation's right to exist. Their attitude was one of polemic resistance. They aimed to persuade other people, by personal example, that resistance and moral courage were not only possible but necessary. They did not sing or demonstrate; they protested with one eye on the public and the other on the occupying power.

Also in this category come pastoral letters and appeals or proclamations of a refractory nature.

In June 1941, the Christian Churches of Norway and Holland rejected Berlin's summons to join a "crusade against Bolshevism." Most clergymen in Norway (1,073 out of 1,100) refused to sign an appeal for volunteers for the Eastern Front.[3]

In Holland, the Catholic and Protestant Churches publicly proclaimed that membership in a National Socialist organization was incompatible with the Christian faith and, thus, prohibited. At the end of January 1941, Roman Catholic bishops sent their priests a pastoral letter expressly forbidding them to administer the sacraments to National Socialists. Attempts to Nazify the country had thus been categorically condemned by all its ecclesiastical authorities.

The Churches carried nonviolent resistance to the limit. They advised Dutch civil servants appointed to conscript forced labor to resign their posts. They forbade believers to collaborate with the enemy, assist in the detention and deportation of Jews, or hunt down students, runaway workers, and escaped prisoners of war. They more than once sent pastoral letters protesting against anti-Semitic measures and the sterilization of Jews married to Christian women. In February 1943 they enjoined the faithful to civil disobedience, even at the risk of losing their jobs and suffering other grave disabilities. Only those in imminent danger of the death penalty or concentration camp were exempt from the duty of disobedience.

In Holland alone, hundreds of ministers of all denominations were arrested by the occupying power. Forty-three Protestant and forty-nine Catholic priests forfeited their lives for engaging in resistance.[4]

In Norway, decrees dated early April 1941 and aimed at politically streamlining the public services encountered polemic resistance, in the truest sense, from the major professional associations. The provincial chairmen of twenty-two such bodies began by lodging a written protest with Reich Commissioner Terboven. In mid-May, forty-three professional associations with a combined membership of 750,000 protested against the banning of political parties and the appointment of provisional councillors of state from the ranks of the Norwegian National Socialists. To cite their actual words, they objected to "official promulgations and decisions" which patently violated "international law, Norwegian law, and the universal concepts of justice" and infringed legal provisions designed to protect the person.

The Germans could not simply lie down under a counterattack launched on behalf of 750,000 organized Norwegians. Their first step was to arrest some of the signatories. The leaders of the forty-three associations were then summoned to the parliament building, surrounded by armed police, and treated to a menacing speech from the Reich Commissioner himself. More arrests followed. Several professional associations were dissolved and others placed under strict supervision.

Now that the ball was back in the Norwegians' court, there were mass resignations from the bodies under supervision. Members of respected professions—doctors, dentists, engineers, lawyers—deserted them almost to a man. But they did not stop there. Professional associations of which only the empty shells remained went underground and gradually built up a hidden infrastructure of organized resistance under eminent leaders who were able to issue precise guidelines in consultation with the government-in-exile in London. This was resistance in the rough, carried on by men with no previous experience. However, the fall of 1941 saw the formation of a steering committee which later assumed the functions of a secret general staff. Still later, in spring 1942, the laws enacted by Quisling's newly formed cabinet unleashed another spate of polemic resistance. Quisling and his ministers had set up a youth movement modeled on the Hitler Youth and founded a National Socialist educational association which all teachers had to join.[5]

Norway's established Church was the first to object to this Nazification policy. Next, Quisling's Education Ministry was inundated with over two hundred thousand letters of protest, complete with names and addresses, from irate parents who declared that they would not permit their children to join the National Socialist youth organization.

The teachers backed the parents. Twelve thousand out of fourteen thousand refused to join Quisling's educational association and condemned the

National Socialist youth movement with equal vehemence. Quisling's Education Ministry retorted by threatening that unless they withdrew their protest by March 1, they would be dismissed on that date. But all to no avail. The united front remained intact.

Quisling had suffered a defeat. To disguise the fact, schools were given a month's vacation on the pretext that there was not enough coal to heat them.

Only force could prevail against these successful acts of nonviolent resistance. In March, a thousand teachers were arrested and sent to concentration camps. In the following weeks, the police detained two hundred more. A further five hundred were piled into a dangerously overloaded coaster and deported to Kirkenes in the far north—a sea voyage of fifteen hundred miles—where they were subjected to forced labor, half starved, and compelled to live in conditions of extreme hardship.[6]

Hitler lent unqualified approval to the Reich Commissioner's measures. His one regret, as he mentioned in the course of conversation, was that German naval personnel assigned to transport the Norwegian teachers had indulged in "another orgy of German good nature." They had apparently shown some initial reluctance to take them by sea because there were insufficient life jackets to go round, instead of reflecting that the Norwegians should be "delighted to be torpedoed by their beloved Britishers and sent to the bottom."[7]

Hitler's cynicism blinded him to what was going on in countries like Norway, which Nazi racial theorists held to be inhabited by "Germanic peoples" who should really have received preferential treatment. It was in Holland and Scandinavia that the persecution of the Jews and essays in Nazification provoked the strongest religious, moral, patriotic, and ideological reactions. Why? Because they were an unpardonable affront, not only to the ethical precepts of the omnipresent Churches, but to the sacrosanct democratic traditions and moral standards of an intact bourgeois society. It was not fortuitous that the occupying power found it harder to cope with polemic resistance in these countries than elsewhere, and that National Socialist propaganda proved wholly ineffective against it.[8]

In Holland at the end of November 1940, when civil servants and university teachers were dismissed for being Jews, non-Jewish teachers and students openly opposed the measure. Students at the universities of Leyden and Delft launched a strike which sparked off demonstrations of solidarity throughout the country.

The occupying power responded by arresting a prominent professor, closing both universities, and banning student clubs and fraternities deemed to be centers of resistance.[9]

Soon afterward, in February 1941, Dutch SA men provoked a number of anti-Semitic incidents in Amsterdam. Hotel and restaurant owners were forcibly persuaded to display signs reading "No Jews Admitted."

Dragging Jews out of buses and streetcars, the homegrown Brownshirts proceeded to jeer and manhandle them in the street. The inhabitants of the Jewish quarter countered by forming vigilante squads, and one of their SA persecutors was killed in a brawl. At this, the German authorities stepped in. They decreed the establishment of a Jewish Council and subjected the Jewish quarter to police raids, during which 425 Jews were arrested and brutally maltreated in public.

Outraged eyewitnesses reported what they had seen. When the local Communist cell distributed mimeographed leaflets appealing for a one-day protest strike and asking the population to shelter Jewish children, the strike call was taken up and obeyed by municipal employees with no left-wing political affiliations. Almost half the municipal work force downed tools. Then the metalworkers and longshoremen struck too.

The German authorities combated spontaneous protest demonstrations in the city center by proclaiming martial law. All curfew violations were savagely dealt with by SS and Security Police patrols, who blazed away wildly and killed seven pedestrians. The mayor of Amsterdam and several of his counterparts elsewhere were removed from office on the grounds that they had failed to take effective action against the protest strike.[10]

At about the same time, theaters in Oslo, Bergen, and Trondheim were closed for weeks on end by a Norwegian actors' strike. This was a protest against attempts at Nazification by the occupying power and its henchmen, one of them being the dissemination of Nazi propaganda by Norway's broadcasting service.[11]

In the fall of 1941, staunch resistance by the teaching staff of Leyden University in Holland foiled an attempt by Van Dam, Undersecretary for Education and Science, to replace dismissed faculty members with National Socialist appointees. The entire staff threatened to resign.

In May 1942, the dismissal of a respected professor of constitutional law provoked another display of solidarity. This time, although only one dismissal was involved, 80 percent of the victim's colleagues made good their threat of the previous year. They resigned their posts, and Leyden University came to a standstill.[12]

In an already tense situation, public resistance could be brought to boiling point by a simple succession of provocative acts. This is borne out by events in Denmark during the last week of August 1943, just before the three-year-old myth of Danish neutrality was finally exploded.

In a wooded area near Aalborg, German and Danish police surprised a Resistance group which was obviously waiting for an airdrop of British arms. A young bank clerk was shot and an engineer arrested in the ensuing skirmish. The rest escaped.

The police not only banned all public gatherings on the day of the bank clerk's funeral but let it be known that the ban would, if necessary, be militarily enforced. For fear of incidents, it was decided not to hold the scheduled ceremony at all, and the dead man was buried secretly in advance.

The citizens of Aalborg needed no funeral to help them express their thoughts and emotions. Over ten thousand people assembled near the cemetery to lay wreaths—expensive wreaths adorned with outsize ribbons and inscriptions such as "To a Courageous Dane." They demanded a minister and a memorial service, and the police gave in. The ten thousand mourners sang Psalms, the "Internationale," and patriotic songs.

The authorities construed this display of symbolic resistance as a provocative act. Police loudspeakers called on the crowd to disperse. A German reconnaissance plane turned up, followed by German troops. Armored cars fired warning shots, and ambulances bore off sixteen wounded civilians.

The shooting of a worker the next day sparked off a protest strike which was joined within hours by all the factories and businesses in town, as well as by the municipal authorities. Seventeen thousand Danes secretly gathered in a quarry and cheered Aalborg's police chief to the echo when he affirmed his loyalty to "Free Denmark." This was symbolic resistance no longer—the crowd were actively protesting. Their spokesmen demanded that German patrols be withdrawn from the town's streets and factories and all Wehrmacht personnel confined to barracks.

The protest strike, a prime example of polemic resistance, had developed into open provocation. The German authorities took hostages. Convinced that their hour had struck at last, Danish Nazis ran amok in the streets. During the course of the afternoon, when it became known that three members of the civilian population had been killed, protest and sympathy strikes broke out in a dozen places in Jutland, Zealand, and Copenhagen itself. The spark had kindled a conflagration. The Germans proclaimed martial law throughout Denmark.[13]

Clandestine Newspapers

In its purest sense, polemic resistance included some of the European Underground's most remarkable and indispensable by-products: clandestine leaflets, newspapers, and books, written and printed in secret, distributed at the risk of people's lives, and possessed of far greater importance than anyone at first thought possible.

They not only transmitted information and propaganda, nor were they merely aids to public awareness, to political debate, to consultation and solidarity. Each clandestine newspaper was the spiritual hub of a Resistance group and, in a sense, the lodestone that held it together and attracted sympathizers. Once equipped with an illegal news sheet, often handwritten and secretly passed from hand to hand, two or three like-minded friends would begin to form a group and recruit fellow fighters for the common cause. Born in the gloomy depths of the Underground but expanding with tremendous speed, the clandestine press became, as it were, the soul of the Resistance.

Hence the staggering and almost unbelievable statistics on record. Under German occupation, Holland and Poland produced roughly 1,200 newspapers apiece, France 1,034,[14] Norway and Denmark 852, and Belgium 500.[15]

In other words, over 3,500 illegal newspapers appeared in occupied Norway, Denmark, Holland, Belgium, and France. Most of them vanished after a short time, ceased publication, merged with others, adopted new names, or ended up in the files of the German Security Police while their editors, printers, and distributors awaited sentence in German-run jails. And still new papers appeared by the thousand and circulated by the million—certainly during the final months of occupation—in almost every country mentioned above.[16]

We must never forget the extent of the problems to be overcome. The French Underground newspaper *Combat* alone consumed three tons of newsprint monthly. Part of it was bought on the black market and part supplied by paper merchants and printers who belonged to the Resistance. Ingenious comrades-in-arms managed to buy more paper from Germany. For this purpose they registered a cover firm whose agents ordered the requisite allocations of newsprint from German sources through the State Rationing Bureau in Vichy.

Substantial amounts of capital were required, together with cash to cover printing costs—a lavish private funding operation undertaken with no prospect of repayment. Premises had also to be found in noisy surroundings where the clatter of the presses would not give the game away.

Newspapers that were later produced in garages, factories, and laundries had at first to be duplicated by the most primitive and laborious means. *Défense de la France,* of which forty-seven editions of 300,000 copies appeared in 1943–44, was produced during its first year by students working in the cellars of the Sorbonne. The only access to the secret subterranean press was the laboratory of the Physical Geography Department, and the key to that was held by a young girl student named Hélène. The youthful printers also turned out serviceable forged identity cards. In January 1944, after *Défense de la France* had transferred to a Resistance printshop of its own, it attained a peak circulation of 450,000 copies.

Underground newspapers were packed in valises labeled with false addresses and left in cloakrooms to be forwarded by railroad employees. Clandestine consignments of newsprint, leaflets, and newspapers were delivered by truck to secret destinations. Following a precise distribution plan, several hundred students went in groups from house to house, street to street, and quarter to quarter, pushing copies under doors. One secret office in Paris, headed from 1943 on by Geneviève de Gaulle, the General's niece, mailed batches of between ten and forty thousand copies of *Défense de la France* to influential figures—and saved on postage by using forged stamps.

More Resistance newspapers were distributed in the course of lightning commando-style operations. Outside churches after Sunday Mass or at movie-house exits, in marketplaces and subway passages, little groups of young men protected by their own surveillance service would suddenly appear, bring out illegal newspapers, and distribute them for minutes at a time—always a risky undertaking but one that sometimes called for humor as well as audacity. In 1943, on the anniversary of the storming of the Bastille, a few distributors managed to thrust their Resistance newspapers into German hands and get away scot-free.[17]

Other occupied countries presented much the same picture. In Holland, sixty newspapers with a combined circulation of 57,000 copies appeared in the first six months. The number of illegal newspapers fluctuated, doubling in 1941 and contracting as a result of harsh repressive measures in the following year, but their total circulation continued to climb. The wholesale confiscation of radio sets in 1943 sent it soaring to a peak of 450,000 copies in December of that year. In January 1945, when the war was drawing to a close, the country's 350 illegal newspapers turned out a grand total of two million copies.[18]

In Holland as elsewhere, the big supraregional newspapers started out in a very modest way. *Vrij Nederland,* published by a group of young Calvinists who later espoused the teachings of the Swiss theologian Karl Barth, had to be mimeographed for nearly eighteen months. One hundred and thirty copies of the first issue appeared late in August 1940. A printed edition of 40,000 copies was produced at the beginning of 1944, and the figure had risen by September of that year to 100,000.[19]

Je maintiendrai, a Dutch Resistance newspaper with a French name, first saw the light in the attic of the International Court of Justice at The Hague. Forty thousand copies of it were distributed in May 1943. Other news sheets were printed at night by firms under contract to the occupying power, and one emanated from a hay barn where the press was powered by an outboard engine.

These dangerous products of the printer's craft were distributed far and wide, sometimes with the aid of official cars, sometimes in official envelopes, and sometimes by couriers as diverse as milkmen and schoolgirls.[20]

Their origins were universally similar. They were the logical development of a spontaneous process initiated by a dozen-odd leaflets, by chain letters and handbills that were read and sometimes passed on, or by written exhortations such as Jean Texcier's "Advice to the Occupied" or "A

Czech's Ten Commandments," which was addressed "To Everyone" and
survived the war in the German Attorney General's files.[21]

Texcier advised his French compatriots to be realistic. "They" were
conquerors, not tourists. They deserved to be treated correctly, but nothing more. The wisest policy was not to understand a word of German and
avoid being drawn into conversation, but not even a mortal enemy should
be refused a light for his cigarette if he asked for one. It was advisable to
reserve one's anger for later, concealing it beneath a mask of serene
indifference. The Czech leaflet also recommended that its readers practice
restraint in public while secretly preparing for the struggle to come. Means
to this end included the compiling of information, names, and addresses,
clandestine military training, and aids to "national invigoration" such as
sports, excursions, and good conversation.

Early pieces of naive and well-meant advice like these were the
forerunners of an important catalogue of patriotic duties. What mattered
was to mobilize the hesitant, strengthen sympathizers in their belief in final
victory, act as propagandists for the cause, and debate knotty problems
such as political murder and its possible justification. People must be
warned against ideological compromise and summoned to engage in active
resistance to the occupying power and its collaborators. Major postwar
problems should be aired and practical advice imparted on how to carry
on the struggle.

Also enlisted were the words of creative writers, the fostering of spiritual tradition, the intellectual and aesthetic practices of symbolic resistance.
Clandestine literary reviews appeared. In France, an Underground
publishing house brought out works by Aragon and Éluard, Cassou,
Chamson, and Vercors; in Holland, eighteen clandestine publishing houses
printed miniature editions of sixty literary works in French and English,
together with poetry by Mallarmé, Baudelaire, and Rimbaud.[22]

In the course of time, ingenious Resistance organizers developed more
sophisticated ways of carrying on the fight. In Denmark, the Underground
press boasted a news agency which maintained a secret telephone link with
its office in the Swedish capital.

One edition of Le Soir, a Brussels daily controlled by the occupying
power and sold as usual by newspaper kiosks, turned out to be an excel-
lent forgery. Readers were startled to discover that its inside pages carried
news and views supplied by the Resistance. The same trick was pulled by a
Resistance group operating in Lyon.[23]

In April 1944, a Resistance commando team invaded the premises of
the Schoonhovense Courant in southern Holland and compelled the staff,
at gunpoint, to print an illegal edition. June saw the appearance of forged
editions of the Haarlemse Courant and other papers.

It is debatable who first devised this trick, which was also used by the
Germans. Having penetrated the jungle of the Underground press, they

tried to mislead the Resistance with forgeries of Resistance newspapers produced on presses of their own and secretly distributed in editions of twenty thousand. These included fake issues of Underground papers as widely known as *Het Parool, Ons Volk,* and *De Waarheid.*[24]

Polemic resistance could take the form of public protests or surreptitious appeals. The only essential difference was that one was legal and the other illegal—one less hazardous than the other. Greater risks and dangers lurked in the shadowy world of the Underground, which was infiltrated by agents of the occupying power.

For a considerable period, the German Security Service carefully followed up every lead that might unmask the editors and printers of *Trouw,* a Dutch Resistance newspaper with a circulation of sixty thousand. Some of its staff had already been traced and detained, so the SD may well have known or guessed that it was produced by young Calvinists. The editors did, in fact, belong to the right-wing Antirevolutionary Party. They appeared to maintain close links with a large Underground movement and a so-called Christian Action Group, which made them a worthwhile target for ruthless detective work.

After some time, the Germans had to acknowledge that the staff of *Trouw* were proof against traditional police methods. In the summer of 1944, the Security Service duly made them an offer through secret channels. In return for the lives of a large number of its associates currently held in German jails, the paper must cease publication. Otherwise, the German authorities would be obliged to shoot them.

The editors refused, and twenty-three prisoners were executed.

Would it ever have been possible to silence the voices of the Underground? *Trouw* alone lost 120 of its associates to German firing squads, yet the weekly circulation of Dutch Resistance news sheets in January 1945 was in the region of two million copies.[25]

Defensive Resistance
or
I Aid and Protect

The defensive resister says: I take the side of those in danger or on the run; I rally to those who protect them; I defend, by force if need be, the human beings and human values endangered by the occupying power.

On this note, we descend into the Underground—the dark and forbidden realm where groups of long-term residents settled at various stages during World War II: in the East, especially Poland and Russia, during the early weeks of the German invasion; in Western Europe, not before the second year of occupation. Until then, for all but a small minority, the Underground was a place of transit, not a permanent abode. Anyone who hid there did so for a particular purpose and a limited period.

The first to go underground in the West were Belgian and French prisoners of war who had escaped from front-line camps, as well as members of the British Expeditionary Force trapped in the Dunkirk pocket by a shortage of time or boats. All needed help, places to hide, civilian clothes, food, and maps or knowledgeable guides who could smuggle them safely across the border into unoccupied France.

It would be fair to say that help was there for the asking. Despite their readiness to collaborate, few Belgians or Frenchmen would have hesitated to aid a soldier who had fought for them and lost. Henri Michel tells of a farmer in the Department of Loire-Inférieure who sheltered three officers and eighteen enlisted men, plus two cars and four horses, at one and the same time.[1]

We do not know how many of these early evaders got away and how many people helped them. However substantial, their numbers were less important than the spontaneous and widespread assistance they received from countless civilians, their families and friends, because it laid the groundwork for a whole web of contacts that was to span Western Europe from Holland to Spain. Solidarity was one of the keystones of the organized Resistance movement.

Its material basis was furnished by those products of friendship and acquaintance that had already proved helpful in the past: a knowledge of useful addresses, safe houses, cellars, double exits, escape routes, and smugglers, and, last but not least, a deep sense of community with many unknown fighters for the same cause. This provided the basis of the large-scale escape networks that developed during the latter half of 1941.

British soldiers who had fled inland from Dunkirk and reached Brussels after a series of night marches were taken in and sheltered by a twenty-three-year-old Belgian girl, Andrée Dejongh, and some of her friends. For almost a year, Andrée brought food to their hideout. She also brought them increasingly depressing news: Hitler was victorious on all fronts, the police were closing in, and food and money were becoming steadily scarcer. An organized escape was their one remaining hope.

Now twenty-four, Andrée took her loose-knit contacts and wove them into a network of escape routes stretching from Brussels, through occupied and unoccupied France, to the Spanish frontier. She procured civilian clothes, false papers, compasses, iron rations, and drugs. Her "Comet Line" was in business. In three years she smuggled eight hundred Britons—officers and enlisted men, fighter pilots and bomber crew personnel—through occupied territory and into a neutral country where they were handed over, whenever possible, to British agents.

Andrée, who was arrested on the Spanish border early in 1943, survived the war in the Mauthausen concentration camp. The Comet Line was then taken over by her father, Paul Dejongh, who fell into a trap and was executed in March 1944.

Many other lines were set up and worked closely together. A British Army captain named Garrow created the "Pat Line," which evacuated seven hundred of his fellow countrymen, and from 1942 the Allied High Command sponsored the establishment of another dozen escape networks. Almost as many more, code-named after French wines, were formed by agents parachuted into France by De Gaulle. The Belgian Government-in-exile also maintained two lines with bases in France.[2]

Once they had proved themselves, the Resistance amateurs of the early days matured into experts with whom other escape route specialists worked in harness.

Allied fighter pilots and bomber crews shot down over Europe carried a whole arsenal of escape aids including compasses in uniform buttons, maps bearing seventy thousand place names but thin enough to be secreted in an ordinary mechanical pencil, uniforms and boots that could be swiftly converted into German civilian clothes, and efficient hacksaw blades concealed in shoelaces.[3]

As soon as an aircraft crashed, scouts from the escape organizations set off to pick up its pilot and crew and take them to a safe house or, if business was brisk, accommodate them under canvas in some remote area in occupied territory.

From 1943 on, this sophisticated defensive Resistance network included the British "Shelburn Line," whose exclusive function was to pick up Allied pilots and get them back to England, either via Spain or by sea from France itself.[4]

The escape networks did not labor in vain. Thanks to their ingenuity, daring, and self-sacrifice, three thousand Allied fliers were rescued and returned to England during the war. In purely financial terms, the recovery of experienced pilots meant a significant saving in pilot-training years and hard cash.[5]

These organizations, which formed part of the Allied war machine, could never have functioned without the cooperation of many thousands of Dutch, Belgian, and French volunteers who were prepared to go underground whenever they were needed, at any fear-ridden, hope-inspiring hour of the day or night.

There they met representatives of all nations, from Jewish refugees and active anti-Nazis to volunteers for service with the Allies and Allied agents on the run. The number of escapes surpassed everyone's boldest expectations. Twenty-eight thousand fugitives were smuggled across the French-Spanish border alone, including twenty thousand Frenchmen (four hundred of them pilots) who were eager to join De Gaulle's Free French forces.

During 1943, traffic across this frontier became so congested that no less than 1,250 Frenchmen and Allied fliers made an intermediate stop at one particular place—the Benedictine abbey of Belloc—before slipping into Spain.[6]

Other networks operated in Scandinavia. Though more loosely organized, they ensured that 44,200 Norwegians were smuggled into Sweden and 5,800 secretly airlifted to Britain. In the case of 38,000 Finns and 35,000 Balts, their trek or passage through the Underground ended in neutral Sweden.[7]

Similar organizations existed in the East, notably in the occupied territories of Soviet Russia, but few precise details of their achievements are known.[8]

How did the Underground come into being, how and why was it populated in the course of time, and what sort of people took the momentous decision to spend the rest of the war leading a shadowy, anonymous existence?

The process took time. The Underground's earliest occupants were birds of passage. Then came illegal organizations, administrative centers, and command posts forming the nucleus of the Resistance leadership. Members of armed combat units did not join them until much later.

The Dutch doctors represent a typical case. As we have already seen, most of them responded to German attempts to "coordinate" the Netherlands Medical Association by resigning. In August 1941, when their country had been occupied for a year, they set up a clandestine professional association headed by a seven-member board and eleven regional chairmen. This was known as "Medisch Contact." Tightly organized in keeping with the established principles of any clandestine movement. Medisch Contact consisted of local cells of five members each. No one doctor knew, or was known to, more than four colleagues who could have betrayed him.

Medisch Contact began its clandestine activities by requiring all members to make certain undertakings. They would never collaborate, never turn over Jewish patients to the police or any other authority, and never reveal the identity of wounded men and women. The regulation enjoining doctors to report and surrender such patients to the German police must not be obeyed under any circumstances, and professional secrecy was to remain inviolate.

Masterminded and directed by the board of Medisch Contact, vigorous concerted action was taken in the fall of 1941, again toward the end of that year, and, finally, in March and summer 1943. Its object on each occasion was to defy a challenge from the occupying power.

In the fall of 1941, the German authorities proposed to establish a State Medical Chamber and compel all doctors to join it. Before this could happen, four thousand members of Medisch Contact signed a letter to the Reich Commissioner condemning the plan and urgently advising him to drop it.

But the Reich Commissioner refused to be dissuaded. In mid-December, he announced that the Medical Chamber had been set up. By a stroke of the pen, all Dutch doctors were declared members whether they liked it or not.

Medisch Contact now urged its members to boycott the new institution and advised them on how to act. They completed no questionnaires, paid no membership dues, and took no notice of what had happened. It was an organized display of symbolic resistance. The new Medical Chamber seemed stillborn.

Over a year passed before the German authorities took action. In March 1943, eighty doctors were punished for denigrating the Medical Chamber and breaking regulations issued by the occupying power. The situation came rapidly to a head. This time, Medisch Contact decided on a trial of strength. It instructed its members to cease practicing and notify the Medical Chamber accordingly.

The summons was obeyed. Over six thousand doctors shut up shop from one day to the next.

Nobody could accuse them of striking or prove that they had broken a regulation of any kind. Each of them had his own reasons for premature retirement.

The six thousand practitioners who had so abruptly developed a need for relaxation took down their plates, closed their consulting rooms, and deleted the "Dr." from their stationery. They also notified the authorities, in six thousand separate letters, that they had ceased to pursue their profession.

They were less intent on attacking the occupying power than on defending their traditional rights, among them the right to practice their profession freely and without regard to political considerations. Theirs was an exemplary instance of defensive resistance, and one that promised to succeed.

The German Commissioner General for Administration and Justice, Friedrich Wimmer, was compelled to back down. He agreed to hold talks with representatives of the medical profession—presumably, spokesmen for its Underground organization. Recognizing the weakness of his position, the man in the seat of power agreed to relax his insistence on compulsory affiliation to the Medical Chamber. The doctors, who had attained their objective with a mixture of firmness and ingenuity, went back to work.

The German authorities continued to browbeat individual doctors and put pressure on them until summer, when the Russians launched their Kursk counteroffensive and the Allies landed in Sicily. Then they struck in earnest. Three hundred and sixty doctors were arrested.

In the sinister lull that followed this resort to force, more and more doctors were reported missing from their homes and places of work. They had prudently gone underground.

Possibly impressed by this surreptitious exodus, the authorities gradually released their detainees. There was no more talk of the new Medical Chamber, and the occupying power took care to moderate its demands.[9]

Thus, Medisch Contact functioned as an Underground organization for two whole years before individual doctors decided to go underground themselves. They did so in self-defense, as an aid to survival and a means of preserving their principles.

Similar developments occurred at universities and colleges in several occupied countries, where German attempts at political streamlining provoked self-defensive measures on the part of staff and students alike. In December 1941, when the professors and lecturers of Brussels University stopped teaching in protest against a demand to admit National Socialist faculty members, a number of students backed them by enrolling at another university. Meanwhile, clandestine teaching on a reduced scale was made available to the remaining students in Brussels itself. Sixty-five teachers enabled four hundred students to complete their studies by giving one hundred and ten unofficial courses to groups of six.[10]

In the spring of 1943, no less than six thousand Dutch students went underground. Having previously refused to make a formal declaration of loyalty to the occupying power, 85 percent of those enrolled had been ordered, on pain of severe reprisals, to report for labor service. Once again, faculty members volunteered to teach students and hold final examinations in secret. The results of these examinations were declared valid after the war.[11]

In December 1943, young Norwegians at Oslo University found themselves in an exceptionally difficult position. The occupying power had closed their seat of learning, arrested several thousand of their number, and shipped some hundreds of them to Germany. Anyone who had escaped the clutches of the Security Police was faced with the choice between running, fighting, or collaborating. Many fled to neighboring Sweden, some resorted to tactical collaboration, and others sought refuge in the Underground.[12]

It is debatable whether these outside recruits to the ranks of the "illegals," or permanent residents of the Underground, should be included in the Resistance proper. Jewish victims of racial persecution, who included fewer able-bodied men than women and children and persons handicapped by age or infirmity, were simply seeking to survive. Only the fortunate were privileged to find shelter because not every Resistance organization was prepared to help and harbor them. Loving your neighbor was a humane duty fraught with danger, and Jewish refugees were clearly identified by the "J" on their identity papers. In Holland the German authorities offered a reward, or "head money," of twenty-five gulden—later increased to forty—for every Jew reported. Anyone who hid a Jew risked losing his own head.[13] Discounting a Zionist youth group which tried to smuggle a thousand Jewish orphans into Switzerland and Spain, no exclusively Jewish Resistance organization took shape in the Dutch Underground. One hundred and four thousand Jewish residents of Holland lost their lives in German extermination camps.[14]

"The British radio speaks of them being gassed. . . ." When fourteen-year-old Anne Frank made this entry in her diary in October 1943, six thousand Dutch Jews had escaped to Belgium and another twenty to twenty-five thousand were living in the Dutch Underground. The people who sheltered them were non-Jews.[15]

More often than not, therefore, the inhabitants of the Underground were not there primarily to fight the occupying power. At the same time, victims of persecution who sought refuge in "illegality" exerted a potent influence on the organized Resistance movements that came to their aid.

The same may be said of the young men who fled to the mountains, forests, and scrub—the *maquis*—of France. Their first thought was to avoid being conscripted for forced labor and sent to Germany. In France they began by congregating in small, unarmed, aimless, and leaderless groups. The Resistance did not bother about them or try to enlist their services until later. Meanwhile, they continued to hide in the remote mountain areas of the Alps and the Jura, the Pyrenees and the Massif Central. How numerous were they? Their importance is generally exaggerated. The total strength of the Maquis in March 1944, four months before the liberation of Paris, has been put at between thirty and forty thousand.[16]

Historians of the Dutch Resistance mention that entire police units took their weapons and went underground. In Denmark, thousands of armed police are reported to have done likewise.

To the Resistance, these disciplined combat units were a gift from the gods. Though armed, however, they at first confined themselves to defensive resistance. In both countries, their primary purpose in going underground was to extricate themselves from an increasingly awkward and perilous predicament.

In Holland they had been compelled to hunt down and round up Jews in broad daylight. They had also gone into action against Dutch strikers, shoulder to shoulder with the German Security Police. Although the relevant orders came from their own Dutch authorities, they could not help suspecting that the undersecretaries had become passive instruments of the occupying power. Disturbed by such doubts, they agreed to let the Resistance overpower them when attacked. It was only a matter of time before smaller units went over to their loyalist compatriots, but the decisive Battle of Stalingrad had long been over when the Dutch police deserted.[17]

In Denmark the police acted in pure self-defense. Everything had been radically changed by the grave political crisis that broke out at the end of August 1943. Having rejected the German demand for a state of emergency after clinging to a policy of negotiation for three and a half years, the Danish Cabinet resigned in protest. The executive powers of government passed to the German authorities, and the Danish forces were taken by surprise and disarmed. From that day on, the attitude of the police changed too.

They refused to take action against Danes who had broken regulations issued by the occupying power. In December, they announced that it would not be their responsibility to combat Danish partisans if the Allies invaded. By May 1944, they were refusing to undertake the protection of Danish factories threatened by saboteurs. In September, the German authorities finally lost patience when again defied in connection with a protest strike against the deportation of 190 Danish citizens. They gave orders for the whole of the Danish constabulary to be arrested forthwith, deported to Germany, and detained in the Buchenwald concentration camp.

On September 19, a mere two thousand policemen were arrested, disarmed, and taken away. Two hundred and fifty-one members of the frontier police were also caught off guard, but the majority of policemen were

alert enough to forestall the Germans. Seven thousand men escaped, their
only recourse a lightning dive for the Underground.[18]

To revert to Holland, it was not by chance that the Dutch produced the
biggest clandestine organizations of all. There could be no question of
launching full-scale attacks on the occupying forces, only of defensive resistance. The terrain was too flat and the road network too open to surveillance to offer any defensive zones where a partisan army could have concealed and organized itself. There were no mountains and no dense forests,
only a few wooded riverside areas where a handful of Resistance groups
did, in fact, manage to hide and even keep German prisoners of war.
These exceptions proved the rule that in Holland, which was one of the
two most densely populated countries under German occupation (Belgium
being the other), only very small Underground groups could assemble in
any one place.[19]

Under these circumstances, defensive resistance would have been impracticable without organized solidarity on a massive scale. As early as
mid-June 1941, the Roman Catholic Church set up a relief fund which
collected fifteen million gulden in three and a half years. Originally intended for Jewish converts to Christianity, this money benefited all fugitives or residents of the Underground who were in need of help. A Protestant relief fund, too, distributed sums running into hundreds of thousands
of gulden.[20]

About six months later, a "National Relief Fund" (NSF) was set up.
Thanks to the good offices of some senior civil servants and the former
director-general of the Netherlands Bank, this fund was subsequently recognized by the government-in-exile in London.

The actual founders of the fund—a retired sea captain, a retired naval
officer, and a banker—were anxious to support the families of seamen serving with the Allies and unable to provide for their dependents until the war
ended. Among many other recipients of their help were the families of detainees and deportees, fugitives in hiding, Jewish fellow citizens, and
workers on strike.

The organization of this illegal fund resembled that of a large-scale
business concern. Working to a precise schedule, approximately fifteen
thousand men, women, and girls cycled the country distributing money to
those in need.

The scheme was not financed by charitable donations. The requisite
sums were raised by means of genuine loans from prosperous Dutch citizens. These loans, which were to be repaid after the war, were fully secured and underwritten by the government-in-exile.

Private loans of less than 25,000 gulden were not accepted. The large
sums involved required loans of corresponding magnitude. By the war's
end, 83,800,000 gulden had been raised. The government-in-exile in-

structed the "banker to the Resistance," as the National Relief Fund came to be known, to disburse 30 million gulden in January 1944 alone. For Jews in hiding, the fund raised a total of 4.7 million gulden.[21]

Late in 1942, a third body—the LO (Welfare Organization for Those in Hiding)—was founded by a Calvinist minister and a housewife. This clandestine organization quickly developed into a mass movement dedicated to the protection of Dutch people living in the Underground.

There was, of course, a perilous contradiction inherent in the wish to enlist mass support and remain secret at the same time. According to its own records, over a thousand members of the LO lost their lives.

The LO stockpiled food and organized its distribution to "illegals" in the towns. It, too, employed about fifteen thousand volunteer helpers, and the scope of its activities steadily widened. In the summer of 1944 it supplied the Underground with 220,000 ration cards. This suggests that it must by then have been supporting two or three hundred thousand people in tens of thousands of hideouts.[22]

To enable it to perform its monumental tasks, the LO maintained three "branches." One forged identity cards with the assistance of civil servants who had joined the Underground, the second produced perfect forgeries of other official documents, and the third consisted of "National Action Groups" (LKP) whose job it was to procure genuine ration and identity cards, if necessary by force.

The Action Groups mounted numerous large-scale raids on food rationing offices during the latter half of 1943, sometimes several in a single day. They usually got what they came for, namely, ration cards, identity cards, and official stamps and seals. Documents and lists of names and addresses that might have helped the German police to combat the Resistance were destroyed on these occasions. The LKP men nearly always managed to catch sentries and office staff off guard. Having gained access to official premises, sometimes by dressing up as German servicemen or members of Mussert's Nazi Party, they could set to work with impunity.

The original purpose of these missions was purely defensive. There was no intention of attacking, killing, or detaining any member of the occupying forces or the Dutch civil service. The raids were simply a means to an end, which was to enable members and residents of the Underground to survive. Force, especially armed force, was only to be used in the direst emergency.

But a change set in as the Action Groups gained experience. They learned the art of surprise and the technique of the perfectly rehearsed coup de main. Their strength increased rapidly, too, rising from three hundred to fifteen hundred men in the first eight months of 1943.

Apart from the fact that LKP teams possessed an inherent dynamism which tended to transform their charitable missions into commando raids, incentives to greater aggression multiplied as time went by. More and more members of the relief organization fell into the hands of the police and were imprisoned, until one day its founder was captured.

The LKP men regarded it as a point of honor to release their chief. Their raid on the jail at Arnhem in June 1944 could not have been more successful. They not only rescued the founder of the LO but released another fifty political prisoners at the same time.

But pleasure at this success was marred by a sinister token of the Germans' reign of terror. A hundred and fifty prison inmates declined to be released and passed up the chance of escape. Such was their fear of brutal reprisals by the occupying power that they voluntarily remained behind bars.[23]

The men of the LKP, who had taken the first crucial step toward offensive resistance, were to play a prominent part in the closing stages of the war in Holland.

Underground Achievements

Even Holland's achievements in the field of defensive resistance pale beside those of Poland, though the conditions that inspired them also defy comparison. For many Poles, resistance was a matter of life and death; for the vast majority of Dutchmen, it was a matter of free personal choice. Unlike the Poles and Russians, the Dutch were not menaced by Hitler's racial mania. For understandable reasons, Poland was the only country under German rule that produced no collaborator in chief, no mass movement or party that subscribed to National Socialism or came anywhere near it. Resistance in Holland was a possibility; for a large proportion of the Polish people, it was a prerequisite of survival.

This was why, when faced with extreme intimidation and the destruction of all things Polish, the entire Polish Establishment went underground.

Soon after Poland fell, a secret apparatus of government—the backbone of an invisible shadow state—installed itself in back rooms and cellars throughout the country. It was made up of government ministries, the secret army then in process of formation, a shadow parliament entitled the "Political Representation," and an official delegation from the London-based government-in-exile, which in turn appointed district delegations to supervise finances and apportion public funds. Not only was the government-in-exile a coalition of Poland's four largest political parties, but a parallel coalition in the illegal shadow parliament enacted laws and tried—as though nothing untoward had happened—to order the affairs of a nation in hiding.

Within this shadow state, newspapers were published, secret factories turned out weapons of war, teachers taught in makeshift schools and universities, authors wrote books, scientists conducted research, judges sat in judgment on ordinary criminal cases, enemy spies and war criminals were tried, and government tribunals passed and carried out some two hundred death sentences.[24]

There are no words to describe the scale of all this clandestine activity. According to figures supplied by the Historical Institute of the Polish Academy of Sciences in Warsaw, approximately one million pupils of all grades were secretly taught by nineteen thousand teachers.[25]

Tens of thousands of illegally printed textbooks were distributed, together with surviving stocks of prewar editions. Clinging to normality, the Polish authorities insisted that parents should continue to pay school fees and that teachers should draw their regular salaries. They also provided for a normal transition from secret school to secret university. Eight thousand school-leavers were examined and passed by Underground boards in Warsaw alone.[26]

The illegal universities grew with amazing speed. At the end of November 1940, the pathetic remains of Warsaw University—fifteen lecturers and forty-eight students—went underground. By 1944, over two hundred professors and lecturers of all faculties were teaching seventeen hundred properly enrolled students under the supervision of an experienced rector and his deans. Four thousand two hundred and thirty-five students enrolled for the winter term 1943–44 and another ten thousand attended semilegal courses of instruction.

The Warsaw Institute of Social Sciences, founded in 1920, also resumed its activities illegally and published the results of its research in secret. One study group conducted an on-the-spot analysis of contemporary history, as it were, by investigating the social effects of German occupation policy on the residents of the Warsaw ghetto. The Institute also published a statistical yearbook running to two hundred pages. Apart from literary and scientific journals, the Polish Underground produced a total of 282 scientific handbooks and monographs.

Before being admitted to an Underground university, students had to sign the following declaration:

"My sole purpose in applying for the courses is to acquire an academic education. I swear, first, to preserve the strictest secrecy about the times, venues, attenders, titles, and contents of lectures and courses, not only in the company of strangers and persons unknown (not to mention enemies of Poland), but also in that of uninitiated friends, and to beware of referring to the same in conversation, especially in public. I swear, secondly, to obey the rules and regulations laid down by the academic authorities in regard to life and work at the university. I swear, thirdly, that I will show myself a true Pole and join no organization hostile to our country, whether public or secret; and that, so far from working for the cause of the alien occupying power, I shall be mindful only of the welfare of the Polish nation and state. So help me God."[27]

The following two instances from Norway, which are far from unique, may serve to show that the essence of defensive resistance was altruistic solidarity with the persecuted on the part of those not directly involved.

Several young men from the Norwegian seaport of Aalesund had fled to England in the summer of 1941 to join the Allied forces. To deter other youngsters who might be toying with the same idea, the German authorities ordered the arrest of the fugitives' parents. Penalizing the families of political offenders was not only a terrible weapon that put any would-be resister to the sternest possible test, it was also a crudely immoral act which so outraged the citizens of Aalesund that five thousand of them spontaneously joined in a public demonstration. By forming a protective cordon around the arrested parents, they upheld the moral precept that forbids the deliberate victimization of the innocent.[28]

The second case had already caused a considerable stir in Norway.

The Provisional Council of State appointed by Reich Commissioner Terboven in September 1940 included members of Quisling's entourage. It was unconstitutional, and so were the laws and decrees enacted by it. To have simply acquiesced in these measures would, for example, have meant accepting a plan to give Norway a "People's Court" on German lines. The Constitutional Court, Norway's supreme judicial authority, countered this proposal by demonstrating that the occupying power was infringing the laws of the land and the international Hague Conventions.

The Reich Commissioner rejected this protest, whereupon the seventy-year-old president of the Supreme Court, ex-Minister Paal Berg, resigned his post. All his fellow judges followed suit. This public refusal to collaborate, which could not fail to impress world opinion, testified to the determination of one of Norway's most authoritative bodies to shield the administration of justice from German attempts at political streamlining.[29]

The same thing happened in Belgium, where decrees issued by collaborationist undersecretaries were pronounced unconstitutional, and therefore null and void, by the Cour de Cassation, or Supreme Court. The occupying power hit back in May 1942 by making all criticism of the administration of justice a punishable offense. Among the recalcitrant lawyers arrested were the members of the Brussels Court of Appeal, who had annulled a law promulgated by Romsée, the Secretary of State for the Interior. An unprecedented situation now arose. To repel this onslaught on their country's legislative foundations, the Supreme Court judges simply stayed away from their place of work. General Eggert Reeder, head of the German military administration, threatened them with the death penalty, but to no avail.

Inevitably, the Germans asked themselves what was to be gained or lost by carrying things to extremes. Having concluded that it would be wiser to yield before matters went too far, they agreed to a compromise which gave the Belgians the satisfaction of having won a total victory: they released the judges from custody and the Supreme Court went back to work.[30]

When and why did defensive resistance succeed, and when and why did it not?

Ulrich Poch explored these questions in his study of eight Danish strike movements during 1943–44. He came to the conclusion that all depended on whether the occupying power was anxious to avoid head-on clashes with the civilian population, the national authorities, or the economically indispensable working class, and, furthermore, on whether or not it might, under certain circumstances, be prepared to negotiate, compromise, or make concessions.[31]

The outcome of numerous other confrontations, both in Denmark and elsewhere, suggests that Poch's rule of thumb is generally valid.

In February and March 1943, for example, Belgian workers leapt to their own defense when labor conscription assumed alarming proportions. As though at a given word of command, sixty thousand men downed tools in the industrial zones of Liège. The strike spread to Charleroi, La Louvière, and other centers of production. Unable, for various reasons, to afford a head-on clash at this particular juncture, the occupying power gave ground. In one instance it dispensed with the recruitment of two thirds of the workers originally requested, and in others it dropped the whole scheme—at least "until further notice."[32]

Somewhat later on, in mid-August 1943, the Danish workers of Odense took offense at incidents provoked by German soldiers and, more especially, at the curfew imposed thereafter. To resist these German "encroachments," they called a token strike without formulating any concrete demands. As a result of further incidents in the days that followed, the German authorities demanded a fine from the Danish Government and humiliatingly insisted on a formal apology. Their arrogance unleashed a storm of protest and brought five thousand workers out on strike. Together with another five thousand who had spontaneously joined them, they assembled at Odense's sports stadium the same day. This was more than a token strike. In an atmosphere verging on uproar, the ten thousand demonstrators passed a resolution sponsored by the strike committee. Among the firm demands it contained were confinement to barracks for members of the occupying forces, the withdrawal of German sentries from Danish factories and dockyards, and the release of all Danish hostages.

Again the Germans yielded. Assessing the situation correctly, they granted the first demand at once and confined their men to quarters for a period of several days.[33]

Photograph taken by a British Mosquito bomber during the air attack on Gestapo headquarters in Copenhagen, a high-precision raid made possible by close cooperation between the Danish Resistance and the Royal Air Force. The Gestapo premises were badly damaged and twenty-seven Resistance leaders released from their cells on the building's top floor.

At the end of June 1944, a hundred Danish Resistance fighters raided an arms factory, seized some weapons, and blew the place up. German reprisals led to riots in which 97 people were killed and 600 injured. A general strike was called, and barricades went up in Copenhagen (above). Germany's long-time "model protectorate" had become a theater of war.

Tito, commander in chief of the only independent "people's army" in Europe, after being wounded in May 1943. He once broke through an enemy cordon five times as strong and led half of his original force of twenty thousand men to safety.

Though spontaneous and sustained by a broadly based popular movement, armed resistance in Italy did not declare itself until the Fascist regime had collapsed late in the summer of 1943 — hence the special characteristics of Italian partisan units and their rapid growth.

Soviet partisan army was the only one to be formed in a country that had not surrendered. Discounting a brief spell of improvisation, it
centrally controlled from the outset and took orders from its own general staff in Moscow, which supplied its component units with
s.

ioed instructions, received from Moscow by a regional partisan headquarters, are conveyed to the rank and file. By August 1943, when
stance in other European countries was only just being coordinated, the 1,131 Soviet partisan units behind German lines maintained 424
o stations which kept them in constant touch with their Moscow headquarters.

Volunteer Resistance fighters undergoing secret military training in a remote Norwegian forest. These members of the paramilitary secret army MILORG (short for "Military Organization") began to receive Allied arms supplies by sea and air in 1944. Similar photographs exist of recruits being trained in almost every occupied country.

Danish sabotage teams delayed German troop trains bound for the hard-pressed Western Front by systematicaly blowing up railroad lines. Workers were forced to repair damaged track under military guard. Here, a suspicious sound in the undergrowth has tightened the trigger finger of a German sentry.

A sunny day in Yugoslavia. "I have fanaticized the masses so as to make them an instrument of my policy. I have roused them, I have
them out of themselves and given them a purpose and function. I have been accused of exciting their baser instincts. What I do is som

An Allied airdrop on July 14, 1944. The receipt of these metal canisters packed with eagerly awaited small arms prompted the Maquisards of Vercors to throw caution to the winds and seize the initiative. The result was predictable. SS units cleaned out their mountain stronghold and killed seven hundred of them.

Partisans waiting vainly for arms and ammunition, their appeals for help ignored. Demoralization was an irresistible and dangerous disease.

"Give my love to Randolph," Churchill radioed Tito on May 24, 1944. His son, a member of a military mission, is here seen with officers of the Yugoslav 8th Partisan Division.

Tito and his partisan commanders discuss the military situation, now tilting in their favor thanks to massive Western aid. Beside him on the left, Eduard Kardelj, his future Foreign Minister; on the far right, Milovan Djilas. Tito only just escaped capture during a surprise raid on his headquarters at the end of May 1943, and was taken to safety by the British.

Draža Mihailović, Tito's inveterate opponent, the staff officer who first raised the banner of resistance in western Serbia.

Chetnik units nominally controlled by Mihailović waged a bloody minor war against Tito's partisans under the independent command of junior officers like those above, who were fighting to restore the monarchy.

Warsaw surrender terms provided for the city's complete evacuation. A hundred and fifty thousand members of the civilian population e dead. The remainder began to move out on October 4, 1944. Resistance groups and lone individuals who still refused to abandon the ggle sought refuge in the sewers and cellars of the deserted capital.

The Warsaw uprising (August–September 1944). Forty thousand men of the Polish Home Army made a desperate attempt to liberate their capital city. Stalin prevented the Western Powers from rendering timely and effective assistance.

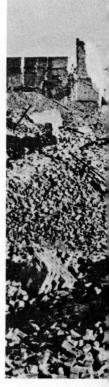

The Warsaw uprising fails: General Bor-Komorowski surrenders to SS General Bach-Zelewski. His units suffered twenty-two thousand casualities, killed and wounded. Though already at the gates of the city, the Red Army stayed put.

General Zervas, commander in chief of the nationalist partisans (EDES), confers in Athens with his rival General Saraphis, leader of the Communist-controlled ELAS units, and General Scobie of the British Army (center).

The news that fighting had broken out between British troops and ELAS partisans, not only in Athens but throughout Attica, provoked a storm of indignation in Britain and the United States. Political principles were in conflict with strategic requirements. Left in the lurch by Moscow, the ELAS units surrendered. Above, a British tank breaks down the gate of ELAS headquarters.

British troops in the streets of Athens early in December 1944, when Greece had already been evacuated by the Germans. Armed with a go-ahead from Stalin, Churchill had ordered the commander of the British expeditionary forces in Greece, General Scobie, to put down a Communist insurrection in the capital.

Fifty Jewish combat groups—a thousand men and women armed with eighty rifles, three light machine guns, a few hundred revolvers, and a thousand hand grenades—put up a desperate fight against two thousand members of the occupying forces under SS General Stroop, who had been ordered to destroy the Warsaw ghetto.

Winston Churchill flanked by two prickly partners. On the left, General Wladyslaw Sikorski, head of the Polish Government-in-exile, who severed relations with Britain's Soviet allies in April 1943. On the right, General de Gaulle, who seriously considered transferring his headquarters and armed forces from England to Russia in May 1942.

One of the British Lysander aircraft which used to ferry couriers and agents to France, where disputes often arose between rival organizations.

Contemporary photograph of the "Kattegat Bridge," a secret maritime link between Denmark and the British Isles. Arms were transferred to Danish fishing boats at sea.

Witold Pilecki (above), career officer and co-founder
of TAP, an armed Polish Resistance movement, procured some false papers and got himself sent to the
death camp at Auschwitz to organize resistance there.
He kept TAP headquarters informed of developments
inside the camp for two and a half years (September
1940–April 1943), part of the time by radio.

When I ply the masses with rational ideas, they fail to understand me. But when I arouse the right emotions in them, they follow the
le slogans I give them" (Adolph Hitler).

Relations between the Allies and the French Resistance labored under suspicions of betrayal. Hitler's armies could hardly be defeated with the aid of pistols dropped by parachute.

Jean Moulin, De Gaulle's accredited representative i France. His attempts to coordinate the Resistance did no eliminate its dangerous internal tensions.

Partisan activity and Allied military operations were coordinated by three-man teams dropped behind the German lines with orders to exploit the special aptitudes of paramilitary units. The latter proved capable of carrying out strategically useful assignments with relatively few casualties.

The Rescue of the Danish Jews

Perhaps the most spectacular example of defensive resistance was the rescue of the Danish Jews.

We are already familiar with the background. Denmark's attitude had an important bearing on German plans for repelling an Allied invasion of Northern Europe, and Danish exports were indispensable to the German economy. It followed that the Wehrmacht and the economy of the Third Reich required a peaceful Denmark.

The German Foreign Office, as we know, was similarly concerned but for different reasons. Its pre-eminent status in Denmark, the one country under its administrative control, could be challenged only if disorders broke out there. The Party, the SS, and other rival agencies and departments could hardly wait for this to happen.

This gave the military and diplomatic authorities in Denmark a common interest, because both took the view that it would, for example, be inexpedient to persecute Jews on Danish territory.

"As long as it remains vital to our conduct of the war and our overall political interests that Denmark's peaceful development be left undisturbed, no consideration can be given to tackling the roots of the Jewish problem there." This excerpt comes from an official report to the Foreign Office dated January 20, 1942, and drafted by the German minister and Reich Plenipotentiary in Denmark, Cecil von Renthe-Fink.[34]

The same view was taken by his successor, Werner Best, who tirelessly employed all the authority he derived from his exalted SS background to ensure that Denmark was shielded from disruptive influences of every kind.

This was why Danish Jews remained unscathed while their fellow Jews throughout the rest of occupied Europe were being harassed, persecuted, hunted, and deported to the East.

The situation changed abruptly, but not until Hitler's wrath had been attracted to Denmark by the political crisis of August 1943. Before long, confidential reports predicting the imminent arrest and deportation of Danish Jews began to filter through. We now know that these reports actually stemmed from an order given by Hitler on September 18, 1943. The departments entrusted with Denmark's "Final Solution" put in an immediate request for three Security Police companies reinforced by fifty experienced officers, together with cargo space for the transportation of at least five thousand people. The arrests were to be carried out on the night of October 1–2.[35]

Presumably anxious to lessen the impact of a shock that might throw Denmark off balance, Reich Plenipotentiary Best decided to inform certain people, in the strictest confidence, of what lay in store. They were the leader of Copenhagen's Jewish community, a head of section at the Danish Foreign Ministry, and the general secretary of the Danish Social Democratic Party.

The Danes' prompt reaction must have taken Best aback. Before the day was out, he received an urgent request from the Danish Foreign Ministry for clarification of the "rumors" alleging that all Danish Jews were about to be arrested. The trade unions weighed in with an equally urgent request for an official démenti. Next day the Danish trade associations sent Best a petition warning him that the consequences of such a step were bound to be disastrous. Then the Danish Foreign Ministry reiterated that it was still awaiting an official German explanation. King Christian himself dispatched a written warning to the German Legation, and the chorus of protest was later joined by senior Danish service officers such as Admiral Vedel and General Gørtz, the chief of the General Staff.

Clearly impressed by such a concerted display of defensive resistance, which strengthened his resolve because it vindicated his assessment of the situation and the policy he favored, Best toed the Danish line. Where the Danish Jews were concerned, he could not and would not take his cue from Hitler. He decided to sabotage the Führer's directive.[36]

On September 29, two days before the "Jewish operation" was due to take place, he sent a member of his staff, Georg Ferdinand Duckwitz, on a highly confidential mission to Stockholm. Duckwitz, the German Legation's shipping expert, was to inform the Swedish Premier, Per Albin Hansson, of Hitler's intentions. Best further instructed Duckwitz to point out that the Swedish minister in Copenhagen had personally drawn his attention, only a few days before, to the Swedish Government's grave misgivings about "certain rumors"—rumors which would soon turn out to be well founded.[37]

In its turn, the Swedish Government hurriedly requested the German Government to comment on the disturbing "rumors" in question and informed Berlin that Sweden would be prepared to grant asylum to all Danish Jews. To lend this démarche as much weight as possible, the contents of the Swedish note were released in Stockholm. When the Germans failed to reply, the Swedish minister in Berlin paid the Foreign Office another visit and asked the German Government to permit at least the children of Danish Jews to leave for Sweden. Berlin brusquely and caustically rejected the Swedish requests.[38]

The Danish operation went ahead, but the Reich Plenipotentiary had not been idle in the last few days and hours.

One of Best's friends, Korvettenkapitän [Commander] Cammann, who was superintendent of Copenhagen harbor, had been directed by him to ensure that the German Navy took no action during the crucial hours. Furthermore, Best enjoyed the wholehearted support of Rudolf Mildner, the

head of the Security Police, who was afraid that the operation would cause
his department a lot of unnecessary headaches. By arrangement with Best,
Mildner instructed the police that no premises occupied by Jews were to
be forcibly entered.

The so-called operation proved a washout. Only 284 Danes of the Jewish faith were traced and arrested, and most of them were too old or sick
to have decamped and hidden somewhere. Fifty had to be released at once
because they were unfit to travel. In the end, 202 Jews—or less than 3 percent of Denmark's Jewish population—were put aboard the *Wartheland*,
the German freighter that was lying in Copenhagen harbor with cargo
space for "at least five thousand persons."[39]

The operation did, nonetheless, cause a stir. The Swiss minister in
Stockholm, Paul Dinichert, referred in his reports to "genuine agitation in
official circles in the capital at the latest news of the Jew-hunt in Denmark." The resulting situation was being described as "calamitous," and
its repercussions in Sweden would be immense. Dinichert emphasized the
Swedish Government's démarches almost as if he would have liked to promote a similar attitude in his own government. This was probably far from
his thoughts. He knew that the "J" on the travel permits of Jewish citizens,
which had sealed their fate in innumerable cases, was the embarrassing
outcome of Swiss-German negotiations and had been unanimously approved by the Federal Government in Bern. The home of the Red Cross
remained silent—had to remain silent—while the monarchs and governments of Denmark and Sweden staunchly championed the victims of anti-
Semitic persecution.[40]

Thus, most of the Danish Jews on Hitler's blacklist had reached the Underground in time. The help they received there was just as humane as the
attitude adopted by Danish officialdom. Copenhagen's clinics and hospitals
promptly "discharged" patients with Jewish names and re-registered them
under pseudonyms without even moving them from one bed to another.
Other clinics took in healthy Jewish families under the pretense that they
were gravely ill. Copenhagen's Bispebjerg Hospital, which had overnight
become an assembly center and transit camp for Jewish refugees, took in
groups of eighty to a hundred at a time, furnished them with food and
money, and passed them on to Resistance organizations. Doctors organized secret collections, and the Danish Medical Association donated a substantial sum. The staff of Bispebjerg Hospital alone raised over a million
kroner, or enough to save two thousand Jews by financing their escape to
neutral territory.[41]

Meanwhile, the Swedish Government instructed its legation in Copenhagen to grant certain refugees Swedish nationality and issue others with
temporary passports and entry visas. Swedish fishing boats sailed to Denmark to pick up Jewish refugees and carry them to safety. Jews who had
gone to ground in Jutland were conducted by Danish Resistance groups to

secret embarkation points, many of them extremely remote. Numerous Danish boats that had put refugees ashore in Sweden returned with arms and ammunition for the Danish Resistance. Although mischance or betrayal increased the Gestapo's haul by nearly three hundred, 7,376 Danish Jews succeeded in escaping to Sweden.[42]

But the Danish rescue operation did not end there. The Jews who had failed to escape deportation were not abandoned. Thanks to the firm and courageous attitude of the King, who had insisted on receiving an assurance from the Germans that his Jewish subjects would come to no harm, the deportees were taken to the Theresienstadt concentration camp, not an extermination center. In mid-1944, unremitting Danish pressure secured permission for them to be visited there by a Red Cross delegation and by Danish Government representatives who brought parcels for all their Jewish compatriots and a personal letter for Rabbi Friediger from the King himself.[43]

Of the 425 Danish Jews deported to Germany, 52 died there of natural causes, mostly at a ripe old age. The others survived the war.[44]

This episode, one of the war's most heartwarming "sideshows," confirms the accuracy of Ulrich Poch's appraisal. The resolute stance of the Danish Government, the trade associations, the trade unions, the police, the medical profession, the man in the street, and the royal house, almost all of whom flatly refused to cooperate in this particular instance, was echoed on the German side by a readiness on the part of the Reich Plenipotentiary, the military authorities, the commander of the Security Police, and the harbor master, to flout a Hitlerian directive which struck them as pointless and detrimental to German interests. Their attitude was reinforced by internal power struggles. Germans and Danes, key representatives of the occupying power and the country under occupation, found themselves working in harness.

Offensive Resistance
or
I Fight to the Death

The offensive resister says: I combat the forces of occupation by every available means. I attack or prepare to attack them whenever the opportunity arises. I regard myself as a soldier—a volunteer member of the Underground.

Under this heading come the resolute men of action who laid mines and hurled grenades; who engaged in ambushes and assassinations, arson and murder; who joined secret paramilitary combat teams or bands of armed partisans on their nuisance raids and foraging expeditions; who belonged to the secret armies that demoralized, harassed, and outmaneuvered units of the occupation forces by attacking them in the flank or rear; and, finally, who enabled the Allies to launch prearranged operations by systematically compiling useful items of intelligence about German dispositions and troop movements and passing them on to Allied headquarters. Theirs was a world apart—a sphere of activity that differed from those devoted to symbolic, polemic, or defensive resistance.

A world apart, yes, but none of these spheres was entirely remote or distinct from the rest. On the contrary, they were forever interlocking, intersecting, overlapping, and supplementing each other. Partisans, too, published clandestine newspapers, promoted displays of symbolic resistance, helped escaped prisoners of war on their way, or enrolled political refugees in their ranks. The same persons, groups, and organizations functioned in different ways at different times. All that characterized and distinguished them from each other was the form of resistance they favored most.

The very earliest form of offensive resistance was intelligence gathering. To fight the enemy, you had to know him. Before armed resistance could be seriously considered, spy rings grew up in the occupied territories.

Any item of intelligence could prove useful to the Allies, and eagle-eyed observers were at work everywhere—in every factory, in every railroad station, in every port, and in every unit of the Todt Organization, the labor service which constructed roads, fortifications, tank traps, and gun emplacements. One can only marvel at the sheer volume of the detailed reports that were secretly compiled and radioed to London from occupied Europe.

In Belgium, nearly ten thousand people, including three hundred Belgian agents trained in England and "inserted" by parachute, fed information to the secret headquarters of thirty-five spy rings which operated telex links and remote-controlled radio stations.[1]

The first secret communications link between Denmark and England was established by a Danish journalist and publisher named Ebbe Munck. This operated via the British diplomatic mission in Stockholm. From 1944 on, there was a direct radio link with London, as well as an ultra-short-wave, high-speed radio link using perforated strips that transmitted bursts of eight hundred characters a minute. The U. S. Embassy in Stockholm acted as a relay station. The reports radioed to London from Denmark during the last fifteen months of the war filled fifteen thousand large, closely written sheets of paper.[2]

All the growing "secret armies" discussed below employed separate intelligence networks in direct and independent radio contact with London. These included the Polish "Home Army," the Czech officers' organization known as "National Defense" (ON), the Prague-based "Central Committee for Secret Resistance" (UVOD), and similar organizations in other countries. Between 1940 and 1942 alone, the Allied High Command in London received no less than twenty thousand radio messages from the various Czech intelligence services operating in the Protectorate of Bohemia and Moravia.[3]

Thanks to their vast army of informants, the Polish intelligence services proved exceptionally productive.

Over a million Poles were working in Germany by September 1941. The most active of them formed cells, helped to rescue stranded Allied airmen or runaway prisoners of war and smuggle them out of the country, and established links with French spy rings through French prisoners of war.

Of the hundred thousand Poles living in France, some twenty thousand belonged to the Resistance. "F2," a Franco-Polish intelligence service run by Polish officers, was another valuable source of intelligence. Every two or three weeks from 1942 on, F2 supplied London with microfilmed reports running to four or five hundred pages.

Operating in occupied Poland, the intelligence service of the Home Army (AK) sent London the first sensational reports of German V-1 test launchings at Peenemünde. Early in May 1944 its agents managed to get hold of a dud rocket, dismantle it, and transport it to Warsaw. Expert Polish aero engineers and radio technicians examined the components and reported their findings to London. In July, a British Dakota took off from Brindisi and collected the dud V-1 from a secret landing strip near Tarnów.[4]

In the case of France, the official record of wartime intelligence services lists no less than 266 networks with a grand total of 89,602 members. The largest organization employed 3,601 informants and the smallest only six, but nearly twenty of them had over a thousand agents apiece.[5]

Most of these networks and a large proportion of their members melted away in the course of the war—either betrayed or detected and eliminated by German Military Intelligence, which maintained twelve outstations in France alone. In 1944 there were still about sixty networks on French soil compiling information gathered by approximately thirty thousand people. By this time, the Gaullist intelligence service (BCRA) maintained a coordinating center and forty-eight clandestine radio transmitters in the South of France.[6]

Espionage activity in France reached its peak in May 1944, on the eve of the Allied landings in Normandy. Little worth knowing remained hidden from Allied Supreme Headquarters, thanks to the 3,700 reports radioed to London during this month alone by intelligence networks based in France.[7]

These achievements on the part of civilian and military Resistance movements probably had a greater effect on the course of the war than any of their other operations. Seldom if ever can belligerent powers have been kept as amply and exhaustively informed about the enemy as the Allies were in World War II. Their intelligence officers reaped a rich harvest because everyone in occupied territory—every child and illiterate—was a potential source of vitally important information.

A Russian report from the Eastern Front proves that this trite-sounding statement may be taken at face value. It tells of an old peasant woman who used to sit sorting peas and beans outside her shack in a semi-deserted village—ostensibly, one of the few surviving inhabitants who had not fled or been driven from their homes. The men in the German armored columns that rumbled through the village took little notice of her, surmising that the old crone was illiterate and incapable of counting beyond ten.

They were right, but that did not prevent her from passing valuable information to the partisan who visited her nightly. For every heavy tank that roared by, she put aside a bean; for every light tank, a pea. Her assortments of peas and beans provided Red Army intelligence officers with a reasonably accurate picture of enemy tank movements in the area.[8]

So the whole Continent was spanned by a close-knit network of silent observers ranging from an illiterate old peasant woman in a Russian village to a future Nobel laureate in Paris, the Irish writer Samuel Beckett, who produced English translations of secret reports for London on behalf of the spy ring known as "Gloria HMS," an organization founded and led by Jeannine, daughter of the surrealist painter Francis Picabia. While the old woman busied herself with beans and peas, the Irish writer went on reconnaissance trips through France armed with an assumed name and false papers. When German Intelligence tracked down Jeannine Picabia's spy ring, which cooperated with others of its kind, the novelist Nathalie Sarraute kept her confrère "Sam" hidden for ten days beneath the floorboards of her attic apartment in Paris.

Though worlds apart, geographically and intellectually, these amateur spies—the babushka of the steppe and the littérateurs of Paris—were servants in the same cause.[9]

Armed Raiders and Murder Squads

Bomb attacks multiplied as the incidence of arson, which was frequent in the early days, declined. The eerie silence of a thousand pinpricks was occasionally shattered by the thunderclap of a large-scale, carefully planned operation. After an early phase characterized by haphazard, individual acts of sabotage designed to be little more than displays of symbolic resistance, Underground combat teams began to learn sabotage techniques and plan and execute their operations with a methodical attention to detail.[10]

This applied to industrial and military sabotage alike. Construction workers, for example, surreptitiously blended their cement with a few pounds of sugar because "sweetened" concrete would one day crumble under moderate stress or even under the blast from a near miss.[11]

Just as stealthily, fitters sabotaged aero engines with subtly calculated defects which, though immune from detection by production controllers, would get fighters and bombers into difficulties after thirty or forty flying hours.[12]

In France, over ten thousand railroadmen are reported to have engaged in nonviolent acts of sabotage, such as deliberately misrouting freight trains and working to rule.[13]

Recorded cases of industrial sabotage in Denmark increased tenfold during the latter years of the war.[14]

In the early days, little or no liaison existed between the numerous Resistance groups that had taken shape in the occupied territories, and few of them were equal to the demands of effective industrial sabotage. Whatever was needed in the way of know-how and equipment, planning and operational precision, could seldom be procured from their own resources—least of all under the wary gaze of German intelligence agents. On the rare occasions when it was required to plan and execute a large-scale operation, possibly of strategic importance, they were dependent on outside help—on fellow countrymen who had learned the requisite sabotage and combat techniques at British training centers and carried out or masterminded the operation with the assistance, and under the direction, of the mammoth British organization known as the Special Operations Executive (SOE).

In 1943, for instance, the Norwegian pyrite mines at Stord were so badly damaged that their output of the precious ore was still 70 percent down two and a half years later. This raid was the work of an Anglo-Norwegian commando unit landed near Bergen by torpedo boats.[15]

Late in February of the same year, a far more important sabotage operation was carried out, after lengthy and elaborate planning, against a Norwegian industrial plant at Rjukan. On this occasion, nine Norwegian saboteurs succeeded in destroying a ton of "heavy water," at that time a substance essential to German research into the development of an atomic bomb.

A scout had installed himself near the plant almost a year before. He was followed in the early fall of 1942 by four more men who prepared landing strips for the two gliders that were to fly in explosives, uniforms, and other items of equipment. Both gliders crashed, and the surviving pilots and crews were captured and shot by the German Security Police.

In February 1943, six more Norwegians parachuted in to join the original group of five. Their plan of action took account of every possible contingency. Wearing uniform, nine of the men climbed an icy rock face, crossed a mountain torrent, scaled yet another rock face on the far side, and thus contrived to reach the heavily guarded plant without being spotted. They overpowered the German sentries, forced their way into the building, and placed their explosive charges in carefully selected positions. Shortly after midnight, the steep sides of the valley resounded to a series of explosions like muffled thunder.

The Germans deployed three thousand men with orders to comb the entire district for the authors of the attack. All eleven managed to escape. Two of them, still in full Norwegian uniform, skied two hundred and fifty miles to the Swedish border. Two more got through to Oslo, where they joined a military Resistance organization. Another four went into hiding near the plant itself.

The bold stroke had succeeded, but the plant had not been totally destroyed and production was resumed. An American task force of 140 Flying Fortresses failed to blast the installation out of existence but did persuade the Germans that it would be safer to transfer their precious stock of heavy water to Germany.

A second Norwegian SOE sabotage team was assigned to thwart this move. The attack succeeded. A train ferry laden with freight cars was sunk in mid-crossing and went down with well over twenty thousand gallons of heavy water on board.[16]

Military sabotage was of no real value unless geared to Allied aims and intentions. The target, location, and exact timing of an attack, or of a sabotage operation affecting an entire theater of war, had to be agreed in advance with the Allied Supreme Command, synchronized with operations conducted by Allied forces, thoroughly rehearsed, and, last but not least, kept strictly secret. If all these conditions were fulfilled, the Resistance could be expected to make a valuable contribution to the war.

One classic instance of this was furnished in the spring of 1943 by the Greek Resistance, whose sabotage operations performed two important functions.

In the first place, they made it seem that the Allies were preparing to invade southern Greece. This impression was fostered by a sudden hectic outbreak of sabotage in precisely those coastal areas where a landing might have been expected. The Germans promptly transferred an armored division from Italy to the south of Greece.

As it turned out, the Allies landed in Sicily. Now needed there, the German armored division was appreciably delayed on its return journey because a rail bridge essential to smooth troop movements had been opportunely blown up by Greek partisans—their second contribution to a major strategic ploy.[17]

This was not a unique case. It became increasingly clear, as time went by, that the paramilitary units of the European Resistance were ideally suited to attacks on railroad lines, bridges, and viaducts. It is fair to say that these constituted one of their most important operational objectives and one of their most rewarding fields of activity.

This, no doubt, is why Resistance sabotage operations were redirected as the war progressed. Their original targets had been factories or plants in the employ of the occupying power. Later on, more and more attacks were aimed at the occupying power itself, and mainly at the railroads it used.

This trend can be fairly accurately plotted with the aid of German statistical records. They indicate that, of all the acts of sabotage committed in France during the first nine months of 1943, the majority (54 percent) were directed against German installations. Of these cases, 62 percent involved railroad tracks and equipment. Until then, sabotage had been directed mainly against industrial plants run by French collaborators.[18]

The same picture recurs everywhere. The demolition of a bridge between Athens and Salonika by Greek partisans under General Napoleon Zervas severely hampered the flow of supplies to the Afrika Korps, 80 percent of which traveled by rail through Greece. In Belgium, attacks on railroad lines and bridges multiplied when the Allies landed in Normandy, and Denmark registered a sharp increase in railroad sabotage at the same period.[19]

In Norway, the destruction of a bridge north of Trondheim in January 1945 severed a rail link vital to German troop movements for a full two weeks. In mid-March, Norwegian sabotage teams damaged the same line at over a thousand points in a single night. This badly delayed the withdrawal of German forces concentrated in Finnmark, which were urgently needed for the defense of the threatened Ruhr.[20] On the Eastern Front, centrally coordinated railroad sabotage by Russian partisans had assumed immense proportions long before, but this will be dealt with in detail in Part Four.

Although its purpose was neither economic nor strategic, another elaborate act of offensive resistance deserves to be mentioned in the present context. This was an air strike requested by the Danish Underground and carried out by the Royal Air Force—an operation of psychological and political importance.

The object of the raid was Shell House, the Gestapo's headquarters in the heart of the Danish capital. This was where all its secret files were kept, among them the central card index on its operations against the Danish Resistance.

One ingenious German secret policeman had hit on the idea of insuring the headquarters and its valuable archives against an Allied air attack by taking as many prominent members of the Danish Resistance as the Gestapo had managed to capture and confining them in the same building. For this purpose, twenty-two concrete cells had been built into the top floor. Their inmates comprised a Danish admiral, two members of the Danish Freedom Council, or central executive of the Danish Resistance, and over two dozen other well-known Resistance fighters. It was hardly to be expected that the Allied air forces would place their lives in jeopardy.

But here the Resistance itself took a hand.

The hostages on the top floor were doomed, a secret transmitter radioed London from Copenhagen in December 1944. It was known that they had suffered gross ill-treatment and would almost certainly be killed by the Gestapo in due course. Would it not be possible to attack Shell House from the air in such a way as to release them unharmed?

A fantastic idea, but was it so utterly impracticable?

The men and women of the Danish Resistance went to work. They procured town plans and marked the exact location of Shell House. They obtained particulars of the materials used in constructing the walls, ceilings, buttresses, and partition walls. They collected photographs showing the building from every angle and in every light. They ascertained who occupied each office and what was kept there. They produced a minutely detailed description of the surroundings of Shell House and appended photographs surreptitiously taken to order. They plotted the location of the German antiaircraft batteries and radar and direction-finding stations in and around Copenhagen. One of their plans even showed the varied coloring of the tiled roofs on all the buildings in the vicinity of the target. The whole of this information was then relayed to London by courier.

After carefully weighing all the arguments for and against this extremely hazardous scheme, the authorities in London decided to risk it. The tactical feasibilities of the raid were tested and pilots rehearsed with the aid of a realistic model of Shell House and its environs based on plans and diagrams received from Copenhagen. By the time eighteen Mosquito bombers and twenty-eight Mustang fighters took off from an English airfield on March 21, 1945, the impending raid had been discussed and rehearsed innumerable times.

The task force commander had been instructed not to use incendiaries. Every effort was to be made to enable the Resistance leaders in their top-floor cells to survive the raid and, if at all possible, to escape. The rest of the building, together with four hundred Gestapo officers and their central filing system, was to be destroyed.

This called for precision work of the highest order. The roof of Shell House was taboo. Bombs were to be aimed at the base of the building, so as to penetrate the cellars at an oblique angle. Three of the four main staircases had to be destroyed and the fourth left intact for the use of escaping prisoners. The pilots and crews knew that, if they were shot down by the German air defenses, they could count on prompt assistance from the Danish Underground.

The bombers and fighters crossed the North Sea at an altitude of fifteen feet. Just off Jutland they climbed to a hundred and fifty. When the first two dozen bombs struck the base of the building, as planned, and the Mustangs began strafing the German antiaircraft batteries on the surrounding roofs, the concrete cells on the top floor housed thirty-two prisoners and four Danish Gestapo informers. A thirty-third prisoner was undergoing interrogation in one of the offices downstairs.

Terrified, a German sentry on the top floor handed over the keys to the cell doors. In the lull between the second and third bombing runs, twenty-seven prisoners made good their escape down the undamaged flight of stairs, though six failed to survive. The building was severely damaged and the central filing system destroyed.

The Royal Air Force lost four Mosquito bombers and two Mustang fighters, together with ten airmen.

Two days after the raid, members of the "Holger Danske" Resistance group searched the ruins of Shell House and recovered a steel filing cabinet. It was found to contain a list of Danish Nazis.

The inevitability of civilian casualties had had to be accepted. Not far from Shell House, eighty-three children and several nuns lost their lives when the Jeanne d'Arc School received a direct hit.[21]

Punitive Assassination

Resistance movements in the occupied territories had gone over to the offensive by engaging in espionage and sabotage. Even before they built up any reasonably effective paramilitary combat units, however, they began to resort to methods that often caused them strong moral qualms. On the grounds that anything was justified in war—in a fight for survival—they deliberately countered German brutality with carefully measured doses of the same medicine.

To this end, the larger Resistance movements and their ancillary organizations formed combat teams and murder squads whose drastic acts were intended to neutralize threats to the Resistance and simultaneously disconcert, and if possible intimidate, the occupying power and its accomplices. Prominent collaborators, senior collaborationist police officers, and Gestapo informers were sentenced to death by secret courts-martial and executed.

For a long time, Resistance fighters who were driven to adopt the tactic of deliberate assassination described their predicament as "tragic." In a "strictly secret and confidential" memorandum addressed to the head of De Gaulle's secret intelligence service in London, the founder and leader of the "Combat" Resistance organization, Henri Frenay, complained that, although it would be years before a French "secret army" could be formed and go into action, the combat teams who had long been operating under the auspices of a "short-term program" could wait no longer for the basic equipment they needed. Every time they carried out a raid, assassination, or sabotage operation, they had first to procure the requisite firearms and explosives at great personal risk. Frenay implored his London-based comrades for aid. In September 1942, he said, his men had been compelled—after vainly awaiting delivery of some pistols fitted with silencers—to dispose of a Gestapo agent with axes.[22]

Holland's National Action Groups (LKP), originally formed as a specialist subgroup of the purely defensive "Relief Organization for Those in Hiding" (LO), killed over forty of Mussert's Nazi supporters and an undisclosed number of German and Dutch agents during a seven-and-a-half-month period in 1943. Once again, none of these operations could be described as a random or arbitrary act of political murder. Each attack was carefully discussed, often with ministers of religion or representatives of legitimate Dutch authorities, and none was approved without a thoroughgoing examination of every conceivable ethical, moral, political, and psychological objection.

At the request of their government-in-exile, Dutch commandos of the LKP and other Resistance organizations were equipped by a British agency with Sten guns which could be easily dismantled and fitted with silencers. These enabled them to gun down active opponents such as ex-War Minister F. E. Posthuma, who belonged to the political secretariat of Mussert's National Socialist Movement, and the Nazi police chiefs of Nijmegen and Utrecht. A commando team from another Resistance organization (RvZ) carried out sentence of death on Holland's erstwhile chief of the

General Staff, General Seyffardt, who had since become head of recruit-ment for the Waffen-SS. According to German sources, the man who fired the shot (he was arrested, condemned to death, and summarily executed) was a "fanatical Catholic." The same squad executed the Dutch Under-secretary for Propaganda, Richard Reydon, who had failed to rebut a charge of unwarranted collaboration with the occupying power.[23]

It will be apparent that most of these early assassinations involved col-laborators who had sided with the occupying power, not German service-men. Murdered Gestapo agents, too, were seldom Germans.

Just as saboteurs switched targets as time went by, so did assassination squads. The more ruthlessly the Germans countered their activities with harsh reprisals, the more they themselves were provoked by deliberate re-taliation on the part of the Resistance. It was a self-perpetuating process.

The same trend developed in Russia, where Communist raiders were the first to launch systematic attacks on German soldiers. However little real damage it might inflict on the German war machine, every act of murder or sabotage seemed to them to benefit and assist their sorely threatened country. Other Resistance organizations might shrink from exposing de-fenseless civilians to the wrath and vengeance of the German authorities, perhaps to no good purpose, and from causing the deaths of innocent hos-tages culled from an already suffering population. The Communists saw this as a positive advantage. Reprisals of any kind, from mass arrests to the shooting of hostages, would foment popular hatred and swell the ranks of the organized Resistance with a growing number of fugitives. In the last analysis—ran one argument—the maintenance of order and the combating of partisan activity tied up German forces that might have wreaked greater havoc elsewhere.

This idea and the Party directives relating to it were what inspired three armed groups drawn from the French Communist "youth battalions" to gun down several members of the occupying forces in August and Septem-ber 1941, including an administrative officer and the German area com-mander at Nantes—murders which resulted, as we already know, in the ex-ecution of ninety-eight hostages. What happened in France was repeated in other countries. In Belgium the partisan army associated with the illegal Communist Party ("Armée Belge des Partisans du Front de l'Indépen-dence") turned assassins from its "Milices Patriotes" loose on German servicemen. In Denmark it was "Bopa," another combat organization owing allegiance to the Communist Party, that drew the German Security Police into a steadily mounting exchange of blows and eventually prompted it to employ an assassination squad of its own.

Almost as a matter of course, the non-Communist Resistance organi-zations also changed tack as time went by. Even French movements in which individual Communists could be found alongside right-wing extrem-ist members of the "Cagoule," a fascist secret society, began ambushing

German servicemen. During the first nine months of 1943, the German authorities in France recorded 281 attempts on the lives of Germans, 97 on French policemen, and 147 on French collaborators. Statistically speaking, 53.5 percent of the incidents involved Germans, of whom as many were killed or wounded (150) as French (149).[24]

That even peaceful Denmark should have become embroiled in this diabolical game of tit for tat was probably attributable to Hitler's exasperation at the open breach that occurred late in August 1943 between his model "Germanic" protectorate and the Third Reich. At all events, he ordained early in January 1944 that Danish "terrorism" should be met with German "antiterrorism." Every Danish assassination attempt was to be repaid in kind. Not long afterward, the atrocities entailed by this projected settlement of scores were christened "clearing murders" by SS-Obergruppenführer [General] Gottlob Berger, the uncouth head of the SS Central Office in Berlin.

Hitler's "change of course" called for each Danish offense to be repaid with "five terrorist acts of equal caliber." The Danes, he insisted, were to be so thoroughly intimidated that they would eventually go down on their knees and beg the occupying power to restore order. Death sentences were ineffective and Danish martyrs undesirable. "Antiterrorism" would produce far better results.

The advocates of offensive resistance were subjected to a prolonged ordeal which began when Ole Bjørn Kraft, a leading parliamentarian, was killed by unidentified gunmen who forced their way into his home and shot him. The next victim was Kaj Munk, the widely admired Danish dramatist, also killed by persons unknown. In quick succession, attacks were made on distinguished doctors, lawyers, journalists, academics, and artists. Then time bombs started exploding in movie theaters and hotel lobbies.

We now know that the German antiterrorist squad worked to a predetermined plan. A detailed card index had been compiled of prominent figures who were to be shot in their homes or in the street, as the case might be, and of buildings suitable for bomb attacks.

In April the antiterrorist squad widened the scope of its activities to include "antisabotage acts." One outrage followed another at an ever more alarming rate.

In mid-April, a truckload of German workers was blown up. Fire broke out at a Todt Organization camp on the island of Fanø, and nineteen German vehicles were vandalized in Odense by persons unknown.

The German authorities retaliated. One student was shot and twelve death sentences were imposed. All the movie theaters in Copenhagen had to close down, travel to Sweden was banned, and postal and telephone links were severed.

A raid on a German arms and ammunition depot in the free port of Copenhagen was countered by bomb attacks on the Copenhagen students' hostel, the Tivoli, and the Royal Porcelain Factory. Officially, the occupying power retaliated with eight death sentences and executions, the introduction of courts-martial, and a movement ban on heavy goods vehicles and commercial traffic.

There followed more murders, the demolition of individual buildings and whole blocks, and the appointment of a summary court-martial which imposed another sixty-two death sentences. These measures were accompanied by an undeclared terrorist war against the Danish press, which suffered badly in the ensuing year. Bombs exploded in the pressrooms or editorial offices of sixteen provincial newspapers, putting them out of business. In the case of the liberal *Kolding Folkeblad,* the proprietor, his daughter, and a janitor all perished in the flames.

The last bomb attack on a building occurred seven weeks before Germany collapsed, the last assassination two weeks before the Wehrmacht surrendered. Where its "clearing murders" account was concerned, antiterrorist headquarters could point to a final credit balance of 797 slaughtered Danes. It had distributed inflammatory leaflets and plastered walls with fake Resistance posters calculated to spark off the disturbances required to justify antiterrorism or intensify its effects, just as it had also distributed strike calls bearing the forged signatures of Danish trade union leaders. All of this was common knowledge, however. Under the very nose of the occupying power, Danish newspapers had summoned up the courage to expose the forgeries by publishing genuine appeals for calm from the heads of the trade associations.[25]

Holland's "antiterrorist squad" chalked up over three hundred murders during 1944. In the Protectorate of Bohemia and Moravia, where the occupying power had perfectly mastered the technique of repression, no such special task force was needed. After the successful attempt on the life of Reinhard Heydrich, Reich Protector and head of the Central State Security Bureau, police and Wehrmacht units moved into the village of Lidice on Hitler's orders, shot its entire population of 173 male adults, dispatched 198 women and 98 children to the Ravensbrück concentration camp, blew up their homes, and burned the remains of the village down. The same fate befell Lezaki, a village near Louka, where the womenfolk were shot as well as the men. Hitler's order of June 15, under which thirty thousand "politically suspect" Czechs were to be shot, was canceled three days later, when Heydrich's two assassins were taken. Nevertheless, German records show that 1,357 Czechs were condemned to death and executed in the two months following the assassination. In 477 of these cases, mere approval of the deed had been enough to send a person to the firing squad.[26]

For and Against Sabotage

The irrational and inordinate brutality of Germany's occupation policy presented Resistance leaders with a serious problem. Their balance sheets disclosed some very heavy losses. Were they justified in sacrificing so many human lives for the sake of putative successes in their campaign against the occupying power? In a book published in Switzerland during the war itself, the Norwegian writer Fridtjof Fjord stated that although resistance and sabotage must always be the work of a minority, given that an entire nation could never go underground en bloc, the men and women of the Resistance badly needed to feel assured that their compatriots were in sympathy with them—that they were, in a sense, fellow residents of the Underground.[27]

But it was in Norway, of all places, that public reaction to the Resistance took an ominous turn. In October 1943, when five Norwegians were summarily shot after a German troop train had been sabotaged, thousands joined in a public demonstration against the saboteurs.[28]

The gravity of this problem was apparent at every stage.

Early in March 1941, a raiding party from the "League for Armed Struggle" (ZWZ), a forerunner of the Polish Home Army, carried out a death sentence passed by a Warsaw Underground district headquarters on Igo Sym, a collaborationist actor who directed the Warsaw Theater. Sym was gunned down in his home. The German authorities thereupon took two hundred-odd hostages, including academics, writers, doctors, artists, and young people. Twenty-one of them were summarily shot and the lives of the others hung by a thread—and all for the sake of a single collaborator.

The Polish Government-in-exile decreed that assassination attempts should henceforth be made only "in the context of self-defense." It had already, at the beginning of the war, clarified the basic question when and under what circumstances the bounds between offensive and defensive resistance were to be crossed in either direction.[29]

Its "Directive No. 1" of early December 1939 embodied the gist of instructions issued to Polish secret army commanders in mid-March 1940: isolated assassinations and acts of sabotage were strictly forbidden unless they served a strategic purpose and had been expressly ordered—as they were, for instance, at the start of the Western offensive in May 1940, after the German invasion of Russia in June 1941, and in association with heavy fighting on the Eastern Front during the fall of 1943 and early in 1944.

Despite the military success of these large-scale operations, however, the same old problem constantly recurred. Two thousand locomotives had been damaged, over 2,500 vehicles destroyed, 125 supply depots damaged by fire, and 76 trains derailed, but the Polish Resistance had sustained such heavy losses that the government-in-exile was compelled to order a total cessation of sabotage after only six weeks.[30]

At about the same time, the disastrous consequences of precipitate resistance evoked a similar reaction from leading expatriate Czech politicians including ex-President Beneš himself: they appealed to the Czech people to bide their time and avoid unnecessary loss of life.[31]

Irate Norwegians were not alone in denying that sabotage served a useful purpose and merited approval. "Anyone who tried to commit sabotage today would probably be condemned by a majority of Danes," wrote Erling Foss, one of the leaders of the Danish Resistance, in a microfilmed report smuggled from Denmark to London during January 1942. The Danish people, he went on, were almost unanimous in supporting their King, who had publicly warned them not to provoke the occupying power by engaging in acts of violence. Secret reports reaching London from Denmark during the first half of 1943 continued to stress that the Danes were not yet "ripe" for sabotage, even though clandestine Resistance newspapers were doing their best to reconcile them to this uncongenial idea. As late as May Day 1943, Socialist speakers contemptuously referred to Underground combat teams as "little groups of fanatical provocateurs."

The public mood of the time was accurately defined by Aage Petersen, who himself belonged to a sabotage team and had been present when some bridges on the southern outskirts of Randers were blown up. The Germans had promptly shot two members of the Resistance who happened to be in their custody. Petersen noted in his diary: "People are utterly scandalized. Nobody dares to shelter us. Nobody will accept an illegal newspaper. People are burning our contribution stamps. They are scared of us." It is consistent with this picture that even the Danish Communist Party did not consider forming a special sabotage group until May 1942.[32]

In reality, this was only one aspect of a far more complex problem. The very arguments that were adduced to condemn sabotage could just as easily be cited in support of it. If strategically important buildings and installations in German-occupied territory had to be attacked and destroyed, Allied air raids would be likely to inflict more civilian casualties than Underground sabotage teams.

In November 1943, 167 Flying Fortresses belonging to the U. S. Eighth Air Force dropped 414 tons of bombs on Herya, near Oslo. Shortly afterward, an even heavier bomb load rained down on Rjukan and Vemork, site of the industrial plants that manufactured the "heavy water" essential to German atomic research. The loss of life was immense; the devastation was appalling but, from a practical point of view, disappointing.

The Norwegian Government-in-exile, which had not been consulted or informed in advance about either of these raids, conveyed its grave concern to the British Foreign Secretary, Anthony Eden, and asked to be consulted about all future operations of any magnitude. More importantly, the Norwegian High Command in London agreed with Allied Headquarters that the destruction of military targets should in the future be left to sabotage teams belonging to the Norwegian secret army and the various Resistance groups.[33]

The Allied military authorities consented to a partial agreement of this kind in the case of the Peugeot Works in France, where an air raid had inflicted heavy casualties and considerable damage but failed to halt the production of tanks for the Wehrmacht. British agents got in touch with the Peugeot family, who were pro-British, and arranged that a sabotage team should lay modest demolition charges at various key points in the factories, thereby crippling production without causing severe damage and loss of life.

These carefully regulated acts of sabotage, which did not as a rule endanger the public, were advocated by numerous Resistance leaders at this period. They were also put into practice here and there, though far from universally. Henri Bernard of the Royal Military Academy in Brussels unearthed what may be a unique case and published it in his history of the European Resistance. According to him, a Belgian sabotage team consisting of scientists and highly qualified technicians, all of whom had conducted thoroughgoing research into sabotage methods, succeeded in disrupting the national high-voltage transmission system so ingeniously that the occupying power lost twenty-five million man-hours.[34]

The problem came to a head in the months preceding the Allied invasion of France. The Allied Supreme Command was planning massive air raids on ninety-three major rail junctions in France and Belgium, which were to be deluged with sixty-six thousand tons of bombs over a three-month period prior to the landings. The declared intention was to transform Normandy into a "railroad desert."

Damage in the vicinity of target areas was bound to be extensive, and civilian casualties were inevitable. In London they were estimated at 20,000 dead and 60,000 injured; in France it was feared that they would amount to 40,000 dead and 120,000 injured. Was such a massacre warranted, however strong the strategic arguments in its favor?[35]

No one took this question lightly. It was carefully studied, not only by Supreme Headquarters, Allied Expeditionary Force (SHAEF), but also by the British War Cabinet in consultation with General Bedell Smith, chief of staff to the Supreme Commander, and with Marshal of the Royal Air Force Sir Charles Portal. It also figured prominently in a remarkable exchange of letters by President Roosevelt and Winston Churchill.[36]

To begin with, the War Cabinet contained a majority against inflicting such heavy casualties on a friendly people. Churchill, too, voiced misgivings. The devastation would be all the greater because the raids were to take place at night. Who could blame the French if they entertained feelings of hatred and loathing for the British and Americans?

The high command of the French secret army was so appalled by the mere idea of this bombardment that General Pierre Koenig, who represented the French Underground forces in London, curtly told Bedell Smith, Eisenhower's chief of staff, "You name the targets and we will see that they are destroyed."[37]

Sabotage or bombing? The fear that acts of sabotage would provoke costly reprisals on the part of the occupying power now seemed less cogent than the arguments against murderous Allied saturation raids. Whoever felt he had chosen the lesser evil, however, would still have the deaths of countless innocent people on his conscience.

Early in September 1944, an Allied bomber force missed its objective and accidentally destroyed the headquarters of the Free French Forces that had by now developed out of the Resistance. General Éon, head of a French military mission in the Brittany area of operations, reported as follows to the general commanding the U. S. Twelfth Army: "Shattering effect on troops in the open, even worse on residential buildings and the civil population. A village is reduced to rubble within minutes, and bodies lie around by the hundred, but the fortifications, even the light ones, remain completely intact." Another French military delegate, Bourgès-Maunoury, radioed to London on another occasion that the air raids on Arles and Marseille would go down in history as "an atrocity committed by the Allied air forces."[38]

Where France was concerned, the decision between sabotage and bombing had been taken by mid-May 1944. At stake was the success or failure of a vast and exceptionally hazardous landing operation whose outcome would determine the duration of the war. No arguments in favor of humane restraint could prevail over the harsh exigencies of warfare. Besides, a swift victory would probably save more lives than would be lost by years of protracted fighting if the invasion went awry.

However regrettable the attendant loss of life might be, Roosevelt wrote to Churchill less than four weeks before the invasion, he was not prepared to subject his commanders to restrictions that might in their view militate against the success of the operation or inflict additional loss of life on the Allied forces.

"This was decisive," Churchill commented in his history of the war. In the event, French civilian casualties proved lighter than everyone had feared. Meanwhile, by sealing off the Normandy battlefield from enemy reinforcement, Allied bombers vitally contributed to the success of the whole operation. "The price," wrote Churchill, "was paid."[39]

The "Secret Armies"

Nations arose and took up arms. Freedom fighters—Underground warriors numbering over half a million in Western Europe alone—threw off the tyrant's yoke, liberated towns and villages, and meted out due punishment to traitors. . . . Medal ribbons and memoirs, monuments and memorials, countless works of history and literature bear witness to this blend of fact and fiction.

Why fiction? Because the story was not as simple as that. No ready-made force or partisan army, no paramilitary unit or makeshift militia ever sprang into being overnight.

The expression "secret army," which was coined by the European Resistance movements themselves, is misleading. Henri Frenay, who built up the secret army of the leading Resistance organization "Combat," and thus made an outstanding contribution to the "French Forces of the Interior" (FFI), stated in a confidential report dated May 20, 1943, that the term "secret army" had caused confusion.

"We have forged no army," he wrote. "This term summons up the picture of a well-organized, mobile, close-knit mass which blindly obeys any conceivable order. In reality, we have raised bands of partisans who would still sooner fight for their own liberties than against the outside enemy."[40]

At the same time, Frenay was a professional soldier whose own secret army was organized on military lines, even if the nature of its clandestine campaign necessitated careful concealment. The same applied to nearly all the so-called secret armies in occupied territory. With the sole exception of Tito, it was professional army officers who took the initiative in building up illegal combat organizations: General Ruge, the ex-commander in chief, in Norway; Colonel Bassin, General Gérard, and other officers in Belgium; Colonel (later General) Mihailović and his Chetnik officers in Yugoslavia; Generals Zervas and Saraphis, and Colonel Psarros in Greece; and General Tokarzewski and fifteen staff officers in Poland. Similarly, the formation, training, and operations of Soviet partisans were directed by a general staff based in Moscow.

Most parallel organizations of a military nature followed the same pattern. Frenay's secret army was placed under the command of General Delestraint. The military organization known as ORA (Organisation de Résistance de l'Armée), which grew out of the French treaty army, was commanded prior to his arrest by General Frère, then by General Verneau, and finally by General Revers. Though not a professional soldier, the chief of staff of the Communist secret army FTP (Francs-Tireurs et Partisans Français) was a general staff officer, Professor Marcel Prenant.

Even the National Military Committee of the French Communist Party originally included a Colonel Dumont,[41] and another professional soldier, Major of Artillery (ret.) Lucien Caré, was one of the founders and senior members of the Communist sabotage organization OS (Organisation Spéciale).[42]

The role of professional soldiers in the European Resistance movement is frequently underrated. It is seldom mentioned, for example, that two of the three founders of the celebrated Paris Resistance organization "Musée de l'Homme," whose members included ethnologists, scientists, university teachers, poets, and authors belonging to the *Nouvelle Revue Française* circle, were Colonels La Rochère and Hauet, both of them regular soldiers.[43]

Little wonder, therefore, that the paramilitary Resistance organizations set up by military experts, much as they varied from country to country, betrayed an expert touch.

Founded in the fall of 1940, the Norwegian secret army MILORG was divided into five military regions and twenty-two districts, each of which had its own recruiting center, a director of military training, a separate logistical organization, and a force of secret security police. MILORG ran sixteen small, well-camouflaged arms factories and employed reserve officers to work out contingency plans for secret mobilization. Late in 1941, it was subordinated to the Norwegian High Command in London. Its strength in the fall of that year was twenty-five thousand volunteers. This number rose during the next three years to thirty-five thousand and attained a maximum of forty-seven thousand at the end of the war.[44]

The various paramilitary organizations that grew up in Belgium styled themselves "armies" even before they merged to form the Belgian secret army proper. Apart from the latter, which the London-based government-in-exile recognized as its only legal armed force, there were two other bodies of note: the "Belgian Partisan Army" (and its commando-style "Milices Patriotes"), which was closely associated with the Communist Party, and the "Belgian Legion," which was founded by reserve officers and later absorbed into the official secret army. Reportedly distributed throughout the country were seventy-five secret mobilization centers equipped with dugouts capable of accommodating one thousand men apiece. In addition, each of the five military districts possessed a proper airfield, secret airdrop zones, and dugout shelters for guerrilla units, all of which had to be inspected and approved by delegates from the government-in-exile. The official secret army alone is reported to have numbered forty-five thousand men, of whom five thousand—mainly engineer and signals officers, technical experts, and three hundred parachutists—were divided into special sabotage teams. Belgium was, incidentally, the one country whose civilian and military Resistance organizations were kept strictly separate and assigned to different ministries-in-exile.[45]

France, too, saw the growth of clandestine combat formations such as the "United Resistance Movements" (MUR), the purely military "Army Resistance Organization" (ORA), and the Communist "French Irregulars and Partisans" (FTP), all of which officially merged early in February 1944. Having been formed by this simple process of amalgamation, the "French Forces of the Interior" (FFI) were then restructured like a proper army, with national, regional, and departmental command centers and twelve military districts subordinate to a general staff. Overall command of the FFI was assumed—though not until the Allies had landed in Normandy—by General Koenig, who had previously spent some months as military delegate to the Provisional French Government in London. The significant feature in France was that paramilitary combat units and the secret army proper had all been spawned by civilian Resistance movements and retained close links with them until the end of the war.

The civilian movements developed independently because of France's division into an occupied and an unoccupied zone. The Resistance was ultimately shaped by three organizations in each of these zones: in unoccupied France by Henri Frenay's "Combat," by the socialist- and trade-union-oriented movement known as "Libération," and by a heterogeneous activist group styling itself the "Francs-Tireurs"; and in occupied France by the "Civil and Military Organization" (OCM), founded by a group of ex-officers, by the socialist- and trade-union-led "Libération-Nord," and by the Communist "National Front." In March 1943, the three southern organizations merged into the aforesaid "United Resistance Movements" (MUR), a body dominated by the numerical preponderance of Frenay's "Combat."

Typical in many ways of this remarkably intimate connection between military and civilian resistance are the "Combat" organization and its originator, once a brilliant graduate of Saint-Cyr, the military academy founded by Napoleon Bonaparte.

Frenay had wept as he ordered the destruction of his unit's guns, colors, and encoding machine after hearing Marshal Pétain's surrender broadcast while encircled in the Vosges with the French XLIII Corps. Determined to avoid capture, he walked by night for three weeks until he crossed the demarcation line. No sooner had he reached his mother's home in the South of France than he proceeded to draw up structural plans for a Resistance movement. In so doing, he defined five separate functions.

The first step was to recruit kindred spirits; the second to weld them together by organizational means. Thirdly, illegal propaganda would be used to swell the movement's ranks and boost the morale of those who were still of two minds. Next, the enemy had to be kept under surveillance and his strengths and weaknesses probed by a secret intelligence service. Finally, consideration would be given to building up an armed force or "secret army." Every form of resistance, from the symbolic to the offensive, was thus to be practiced under central control. The creation of a "secret army" was only one task among several.

The plan soon took shape and was put into effect, step by step. Frenay contacted all the trustworthy friends he could reach and persuaded many of them to join him—to pass on his ideas and recruit friends of their own who could later be entrusted with special assignments. No one was to venture outside his own immediate circle. Each group of six formed an isolated and undetectable stronghold, and only one of the six had access to his superior, who in turn controlled only five groups of six—in other words, a unit of thirty conspirators. These larger units, all as unknown to each other as their constituent groups, were linked to a secret communications network of regional and departmental magnitude, and thus maintained indirect contact with an operational and administrative headquarters which was naturally sited in the farthest and darkest recesses of the Underground.

Within this basic structure, various tasks were allotted to various groups. The secret intelligence service, which was the first to function, established contact with London at the end of January 1941. Operating under the code name "Kasanga," it later supplied a weekly average of two hundred closely written pages of military information. It also employed over seven hundred permanent and part-time informants, of whom twenty-four were captured and shot by the occupying power.[46]

Another group handled the editing, printing, and distribution of clandestine publications and leaflets. It also brought out the Resistance newspaper *Combat,* which attained a circulation of 40,000 in 1942 and 250,000 two years later.[47]

Surreptitious industrial sabotage was coordinated by a "workers' operation," the sabotaging of railroads and other installations of use to the occupying power by another special section organized on military lines.[48]

Overt acts of violence intended to jolt and rouse the public, as well as coordinated bomb attacks, assassinations, and punitive expeditions against collaborators and enemy agents, were carried out by "Groupes francs," or special task forces recruited for that purpose.[49]

Other groups were responsible for the manufacture of false papers, for concealment and subsistence in the Underground, and for supporting the dependents of colleagues who had been arrested or executed. Others, again, organized the infiltration of the public services, ran the overseas courier service, supplied the Maquis, and, last but not least, administered the so-called Secret Army.

"Combat's" organization chart for March 1943, which Frenay published after the war, clearly illustrates the equal and parallel status of its political and military wings. The Secret Army is shown as only one of four subsections in the "Military Affairs" branch. Almost as if "Combat" were an independent state, its leader maintained relations with the Western

Powers' diplomatic agencies in Bern, with their intelligence services, with the intelligence service of the Swiss armed forces, and with the International Committee of the Red Cross in Geneva. Frenay himself and four of his associates later belonged to the directorial committee of the first Provisional French Government, whose Foreign Minister was Georges Bidault, president of the National Security Council.

The invisible strength of "Combat's" secret army was estimated at fifteen thousand in September 1942 and eighty thousand in June 1943.[50]

It was not, of course, a standing force of well-armed, well-trained soldiers, but a body of volunteers who would turn out for duty on demand. It did, however, possess the organizational framework and infrastructure required to mobilize paramilitary guerrilla units.

If Frenay had not said so himself, it would seem incredible that even in March 1943, when its organization chart listed fourteen national departments, "Combat" got by with only 102 permanent staff, all of them residents of the Underground.[51]

Frenay had no illusions about what could be expected of such a "secret army." He assigned it three tasks: first, the immediate "neutralization" of selected industrial plants (sabotage); second, on the day Allied forces landed, the disruption or destruction of overland supply lines used by the Wehrmacht; and, third, after the invasion, the disruption of German troop movements by means of continuous harassment on the part of organized guerrilla units.[52]

The commander of the Belgian secret army, General Gérard, was thinking along similar lines. He hoped that, once his men had been mobilized and deployed in their prepared dugouts and mobilization centers, the Allies would supply them with arms by air. They would then, as it were, adopt the role of paratroops dropped behind the German lines and disrupt the enemy's troop movements and lines of communication.[53]

We can correctly assess the achievements of the "secret armies" only if we clearly recognize that they did not resemble armies in the conventional sense. Cadres and infrastructures apart, they lacked almost everything that goes to make up a modern fighting force. They were wretchedly ill-armed or not armed at all. Scantily equipped and inadequately trained, they were a motley assortment of men, the bulk of whom had fled to the *maquis,* or "scrub," from which the French guerrillas took their name.

As soon as the occupying power started hunting down conscripts for forced labor in Germany, many young Frenchmen sought refuge in the mountains, individually or in small groups. They threaded their way from village to village, sometimes with the aid of a password, sometimes directed or guided by unarmed middlemen, until they reached an assembly point where they were met and interrogated by other young men, examined on their bona fides, and finally "accepted." Quickly recognizing that an ideal field for recruitment was opening up, the various Resistance movements set to work to organize the Maquis.

Less than one third of France's territory was occupied by German forces, they pointed out. The bulk of it was administered and controlled by French collaborators—Vichy officials and their notorious militia—under the watchful gaze of German agents. The task of the Maquis was to gain control of these 150,000 square miles. Liberating the rest would be up to the Allied invasion forces.

The Maquis proper consisted of "camps"—mountain cabins, stables, charcoal burners' shacks, caves, or subterranean dugouts. The larger camps housed as many as five or six hundred men. Henri Amouroux describes how the men of the Souesmes Maquis constructed twenty or thirty huts of branches woven in two layers and tightly packed with foliage. These huts were linked by communication trenches five feet deep and enclosed by a circular perimeter trench. The Maquis kept their "transportation fleet" inside the huts themselves. It comprised sixty or seventy bicycles and half a dozen motorcycles, but not a single car.

The men were dependent on friendly farmers for their food, but they also acquired much of what they needed by means of theft or "confiscation." Many of them preferred to go hungry.

Arms were in very short supply. Some camps had only a handful of rifles, but others were better equipped. According to Amouroux, the one hundred and fifty members of a Maquis in the Creuse district possessed an arsenal of thirty-five revolvers, thirteen rifles, three submachine guns, and six grenades.

The Maquis generally began their day at six-thirty, when reveille was followed by camp chores. Twice a day, one or two hours were devoted to fieldcraft, crawling, camouflage, mock attacks in forest clearings or open country, and—from the summer of 1944, when the Allies began to airdrop arms on an extensive scale—to training in the use of submachine guns, explosives, and other military equipment. The hours of darkness, during which a strict blackout was observed, were devoted to combat or reconnaissance patrols, foraging expeditions, sabotage, and assassination.

It is recorded that seven thousand individual attacks, six thousand on Frenchmen and one thousand on Germans, were carried out in six weeks (mid-May to the end of July 1944) in the South of France alone.

In February 1944, the Maquisards of Beyssenac were attacked by SS units based at Limoges. Fighting continued for hours, but the Maquis commander later reported that his unit had been completely wiped out "without even wounding a single SS man."[54]

Hundreds of miles to the east, similar guerrilla bands took shape in the wooded country southwest of Prague, in eastern Moravia, and in the Baltic States. These, too, consisted mainly of young men who had taken to the forests rather than do forced labor, and their numbers were augmented by escaped Russian prisoners of war.[55]

It was no easy task to weld these recruits into an effective paramilitary fighting force. Research has also disclosed that each full-time member of a French Maquis cost the Resistance organization supporting him between 600 and 2,300 francs a month.[56]

How many Maquisards were there in all?

In latter years, historians have thrown out some of the more fanciful statistics that were current for so long. With remarkable attention to detail, they have collated extant records and data, compared contemporary estimates, and compiled lists of all the Maquis camps, Resistance movements, armed and unarmed Resistance fighters, and paramilitary units whose existence has been officially verified. It may now be assumed with a high degree of probability that, in 1944, the Maquisards of the South of France numbered approximately twenty-two thousand.[57] Reliable estimates for the whole of France in March 1944 point to a figure between thirty and forty thousand.[58]

Figures now available indicate that in July 1944 France had a total of 821 Resistance "centers," only some of which had previously existed as Maquis of the sort described by Amouroux. Then top secret, an official estimate based on innumerable intelligence reports collated by Allied Supreme Headquarters puts the total number of resisters mobilized throughout France on July 11, 1944, or exactly five weeks after the invasion, at 393,470, though only 116,215 of these, or less than 30 percent, possessed firearms of their own. The remaining 277,255 were either unarmed or, at best, armed with pistols. More detailed figures may be found on pages 326–27.[59]

So there were 400,000 Resistance fighters—an impressive number, even if most of them were unarmed. Some critics have wondered how many of them were Frenchmen who did not join in until the worst was over— "Resistance fighters of August 32," as they were sarcastically known in France.

Gordon Wright of Stanford University puts the figure still higher but also points out that even the most liberal estimate cannot disguise the fact that less than 2 percent of the adult French population belonged to the Resistance. The former chief of staff of the French Underground's military intelligence service goes so far as to opine that there were no more than 45,000 "true Resistance fighters" in the whole of France, or 0.15 percent of the adult population. The commander of the German Security Police in Holland came to a similar conclusion. He estimated that less than 1,200 Dutchmen, or 1 in every 5,000 adults, were exclusively engaged in resistance before June 1944.[60]

These estimates probably come close to the truth, given that they relate to cadre members. At the same time—to take only one example—Henri

Frenay's permanent staff could fall back at a moment's notice on many, many thousands of people who, though not "professional" *résistants,* periodically took part in limited operations and held themselves in readiness for the day when they would stand forth and prove their mettle as full-fledged Resistance fighters. For hundreds of thousands of Frenchmen and Frenchwomen, this day dawned in June 1944, when troops of the Western Alliance breached the Atlantic Wall in Normandy. Then, 2 percent of the adult population showed themselves ready to wage overt and armed resistance. Before that, resistance had been the business of a small minority. Henri Michel and other leading authorities on the subject have often stressed this unpalatable truth.

Ill fed and living in hazardous conditions, the original Maquisards found themselves abruptly inflated into a sort of "people's army." The problems arising from this sudden metamorphosis could not be resolved in the brief time available after June 1944. Furthermore, even the existing groups did not form close-knit units, so many fought against as well as alongside each other.

Two thousand escaped Russian prisoners of war—officers and enlisted men—banded themselves together into a Soviet partisan regiment under a general staff of their own. An isolated but compact fighting force, they helped to liberate the city of Nîmes. Other Red Army men were represented in thirty-five different units of the French secret army. They, too, had managed to escape from German prisoner-of-war camps on French soil, which in 1943 housed approximately twenty-five thousand Russian soldiers.[61]

Of the eighty thousand Poles who had fought on the French side in 1940—five whole divisions, of which two escaped to England and one to Switzerland—many were still active in the ranks of the French Resistance.[62] Other foreign recruits included German, Italian, Czech, and Spanish anti-fascists, Dutchmen, Belgians, and refugees from many other countries. Although this caused innumerable problems, the overnight emergence of solidarity among the heterogeneous components of the European Resistance was a tremendous boost to morale.

On the other hand, the various national movements were ideologically split. Clashes soon occurred between Communist and non-Communist groups—irreconcilable rivals and antagonists whose eyes were fixed on the future. This friction was mildest in the old-established Northern European democracies of Norway, Denmark, and Holland, more intense in Belgium and France, and marked by savage, bloodthirsty fighting in Poland and the Balkans. Most Western Communist movements isolated themselves from the rest, conserved their strength, and prepared to step in and establish regimes of their own in the power vacuum that would result when Germany collapsed. Certain other Resistance groups led by ex-officers resolved to prevent this.

Although the Communist Resistance movements took a considerable time to become active after Hitler violated his pact with the Soviet Union, they managed to assume a dominant role. The Belgian Communist "Independence Front" (FI), with its secret army and "Milices Patriotes," developed into the country's strongest Resistance movement. In France the Communists secured a majority on the Departmental Liberation Committees and also gained control of the Military Committee of the "National Resistance Council" (CNR), formed in the spring of 1943. In Italy, approximately 40 percent of freedom fighters belonged to the predominantly Communist "Garibaldi" partisans.

These successes were attributable not only to efficiency, discipline, and fanatical self-sacrifice, but also to the Soviet Union's reputation, among Communists and non-Communists alike, as the premier Resistance power. In addition, universal criticism of prewar regimes in occupied countries—regimes that were blamed for their military defeat—aroused nebulous but fervent revolutionary expectations to which even anti-Communist professional soldiers like Henri Frenay were not immune.

The National Congress of Frenay's "Combat" movement, an amalgam of socialists and trade union leaders as well as ex-officers, technocrats, industrialists, and intellectuals, met at Algiers in August 1944. It unanimously adopted a "revolutionary charter of free people," one of whose avowed aims was "the destruction of the bourgeois spirit"—a spirit allegedly characterized by fear, egoism, conformism, and love of order at any price. The same statement of principle went on to demand that the production and distribution of goods be entirely subordinated to consumption "on the ruins of capitalism," that total freedom should prevail, and that all who lied to the public should in the future be punishable by law.[63]

Such were the high-flown ideas, and such the consoling dreams of the future, with which many Resistance fighters embarked on the final battle, either in or in concert with their national secret armies.

Armed Resistance and Its Handicaps

Before that day came, however, the European Resistance movements had a long and arduous road to travel. Every country presented its own set of difficulties, and almost every one had a special handicap to be surmounted.

Holland's handicap was her terrain. She was almost completely cut off from the rest of the world, geographically and militarily. Fifty thousand Norwegians made good their escape to Sweden or Britain and over thirty thousand Frenchmen to Spain, but less than a thousand Dutchmen escaped to England across the North Sea or to Switzerland through occupied territory. Holland was longer out of touch with the free world than any other occupied country.

The Dutch Resistance took nearly two years to set up a reliable courier service to Sweden and even longer to set up a reliable communications link with Switzerland. It was two years before the first Dutch Resistance newspaper reached London and three years before the Dutch secret intelligence service could be said to have made a serious start on useful work for the Allies. For eighteen months, from mid-1942 to April 1944, German Military Intelligence virtually paralyzed communications between the Dutch Resistance and the outside world by means of "Operation North Pole," of which more will be said at a later stage.[64]

So Holland's most active organization, the "Resistance Council" (RvZ), whose two thousand members operated throughout the country in groups of three, was isolated from the outside world, dependent on its own resources, and confined to sabotaging German military installations. Aided when necessary by the large-scale Underground relief organizations, and joined in the summer of 1942 by one of the smaller Communist sabotage teams, the RvZ built up an astonishing record of achievement.[65]

Its worst handicap, as we have already said, was that the open plains of Holland did not lend themselves to guerrilla warfare. This was why the "Internal Netherlands Armed Forces," command of which was assumed by Prince Bernhard, attained no military importance after their belated formation in September 1944.

The same went for Denmark, as all the leaders of the principal sabotage organizations agree in their war memoirs.[66] Here, however, the Resistance suffered from an additional problem: it could not legitimize itself.

In whose name could the Danish Resistance claim to be acting?

Born in opposition to official policy, it had nothing to invoke—neither a government-in-exile nor a moral obligation to bear arms against a neighboring country with which Denmark was not even at war. In practical terms, the Danish Resistance organizations were sustained by individual citizens who assumed full responsibility for breaking the laws of the land, defying their own authorities, and rebelling against an occupying power to which their government, with parliamentary approval, had granted certain powers and prerogatives. Even the political parties failed to relieve them of this responsibility, so it remained their self-imposed task to combat and agitate against the convenient fiction of Danish neutrality. In this case, the scope for offensive resistance was smaller than usual.

Not until the fall of 1943, after Denmark's open breach with Nazi Germany, could thought be given to the recruitment of clandestine armed forces. By the spring of 1944, their framework was complete.

They consisted of two paramilitary organizations which were founded at roughly the same time and then, after a fairly short interval, subordinated to the Danish "Freedom Council." This had itself been founded in September 1943, and was the product of a merger between the country's major Resistance organizations, Communist groups included. The leaders of the two "secret armies" had twenty-five thousand men under their command by January 1944 and roughly forty-five thousand in the closing days of the war.[67]

Norway suffered from a different problem, namely, the simultaneous existence of several secret armies. Norway's MILORG had a British rival in the Special Operations Executive, an organization originally set up to aid the formation of secret armed forces in all the occupied countries. Where Norway was concerned, the SOE began by totally ignoring MILORG, which was already in process of formation.

Having founded a Norwegian section in London at the beginning of January 1942, the SOE proceeded to build up an on-the-spot organization of its own. In the course of the year, twenty-one British-trained Norwegian SOE men were parachuted into the country, where the organization maintained thirteen radio stations in addition to the sixteen simultaneously working for Britain's Secret Intelligence Service. The SOE not only mounted commando and sabotage operations but trained a force of guerrillas designed to do useful work—under British command—when the Allies reinvaded Norway.

This juxtaposition of mutually evasive and mistrustful organizations took its toll—so much so that in the summer of 1942 MILORG seriously considered disbanding its skeleton establishment. It was not until May 1943, when both parties had suffered grave reverses, that they finally came to terms.

Before that happened, however, a Gestapo team unearthed an SOE arms and ammunition dump at Televaag, together with a clandestine radio station. An SOE radio operator and two Gestapo officers were killed in the ensuing shoot-out, eighteen members of the Underground organization captured and executed, all the buildings in Televaag razed to the ground, all the local fishing boats sunk, seventy-two male inhabitants sent to a concentration camp in Germany, and the remaining two hundred and sixty interned in Norway. During October and December, the Gestapo netted forty-two leading members of MILORG, thirty-four of whom were executed.[68]

There could be no further justification for frittering away scarce resources, human and material. In 1944, when Norway resumed a certain role in the Western Allies' strategic calculations, the long-forged agreement to cooperate began to bear fruit. MILORG units were more generously supplied with arms by the SOE. Thanks to 1,241 Allied airdrops of which 717 landed on target, MILORG not only received explosives, ammunition, uniforms, radio sets, and medical supplies, but was reinforced by hundreds of trained agents. These consignments were supplemented by others smuggled across the Swedish border or delivered by sea (194 secret landings were made in a single year).[69] The possibility that paramilitary units might take part in the liberation of Norway, too, was at last in the cards.

The major handicap of the Italian Resistance, universally present and effective but seldom reducible to a common denominator, was rooted in its own history.

Resistance in the true sense could not rear its head until the outcome of the war was decided. Allied armies were already on Italian soil and the Fascist regime had collapsed before the first Italian partisans could think of taking up arms. Moreover, the country's recent history had been enacted against the backcloth of a Fascist dictatorship which dissolved itself with positively Latin elegance and briefly survived its downfall in the bloodthirsty puppet republic of Salò, Mussolini's rump state in the north of Italy.

Rudiments of a Resistance movement had existed under Mussolini ever since December 1942, when Communists, Socialists, and Liberals united to form a "National Action Front." Thereafter, the anti-Fascist parties had published illegal newspapers on a monthly or semi-monthly basis. They were not, however, behind the industrially motivated strikes that hit Turin, Milan, and Genoa in March 1943, nor did they bring about the collapse of Fascism. It was the Fascist Grand Council itself which effectively passed a vote of no confidence in Mussolini on July 25, 1943. Mussolini submitted his resignation to the King, who accepted it and had him arrested. Only when the Italians unconditionally surrendered did the Wehrmacht occupy their major cities and disarm their fighting forces, and only then could resistance to yesterday's ally—the German occupying power—come into its own.[70]

The political foundations of the Resistenza had been laid by anti-Fascist refugees abroad. Exiled Republicans, Socialists, Communists, and Liberals had agreed that close cooperation by all anti-Fascist forces was essential. With this thought in mind, they returned to Italy after the fall of Fascism.

There followed violent and spontaneous eruptions of activity on the part of large-scale partisan movements whose emergence conflicted with the expectations and intentions of the Allied powers.[71]

Its origins speak for themselves. Resistance arose when Allied prisoners of war, who were the targets of a particularly unbridled Fascist hate campaign, needed assistance. A few thousand bold and battle-hardened Yugoslavs, Russians, and Czechs—their precise number has never been ascertained—elected not to go home or rejoin their units. Instead, they joined the earliest Italian partisan units, which were just being formed, and gave them an injection of the military élan and experience they so urgently needed. Meanwhile, town and country were in turmoil, as were the universities of Tuscany and the north. Groups took shape, and from them sprang

King Christian X of Denmark used to astonish the German authorities by riding through the streets unescorted and passing the time of day with his subjects. He and his government practiced tactical collaboration as a special form of resistance. They managed to collaborate and resist simultaneously, forever giving ground or standing firm at the psychological moment.

The success or failure of tactical collaboration depended on the willingness of the occupying power to grant national governments a measu~
of sovereignty. This was so in Denmark. Under the auspices of the German Foreign Office and of Werner Best (above), the Reic~
Plenipotentiary, the Danish authorities gained sufficient scope for years of semi-independent action.

Jewish women and girls in the Jewish Council sewing room at a theater building in Amsterdam, the hub of Holland's Jewish community and a provincial deportation center. They are refurbishing old clothes for the needy internees of the Westerbork camp—and waiting, like them, for "resettlement" in the great unknown. The Jewish Council of Holland was a vast organization employing up to 17,500 helpers.

The best of Jewish citizens were impelled to collaborate and work with the Jewish Council by moral constraint, a religious duty to succor those in distress, or the hope of preserving their community from destruction and saving lives. The Council's social services covered education and guidance, legal and medical facilities, child welfare, and clothing distribution centers for the destitute (above).

The Dutch "Jewish Council," an organization which was forced, for good or ill, to cooperate with the authors and instruments of the "Final Solution." Tactical collaboration, whether demanded or extorted by the occupying power, was always intended as an aid to the persecuted, never to Hitler and his regime. Jewish Councils were also active in ghettos and extermination camps.

A "flying squad" of Jewish police auxiliaries at Westerbork, the Dutch camp where batches of prisoners were assembled for forwarding to extermination camps. The Jewish police force, a legally constituted body, performed a dual service for the Jews and their murderers. Like the Jewish Council, its members ended up in gas chambers and mass graves. Till then, they sent others to their deaths.

Hand-knitted caps in the colors of the Royal Air Force. Thousands copied the Dane who hit on this idea. The caps became a profession of faith, a symbol of resistance, and a token of their wearers' consoling knowledge that they were spiritually at one with the free world.

The statue of the Dutch Queen Mother, smothered in flowers and surrounded by a large crowd of loyal citizens. All over Holland, m
women, and children celebrated the twenty-ninth birthday of Prince Bernhard, in exile in London, by wearing his favorite flower
carnation, in their hair or buttonhole — a massive and spontaneous display of symbolic resistance only seven weeks after Holla

...rrendered. Similar demonstrations were held on a Sunday evening in September 1940 by two million Danes—two thirds of the population ...ver the age of fourteen—who gathered to sing folk songs in the squares of villages and towns throughout the land. Here too, symbolic ...sistance helped to salve the wounded pride of an outraged nation.

The scuttling of the French fleet at Toulon on November 27, 1942, sixteen days after the Germans marched into unoccupied France. By staging this spectacular display, the Navy opted for symbolic resistance instead of sailing for Africa and joining forces with the Allies.

Symbolic resistance in Prague on the anniversary of the Munich Agreement. Normally crowded, the streetcars are running empty — boycotted in response to an appeal from two Resistance groups. The dismembered Czechoslovak Republic gives a mute and eerie demonstration of unbroken national pride.

ompulsory labor service and the deportation of young men to Germany for forced labor sparked off an exodus to remote areas of mountain d forest which became known as the *maquis* (originally, bush or scrub). Small groups of evaders gathered in makeshift camps like the one ove, later to organize themselves into Resistance combat units.

Countless fugitives and advocates of defensive resistance in the occupied territories of Europe went underground in the literal sense. Conservative estimates of the Dutch Underground population, two of whom are pictured above, range between two and three hundred housand. Poland had a complete "shadow state" with its own army, civil service, schools, and universities.

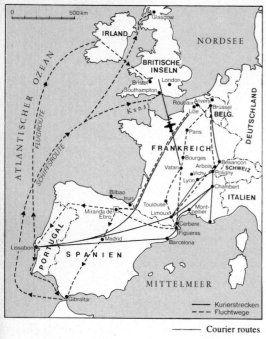

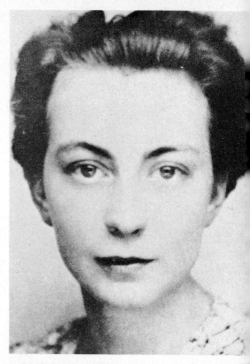

Escape networks, which fulfilled a purely defensive function, sneaked escaped prisoners of war and Allied airmen into Spain and back to England by secret routes.

Andrée Dejongh (above), a twenty-three-year-old Belgian girl organized the first escape network. Three thousand strande Allied airmen made it back to England.

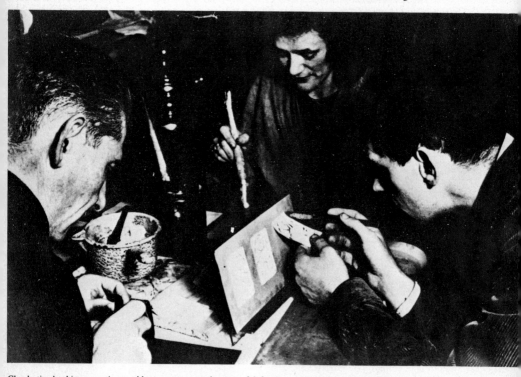

Clandestine banking operations and loans were as much a part of defensive resistance as the workshops that forged identity cards, rubber stamps, signatures, and official documents (see picture), or the armed raiders who seized ration cards for members of the Underground or destroyed lists of names and addresses that might have been useful to the German Security Police.

Hitler's Europe was deluged with Underground leaflets, pamphlets, and news sheets. Over a thousand Resistance newspapers were printed in Holland, as many again in France, and 852 in Norway and Denmark. Handwritten chain letters were followed by the products of secret amateur presses (above) and eventually by huge editions of newspapers devoted to argument, protest, and information.

Poets, novelists, and publishing houses went underground, eager — in the words of the French poet Paul Éluard — to rediscover "free expression" under German occupation. Intellectuals and artists, who were particularly hard hit by Nazi tyranny, joined distinguished writers like Louis Aragon and Elsa Triolet (above) in becoming spokesmen for the Resistance.

Albert Camus, co-founder of the clandestine newspaper *Combat* and Nobel laureate in 1957, produced his novel *L'Étranger* and his main philosophical work during the Resistance era.

Paul Eluard (above) wrote "Liberté," the celebrated Resistance poem, in 1940. Éditions de Minuit, the underground publishing house co-founded by Vercors, published his novel *La Silence de la mer* in 1942.

A TOUS LES FRANÇAIS

La France a perdu une bataille!
Mais la France n'a pas perdu la guerre!

Des gouvernants de rencontre ont pu capituler, cédant à la panique, oubliant l'honneur, livrant le pays à la servitude. Cependant, rien n'est perdu!

Rien n'est perdu, parce que cette guerre est une guerre mondiale. Dans l'univers libre, des forces immenses n'ont pas encore donné. Un jour, ces forces écraseront l'ennemi. Il faut que la France, ce jour-là, soit présente à la victoire. Alors, elle retrouvera sa liberté et sa grandeur. Tel est mon but, mon seul but!

Voilà pourquoi je convie tous les Francais, où qu'ils se trouvent, à s'unir à moi dans l'action, dans le sacrifice et dans l'espérance.

Notre patrie est en péril de mort.
Luttons tous pour la sauver!

VIVE LA FRANCE !

GÉNÉRAL DE GAULLE

QUARTIER-GÉNÉRAL,
4, CARLTON GARDENS,
LONDON, S.W.1

Inspiring words from general de Gaulle, whose appeal to the French people to fight on, broadcast from London on June 18, 1940, was not widely heard. France had lost a battle, he declared, but not the war. The enemy would one day be crushed by the vast and uncommitted forces of the free world. France must be in at the death, ready to regain her liberty and greatness.

Henry Frenay, head of one of the foremost Resistance organizations in occupied France.

General Delestraint, De Gaulle's onetime superior, assumed command of the "secret army" in 1943.

General Koenig, commander in chief of the French Forces of the Interior after D-Day.

STRUCTURE OF THE "COMBAT" ORGANIZATION

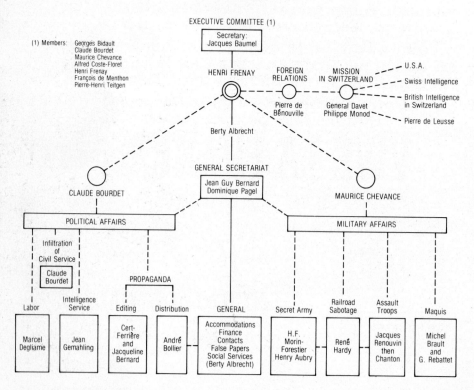

Structure of the "Combat" Resistance organization. Political and military affairs enjoyed precisely equal status. The executive body had a permanent staff of 102, all drawn from the Underground. Five members of the Executive Committee later joined the first French Provisional Government, among them Henri Frenay and Foreign Minister Georges Bidault.

The Czech parachute agent Jan Kubis, trained at a British center for "ungentlemanly warfare," threw the grenade that fatally wounded Reinhard Heydrich, Reich Protector and head of the German Security Police.

Four Czechs, parachuted into the Protectorate with arms and radio sets, were assigned to kill Heydrich. Jan Kubis did the job with a grenade when Josef Gabcik (above) found his submachine gun jammed.

SS officers standing over the dead assassins in their hideout, the catacombs of an Orthodox church in Prague. The German authorities, who had offered a reward of one million reichsmarks for their capture, found a convenient traitor. They then retaliated by arresting 3,000 innocent civilians and members of the Czech Underground and sentencing 1,357 to death.

Sabotage or aerial bombardment—a problem that exercised the European Resistance movements and the Allied Supreme Command. Allied saturation raids inflicted heavy casualties on the civilian population; organized sabotage provoked German reprisals which likewise claimed the lives of many ordinary people.

The hydraulic plant at Rjukan in Norway manufactured the heavy water required for German atomic research. Norwegian sabotage teams succeeded where Allied bombers had failed. They not only crippled production but destroyed irreplaceable stocks of heavy water bound for Germany.

the smaller combat units that now attempted to gain control of villages, roads, and mountain valleys.

The political parties strove to exert a coordinative influence on this chaotic popular movement. Whereas Resistance movements in other countries had taken years to achieve political fusion, the process was complete only twelve days after Italy's declaration of war on Nazi Germany, less than five weeks after her surrender to the Allies, and despite the political and ideological differences between one group or party and another. In Rome the parties jointly formed a "National Liberation Committee" (CLN) made up of such prominent figures as De Gasperi and Gronchi, Romita and La Malfa, Amendola and Nenni. Soon afterward, Milan became the headquarters of a similar political lineup known as the "National Liberation Council for Northern Italy" (CLNAI), which established a permanent delegation in Lugano, just across the Swiss border, at the end of March 1944.[72]

So the Resistenza was animated by a strong tendency toward offensive resistance from the very first. What became of it?

In the south, regular Italian Army units amounting to roughly one division fought alongside Allied ground forces.[73] In the north, despite their formal amalgamation, the Resistance and partisan groups split up into a multitude of independent entities. Almost every place of any size had its own liberation committee, and every committee had a secret local fighting force obedient to the orders of the predominant political party or coalition. Although everyone shared a common commitment to the dual aim of liberating his town, district, or province from the Germans and the Fascist regime, there was no political or military authority that could have welded such a random and diverse alliance into a unified and compact secret army.

In this state of chaos, two attempts to steer offensive resistance in a particular direction came to nothing. One aimed at a revolutionary upheaval timed to coincide with liberation, and the other at the immediate establishment of a democratic system on every patch of liberated soil.

The revolutionary movements petered out because the Soviet Union and the Italian Communist Party thought it expedient to team up with conservative forces, so the relatively strong Communist partisan units were politically neutralized.

The democratic movements succeeded in founding fifteen small and thirteen larger partisan republics during the summer and fall of 1944, but only briefly. The most prominent of them, the so-called Republic of Ossola, was administered by a provisional government comprising four representatives of the bourgeois parties, two Socialists, and one Communist. This miniature republic, which commanded a strategically important area of just over six hundred square miles and a population of eighty-two thousand, owed its precarious existence to a force of between 3,500 and

4,000 partisans. After a life span of only forty-three days, it was recaptured by the Germans. The partisans of Ossola were crushed in two weeks' fighting by twelve thousand members of the German armed forces and police.[74]

Allied assistance, though ardently desired and expected, was not forthcoming. Events in Italy showed, yet again, that all Resistance movements were ultimately and wholly dependent on the grace and favor of the Allies. Not until December 1944, when the principles governing cooperation between Italian partisans and the Allied High Command had been defined by the so-called Rome Protocols, were orders given to open the floodgates that had so far held up the flow of arms and equipment to Italy's secret army. The partisans of northern Italy, variously estimated at between two hundred thousand and a quarter of a million men, were now able to take part in military operations.[75]

The Final Phase

When their day finally dawned, how much did the secret armies accomplish and what were their allotted tasks?

In Norway, MILORG received instructions from the Allied High Command to avoid becoming embroiled with the Wehrmacht. No Allied forces would be committed there. Instead, the Germans would be allowed to withdraw men from Norway and throw them into the fighting on the Western Front, where Allied superiority would in any case prove invincible.

Hitler's Ardennes counteroffensive prompted a change of plan, however. It now seemed expedient to disrupt German troop movements in Norway, and this was the task performed by MILORG's large-scale sabotage operations against the country's rail network.

The Norwegian secret army was also assigned a defensive and security role. There was a likelihood that, like the Soviet Union, Norway would be subjected to the German "scorched earth" strategy. MILORG assumed responsibility for the protection of power stations and harbors, industrial complexes and road and rail junctions. In the event of a German collapse, it was also to maintain internal order until the arrival of Allied troops.

In fulfilling these assignments, MILORG was assisted by thirteen thousand men belonging to Norwegian police units which had been formed, trained, and armed in Sweden during the war, despite vigorous protests from the Third Reich.

In Norway, the Wehrmacht laid down its arms on May 8, 1945. The German forces of occupation—350,000 rested and well-armed officers and men—surrendered without incident to MILORG's 40,000 freedom fighters.[76]

However notable this achievement, it cannot disguise the fact that the paramilitary forces of the Norwegian Underground never—any more than the Dutch and Danish secret armies—participated in the final phase of the war as close-knit combat formations fighting shoulder to shoulder with the Allies. In Holland, where the Wehrmacht surrendered on May 4, Dutch Resistance forces had not been placed under unified military command until March—too late to become truly effective.

In Belgium, the secret army should have cleared the Allies' line of advance, but it never had to. German forces fought no rearguard actions except when absolutely necessary. Though hampered by sporadic guerrilla activity, they withdrew from Belgium almost without firing a shot. As Allied fliers reported at the time, Belgium looked from the air like "an untouched expanse of glorious gardens between devastated Normandy and blazing Holland." The Belgian secret army did, however, round up ten thousand German prisoners.[77]

One exception was Antwerp, where the Resistance carried out methodical sabotage attacks on the harbor installations for a week. The city and its port were finally liberated at the beginning of September 1944 by units of the secret army and a British armored regiment.[78]

The situation in Italy was more complex. In the south, as we have already mentioned, Italian regulars were fighting on the Allied side—fifty-four thousand of them by October 1944. North of the Gothic Line, an assortment of politically disunited and poorly armed partisan units was confronted by two powerful foes—the Wehrmacht and Mussolini's Fascist forces, which alone numbered two hundred thousand men—and a highly mistrustful partner in the shape of the Western Allies, who had promised arms but long withheld them.

Though universally inferior to their enemies, however, the partisans contrived to be militarily useful. Field Marshal Albert Kesselring, Hitler's "Commander in Chief South," estimated that his partisan-inflicted losses for the period June–August 1944 amounted to at least seven thousand killed and missing and fourteen thousand wounded.[79]

Partisan units with no form of regular military organization occupied approximately one hundred towns before they were entered by Allied troops.[80] They also helped to liberate cities such as Florence and Genoa and were persuaded to save North Italian industrial installations and harbors from destruction by the Germans. They are further reported to have captured some forty thousand German and Italian Fascist soldiers in April 1945, as the war drew to a close.[81]

It was clearly a great advantage that their numbers had not been whittled away and their morale impaired by the years of attrition which Resistance fighters in other countries had been forced to endure. In their case, final victory was assured by the time they took up arms. Fascism had already been overthrown and Hitler's armies were retreating on every front.

What role did France's secret army play in the final act of World War II?

The question is doubly interesting because regular and irregular French forces came face to face on the battle-riven soil of their native land.

By September 1944, General de Gaulle's Free French Army (7,000 strong at the end of July 1940 and 70,000 strong two years later) had grown to 560,000 men, of whom 91 percent were colonial troops and 45 percent natives of Africa.[82]

Despite this, not a single French soldier landed in Normandy with the Allied Expeditionary Force in June 1944. On August 15, three French divisions went ashore in the South of France and liberated Toulon and Marseille. Then they combined to form the French First Army, commanded by General Jean de Lattre de Tassigny, and marched north with their allies.

The irregular secret army (FFI), an umbrella organization in which paramilitary Resistance combat units had not been integrated until the beginning of February 1944, was everywhere and nowhere at once. It was scattered throughout the country in 821 secret Resistance centers. It possessed no artillery or armor, no antitank or antiaircraft guns, no aircraft, and a slender supply of small arms and ammunition.[83]

In Normandy it was hardly in evidence at all after the invasion forces landed. In Brittany, five thousand men distributed over five Departments were deployed against railroad lines in small sabotage teams. By the end of July, enough volunteers had come forward to make twenty thousand men available for guerrilla operations. By mid-August they numbered eighty thousand.[84]

In the South of France the FFI provided flank defense for the Allied troops advancing north, among them the French First Army. It seemed logical to try to effect an organizational merger between the regular and irregular French forces, but this process did not succeed as fully as expected or desired.

On December 19, 1944, General de Lattre de Tassigny wrote to General de Gaulle: "From one end of the political edifice to the other, one gains the impression that the people want nothing to do with us and are letting us go hang. Some go so far as to believe that the regular Army, which has come from outside the mother country, is performing a task that devolves on it alone. The underlying reason for this sorry state of affairs is that the nation has taken no part in the war." The commander of the First Army concluded by requesting that it should "enroll eight to ten thousand young Frenchmen in its ranks, this being essential to the preservation of its morale and combat strength."[85] (By contrast, Marcel Baudot claims that seventy-five thousand irregulars had already been absorbed into the First Army in November, and that twelve thousand saw action.[86])

Generally speaking, the FFI's paramilitary formations and regular French units seem to have operated independently and gone their separate ways in stubborn adherence to their own individual scheme of things.

Anyone inquiring into what the Resistance accomplished will, nevertheless, find a whole corpus of literature at his disposal—all of it glowing
with admiration. FFI units seized control of Savoy, we are told, as well as
the southern coastal and frontier areas and no less than twenty-eight Departments in central and southwestern France. They took fifty thousand
German soldiers prisoner in Brittany and Provence and fought as makeshift infantry, supported by American armor and artillery, in the Departments of Drôme and Isère. According to Henri Michel, General Eisenhower likened their military value to that of fifteen regular divisions.[87]

We shall have to revert to this later.

The East and the Balkans

Resistance in the East and the Balkans had little or no contact with the
Resistance movements and secret armies of the West. It grew up in the
shadow of the Soviet Union, under conditions and circumstances of a special nature.

It would, to take only one example, have been utterly absurd for someone in the East to have opposed Hitler's genocidal policy by wearing a carnation or singing the national anthem. This type of symbolic resistance did
occur in the occupied areas of Czechoslovakia. In Poland and the Soviet
Union, however, the millions who were persecuted and in fear of their
lives had only one course open to them apart from a policy of extreme tactical collaboration, and that was to go underground—to fight the enemy
from a place of concealment.

This was why the Polish Resistance movement began to take shape at
an exceptionally early stage, on the very eve of Warsaw's surrender. The
Poles knew what to expect. Polish staff officers were already aware of German manhunts and alert to the unmistakable portents of Hitler's extermination policy, so the first step was taken while the Polish capital was still
reeling under a murderous German bombardment. General Juliusz Rómel,
commander of the "Warszawa" army corps, entrusted his colleague General Michal Tokarzewski with the organization of an illegal armed Resistance movement and placed a preliminary sum of 750,000 zlotys at his disposal.

As soon as Warsaw surrendered, Tokarzewski went to ground in a hospital on the city's outskirts and assumed the guise of a medical orderly.
Here, working with a team of fifteen staff officers, he took only two weeks
to devise a complete administrative structure, draw up a constitution for
his new organization, which he christened "Service for the Victory of
Poland" (SZP), and forward it to the commander in chief and the Premier
of the government-in-exile in London. After another two weeks, on December 4, 1939, the SZP was renamed "Armed Combat Association"

(ZWZ) and officially integrated in the Polish regular forces by the government-in-exile. By September 1940 it had attained a strength of 140,000 men.

Apart from the ZWZ, the military formed between a hundred and a hundred and fifty other political organizations in the period up to June 1940, though by 1942 these had merged into twenty groups or "movements" at most and were largely integrated into the Home Army. Contemporary estimates of the number of Resistance organizations diverged widely, as we can see.[88]

Partisan Resistance in occupied Soviet territory followed an entirely different course of development. Here, discounting the spontaneous formation of groups by local Party authorities, it was initiated by orders, directives, and official instructions from the Party leadership and Supreme Command of the Red Army—in other words, from the very apex of the Soviet hierarchy. Only a week after the Germans invaded, the Central Committee of the Soviet Communist Party enjoined all Party organizations in threatened areas to prepare to go underground. Four days later, Stalin called on Party members and Soviet citizens resident in areas already occupied to attack the enemy in the rear. This appeal was followed at the end of July by precise instructions from the Central Committee on how to organize combat operations behind the German lines.

In western areas that had been overrun by the Wehrmacht during the first few days, weeks, and months, guerrilla warfare was temporarily out of the question. The swift collapse of the Soviet defenses had dealt their inhabitants a numbing blow and robbed them of the power of decision. Few of them were prepared to make a definite stand. For the moment, therefore, partisans could not expect to receive firm backing, total solidarity, and effective help from the civilian population.

The Central Committee's instructions were nonetheless obeyed by some faithful Party officials who promptly withdrew to makeshift hideouts and made preparations to resist the enemy.[89] A firsthand account of their approach to the problem has been given by Aleksei Fyodorov.[90]

Together with half a dozen Party members whom he knew to be trustworthy, Fyodorov set up a so-called district committee and assigned it various tasks. These included forming a clandestine organization, establishing hideouts and supply depots, recruiting cadres, ensuring central coordination and permanent supervision, putting out propaganda, and paving the way for armed resistance.

To begin with, the committee members were brought a daily total of ten to fifteen Party members whose loyalty was beyond question. After six weeks or so, they had assembled five hundred men. The clandestine nature of the organization required them to be issued with identity papers bearing false names. Only the leaders of the district committee were permitted to know the location of arms dumps and caches of equipment hurriedly installed in forest hideouts by selected Party members.

Still on Party orders, Fyodorov proceeded to form a mounted detachment, a demolition squad, and infantry detachments totaling between a hundred and eighty and two hundred men. These recruits were taken to remote areas of forest or marsh to be trained in groups of thirty. Any Red Army stragglers they came across were compelled to join them.

Finally, Fyodorov appointed one Party member in every village in his district to create the psychological and material prerequisites for resistance under German occupation. Preparations were far enough advanced by mid-November for Fyodorov's group to be merged with others.

Developments followed a similar course in other places. Makeshift partisan units were formed here and there in obedience to orders, though it was not easy to coordinate them under the Germans' noses. In one reported instance, liaison between illegal cells and groups was maintained by a Red Army lieutenant posing as an itinerant accordion player. Parachutists were dropped in occupied territory to seek out widely scattered groups and put them in touch with each other, but few attained their objective. Some were killed and others betrayed by Russians who had been quick to range themselves on the Germans' side and come to terms with them.[91]

Operating under these circumstances, the earliest partisans suffered enormous losses. Their position soon deteriorated to such an extent that many large areas were virtually denuded of them. This was especially true of the Ukraine, whose intimidated population was far from well disposed toward freedom fighters. Some surviving partisans fled into the forests or went underground in villages, while others fought their way through to the Red Army or resigned themselves to collaboration and put their services at the Germans' disposal. Thus the first chapter in the annals of Soviet partisan warfare ended on a disastrous note. Like public morale, the situation did not improve until the German advance on Moscow ground to a halt and the Red Army proved that it possessed the strength to stem the enemy onslaught.

Then, sustained by a resurgence of hope, new partisan groups were formed. These units, which were mainly to be found in White Russia, in the forests of Bryansk and farther north, now received a substantial measure of assistance from two quarters.

In the first place, the political and military authorities in Moscow now made supreme efforts to concentrate their forces behind the German lines and submit them to strict supervision by experienced and reliable commanders. They also kept these new partisan formations liberally supplied with arms and ammunition, either by air or via the so-called "front corridors."

The second source of aid was at least as important. Millions of Soviet soldiers had been encircled and captured during the summer and fall of 1941. Hundreds of thousands starved to death in open-air barbed-wire cages, but tens of thousands managed to escape and form a sort of Russian Maquis in the forests. Although most of them were fugitives intent on survival and as politically neutral as only those faced with extinction can be, they were well armed and inured to the horrors of modern warfare.

Rounded up and concentrated by Red Army paratroops, these lost soldiers formed the basis of the regional partisan brigades, ranging in strength from three hundred and fifty to two thousand men, which first embarked on local operations in the summer of 1942. Their initial importance lay less in their military potential than in the fact that their mere existence, and their rapid dissemination over large tracts of occupied territory, acted as living proof of the undiminished power of the Soviet regime.

Another fundamental change occurred when the Soviet High Command reinforced partisan units and their mounted detachments with airborne troops of the Red Army and assigned them to attack road and rail links in White Russia. At about the same time, heavy weapons were flown across the German lines and landed on airstrips prepared by the partisans.

An equally significant development occurred in Moscow at the end of May 1942, when the Soviet authorities set up a "Central Staff of the Partisan Movement." This was a sort of supreme general staff comprising all the usual branches plus three regional staffs for the Ukraine, White Russia, and the Kuban area, which in turn maintained permanent contact with partisan commanders in German-controlled territory by radio, air, and couriers.

Although Soviet partisan formations were organized on Red Army lines and incorporated into an umbrella organization which also included the Party and the armed forces, they were as far from attaining the status of an army as their counterparts in the West. They were and remained a mere auxiliary corps which swiftly concentrated behind the enemy lines as ordered, disrupted German troop movements by launching surprise attacks on railroad lines, and just as swiftly dispersed. At the same time, their militarization and submission to discipline were carried to absurd extremes. Fyodorov describes how, when inspected by a Red Army general and the Secretary of the Central Committee of the Ukrainian Communist Party, partisans in the field were obliged to goose-step past a saluting base.[92]

In time, however, they demonstrated their military value. Although they failed to affect the course of operations during the summer and fall of 1942, their increased activity provoked German countermeasures which ultimately benefited the Soviet cause.

In the belief that they could be starved out, German security forces took to systematically destroying crops and stocks of foodstuffs. In the additional belief that ruthless reprisals would deprive them of support among the farmers and cut off their sources of supply, they burned whole villages to the ground and rounded up hordes of young men for forced labor.

In the event, these measures proved counterproductive. The civilian population became increasingly pro-Soviet, and the young labor conscripts, itching to get their own back on the occupying power, sought refuge with the partisans.

They got a chance to win their spurs in summer 1943 and the following winter. During the great Russian counteroffensive at Kursk, they blew up roads, bridges, and railroad tracks in at least twenty thousand places in July alone. During August, a strong force of partisans occupied and held a strategic key point behind the German lines in the forests of Bryansk. When winter came, they set off on a long march to the Ukraine. Even then, however, the political and psychological effect of these operations far outweighed their military value.[93]

The partisans' military usefulness and the true extent of their contribution to the Soviet war effort are questions that will be examined at the end of this book. Our present concern is with the peculiarities of the Russian Resistance, which differed so fundamentally from every other Resistance movement in Hitler's Europe.

No other secret army enjoyed greater advantages than the Russian partisan movement, whose dependence on its own resources lasted a very short time. Its requirements were soon met with the same care as those of the Red Army. It was not an ill-equipped and isolated band of forlorn-hopers like the French Maquis. By August 1943, 1,131 partisan units behind the German lines had access to 424 radio stations in permanent contact with their general staff in Moscow. As early as spring 1942, 25 percent of them were receiving regular airdrops of arms and ammunition, and that figure had doubled by 1944. In contrast to all other freedom fighters in German-occupied territory, they were doing battle for a still undefeated country and did not have to await liberation by foreign powers before taking up arms at the eleventh hour. From the first day of the war to the last, they enjoyed the protection of a powerful air force which was superior, in their own theater of operations, to that of the enemy.[94]

Their numerical strength was remarkable in itself. One East German study of partisan warfare in Europe puts it as high as a million,[95] though Russian and German estimates based on national records present a different picture. The number of organized, armed, and militarily effective partisans is given as 30,000 at the beginning of 1942, 120,000 a year later, 200,000 in mid-1943, and 175,000 in mid-1944.

Partisan units began to disband during 1944 on orders from Moscow, whose policy was that their members should be gradually regrouped and assigned to Red Army assault detachments which had little prospect of surviving the war. Most of their officers were demoted. It would appear that men who had spent years in the wilderness—men who had learned,

when necessary, to act on their own initiative and think for themselves—
were not overpopular with the supreme political arbiters of their native
land.[96]

We have already touched on the entirely different circumstances governing
the development of partisan warfare in Yugoslavia. Here the Resistance
was up against four occupying powers, not one. The Italians, who had not
only annexed and occupied parts of western Slovenia, Dalmatia, and Montenegro but controlled Mussolini's newly created Kingdom of Croatia, held
sway over more than half the country. German forces wielded authority in
less than a third of it, namely, the annexed portions of Carniola, occupied
Lower Styria, Serbia, and the Banat. The two remaining powers, Bulgaria
and Hungary, had established control over a fifth of the country: Hungary
over the annexed areas of Bačka, Baranya, and part of eastern Slovenia;
Bulgaria over northern Macedonia. Furthermore, the Kingdom of Croatia
was divided into two roughly equal zones which could be occupied in an
emergency by German forces advancing from the east and Italian from the
west. In addition to being occupied by troops from four different countries,
Yugoslavia had a puppet government in Belgrade headed by Milan Nedić,
the Serbian general. Both he and Ante Pavelić, dictator of the Axis-spon-
sored Kingdom of Croatia and authoritarian leader of the fascist Ustasha
movement, controlled police and paramilitary forces of their own. Yugoslavia was a geographically divided country traversed by rugged, impassa-
ble mountain ranges providing ideal places of concealment for partisans.

The beginnings of the struggle were unexceptional. A professional staff
officer, Colonel Draža Mihailović, was the first Yugoslav to refuse to surrender. Instead, he took his men and withdrew to the Serbian highlands,
where he joined with officers loyal to him in setting up partisan units
which he christened "Chetniks," after the irregulars who had fought the
Turks at the turn of the century. His idea was to build up an army for the
final showdown, not to pit his forces against the Wehrmacht's overwhelming superiority and get them wiped out.[97]

Meanwhile, the twelve-thousand-strong Communist Party led by Tito,
who had faithfully defended the German-Soviet friendship treaty until
June 1941, was forming partisan detachments numbering between five and
fifteen men. Official Yugoslav war historians state that these groups, which
were scattered throughout the country, took only six months to attain a
strength of eighty thousand men.[98]

In October 1941, a merger took place between the partisans commanded by Mihailović, the royalist colonel, and Tito, the senior Communist Party official. They formed joint general staffs, shared out captured
rifles held at a factory in Užice, and established joint commands in places
under their control.

The alliance lasted only six weeks. When several independent Chetnik commanders defected to the Germans and Mihailović declined to join Tito in taking ruthless action against all "hostile Chetniks," an open breach occurred. By the end of October, fighting had flared up between the Serbian nationalists and Tito's Communist partisans.[99]

But that was only one of the internal battle fronts that threaded the country and were to intersect as disastrously as they had at the time of the Napoleonic Wars. Now split six ways, Yugoslavia became the scene of various secondary but sanguinary wars.

It was all against all. The Chetniks fought Tito's partisans and the German and Italian forces of occupation, though some of their leaders and units collaborated with the Germans or Italians while simultaneously maintaining a defensive posture against the Ustashi, who massacred half a million Orthodox Serbs in northwestern Bosnia and impelled large numbers of Serbian refugees to throw in their lot with Tito or Mihailović. The Germans not only fought the Chetniks and Tito's partisans but later, in September 1943, attacked the renegade Italian forces that had hitherto operated against Tito's partisans in tacit collaboration with Chetniks pursued by German "hunting parties." And while some Chetnik leaders made occasional deals with General Nedić, the Berlin-sponsored head of Belgrade's puppet government, the Wehrmacht launched a campaign to wipe out Mihailović's partisans in Herzegovina and Montenegro during the spring of 1943.[100]

Throughout these chaotic years of hostility and subsidiary wars, Tito's partisans fought a protracted duel with those of Mihailović. Meantime, their sabotage teams and assassination squads caused so much concern to all four occupying powers that Hitler ordered their annihilation.[101]

He nearly succeeded. It is understandable that Yugoslav historians should divide their country's war history into phases corresponding to the German offensives that so often brought Tito to the brink of disaster. He and his partisans fought their way out, time and again, because he skillfully and doggedly exploited the weaknesses of the occupying powers—inadequate coordination and the absence of a central high command—as well as the natural protection afforded by rugged mountainous terrain. This was what earned Tito the reputation that prompted even some Chetniks to desert to him.

In 1943, he and his partisans entered the higher realms of international politics. Stalin had ignored Tito's appeals for aid and left him in the lurch. Churchill, on the other hand, correctly assessed the political and military importance of the Yugoslav partisan leader, who still commanded nearly three hundred thousand men despite losses of eighty-five thousand. In May the Prime Minister assigned him a permanent British mission. At the end of the same year he began to supply him with arms.[102]

This drew Tito into the field of tension between two allied but antagonistic world powers which were already jockeying for a favorable position in the postwar world. Politics took over from strategy, and the Yugoslav Resistance acquired a new dimension of which more will be said in Part Four of this book.

In Greece, the Resistance was in many ways reminiscent of Yugoslavia. Here, too, were mountains affording sanctuary; here, too, bitter conflicts raged between Communist and non-Communist partisan armies; and here, too, a bloody civil war broke out. The Communist "People's Liberation Army" (ELAS) wiped out the partisans commanded by General Saraphis and Colonel Psarros in a series of campaigns, but British expeditionary forces violently nipped a Communist takeover in the bud, just as we shall see they did—less violently—in Belgium. This move was made with the approval of Stalin, who had expressly given Churchill, his ally-cum-adversary, the green light shortly before. But more of this, too, later.

As for resistance in the countries bordering the Soviet Union, which were allied with Nazi Germany but closely monitored by the Gestapo, it was doomed to a lingering and terrible death by asphyxia. Its sole bequest to posterity was the mute tragedy of many lives sacrificed in vain.

In Hungary, for example, all vestiges of organized resistance had disappeared by early 1943. In the Protectorate of Bohemia and Moravia, German forces annihilated the last surviving partisan detachments at the end of 1944. Partisans smuggled in from the Soviet Union first appeared in Hungary during the fall of that year and surfaced in Bohemia and Moravia even later, in the spring of 1945. The German spell was not, however, broken by them when the hour of liberation drew near. In Prague and Sofia, it was non-Communist army officers who proclaimed and led a revolt against the Germans. In Prague, as we have already heard, military and police powers were assumed by a handful of officers who had survived the violent end of ON, the military Resistance movement, and took control four days before the Red Army entered the city; in Sofia, officers belonging to the "Zweno League," a secret military society high in the councils of the "Patriotic Front," unexpectedly forestalled the Russians by a full week.

But the Russian steamroller flattened these obstructions and cleared a path for all who were willing to be harnessed to the Kremlin's foreign policy.[103]

Resistance Enchained
or
Freedom Fighters in Camp and Ghetto

One of the leading members of the Underground at Auschwitz, the notorious concentration and extermination camp, was a Polish officer named Witold Pilecki, joint founder of the Polish secret army known as TAP (Tajna Armia Polska), which was formed in the fall of 1939 and later merged with the government-in-exile's officially recognized "Home Army." Pilecki was forty years old, twelve years married and the father of one daughter, when he submitted his audacious plan to higher authority in the fall of 1940.

It was known that a concentration camp for Polish detainees had existed at Auschwitz since mid-June 1940. A preliminary consignment of between one and two thousand prisoners had been sent there in the middle of August. They included members of the TAP, some of whom were officers who had failed to surrender for internment as prisoners of war pursuant to an order issued by the German military authorities in December 1939. All officers detained during house searches or identity checks were sent to Auschwitz as a matter of course.

This fact formed the basis of the plan which Pilecki, acting with his superiors' consent and on their instructions, put into effect in September 1940.

Pilecki behaved so suspiciously during a street check in Warsaw that the Germans demanded to see his papers. He duly produced an officer's identity card in the assumed name of Tomasz Serafinski. As foreseen, he was arrested on the spot and sent to Auschwitz a few days later.

Pilecki planned to organize resistance in Auschwitz and keep TAP headquarters regularly informed of conditions and developments inside the camp. Arrangements had been made to maintain contact between the camp and the secret army headquarters through men and women couriers, who were already standing by, and code words had been issued. Pilecki's intelligence network functioned so efficiently that his first report reached Warsaw in December 1940.

Pilecki, alias Serafinski, Auschwitz Prisoner No. 4859, spent two and a half years inside the hellhole where daily mass gassings began in mid-May 1942. His reports, which were forwarded to London, provided the first authentic and detailed evidence of these horrors, though the initial reaction to them was one of incredulity.

At the very period when Auschwitz, by then a gigantic complex embracing thirty-nine subsidiary camps, was being converted into a center for industrialized mass murder, a secret transmitter within its gates was maintaining direct radio contact between Pilecki's Resistance group and the Silesian headquarters of the secret army. Thanks to the couriers who kept the latter informed of wavelengths and transmission times, it continued to do so for seven whole months.

The transmitter had been laboriously put together from components smuggled into Auschwitz one by one. Concealed in a typhus-infested part of camp which the SS tended to avoid, it ceased to operate as soon as its existence seemed in danger of detection.

Nowhere did polemic resistance—which was what Pilecki's intelligence service engaged in, to the extent that its reports from Auschwitz enlightened and shocked world opinion—make a stronger or more effective impact.[1]

Pilecki's Resistance group was only one of several which took shape in Auschwitz and its subsidiary camps, independently of each other and with varying objectives. By the end of 1942, however, Pilecki had largely succeeded in merging them and coordinating their activities.[2]

No consideration could be given to defensive resistance until he and his group had secured the tacit support of those inmates whom they could safely take into their confidence. This took time, courage, perseverance, and strength of mind. In December 1940 Pilecki's team numbered six prisoners including himself. By the spring of 1941 there were eight of them; by mid-1942, eighteen months later, five hundred. Józef Garlinski, who himself belonged to the Polish secret army and knew Auschwitz at first hand, has stated that "several thousand" inmates belonged to the camp Resistance groups by August 1943.[3]

Defensive resistance began with the systematic infiltration of the entire administrative system, insofar as it was accessible to prisoners. Pilecki's organization tried to insinuate its best operatives into offices and kitchens, camp hospitals and stores. Its aim was to supply the maximum possible number of "Kapos" from its own ranks—prisoners in charge of working parties—so as to avoid unnecessary brutality and ill treatment. It also made a deliberate practice of tactical collaboration, as the Jewish Councils did, so that prisoners who stood a better chance of survival were selected for transfer to other camps, construction projects, and similar assignments.

Organized breakouts—those desperate attempts to escape from a hell on earth—would have been unthinkable without a close-knit system of defensive resistance.

A total of 667 Auschwitz inmates managed to escape, though we know for sure that 270 were recaptured. Escorted by members of the socialist Resistance, fugitives were taken by night to a safe house in Cracow, where doctors removed the tattooed numbers from their arms. Then, armed and equipped with false papers, some of them returned to hideouts in the neighborhood of Auschwitz, where they could assist in further breakouts. Four partisan groups were stationed near the camp in readiness for the day of liberation and became involved in actual fighting. Of their 780 members, sixteen were ex-inmates whose names are on record. Pilecki himself broke out of camp at the end of April 1943, rejoined the Polish secret army, and fought in one of its units during the Warsaw uprising of August–September 1944.[4]

SS guards who treated prisoners particularly harshly were infected with typhus bacilli. This came under the heading of offensive resistance, as did the procurement of arms—an exceptionally difficult task—and the planning of the revolt that would not be launched until there were signs that the Germans intended to destroy the camp in toto, complete with its inmates. Even those who witnessed the daily mass murders and were compelled to perform the grisly chores associated with them stood in various degrees of mortal danger. Here, too, there was a final threshold of provocation—a point at which the worm would turn—but to strike too soon was to strike oneself down in the process.

This happened at Birkenau, the death camp attached to Auschwitz, early in October 1944. Secretly armed and itching for a fight, a working party blew up the crematorium, shot three SS men dead and wounded another twelve, but every one of the 262 inmates who took part in the ensuing breakout was killed.[5]

A year earlier, in October 1943, an armed revolt at the Treblinka extermination camp ended in a welter of blood. Although six hundred prisoners fled to the nearby forests, only forty escaped with their lives.[6]

Armed insurrections in the Warsaw ghetto in April 1943, in the Bialystok ghetto in August, in the Sobibor death camp in October—all these added more dark chapters to the history of the European Resistance.

Many accounts have been written of the uprising in the Warsaw ghetto, which probably holds a greater fascination for modern observers, and Jews in particular, than any other similar revolt. Diaries and notes, eyewitness accounts and documents such as the official reports of General Jürgen Stroop, the German commander who ordered the ghetto's destruction, have long since become woven into a Warsaw epic.

On January 21, 1941, the day when the German authorities sealed it off, the Jewish quarter of the Polish capital was inhabited by 450,000 people living in twin ghettos separated by broad thoroughfares. Apart from a thin upper crust of prosperous businessmen, they lived in wretched conditions (on average, fifteen to an apartment and five or six to a room). Of the fifty thousand children of school-going age, only about seven thousand were receiving a meager education because most were sick and debilitated, others had no shoes, and many roamed the streets begging.[7]

Despite widespread hardship and deprivation, cultural centers such as the Jewish library were not only kept in being but heavily patronized. Five theaters, of which three presented plays in Yiddish and two in Polish, were regularly sold out at prices which all but the poorest could afford. Five hundred young people were undergoing two-year medical and pharmacological courses of university standard. The Grand Symphony Orchestra gave well-attended concerts of classical, sacred, and modern music, and the affluent few could satisfy nearly all their needs in a score of coffeehouses and restaurants.[8]

On July 22, 1942, eighteen months after the ghetto was sealed off, notices posted by the Jewish Council informed its inhabitants that the Jews of Warsaw (except for the forty thousand factory workers employed by the German Munitions Department and members of the Jewish Council and Jewish auxiliary police) were to be resettled in the East, where families would allegedly be housed together in surroundings that afforded sufficient employment and residential accommodation. Baltic and Ukrainian SS units were deployed around the ghetto, and the deportations began.[9]

Over twenty thousand volunteers reported during the first week. Fifteen thousand of them were taken to Treblinka, where work on the first gas chamber had just been completed.[10] Two hundred thousand Jews had been deported by mid-August and a further hundred thousand followed during a single week in September, among them over three thousand Jewish police auxiliaries. By the end of October 1942, all that remained of the ghetto's erstwhile population of four hundred and fifty thousand were sixty or seventy thousand young, fit, and able-bodied men and women.[11]

What had become of the deportees, and what did "resettlement in the East" imply?

People might have guessed, even inside the ghetto, but very few were disposed to accept the truth. Since February 1942, fifty-six Underground newspapers (twenty-six in Yiddish, twenty in Polish, and ten in Hebrew, mostly of two or four pages only) had been publishing lurid reports of mass shootings of Jews in Poland and the Baltic States. What was more, a group of Warsaw Jews had managed to escape from Treblinka in mid-August, so they were able to give their friends in the ghetto credible firsthand accounts of the wholesale executions there.[12]

As a result of these reports, which were fully borne out by the messages then being transmitted from Auschwitz by Pilecki's secret radio, more and more small groups began to form inside the ghetto with a view to resisting further deportations by force of arms. A coordinating committee entitled the "Jewish Combat Unit" (ZZW) had already amalgamated the existing groups of activists and was in touch with the Polish Home Army. In December 1942, a "Jewish Combat Organization" (ZOB) was also formed on the initiative of a relatively strong Communist group.[13]

Would armed resistance be of any benefit at all to those who still belonged to the dwindling band of survivors? This question was hotly debated inside the ghetto. As in the occupied countries of Western Europe, the active Resistance fighters found themselves in a minority. One of those destined to survive was Marek Edelman, the leader of a socialist faction in the ZOB. "Unfortunately, everyone was against us," he wrote later. "The entire population of the ghetto felt that the slightest resistance would inevitably provoke savage repression on the Germans' part, but that, provided the Jews delivered up their due quota, all the rest would be saved. The instinctive urge to survive causes human beings to think primarily of their own salvation, even at the expense of others." Consequently, Edelman went on, the ghetto became divided into two Jewish camps—"one doomed to die, the other hoping to survive. The latter sent the former to its death in the vain hope of saving itself."[14]

Communist attempts to persuade the ghetto elders that an armed breakout should be tried were just as fruitless. One Communist group numbered roughly five hundred men and was led by Finkelstein-Lewartowski, a former member of the Central Committee. He was eventually obliged to inform his comrades on the outside that he was getting nowhere. "Our proposals are being rejected," the illegal Party directorate radioed Moscow late in October 1942, "on the pretext that they would only hasten the end of the ghetto."[15]

The legendary uprising might never have taken place at all, had not matters come to a head in the spring of 1943.

In mid-January of that year, some young men who were to be resettled on the orders of the Munitions Department decided to resist. While being led away, they produced guns from their pockets and opened fire on their escort of SS and militiamen. They belonged to Resistance groups in possession of arms and ammunition—automatic pistols and hand grenades purchased outside the ghetto and smuggled in by various routes including the sewers. Having shot up a building in which four Resistance groups had barricaded themselves, the SS withdrew.

Heinrich Himmler, the Reichsführer-SS, promptly decreed that the ghetto should be "evacuated" and destroyed. The residential quarter previously occupied by "five hundred thousand subhumans" was to "disappear from the map."

The Jewish Council now sided with the Resistance. Its members refused to cooperate with the German authorities on the grounds that they had lost all influence over the ghetto's inhabitants.

The "evacuation" began on April 19, 1943, under the command of Jürgen Stroop, who held the twin ranks of SS-Brigadeführer and Major General of Police. He moved in with a force of two thousand men, including 858 Polish and Lithuanian police and militiamen and members of the Warsaw fire brigade.[16]

They were opposed by about fifty Jewish combat teams—a total of one thousand men and women armed with eighty rifles, three light machine guns, a few hundred revolvers, a thousand hand grenades, and a quantity of explosives.[17]

Describing the course of the fighting on April 24, General Stroop reported as follows: "At 1815 hours, after sealing them off, armed search parties entered the buildings and ascertained the presence of a large number of Jews. Since most of the Jews offered resistance, I gave the order to burn them out. It was not until the streetcar and all the courtyards on either side were ablaze that the Jews emerged from the blocks, some of them on fire, or tried to escape by jumping from windows and balconies into the street, into which they had previously thrown beds, blankets, and other articles. It was often noticeable that, although in imminent danger of being burned alive, the Jews and bandits chose to return to the flames rather than fall into our hands."

"In all of our members' dugouts, there is not enough air left to light a single candle." Thus wrote twenty-four-year-old Mordechai Anilewicz, who was reportedly elected leader of the Resistance during the fighting, in a letter dated the same day and smuggled out of the burning ghetto. Here is General Stroop, commenting on the same subject: "On several occasions, we broke open dugouts whose occupants had not been to the surface since the operation began. In a series of instances, the occupants . . . were almost incapable of crawling to the surface."[18]

Where Resistance fighters had ensconced themselves in sewers, smoke bombs were dropped down manholes.

"I myself," the historian Emanuel Ringelblum noted in his diary, "have seen Jewish women firing a machine gun from a rooftop."[19]

Meanwhile, men of the Polish Resistance armed with submachine guns attacked the ghetto sentries from outside and tried to blow up the walls. They also took charge of the few exhausted men and women who managed to escape through the sewers and escorted them to safety—to join the twenty thousand other Jews whom Polish historians estimate to have been previously hidden, notwithstanding their traditional anti-Semitism, by thousands of Warsaw families.[20]

"The Jewish quarter of Warsaw is no more," General Stroop reported on May 15, 1943. According to his figures, approximately seven thousand ghetto dwellers were killed on the spot, another seven thousand sent to the gas ovens at Treblinka, and over fifty-six thousand taken prisoner. Stroop further estimated that between five and six thousand Jews perished in the flames or were entombed by rubble. German losses he gave as sixteen dead and ninety wounded. The remains of the ghetto were razed to the ground.

What impelled the Jews to engage in this forlorn and desperate struggle? What inspired their hopeless attempts at self-defense and their furious counterattacks?

The word that so often recurs in oral accounts, letters, diaries, and court testimony is "honor": "Let us die in *honor* . . ."—"not to stand aside at the expense of our honor . . ."—"to avenge murder by fighting to preserve our *honor* . . ."—"We were not intent on saving our own lives. . . . We were looking for ways of saving them (our mothers, brothers, and sisters) or their *honor* . . ."[21] The Jews wanted to demonstrate, to themselves and the outside world, who they were.

And so they took up arms because they believed that by unleashing resistance—by fighting and dying in a death camp or blazing ghetto—they would bequeath to the world an imperishable symbol of defiance.

PART FOUR

Prickly Partners

The Third Front
or
General de Gaulle Stands Aloof

Though natural comrades-in-arms, the Allies and the European Resistance movements developed an extremely uneasy relationship. They undoubtedly agreed that the war must be won, but their views and aspirations differed so widely in every other respect that the Resistance often regarded the Western Powers' attitude as hostile and provocative.

The underlying reason was their lack of contact, especially the relaxed and friendly contact that springs from basic unanimity.

To the military leaders of the Western Powers, the Resistance was merely a side issue and remained so until the war ended. At no stage did it constitute a clear-cut organization. Composed of a multitude of small or minuscule groups, it resembled an amorphous mass, forever in a state of flux and impossible to pin down. There was no sure way of foreseeing or assessing the importance it might someday acquire or the direction it would take.

Its deep internal divisions were another liability. It emitted every color in the political spectrum and contained every party, school of thought, and ideology from the extreme left to the far right. It could adopt the slogans of social revolution or even of fascism, depending on which group predominated where. Churchill watched the revolutionary stirrings in the European Underground with a wary and suspicious eye, while Roosevelt saw General de Gaulle as a budding dictator—possibly, even, as a new fascist leader.

This had little to do with the requirements of waging war on Nazi Germany. All that can be said for certain is that those responsible for overall strategic planning never felt able to employ the Resistance as a factor of determinate magnitude and thought that it might, at most, fulfill a modest ancillary function in the closing stages of the war. Professional soldiers, who had a low opinion of guerrilla warfare at the best of times, were even afraid that armed irregulars might prove obstructive to large-scale military operations. In the summer of 1942, acting on this assumption, the Allied chiefs of staff decided to exclude the Resistance from their strategic calculations.

For the Resistance, this momentous decision amounted almost to a death sentence, because it was henceforth considered inexpedient and undesirable to provide the freedom fighters of Europe with Allied arms. The decision was only partially revised in 1944.

Was it disastrous or fortunate that the Resistance failed to recognize its true position at the time? Though written off as a military factor, it received continuing Allied encouragement to fight the common foe, and thus subsisted on the belief that it was needed.

This belief was not altogether unfounded. The escape networks, those spontaneous products of defensive resistance, had proved their worth at a time when Britain herself was still in danger, so London naturally supported them. Resistance organizations also turned out to be invaluable gatherers and purveyors of secret military intelligence, so they had to be utilized, organized, and pointed in the right direction. Last but not least, Resistance combat teams lent themselves admirably to selected sabotage operations. Central control was the sole requirement.

This was to be one of the tasks of a formidable secret organization to which several references have already been made: the Special Operations Executive, or SOE, which masterminded the attacks on the Norwegian heavy-water plants and the air raid on Gestapo headquarters in Copenhagen. The SOE had been set up on Churchill's orders in July 1940 and subordinated to what he called, only half in jest, his "ministry of ungentlemanly warfare."

Churchill envisaged that the SOE would not only carry out sabotage on a grand scale in permanent consultation with the Allied High Command and the governments-in-exile in London, but become the world headquarters of the Resistance. Wherever they were active, Resistance movements would have to be provided with arms, radio sets, advice, and agents, at first in Europe and then in the Far East.

The personnel recruited and employed by the SOE were as international as the war itself, and included volunteers from nineteen countries. These operatives were specially rehearsed for their missions by expert instructors at sixty British training centers. Their curriculum covered the most sophisticated espionage and sabotage techniques, the secrets of silent close combat and clandestine radio procedure, and the subtlest arts of dissimulation and concealment. Graduates of these schools rated as qualified "parachute agents."

The three headquarters for Western Europe and the Middle and Far East were sited in London, Cairo (later Bari), and Delhi respectively. By the end of 1944, the SOE's own communications center, equipped with radio transmitters and receiving stations, was handling internal radio traffic amounting to two million words a week.[1]

This was no amateur Resistance organization run on the usual do-it-yourself lines. The SOE developed into an exceptionally efficient, reliable, and precisely controllable instrument of military complexion. At the end of 1944, its headquarters staff and central elite—all of them true-blue Britons who welded the apparatus together and had to prove their mettle in a variety of daring operations—numbered 12,800.

The achievements of this unique organization may be roughly gauged by comparing its beginnings with its end.

Early in 1941, the first two black-painted Blenheim bombers flew to Poland, manned by Polish crews, and the first French sabotage experts to have been trained in England landed in northern France by parachute. They started transmitting secret information to London in May but were silenced by the end of the year. German Intelligence had detected and captured them. In 1942 the SOE had to begin again from scratch.

And yet, by the end of 1944, the following balance sheet could be drawn up. Seven thousand trained agents of every European nationality had been "inserted" into occupied territory, including fourteen hundred into France, over a thousand into Greece, and 365 into Poland. The SOE had also supplied paramilitary Resistance groups with large quantities of equipment. The French, for example, received ten thousand tons, an amount equivalent to the cargo of a sizable oceangoing freighter, but one which had had to be parachuted onto Resistance landing zones in countless metal canisters.[2]

The European Underground was, however, compelled to wait a long time before receiving this deluge of arms and ammunition. The British staff directive that no arms should be supplied except for coordinated acts of sabotage remained in force until 1943, when events in Yugoslavia and Italy proved that even guerrillas could be militarily useful. Until then, the Resistance was consumed with impatience and despair.

Claude Serreules, General de Gaulle's official delegate to the French Resistance, radioed London that he was "besieged, day after day, by the heads of the organization, who complain bitterly that they are unable to arm their men." Another plea, this time from Jacques Bingen, who succeeded Serreules: "It is tragic. The essential thing . . . is to feed and clothe the young men for whom we have assumed responsibility—in short, to prevent them from starving to death." Many such despairing appeals for help are on record. The complaint, which never varied, was often couched in the selfsame words.[3]

One report brought to London by two secret couriers in mid-July 1943 is worthy of special note. Its author was Philippe Monod, permanent delegate to the "United Resistance Movements" in Geneva and an official liaison officer between London and the French Underground.

A levelheaded and dependable observer, Monod wrote that the Resistance was in a dramatically unstable condition. "The leaders have become discredited because they are no longer able to provide for their men. Disunity is rife. The men of the Maquis and the Secret Army cannot be restrained from taking action, from looting and going over to the offensive. Reports reaching us here, together with the incidents that have already occurred, leave no doubt at all that this is the prevailing situation."[4]

The date of this report, July 1943, is important. German faith in victory had long ago been shaken by the fateful Battle of Stalingrad, the Russians had recaptured Kursk, Rostov, and Kharkov, German forces in Africa had surrendered, and the Allies had landed in Sicily. The tide of war had turned, heralding the defeat of Nazi Germany, by the time the French Resistance bewailed its total dependence in such bitter and resentful terms.

It was at the same period, mid-July 1943, that Henri Frenay paid a second visit to London and had his third interview with De Gaulle. Acting as spokesman for his compatriots in France, who had been condemned to live with the enemy, Frenay drafted two reports for the General and his staff. "The French armed forces," he wrote, "look upon the Allies as their worst enemy."

Then came an extremely ominous statement: the French, wrote Frenay, were fighting in occupied France against the Germans, in unoccupied France against Vichy, and in London against the Anglo-Americans.[5]

Frenay was clearly filled with intense concern by what he ventured, with such startling candor, to describe as a war on three fronts. While organized resistance in France was being cut to pieces on two fronts, events in London could not but seem incomprehensible and reprehensible to the men and women of the French Underground. On this third front, far from the secret war in Europe, fierce differences had arisen between two ill-matched partners: a lonely general named De Gaulle and the up-and-coming Western Powers on whom De Gaulle himself, as well as the Resistance movements on the European mainland and all French people throughout the world, were wholly dependent.

This was extremely disturbing because it posed the question who, if not De Gaulle, could represent the French Resistance in London and Washington. There was, after all, no central Resistance organization in France itself that could have delegated representatives to Britain and the United States. The "French Committee of National Liberation," which had just surfaced in Algiers, lacked the authority that only formal Allied recognition could have conferred, and none had been forthcoming.

Was General de Gaulle the founder, organizer, and leader of the clandestine Resistance movement in the French motherland—in other words, its natural representative? This legend, better described as a pious myth, had yet to be invented.

Today it is deeply rooted in the public mind. The appeal for continued resistance which De Gaulle broadcast from London on June 18, 1940, now passes for the glorious inception and inauguration of the French Resistance, even though it has been sufficiently proved that almost no one heard it. A year later, nine out of ten French people were still unaware that De Gaulle had broadcast it at all.[6]

For the better part of two years, De Gaulle paid absolutely no heed to the Resistance. Whoever built up organizations or embarked on hazardous ventures in occupied and unoccupied France did so without his knowledge and cooperation. Not a word of inquiry about the state of the organized French Resistance escaped him in March 1942, during his first interview with one of its leading representatives, Christian Pineau, even though he knew he was dealing with the head of a Resistance organization and the founder of an important clandestine newspaper printed in occupied France.[7]

Pineau, whose sole reason for visiting London was to consult De Gaulle on problems affecting the Resistance, was taken aback to discover that the General had no knowledge of the subject. Other prominent members of the Resistance were struck by the same thing—even Colonel André Dewavrin ("Passy"), De Gaulle's own secret service chief.[8]

In the General's view, the "third front" headed France's list of strategic priorities. He deemed it his most urgent task to be a thorn in the side of his powerful and uncomfortable bedfellows. Instead of concentrating on Hitler, he began by tackling Churchill and Roosevelt with a view to asserting himself and the authority he claimed. He insisted that he, Charles de Gaulle, personified eternal France, and that his demands were the legitimate demands of his nation.

Giants like Churchill and Roosevelt were bound to regard this as overweening arrogance. Who, after all, *was* De Gaulle?

A general in exile. A solitary, stubborn, lanky professional soldier who had, at a dark and turbulent moment in his country's history, appointed himself "leader of fighting France" and head of a defeated great power—a head of government without a government, without any constitutional legitimation.

On June 17, 1940, when Pétain publicly announced the surrender of the "*Grande Armée*," De Gaulle had gone to the airfield at Mérignac with a British companion, General Edward Spears, and taken off for London in a light aircraft. After winging his way across the black pall of smoke enshrouding the towns and villages of Brittany, he reached England and was taken at once to Downing Street, where he told Churchill that he intended to fight on at Britain's side. Why had he brought him such an undistinguished figure, Churchill reportedly complained to Spears after De Gaulle had left—why not a big name?[9]

One Foreign Office official seriously thought "De Gaulle" was a humorous pseudonym, and William D. Leahy, the U.S. ambassador in Vichy, still believed in June 1941 that the French people who called themselves "Gaullists" had taken that name in memory of the old French geographical designation "Gallia," not borrowed it from a certain Monsieur de Gaulle.[10]

The General received no special favors from the BBC on the day of his historic proclamation. It never occurred to anyone to record his appeal, which he read in French from a prepared draft (though De Gaulle later remedied this omission in a private recording studio).[11]

These were ill omens for De Gaulle's chosen role on the "third front." Just as unpropitious was the slender military following commanded by the self-appointed head of state, whose lack of support was universally apparent. Seven thousand men in July 1940 and seventy thousand in April 1942 were a meager enough haul, considering that the French colonies and mandated territories were a human reservoir of sixty-seven million inhabitants. In Syria, only one soldier in five—127 officers and 6,300 enlisted men under the command of General Henri Dentz—had decided to join De Gaulle in 1941.[12]

As for the General's standing in France itself, information reaching the Foreign Office and the State Department hardly suggested that he was a power in the land. As President Roosevelt was informed in mid-1942 by Cordell Hull, his Secretary of State, "95 percent are against Hitler, but over 95 percent are no Gaullists."[13]

De Gaulle had no illusions on this score. His memoirs do not disguise the fact that he long refrained from devoting time and effort to the cares and concerns of the internal French Resistance. For years, his thoughts and actions were directed almost wholly toward regaining his defeated country an equal place among the great powers and future victors of World War II. Grumbling and importuning, raising the dust and harping on France's traditional rights, fuming and threatening—not even balking at the well-nigh ludicrous pose of an uncrowned king—he missed no opportunity to impress on the British and Americans that France differed from every other defeated and occupied country in Europe. "*La grande dame France*," he never tired of proclaiming, was still a great power. She not only possessed the second-largest colonial empire in the world but could provide the Allies with an ideal springboard for the invasion of Europe and the final showdown with Nazi Germany. Whether they liked it or not, even the world's most powerful men and nations would have to take account of France and, thus, of Charles de Gaulle. For his part, he was firmly resolved that he and his fellow exiles would one day return to France, not in the victors' baggage train, but marching at their side.

It took years for it to dawn on people that the Don Quixote of the early 1940's was a statesman—a shrewd and exceptionally adroit political strategist who had gambled for maximum stakes, empty-handed, and come away a winner. Although he could not have entered liberated Paris as a feted national hero without the acquiescence of the real conquerors, he steadily and unswervingly attained his lofty goal: France was included among the victorious powers. The French people honored his unsecured loan and made him their head of state.

Vain appeals for help, false hopes, and countless squandered lives attest that the internal French Resistance paid dearly for this successful confidence trick. Were De Gaulle and his obsessive patriotism to blame?

Much of this question has been answered above. Even before De Gaulle could lift a finger, the fate of the Resistance had been partly determined by the minor role assigned it in the Western Powers' calculations. But other factors were also involved.

The General had sent trusted emissaries from London to France very soon after the armistice. Even in the fall of 1940, a certain number of French people supported him and styled themselves "Gaullists," though no "Gaullist" Resistance organization had yet been founded. For most inhabitants of the motherland, however, De Gaulle first emerged as a political force early in January 1942, when he sent ex-Prefect Jean Moulin to France as his personal representative. Moulin's task was to coordinate the larger Resistance organizations and persuade their chiefs to join a political coalition under the General's leadership.

De Gaulle was fortunate in being able to send his delegate to France armed with powerful arguments in the shape of funds to be distributed on his behalf. Few Resistance groups were in a position to reject such help. De Gaulle's inflexible attitude had paid off in terms of British financial aid, which eventually totaled more than 120 million dollars. U.S. aid, which started to flow in 1942, amounted to over 11 billion dollars.[14]

Another point in De Gaulle's favor was that the badly fragmented Underground needed someone to lend it a respectable appearance of unity, at least in Allied eyes. The identity of this man mattered less than his ability to be accepted as a symbol of national resistance.

Fundamentally, the Allies thought likewise. They were less interested in De Gaulle's person than in knowing, from a coldly practical point of view, how many French fighting men would be prepared to obey him when it came to the pinch.[15]

Here, however, the threads of destiny became entangled.

One result of De Gaulle's stubborn stand against the Allies was that each British combat organization had an independent French counterpart. Until 1944, for example, there existed a French section of the SOE and a corresponding organization maintained by De Gaulle. This duality was persistently carried to extremes. The Gaullists made studious efforts to shield their secret contacts with the European mainland from British surveillance, and relations were almost severed because of the friction that inevitably resulted.[16]

With compelling logic, this state of affairs transmitted itself to the whole of the Resistance. Dissipation of strength had ceased to be an evil and become a deliberate feature of higher French policy. And this, in turn, could only reinforce the tendency of numerous Resistance groups to cling to their independence and decide for themselves when, whether, and where to strike. Even their formal integration into the National Resistance Council in 1943 did little to alter this.

Nothing could now have averted the tragedies that were brewing in the Maquis. How to organize, control, arm, and usefully employ the men who had fled to the mountains were problems which De Gaulle and the SOE approached by separate routes. While the SOE was busy flying in officers specially trained in guerrilla warfare, De Gaulle was endeavoring to bring certain groups under his control. At the same time, the Communists—and they were not alone in this—strove to incorporate still other groups into their highly disciplined partisan units. Open rivalry for internal positions of power had broken out under the banner of national liberation.

In the two months preceding the invasion and during the battles in Normandy, the Allies, whose attitude had meanwhile changed, began to supply the Maquis with arms. British and American planes carried out 2,365 airdrops in three and a half months. Thanks to these, Resistance forces were showered with approximately 104,000 handguns, 17,000 rifles, 4,000 other firearms, explosives, and assorted military equipment—consignments which had been procured for them (in a ratio of six to four) by the SOE and the Gaullist authorities in England.

This was enough to dissuade the Maquisards from patiently awaiting an order from Allied Supreme Headquarters but too little to give them adequate protection against the Germans. No heavy weapons had been entrusted to them for fear they might fall into the hands of a revolutionary movement.[17]

At least eight schemes were submitted to the Allies by the Resistance, but only one could be incorporated into their overall military planning. This related to prearranged attacks on rail networks during and after the disembarkation of Allied troops. All the rest were rejected, notably the Vidal Plan, which provided for the seizure of extensive areas by armed Resistance units. The attractive feature of this plan was that it might have secured useful bases for Allied airborne troops and airlifts of arms and ammunition. It would, however, have called for logistical preparations of such magnitude that the place and timing of the invasion could not have been kept secret.

Events ran their course with dread inevitability. During the weeks and months preceding the invasion, so-called Jedburgh missions had been flown in from England. These were threesomes, each consisting of one French, one British, and one American officer, whose task it was to make a last-minute, on-the-spot evaluation of the forces available, weld them together, and set them in motion in line with an overall strategic plan. But these hurried attempts to iron out the "third front" came too late. Here and there, in the Vercors and the Massif Central, Maquis units jumped the gun when they learned that the Allies had landed in Normandy. Eager to liberate French territory by their own efforts, they made independent attempts to proceed with the discarded Vidal Plan.

They did not get far. The Germans responded with massive counterattacks, throwing in tanks, artillery, and aircraft against inexperienced opponents armed largely with handguns. Gliders laden with veteran SS men landed on the Vercors highland plateau, which was ringed with mountains and supposedly inaccessible. Every spark of resistance was extinguished within a matter of days. Nobody remained to bury the seven hundred slaughtered pistol-fighters apart from a few horrified civilians.[18]

The "third front" was simply an established fact, and not to be abolished overnight. Despite a good deal of useful cooperation between Churchill and De Gaulle, it had often become the scene of melodramatic skirmishes during its years of uninterrupted existence.

One such clash occurred in December 1941, when De Gaulle launched a military operation, not against Nazi Germany, but against the United States. He ordered Admiral Émile Muselier to take three corvettes and head for St. Pierre and Miquelon, off the Newfoundland coast, where he was to land French marines and occupy both islands. His order was carried out, even though it blatantly violated his pledge to the United States that he would leave the islands under the administration of their Vichy governor. This was an affront whose prior history was temporarily less important than that it occurred on Christmas Eve, just two and a half weeks after the Japanese attack on Pearl Harbor.

The Americans' reaction to this pinprick from a difficult French ally—whom they had just offended, in their turn, by quietly confiscating fourteen French ships—was somewhat excessive. They demanded the immediate withdrawal of the marines and the three corvettes. De Gaulle rejected this request so brusquely that Washington considered restoring order with the aid of a small task force consisting of one cruiser and two destroyers. When Anthony Eden, the British Foreign Secretary, asked what would happen if American warships entered the islands' territorial waters and refused to be warned off, De Gaulle snapped, "We shall open fire." As it turned out, this budding naval battle on the "third front" ended in a mere exchange of words and a tame compromise.[19]

It was not, however, a unique case. De Gaulle had become so incensed with his British allies in June 1941, over the Syrian issue, that he flatly threatened the Minister of State, Oliver Lyttelton, with the possibility of a formal severance of relations.[20]

A mere unfounded hunch that the British might be planning to land forces in Madagascar was sufficient for De Gaulle to warn both the Western Powers in May 1942 that France would cease to cooperate with them and go her own way if a square foot of French soil were lost to Britain or the United States.[21] Although the General undoubtedly suffered from an obsessive fear that the Americans were seeking to extend their influence at France's expense, his suspicions have since been rebutted by thorough historical research.[22]

De Gaulle's mistrust and irascibility, brusque manner and deliberate condescension, were nonetheless a factor of some political importance. They provoked dislike and resentment in Washington, and particularly in the President himself. Many leading Americans came very close to adopting a turn of phrase used by Pétain in conversation with Admiral Leahy, the U.S. ambassador in Vichy and a personal friend of Roosevelt's, when he called De Gaulle "a traitor to his country."[23]

The imponderables of emotion and sentiment can sometimes outweigh concrete political interests, and this was so with the Allies and De Gaulle. Twenty-seven countries subscribed to the principles of the Atlantic Charter in January 1942. Haiti, Panama, Luxembourg, and Costa Rica were all invited to sign the declaration, but not De Gaulle's Free France.

Churchill mortally offended the General by informing him of the Allied landing in North Africa, in which not a single Frenchman took part, only when the operation was well under way. As for the Allied landing in Sicily, De Gaulle heard it reported on the radio long before Churchill deigned to tell him about it.

It is clear that the General contrived to alienate everyone on whose good will he was ultimately dependent. Even at the Teheran Conference late in 1943, Stalin himself declared that Pétain was the true representative of France, not De Gaulle.[24]

The General's strained relations with his allies entered a peculiarly critical phase on the day of the Normandy landings. General Eisenhower's announcement of the assault on "Fortress Europe" contained no mention of De Gaulle's Free French. Heedless of Churchill's furious insistence, De Gaulle in turn refused to add a word to Eisenhower's broadcast statement.[25]

Churchill then lost his temper and lectured De Gaulle like a schoolboy in the presence of Pierre Vienot, the French ambassador.[26] A letter written the same day requested him to leave England forthwith, but this was intercepted and destroyed by Foreign Secretary Eden.[27]

One week later and ten weeks before the liberation of Paris, Roosevelt told Henry Stimson, his Secretary of War, that De Gaulle would "crumple" and that his British supporters would be "confounded by the progress of events."[28]

De Gaulle himself often thought of quitting London, where he was subjected to "the mistrust of the Foreign Office and the colonial ambitions and intrigues of the Intelligence Service," and taking refuge in French-owned Brazzaville.[29]

At the end of May 1942 he unburdened himself to Molotov, the Soviet Foreign Minister. Not long afterward, he asked the Soviet ambassador in London, Aleksandr Bogomolov, whether the Soviet Union would be prepared to admit him and his armed forces to Soviet territory if he severed relations with Britain.[30]

Mutual Aggravation
or
Three Ideological Ricochets

Less complicated than De Gaulle's relations with Roosevelt and Churchill, but no less important, were Tito's relations with Stalin. As in the West, so in the East, what was at stake was the weal or woe, the success or failure, of the Resistance.

As soon as the German-Soviet friendship treaty came to an abrupt and violent end, Stalin hastened to establish good relations with every member of the anti-Hitler bloc, large and small. Three months after the Germans occupied Yugoslavia and only four weeks after they opened hostilities against Russia, he approached the Yugoslav Government-in-exile and expressed a wish to resume diplomatic relations.

Shortly afterward, at the beginning of September 1941, a Kremlin envoy was accredited to the Yugoslav court in London.

A direct radio link already existed between Tito and Moscow at this stage, so the Comintern must have known that the General Secretary of the Yugoslav Communist Party, Josip Broz Tito, had been appointed "Supreme Commander, General Headquarters of the National Liberation Partisan Detachments"—a somewhat high-flown title for the leader of what was still a collection of diminutive guerrilla bands.

For the moment, Moscow had other worries. It did not look as if the German advance would be quickly stemmed. With large tracts of her territory already controlled by the Wehrmacht, Russia was close to disaster.

The Soviet authorities did not, however, ignore the other occupied territories. In mid-September, their press and radio published the first reports of a burgeoning Resistance movement in Yugoslavia. Officers and men of the Yugoslav Army were said to have risen against the Germans in Serbia. No mention was made of Tito and his partisans.

During October and November, the Kremlin and the Yugoslav Government-in-exile held diplomatic discussions on the subject of whether it would be expedient to place all Yugoslav Resistance groups under a single commander, to wit, Colonel Draža Mihailović of the Royal General Staff. Once again, Tito's name did not crop up. In November the BBC hinted that it might be to Russia's advantage if Mihailović assumed command, and Radio Moscow's glowing references to the Colonel clearly conveyed Russian approval.[1]

Tito had been soliciting help from Moscow since August. Radio messages of growing urgency suggested that he should prepare airstrips or dropping zones for the delivery of arms, ammunition, and other military equipment by air. He would then inform Moscow when and where landings or airdrops could be made without risk to Russian aircraft. No answer. Tito renewed his concrete proposals and appeals for assistance in mid-November and late December.[2]

In contrast to the Russians, the SOE had been on the spot since October. Its British-manned military mission to Colonel Mihailović was gratified to discover, on arrival, that he had reached agreement with Tito, set up joint general staffs in western Serbia, and was fighting the Wehrmacht alongside Tito's partisans in the Valjevo district. The alliance fell apart after only six weeks, however, and by the end of October the Chetniks and Tito's men were at each other's throats. Early in November, during the fighting around Kraljevo, this "second front" degenerated into open civil war.[3]

Tito hurriedly informed the Russians and protested against Radio Moscow's reports of battles between the Chetniks and the German forces of occupation. He pointed out that Chetnik units had actually defected to the Germans and were now attacking his partisans. Moscow remained silent and the Comintern made no move.[4]

Tito and his partisans gained some successes in the ensuing months. Though completely encircled during the battle of Kraljevo, they managed to fight their way out and escape into Italian-occupied Montenegro, where they gained a firm foothold. Tito was now able to inform Moscow that a second Soviet Republic had been established in Yugoslavia.

At the end of 1941 he had proclaimed the small town of Užice, which was then jointly occupied by himself and Mihailović, a "People's Republic." Now, early in February 1942, he proclaimed a Soviet "People's Republic of Montenegro" in the mountainous terrain around the Durmitor, Montenegro's highest peak, an area unclaimed by the Germans and neglected by the Italians.

If Tito expected the Kremlin to show gratitude for this New Year's gift, he must have been bitterly disappointed. Radio messages received from Moscow early in March proved an eye opener. What was the point, asked Moscow, of forming a "proletarian front"? Why reinforce the suspicions of the Yugoslav Government-in-exile and the world at large that Moscow was aiming at the "Sovietization" of Yugoslavia? Why brand the partisan

movement as Communist instead of turning it into the country's "only true
National Front"? Tito's complaints that Mihailović was fighting on the
German side would not hold water, Moscow declared. He must undertake
a thorough revision of his attitude, which was dismissed as "sectarian
deviationism"—perhaps the harshest and most ominous condemnation in
the Party's store of jargon.[5]

Not long afterward, Tito received a reply to the cries for help that had
gone unanswered for six long months. Moscow informed him that every
effort would now be made to supply him with arms, but that the technical
problems were immense and could not, unfortunately, be surmounted in
the immediate future. Until they were, Tito's partisans must contrive to
capture weapons from the enemy and husband them with care.[6]

Moša Pijade, a member of the Party's Central Committee and holder of
the honorary title "People's Hero," later described how he and his comrades desperately strove to delude themselves at this period. "When no Soviet aircraft turned up," he wrote, "we were fully aware of the true reason.
Rather than annoy King Peter and the government-in-exile, Moscow chose
to deprive us of overt material and moral support. We nonetheless forced
ourselves to credit the existence of technical problems of some kind."[7]

Milovan Djilas tells in his second volume of memoirs how the Yugoslav
Resistance fought its weary way through 1942, dogged by internecine strife
and sanguinary clashes on the "second front." Wherever this minor but
self-lacerating war raged, it left a trail of misery, unquenchable hatred, and
charred ruins. Tito repeatedly urged the Comintern by radio to denounce
Mihailović as a class enemy and his Chetniks as collaborators, but the
Comintern held its peace.[8]

Finally, in September 1942, a signal arrived from Moscow. Tito was
requested to submit conclusive documentary evidence of Mihailović's alleged collaboration with the occupying power, but to check it carefully beforehand. It was not beyond the bounds of possibility that "certain documents" had been "deliberately forged by the conquerors." This could only
be a backhander at Tito and his associates, whom Moscow apparently suspected of manufacturing evidence against Mihailović.[9]

Meanwhile, the Kremlin had promoted its diplomatic representative
with the London government-in-exile to ambassadorial rank.

Loyalty and devotion, fighting spirit and ideological incorruptibility
were not enough, nor was it sufficient to be a staunch member and veteran
General Secretary of the Yugoslav Communist Party, to gain the respect of
Moscow. In mid-November 1942, Stalin offered the government-in-exile
the help he had denied to Tito. Without even being asked, he volunteered
to send a Soviet military mission led by senior Red Army officers to the
headquarters of the commander in chief of the Yugoslav Resistance, Draža
Mihailović. He also offered to make aircraft available to supply the Chetniks with arms, ammunition, and other equipment. Last but not least, he

broached the possibility of a pact in respect of political propaganda broadcasts.[10]

If this démarche had resulted in an agreement acceptable to Moscow, Tito would have found himself in an even more critical position on his own "third front" than De Gaulle in the West. The Yugoslav leader had nothing to fall back on—neither the resources of a colonial empire, nor regular troops, nor Anglo-American loans.

It was not Moscow's fault that no agreement was reached. The Yugoslav Government-in-exile stipulated that Mihailović should additionally be appointed commander of Tito's partisans, but the Russians were incapable of making such a commitment. Their authority would have been insufficient to dragoon Tito into surrendering to the "class enemy" on whom he had been waging war for a year.

It was not the Russians who came to Tito's aid, but the fortunes of war.

A second British military mission, which had been attached to Mihailović's headquarters since March 1942, ascertained that the areas he controlled were completely clear of German forces. The only battle front of interest to the Allies had melted away, as it were. That, coupled with the unwelcome suspicion that some of Mihailović's junior commanders had come to terms with the Italians and were receiving arms from them, transferred the Western Powers' attention to Tito.[11]

So far, only Mihailović had derived benefit from the SOE, which supplied the Yugoslav Government-in-exile with hundreds of tons of military equipment and six radio transmitters, as well as a hundred thousand dollars in cash, at the end of December. A transmitter in Jerusalem was also placed at its disposal for radio propaganda by the British military authorities in the Mediterranean area. Further aid agreements had been signed with the British and U. S. Governments in spring 1942—but what was the point, if Mihailović's combat troops were no longer in a position to harass the Germans?[12]

London decided to check for itself. During April and May 1943, Croatian and British liaison officers were flown into Tito's partisan domain. At the end of May, the first permanent British military mission arrived at his headquarters to conduct a detailed on-the-spot survey of the military situation. It was led by F. W. Deakin, who had once been Churchill's literary secretary and worked with him on his life of Marlborough. Deakin reached Tito's headquarters just as heavy fighting was in progress.

Enemy forces were making their fifth concerted attempt to dispose of Tito once and for all. According to Deakin's account, which was not published until 1971, over a hundred thousand men were deployed for this large-scale operation, including Italian and Bulgarian regulars, Ustashi, Chetniks, and a German mountain division supported by artillery, tanks, and aircraft.

Miraculously, ten thousand partisans succeeded in escaping from the pocket after a month's fierce fighting. They took ninety days to cover the three hundred-plus miles from Bosnia to Montenegro on foot, taking three thousand wounded with them. Of these, two thousand died. Thirty doctors and twenty nurses who had stayed behind to tend the wounded were shot with their patients. Deakin cites German documents which indicate that 5,697 partisans were killed in action and 411 out of 498 prisoners executed. Of the 11,000 civilians who had once inhabited the battle-scarred area, 2,357 lost their lives. Fifty villages were burned to the ground when fighting ceased.[13]

Tito had lost a battle but won his personal war. Deakin's reports convinced London of his partisans' military potential, and the War Cabinet decided to back him from now on. It was agreed that, with the invasion of Sicily imminent, Tito merited vigorous support.

But his fortunes continued their dramatic ups and downs. Although two armed Italian divisions defected to him after their country's surrender, he was seriously threatened by German forces and driven back into the mountains during the last three months of 1943. The SOE now came to his aid with over 2,000 tons of supplies. A further 6,700 tons of military equipment reached the partisans during the first quarter of 1944 and 8,600 tons during the second. Nearly 12,000 wounded partisans were flown out for treatment at Allied field hospitals in Italy.[14]

And Moscow?

The "National Liberation Council of Yugoslavia" (AVNOJ) had convened at Jajce late in November 1943 and invested itself with the powers of a provisional government, simultaneously depriving the government-in-exile of authority over Yugoslav territory. The King was forbidden to return to Yugoslavia and Tito appointed Marshal and War Minister of the Provisional Government.

This provoked an angry response in Moscow, where the representative of the Yugoslav Communist Party, Veljko Vlahović, was sharply rebuked. Stalin gave him to understand that he regarded the Jajce resolutions as "a stab in the back of the Soviet Union."

But the decisions reached at the Teheran Conference vindicated Tito and implicitly confirmed that Mihailović had had his day. Recognition of Tito as a member of the East-West alliance was virtually an accomplished fact.[15]

At long last, in mid-April 1944, a Soviet military mission was dispatched to Tito's headquarters. The British had preceded them by a year and the Americans, who arrived in March, by a month.

SOE aid assumed substantial proportions. Tito received 5,000 antitank guns, 346 aircraft, over 2,000 trucks, 134,000 automatic weapons, and a fully equipped armored brigade manned by partisans hurriedly trained in Italy. The United States supplied 100,000 rifles, 175,000 combat uniforms, and other equipment.[16]

Military operations in Yugoslavia were at this stage coordinated by the British. The theater of operations was divided into sectors, and the partisan commanders who took them over in August received detailed instructions from British officers. The latter were also responsible for calling in British naval and air support as required.[17]

During the third week of September, Tito startled the Western military missions by disappearing without prior warning or explanation. They later discovered that he had gone to Moscow.

It was not until after his return, at the end of September 1944, that the Russians, too, began to supply him on a massive scale. Their consignments included nearly 70,000 automatic weapons, some 20,000 pistols, a quantity of artillery, and 3,800 armored vehicles.[18]

By the time Soviet aid did start flowing, however, the Red Army stood poised on Yugoslavia's eastern border, Paris and Brussels had already been liberated, and British and American troops were nearing the frontiers of the Third Reich. Soviet aircraft using the British air base at Bari, in Italy, flew 1,460 sorties and delivered 3,000 tons of military equipment.[19]

"Tito wanted to be Moscow's friend, not its servant," writes Franz Borkenau. The only Eastern European leader to preserve his country from long-term Russian occupation, he secured the complete withdrawal of Soviet troops late in March 1945. The Yugoslav Resistance movement was alone in founding a new and independent state.[20]

As for the Soviet Union, it was more than just a difficult ally to those who carried on armed resistance in Yugoslavia—it was a positive threat. Had it rested solely with the Russians, Tito's partisan army might well have been sacrificed on the altar of Soviet foreign policy.

Skirmishes in Greece, Shots in Brussels

Italy's surrender in September 1943 abruptly and radically transformed the strategic situation in the Mediterranean area. From the British and American point of view, this was not an unmixed blessing because welcome military developments in Italy raised serious problems elsewhere.

There was a likelihood that German forces would withdraw from northern Greece or evacuate the whole country, and that rival Communist and non-Communist Resistance organizations would seize the chance to fight it out. Civil war seemed inevitable and the victory of the Communist-led ELAS units virtually assured. The strategic and diplomatic consequences of such a development would be not only far-reaching but extremely detrimental to the Western Powers.

Well-matured plans to avert this contingency by landing British troops were shelved when it turned out that the Wehrmacht was not, after all, abandoning its positions in the Balkans.

What could not be averted, on the other hand, was the civil war which ELAS forces inaugurated with an all-out campaign against their inferior opponents, the non-Communist EDES partisans. By promptly cutting off supplies of arms to ELAS, the SOE starved it of strength to such an extent that both Resistance movements appealed to the Allies to negotiate a cease-fire toward the end of the year. This armistice came into effect at the beginning of February 1944.[21]

The conflict was not resolved, however, merely postponed until the Germans withdrew. Meanwhile, everyone prepared for that day: the Communists by gaining control of the capital and as much of the country as possible, so as to pave the way for a successful coup d'état; the British by planning to forestall them and making every effort to ensure that Greece did not vanish behind the "Iron Curtain," which Churchill did not introduce into the vocabulary of international relations until two years later.

Both sides had taken up their positions by the end of November 1944. Eisenhower's troops were already fighting on German soil near Aachen, far to the northwest. The Russians had liberated Budapest and Belgrade and concluded an armistice with Bulgaria, Greece's immediate neighbor. The British High Command had by this time transferred 22,600 men and five squadrons of aircraft to Greece, sent for another division from Italy, and stationed a reserve force on the Greek mainland consisting of another division and a Greek mountain brigade. ELAS, whose estimated strength was eighteen to twenty thousand men, had meanwhile succeeded in occupying large areas of the country and numerous provincial capitals since evacuated by the Germans. Some of its forces were concentrated near Athens. The British had taken the precaution of occupying the capital itself in mid-October, first with paratroops and then with five thousand reinforcements.[22]

The pace of events quickened early in December. After clashes had occurred inside the city, the British commander, General R. M. Scobie, ordered ELAS to quit Athens. ELAS refused and went over to the attack. Its partisans stormed the police stations and seized so much of the capital that only the city center remained under British control.

On December 5 Churchill sent General Scobie a sharply worded telegram—even he called it "somewhat strident"—instructing him to proceed against ELAS. He, Scobie, was responsible for maintaining order in Athens and for neutralizing or destroying all ELAS forces approaching the city. He should have no hesitation in acting as if he were in a conquered city where a local rebellion was in progress. Athens must be held and dominated. It would be "a great thing" if Scobie succeeded in doing this without bloodshed, but he should not shrink from bloodshed if necessary.[23]

Churchill had no need to tread with care: he knew for certain that the Soviet Union would not back the Communist partisans in Greece. While negotiating with Stalin in Moscow only two weeks before, he had pushed a sheet of paper across the table bearing the terms of a startlingly simple deal: "Roumania: Russia 90%; the others 10%. Greece: Great Britain (in accord with U.S.A.) 90%; Russia 10%. Yugoslavia: 50–50%." Stalin had ticked this share-out with a big blue pencil and pushed it back, so perfect unanimity reigned.[24]

Stalin kept his part of the bargain. The Soviet press passed over the ELAS rebellion in silence, and Soviet propaganda devoted not a word to the battles raging in the center of Athens and the area between the capital and the port of Piraeus. ELAS waited for Russian parachute agents and military assistance—for a show of Russian solidarity—but in vain.[25]

British troops managed to clear the partisan-controlled area around Athens and, by degrees, the whole of Attica. Meanwhile, more British reinforcements had arrived in the Greek capital, which was also visited by Field Marshal Alexander. In view of the gravity of the situation, Churchill decided to fly there himself, accompanied by Foreign Secretary Eden. At Churchill's invitation, ELAS came to the conference table on Boxing Day. Those present included the U.S., French, and Soviet ambassadors, the last of whom adhered strictly to Stalin's instructions.

In mid-January, after six weeks of savage fighting, a truce came into force. ELAS had undertaken to withdraw from Athens and the seaports of Salonika and Patras and disband its forces in the Peloponnese. It did so, and was dissolved in mid-March. With the exception of two divisions, British troops could now be withdrawn from the Greek "third front" and redeployed against the Germans in Italy.[26]

British intervention in Greece unleashed a storm of indignation at home. Newspapers as prestigious as the *Times* and *Manchester Guardian* castigated the Prime Minister for what they called his "reactionary policy," and Parliament was thrown into turmoil. Compelled to justify himself in the Lower House, Churchill did so in a speech so eloquent and persuasive that he finally secured an overwhelming vote of confidence.[27]

In the United States, government circles and public opinion were thoroughly dismayed. The mere idea that Allied troops were using force against partisans who had fought the Germans seemed intolerable. There were "limitations," President Roosevelt telegraphed to London. The traditional policies of the United States and the adverse reaction of public opinion made it impossible for him and his government to back Churchill openly.[28]

Roosevelt's special adviser Harry Hopkins informed Churchill of his deep concern, and Edward Stettinius, who had just been appointed to succeed Cordell Hull as Secretary of State, issued a public protest on behalf of the U. S. Government against "military attacks on Resistance movements and their leaders" and against British attempts to seek a "reactionary solution" in the liberated territories.[29]

That, however, was an allusion not only to "the Greek affair" but also to British military policy in newly liberated Belgium, where events had followed a similar and almost simultaneous course.

At the end of November 1944, riots and shooting had occurred outside government ministries in Brussels. The General Secretary of the Belgian Communist Party called a general strike "to liberate the country from the government by any expedient means." Churchill reacted promptly by ordering the commander of the British 7th Armored Division, General G. W. E. Erskine, to restore order by force. On December 2, Erskine was able to report that his troops had foiled a Communist march on Brussels and nipped an attempted revolution in the bud.[30]

American criticism of British policy was also leveled at Churchill's unflagging efforts to influence events in Italy in favor of the monarchy. One result had been the resignation of Count Sforza, an anti-Fascist republican who had recently returned from political exile to join the Italian Government. This, too, had aroused fierce protests in the United States.

Strangely enough, therefore, it was the Resistance that brought these political differences to the surface and made it clear that the great powers themselves could be prickly partners.

But the Resistance nearly always came off badly. By moving out, the Germans deprived it, in a sense, of its *raison d'être*. All that remained was a weapon without a target and an organization without a purpose—unless, of course, its aim was to transform a country's internal power structure, in which case the great powers closed ranks against it.

To Britain, the ELAS movement in Greece was an interference factor requiring elimination. So it was to the Soviet Union. Even though a Communist takeover would have been in the Soviet interest, the war was still in progress and political preferences had to be subordinated to military exigencies. The Russians therefore bowed to strategic necessity and ditched their faithful Greek supporters. In the political judgment of the far-off Americans, British concern about the balance of power in the Mediterranean area carried less weight than the foreign policy principle of self-determination, which they considered essential to any secure peace. To them, Churchill's violation of this principle seemed to merit a public rebuke.

So the ELAS partisans were consigned to their doom by all three great powers when the Wehrmacht withdrew. One crushed them by force of arms because they militated against its political scheme of things; another left them in the lurch for reasons of strategic expediency; and the third merely lamented their passing because they were the victims of a flouted political doctrine—of Winston Churchill's supposed dereliction of duty.

The Warsaw Uprising

A similar tragedy had occurred in Poland a few months before, though there the roles were reversed. There the victims of strategic expediency had not been left-wing partisans but a secret army at grips with two occupying powers, German and Russian, and there it was Churchill, not Stalin, who was forced to leave the Resistance in the lurch. The Germans were on the retreat but had not yet evacuated the Polish capital when the Warsaw uprising broke out. It lasted sixty-three days.

Only two months elapsed between the Polish Home Army's surrender in Warsaw and Churchill's order to neutralize or destroy the ELAS partisans in Greece. During this brief period, Churchill had hurriedly secured Stalin's assent to his provisional share-out of spheres of influence and transferred British forces to Greece for the subsidiary war against ELAS. His doggedly determined stand during the Greek crisis cannot be fully comprehended without regard to his recent experience of Stalin and the Warsaw uprising.

On the night of July 29, 1944, Radio Moscow broadcast an appeal in Polish to the population of Warsaw: "If you attack the Germans at once—everywhere, in the streets, in buildings, factories, and warehouses—the hour of liberation will strike sooner." The next day another Russian transmitter broadcast a similar appeal on four separate occasions: "The Soviet Army is on the offensive. . . . It is coming to bring you freedom. People of Warsaw, to arms! Attack the Germans! Help the Red Army to cross the Vistula. . . . A million inhabitants of Warsaw will be a million soldiers driving out the German invaders. . . ."[31]

After another twenty-four hours, the German High Command reported that the Russians had begun their general assault on Warsaw. The Polish provincial secret army commander confirmed that the Red Army had advanced some six to nine miles nearer the capital.[32]

Inside Warsaw itself, German civilians had already packed their bags. German newspapers had ceased publication, and restaurants and bars were closed. Heartened by the sight of trains standing by to evacuate German civilians, the people of Warsaw feverishly awaited the signal to strike. On the afternoon of August 1, the supreme commander of the Polish Home Army, General Count Tadeusz Komorowski, generally known as Bor-Komorowski, launched an all-out attack on the occupying forces.

Of the forty thousand men under his command, only about twenty thousand were armed with rifles and submachine guns. Although reserves of ammunition were sufficient for only seven days, the insurgents managed to capture appreciable quantities of arms and foodstuffs, plus two Tiger tanks, in the first assault. They also succeeded in occupying most of the city center and the working-class district of Wola, but failed to press home their attacks on airfields, German administrative buildings, and the strategically vital bridges over the Vistula. Bor-Komorowski was nonetheless able to report to London that he could hold his present positions until the Red Army arrived. On August 4, his combat units were joined by the Communist partisans of Warsaw.

Meanwhile, the Russian advance had been halted by the loss of an armored corps defeated northwest of the capital. The thunder of Russian guns died away, and the Red Air Force—which had hitherto dominated the Polish skies—was withdrawn. This gave German bombers unlimited freedom to launch low-level attacks on the insurgents' positions as often as fifteen times a day. To oppose the rebels on the ground, the German High Command deployed General Kaminsky's Russian SS men, the dreaded daredevils of the Dirlewanger SS and Police Regiment, a number of Transcaucasian mercenaries, and men of a German police security regiment—in short, a motley but effective force equipped with tanks, artillery, and mobile, remote-controlled explosive charges. Stalin and the Red Army still held back.[33]

On August 4 Churchill informed Stalin in an "urgent, secret, and personal message" that he proposed to airdrop arms and ammunition into the southwest quarter of Warsaw at the urgent request of the Polish Underground Army, which was under attack by one and a half German divisions. The Poles had also apprised him of their wish to appeal for Russian help, which seemed so close at hand.

Stalin replied the next day that Churchill's information from the Poles was a gross overstatement. The Home Army really consisted of a few detachments, wrongly called divisions. It had no artillery, tanks, or aircraft. It was unthinkable that such "detachments" could capture a city defended by four German armored divisions.

Five days later Churchill informed Stalin that, during the previous night, Polish pilots of the Royal Air Force had made a renewed attempt to bring help to the Resistance fighters of Warsaw.[34]

In fact, twenty-three aircraft had attempted to fly arms and ammunition to Warsaw from Italy in the preceding six days. Only twelve planes reached the dropping zone and six had been lost.[35]

Another agonized appeal from Warsaw prompted Churchill to address a second telegram to Stalin. The Poles, he said, were begging for machine guns and ammunition. Couldn't Stalin help?

Once again, twenty-three aircraft tried to bring help from Italy. Eleven of them were damaged and another eleven destroyed before Stalin's reply to Churchill's inquiry arrived. The Soviet High Command had resolved to dissociate itself from the Warsaw "adventure" and assume no direct or indirect responsibility for it.[36]

London and Washington were both alive to the gravity of the situation.

Various attempts had been made to supply Bor-Komorowski from the air that spring, but only two out of twenty flights reached their objective. Equally heavy losses had been sustained during an even earlier attempt in September 1943. The costly experiment had in any case to be discontinued because Stalin curtly intimated that, from his own point of view, the arming of this particular Resistance movement was highly inopportune. Aiding the Warsaw insurgents without his assent and cooperation was therefore not only difficult but dangerous.[37]

Churchill and Roosevelt now made a joint attempt to change Stalin's mind. They pointed out how world opinion would react if the three great powers effectively abandoned the anti-Nazis in Warsaw. All three of them should surely do their utmost to save as many of the "patriots" there as possible. Would Stalin agree to supply the Poles by air or assist British and American planes in doing so? "We hope you will approve," they concluded. "The time element is of extreme importance."

Stalin's reply dashed all their hopes for good. Sooner or later, he telegraphed, the truth about the clique of power-hungry "criminals" who had embarked on the Warsaw adventure would become known to everybody. These individuals had exploited the good faith of Warsaw's inhabitants and pitted many almost unarmed people against German guns, tanks, and aircraft. The effect of this would be to exterminate the civilian population, not liberate Warsaw.[38]

The men of the Resistance, those "power-hungry criminals," fought until they could fight no longer. It was forty days before operations were resumed by the Russian troops who had lingered outside Warsaw for so many weeks. Between the forty-fifth and sixtieth days of the revolt, Russian aircraft carried out twelve airdrops of arms and ammunition over the capital, either without parachutes or with parachutes so defective that the equipment was damaged on impact.

The Western Powers gathered themselves for a last belated effort. On the forty-ninth day of the fighting, 110 USAF heavy bombers took off from bases in England and flew to Warsaw. They managed to drop less than a third of their payload over the city center. One hundred and seven canisters filled with arms and ammunition drifted down by parachute, but only fifteen are recorded as having fallen into rebel hands.[39]

Bor-Komorowski's combat units sustained such heavy losses—10,000 killed, 7,000 badly wounded, and 5,000 with lesser injuries—that on October 2, 1944, the exhausted survivors laid down their arms. The Germans are reported to have lost 2,000 killed and 9,000 wounded. Over 15,000 civilians lay dead in the city's streets and ruins, and total civilian fatalities were estimated at 50,000 to 150,000.[40]

Under the terms of the surrender document, Warsaw had to be completely evacuated. The surviving inhabitants and Polish prisoners of war began their exodus on October 4. Only a few armed men continued to lurk in the sewers and ruined buildings, among them a group led by an SOE parachute agent and a Jewish combat team which had joined the Warsaw Resistance after the ghetto's destruction less than five months earlier. They did not emerge into the light of day until the Red Army marched in.

Later, they told of a last-ditch Resistance fighter named Arès, whose exploits are confirmed by German reports dating from the period after October 10, 1944.

Flitting through the ruins like a ghost, this lone wolf crept up on German sentries from behind and slit their throats with silent and sinister dexterity. Having done so, he scratched his name on walls and left signed warnings addressed to German patrols. All attempts to capture Arès failed, even when a special detachment went after him with police dogs.

One patrol thought it had finally run him to earth when the distant strains of some march music came drifting down a deserted street. Tiptoeing nearer, the Germans discovered that its source was a partially damaged house. They stormed the building, only to be wiped out when a mine exploded under the stairwell. It was later established that the faint music had been issuing from a second-floor window. The record was still spinning on an ancient phonograph hooked up to a loudspeaker.

Undaunted to the last, Arès cheated the Germans by blowing his brains out. He had eaten some poisoned sausage left for him in the ruins like bait for a marauding rat. He was writhing in agony when he fired his penultimate round at the patrol that found him in his death throes.[41]

Even before the battle for Warsaw came to such a macabre end, something decisive had occurred on the political front. A week before the insurrection broke out, a "National Polish Liberation Committee"—a sort of rival Communist government—had been set up in Lublin. The government-in-exile in London promptly protested, and Bor-Komorowski led his Home Army into action partly because he and his men hoped to secure Poland against Soviet domination by liberating the capital with national Resistance forces before the Red Army arrived on the scene.

Telegrams exchanged by Stalin, Churchill, and Roosevelt during the battle for Warsaw attest how the paramount political problem of our century, then in its infancy, was shelved at the expense of the Polish Home Army.

It was clear that Allied bombers bringing help to the Resistance fighters of Warsaw would be dependent not only on long-range fighter support but also on an ability to refuel at Russian airfields before returning to England. This practice had already proved an effective aid to bombing raids on Germany in June. Now, however, when Churchill requested landing rights for aircraft engaged in relief flights to Warsaw, Stalin procrastinated. His initial response was silence.

Determined to enforce his cooperation, Churchill drafted a telegram and submitted it to Roosevelt. In it, he proposed to inform Stalin that he would send his bombers on to refuel in Russia unless the Marshal expressly forbade it.

At the same time, Churchill told Roosevelt that he intended to risk a trial of strength. If Stalin again proved evasive, he would simply order British planes to fly on to the Russian air base at Poltava and land there. They would then see how their Russian partner wriggled off the hook.

Roosevelt opined that it would not prove "advantageous to the long-range general war prospect" if he took Churchill's side in this matter. It had to be recognized that Stalin had already, in essence, refused permission for the aircraft to land.

Churchill now contemplated the possibility of an open breach with the Soviet Union—indeed, he even felt tempted to threaten Stalin with the immediate cessation of all British convoys. It was with this thought in mind that he called a meeting of the War Cabinet on the night of September 4.

Here he encountered grave misgivings. With the Allies and Hitler locked in one of the most murderous armed conflicts in history, would it really be warrantable to provoke a crisis so grave that the Alliance itself might fall apart in consequence?

The Prime Minister eventually yielded. Years later, when writing his war memoirs, he frankly admitted how much he deplored "the terrible and even humbling submissions that must at times be made to the general aim."[42]

Stalin granted permission for American bombers to land in Russia only when it became obvious that the Warsaw Resistance fighters were past saving.

Thus, Churchill had acted just as Stalin was to do a few weeks later. Each war leader sacrificed a politically friendly Resistance group, one in Poland and the other in Greece, one on the right of the political spectrum and the other on the left. This exhausts our scope for meaningful comparison, however, because the background and circumstances of each case were fundamentally different.

Stalin's aims in Poland were territorial aggrandizement and the expansion of Russia's power base, and for their sake he tolerated the slaughter of Resistance fighters who had risen against the Germans during the final battle for Poland. He deliberately gave Hitler's forces enough of a breathing space to smoke out the seat of non-Communist resistance, and he coerced the Western Powers into a similar policy of abandonment.

Churchill's object in Greece, by contrast, was to preserve a long-standing balance of power. While ELAS forces were fighting the Germans, they enjoyed, like Tito's partisans, the support of the Western Powers. As soon as they tried to install a Soviet-style regime in liberated Athens after the German withdrawal, British troops stepped in and Stalin unhesitatingly sacrificed his political allies in the interests of foreign policy.

The renunciation of ideology—a historical commonplace whenever great powers struggle for supremacy—was one of the most conspicuous features of World War II. It was Stalin, not Churchill alone, who backed the King of Italy in the spring of 1944, when the Italian Resistance called for his abdication. It was Stalin again, not De Gaulle, who disarmed the Communist partisans in France by instructing the General Secretary of the French Communist Party to call for the disbandment of all "irregular formations" and see that it was carried out.[43] It was Hitler, harnessed to his ideological archenemy Stalin by a treaty of friendship, who tolerated the existence of Communist parties in occupied Scandinavia, Holland, and Belgium, and allowed printed matter to be produced in Germany for the French Communist Party. French Communists were levered into cabinet posts by a conservative named De Gaulle, and thousands of Jews were saved with the connivance of a senior SS officer in Denmark.

All this points to two conclusions. In the first place, the war gave birth to a variety of human impulses which had not existed before it broke out. This applies as much to De Gaulle's cooperation with Communists as it does to Best's protection of Danish Jews. Secondly, though hard to define and often declared extinct, the element of nationality emerged during the war as a force by which all ideologies were temporarily absorbed and assimilated. World War II was a war of nations, not ideologies—nor, least of all, was it a class struggle in disguise. Even the Soviet Union waged a "national war," and there was no Communist Party in the whole of Europe that did not style itself a "national front" or "national Resistance movement."

This was the source from which the major Resistance movements drew their entire strength. Too close an adherence to ideology brought them into conflict with political reality and exposed them to the perils of their extremely vulnerable position—their inescapable dependence on the great powers and the vicissitudes of war. Henri Michel once said, quite rightly, that the Allies were the victors of World War II but the men and women of the Resistance its direst sufferers.

Resistance to Resistance
or
The Question of Military Value

It is not entirely clear, even today, how much of a practical asset or liability the Resistance was to its prickly partners in the outside world.

Books devoted to recounting the achievements and victories, sacrifices and sufferings of the various national Resistance movements tend to inundate the reader with facts and figures. These conjure up a picture of sinister destructive power so immense as to suggest that, at certain times and places in occupied Europe, there can have been scarcely a single undamaged railroad track, few serviceable bridges and telephone lines, and no roads safe for German troops to use.

The numerical language of this historical stocktaking exercise is quite overwhelming, and most of its data are probably accurate. To attempt to double-check them at this stage would be pointless in any case, because the achievements of the Resistance are beyond dispute. What is more important is to distinguish between performance and effect.

To take a single example: A Resistance movement manages to blow up a railroad line in a thousand places, rendering it temporarily unusable for troop movements by the occupying power. This is a signal feat of sabotage, yet its practical utility may be less than nil. Why? Because the line's importance may have been wrongly evaluated or the charges detonated at the wrong time or in the wrong sections, or because sabotage on such a massive scale may prod the occupying power into punitive measures that take a disproportionate toll of the local population and the Resistance itself. Effect, not performance, constitutes the prime criterion of military value, that of the Resistance included.

This, needless to say, is a point on which opinions differ widely.

The French historian Marcel Baudot asserts that Resistance units in France temporarily obstructed 150,000 German troops, appreciably delayed the transfer of some ten divisions to Normandy, and held up German armored forces hurriedly summoned from the South of France.[1]

According to the Allied Supreme Command, Resistance forces south of the Loire delayed the arrival of German reinforcements by approximately forty-eight hours.[2]

Writing in *Revue Nationale,* an officer of the French Army's Historical Services claimed that the Wehrmacht was demoralized by the threat to its supply lines. He went on to state that the combat units of the French Resistance represented a military force equivalent to twenty regular divisions.[3]

Quite a different picture emerges from a report by the senior intelligence officer of German Army Group G, Southern France. Far from disparaging the achievements of the Resistance, he assessed them—as we now know—with remarkable accuracy.

He began by reporting that French Resistance movements had stepped up their offensive operations throughout his army group's area, as foreseen, when the Allies landed in the South of France on August 15, 1944. "The focus of activity," he went on, "was in the Rhône Valley, where supply columns and disengaging movements were unpleasantly but not significantly disrupted. Rail traffic, on the other hand, was completely paralyzed by sabotage. Unified command of the numerous guerrilla bands was either deficient or unable to make itself felt. Systematic arming, equipping, and military training had been initiated but was not yet of a high standard. Strong political dissension within the French Resistance movement resulted in a dissipation of strength, so that, viewed as a whole, it played no decisive part in the fighting."[4]

So the Maquis caused "unpleasant but not significant disruption" and "played no decisive part . . ." The German intelligence chief was far from alone in this view, which was later endorsed by military experts as distinguished as B. H. Liddell Hart.

Liddell Hart concedes in his well-known work *The Defence of the West* that armed Resistance groups had undoubtedly imposed a heavy strain on the Wehrmacht, and that its effect had been most pronounced in France. "General Blumentritt, Chief of Staff to Field Marshal von Rundstedt in the West, told me how operations of the Maquis interfered with the switching of German forces to meet the Allied invasion. Headquarters had to be strongly guarded and generals accompanied by armed escorts when driving about."

Qualifying this, he goes on: "But when these back area campaigns are analysed, it would seem that their effect was largely in proportion to the extent to which they were combined with the operations of a strong regular army that was engaging the enemy's front, and drawing off his reserves. They rarely became more than a nuisance unless they coincided with the fact, or imminent threat, of a powerful offensive that absorbed the enemy's main attention. At other times they were less effective than widespread passive resistance—and brought far more harm to the people of their own country. They provoked reprisals much severer than the injury inflicted on the enemy."[5]

As a brief survey will show, this verdict applies to all the occupied territories in Europe.

Where Italy is concerned, the Wehrmacht war diary for the summer of 1944 contains situation reports in which the same turns of phrase crop up. The Germans' movements, we are told, with special reference to reserves, were "hampered" and their communications and supply lines "disrupted."[6]

Wherever armed partisans worked in concert with the Allied High Command, on the other hand, they could contribute valuable assistance to a large-scale operation, for instance by protecting communications and industrial plants.[7] The successful bomb attacks on railroad installations in Norway during the winter of 1944–45 were likewise attributable to cooperation between MILORG and the SOE. Only one German division per month could be withdrawn from Norway instead of the four that had previously been pulled out in the same span of time.[8]

Working on instructions from London, the Polish Home Army destroyed approximately 20,000 railroad cars, 7,000 locomotives, and 4,000 tons of gasoline during the period 1940–42. Poland's geographical position rendered this extremely useful to the Allied war effort because 70 percent of all major communications routes and five arterial roads linking the Third Reich with its forces in the Soviet Union passed through Polish territory. This proves, yet again, that Resistance operations acquired real value only when they were systematically incorporated into overall strategic planning.[9]

Liddell Hart supplies a similar answer to the vexed question of the Warsaw uprising, which Bor-Komorowski launched without the Allies' knowledge. The Polish Government-in-exile had authorized him to do so— probably on the strength of a false assessment—but omitted to consult the Allied Supreme Command in advance.[10] A mere attempt to reach prior agreement with London and Washington might well have deterred the Resistance and the population of Warsaw from squandering lives that purchased nothing of value and prevented nothing of consequence.[11]

Russia and Yugoslavia, of course, were peculiarly rich and instructive sources of practical experience.

Where Russian partisans were concerned, German situation reports often struck an alarming note. In December 1943, for example, the general in charge of transportation for the four armies comprising Army Group Center reported that guerrillas had severely hampered rail traffic by blowing up sections of track. He also stressed that the campaign was "centrally directed with an eye to operational factors" so as to "hit us where it hurts most."

The effects of this disruption were listed as follows: prolonged turnaround times for locomotives and rolling stock, crashes between trains immobilized by breaks in the track and others following on behind, and a rapid buildup of congestion in junctions to the rear.

The final sentence of this report had a particularly ominous ring: "Large-scale operational attacks by guerrillas . . . can, in difficult situations, prove decisive."[12]

But did they?

Erich Hesse, who conducted a detailed study of Soviet partisan warfare, came to the conclusion that, although partisans never matched regular troops in combat effectiveness, they were capable by 1943 of performing eight valuable tasks. They isolated German combat troops from their rearward lines of communication, impaired their combat strength by launching surprise attacks, encircled smaller garrisons, carved out corridors for advancing Soviet troops, prepared facilities for river crossings, plugged gaps in the front, and—in the north—converted every rear area into a battlefield.

According to Hesse, the decisive factor in these successes was "the inclusion of the partisan army in strategic planning"—in other words, precisely what Liddell Hart considered so essential to purposeful and effective guerrilla activity.[13] One indication of the extent to which this requirement was actually met in the Soviet Union is that, as early as 1942, partisans were officially termed "soldiers of the Red Army behind the enemy lines."[14]

But there were other reasons for their success.

Russian partisans were not fighting in a country that had lost the war. They took part in large-scale operations which were gradually wearing down an enemy inferior to the Red Army in numbers and equipment. By mid-1942, moreover, the Soviet Air Force had gained superiority on every front.

Yet another factor was that the German forces never, from the outset, had enough tanks and other heavy weapons to eliminate the partisans, who received their supplies by air.[15]

The Germans suffered from sheer lack of manpower. In October 1941, all they could muster to control the territory behind their central sector— an area one and a half times the size of Great Britain or the Federal Republic of Germany and bigger than Italy and Switzerland combined— was three holding divisions, two second-rate infantry divisions, and an SS brigade. One understrength division, consisting of two infantry regiments and a motorized transportation company, had to repell partisan attacks and provide internal security in an area twice the size of Switzerland and larger than the three Benelux states put together.[16]

This means that the partisans' achievements must be set against their enemy's weakness as well as measured by their strategic utility. According to official Soviet war historians, Russian partisans disabled over a million enemy soldiers and auxiliary personnel, derailed eighteen thousand trains, and destroyed eighty-five thousand railroad cars.[17] By themselves, however, these figures tell us little. We may marvel at such feats, but their practical evaluation demands a thorough knowledge of the concomitant strategic circumstances.

Discounting many other carefully compiled studies published in Europe and the United States, these circumstances owe their elucidation primarily to a group of American historians who conducted research into the major aspects of partisan warfare in Russia, initially on behalf of the U. S. Government and later as an independent research team.

Edited by John A. Armstrong and published by the University of Wisconsin in 1964, their findings are embodied in a large symposium containing case histories and excerpts from documents of interest as well as analytical studies.[18]

Armstrong and his colleagues came to the conclusion that, notwithstanding their remarkable achievements and their integration into the Red Army, Russian partisans exerted no significant effect on the strategic situation and the course of the war. Although they disrupted or delayed supplies like irregular combat units in other countries, they never managed to suspend German troop movements or block them entirely. As for the joint operations occasionally mounted by large partisan formations and units of the Red Army, their practical utility was on the meager side.[19]

Another American expert, Edgar M. Howell, had earlier explored the possible reasons for this. He ascertained that to the rear of Army Group Center, where partisan units were active on a grand scale under centralized command, over fifteen thousand sabotage attacks were made on railroad installations during the single month of August 1943. Five hundred attacks a day seemed a remarkable achievement.

But Howell also discovered that the most vital rail link in the whole area, the Brest–Minsk–Smolensk section, was damaged in only 903 places, that another twin-track section four hundred miles long sustained serious damage at only four points, and that the partisans squandered precious lives and equipment in over two thousand attacks on unimportant subsidiary lines. Compared with a total of fifteen thousand incidents, this was an exceptionally poor showing.

Furthermore, intervals between sabotage attacks had often enabled the Wehrmacht to repair the damage quickly enough to avert its intended effects. Finally, it turned out that the partisans' sabotage technique was not always up to the mark.

This was why their immense efforts and apparent successes proved ultimately unproductive. For all the undoubted damage they caused, their strategic objective—to paralyze the flow of German supplies and reinforcements and sever lines of retreat—was never attained. Howell ascertained that German forces were, in fact, able to retreat westward in a smooth and almost methodical manner, and that their losses of men and equipment were small in relation to the exceptional hazards of the general situation. From a strategic point of view, the partisans' large-scale operations resembled a dazzling display of pyrotechnics.[20]

Howell pointed out that it is practically impossible to supervise and control a force of over one hundred thousand men at a range of several hundred miles, still less an "army" whose structure and training, equipment and discipline fall short of regular army standards. All the European Resistance movements, that of Russia included, suffered from lax organization, civilian indiscipline, and erratic and volatile behavior.[21]

This view is now shared by most authorities on the subject. The Soviet Union was conspicuously late in supplying the Resistance organizations and Communist partisans of Eastern Europe with arms, so its peculiar reluctance may be an indication that Soviet military experts took much the same view of them as their counterparts in the West.

In the public mind, however, other ideas live on because legends—like all forms of exaggeration—are possessed of great persuasive power. Fantastic estimates of the losses supposedly inflicted on German forces by Soviet partisans are incessantly broadcast, cited, and reproduced. It is claimed, for instance, that they killed 147,835 German soldiers in the Orel district alone, whereas Armstrong's research has established that total partisan-inflicted casualties on that front were really in the region of 35,000.[22]

Many similar exaggerations were, and are, current in respect of Tito's partisan war.

Tito Hits and Runs

Yugoslavia engendered a partisan army that was wholly dependent for years on itself and its own resources. For most of the time it received no arms, ammunition, or other military equipment from any quarter. Nobody took any notice of it until the first British military mission arrived.

In contrast to the partisans of Russia, Tito's combat units could best be likened to wild guerrilla bands. Constantly harassed and often hounded to death, they survived only because their dwindling ranks were replenished by a steady stream of fugitives from minor wars of the most terrible and chaotic nature. Individual groups and formations were nonetheless held together by a unified high command which never became separated from them during their almost continuous retreats. Having grown out of nothing, this irregular "people's army" not only became a source of grave concern to the principal occupying power but eventually emerged victorious from its duel with a far superior opponent.

A historical marvel?

We have already spoken of Yugoslavia as a divided country under six-fold rule. In addition to the rabid and murderous police units commanded by Milan Nedić of Serbia and Ante Pavelić of Croatia, military forces belonging to four occupying powers—Germany, Italy, Bulgaria, and Hungary—looked after the internal and external security of their allotted areas.

This was an asset to Tito's partisans. When hard pressed by one occupying power, they usually succeeded in dodging into the territory of another because operations by the multifarious security forces were not coordinated. Another asset was the rugged mountainous terrain, which afforded ideal places of refuge and precluded the deployment of tanks and heavy artillery.

Tito's answer to attacks by superior forces was flight and evasion. On one occasion he withdrew from western Serbia to the Croatian mountains, on another from Montenegro to eastern Bosnia. From the strategic aspect, all that saved him and his partisans from annihilation was an acceptance of defeat by stages.

Once again, this is inconsistent with the views that have taken root in the public mind.

Tito's partisans were holding fifteen German divisions at bay, declared a British M.P., Sir James Grigg, in January 1944. The Yugoslav historian Dušan Plenca later outdid him by claiming that Nazi Germany was compelled to maintain twenty-four divisions in Yugoslavia, the obvious implication being that this substantial military force had been stationed there to combat the partisans and was therefore "contained" by them. This seemed proof positive that the partisan army had been of military—indeed, strategic—service to the Allied powers.

Unfortunately, this is yet another overstatement. Robert M. Kennedy of the U. S. Army's Historical Section in Washington established on the strength of German documents that only thirteen Wehrmacht divisions were stationed in Yugoslavia at the end of 1943, including one division of Russian legionaries. In December 1943, the period to which Grigg and Plenca were alluding, only five of these thirteen were briefly assigned to eastern Bosnia for the antiguerrilla operations "Kugelblitz" [Globe Lightning] and "Schneesturm" [Blizzard]—a numerical peak that had not been equaled since the end of 1941 and was never attained again.[23]

The immense concentration of German forces on the Russian front had, after all, to be achieved at the expense of other areas. Between April and July 1941, German forces of occupation in the Balkans were reduced from twelve to seven divisions. Of these, Yugoslavia was assigned only four reserve divisions, more than half of whose personnel were World War I veterans. The military defense and policing of Southeastern Europe, though not of the German-occupied zone, had to be undertaken by thirty-two Italian divisions, twenty of which were stationed in Yugoslavia and Albania.[24]

In December 1941 and January 1942, the German forces had to release a mountain corps and another two infantry divisions for the Eastern Front. This left them genuinely too weak to combat the partisans effectively, and the German High Command was forced to enlist the help of Bulgarian troops in southeastern Serbia. In 1942 the German forces of occupation had to be increased to a total of six divisions. When the twenty Italian divisions stationed in Yugoslavia were canceled out by Italy's surrender in September 1943, all that could be scraped together to replace them was an additional force of seven German and four Bulgarian divisions.

Only between one and two of the thirteen German divisions in Yugoslavia were employed in major antiguerrilla operations during 1944. Bulgarian, Croatian, and other allied forces had to bear the brunt of the fighting because many of the German troops were too overage or exhausted to endure the rigors of mountain warfare.[25] Apart from this, absolute priority now went to other tasks such as securing the coasts against an Allied invasion, protecting essential military and industrial installations, and guarding consignments of strategically important raw materials bound for Germany.[26]

In 1943, to cope at least partly with the growing difficulties of their position in Yugoslavia, the Germans proceeded to build up a network of strongpoints patrolled by armored cars equipped with searchlights and heavy guns. The areas outside this security zone were only occasionally penetrated by raiding parties of the sort employed in Russia. These consisted of seasoned combat troops inured to living under conditions of extreme hardship. Dressed in civilian clothes or partisan uniforms, they stalked the guerrillas or infiltrated and reconnoitered their positions, then summoned reinforcements and took them by surprise.[27]

This security system, which effectively left the partisans and Chetniks free to "liberate" substantial parts of Yugoslavia, accounts for another misconception.

Although Tito's partisans controlled a "liberated" area the size of Switzerland during the latter half of 1943, this did not mean that they had wrested it from the Wehrmacht in battle. The Germans had deliberately, albeit unwillingly, relinquished it to them—a military situation outside the realm of victory or defeat. In the same way, the fact that territory had been "liberated" from the chetniks was of absolutely no strategic use to the Allies.

The new situation nonetheless benefited Tito's partisans by presenting them with a steadily expanding area in which to create, almost unmolested, the political and military infrastructure that was to prove its worth during the final phase of the war and, even more so, in the immediately ensuing period. As soon as Churchill tipped the scales in Tito's favor, the partisan leader saw his big chance.

In the spring of 1944, when SOE arms supplies were already coming in, Tito suffered a grave but temporary reverse. An antiguerrilla operation code-named "Rösselsprung" [Knight's Move] inflicted heavy casualties on his men, killing six thousand of them, and he himself so narrowly escaped capture by German paratroops that he had to be taken to safety on the island of Vis with British help. As soon as the Allied High Command assigned his forces definite tasks within the context of an overall strategic plan, however, they at last attained the military importance that had so far been denied them.

What price did Tito's partisans have to pay, over the years, for the uncertain prospect of success? According to German figures, 65,000 killed in their battles with the Wehrmacht alone; according to Yugoslav figures, which also take account of operations against the Chetniks, nearly 300,000 killed and 400,000 wounded—strategically speaking, an immense waste of effort and manpower.

In August 1944, Tito's forces were still put at 120,000 men by the Germans and at 370,000–500,000 by Eastern European postwar writers.[28]

Yugoslavia's experience thus accorded with that of other occupied countries. The achievements of the armed Resistance could be substantial, but its loss of life was colossal, its military value not outstanding, and its strategic value surprisingly low. Whether such a loss of life was justified is a political and moral question which victors and vanquished see in two different lights. Fruitless sacrifices are harder to endure than those that lend belated luster to success.

However useful the European Resistance movements may have been to the Allies, a balanced view must also take account of the harm they did, or simply of the disadvantages accruing to Allied strategy from their mere existence. The problems of the partnership were not, after all, the invariable responsibility of one side alone.

In November 1944, for example, the activities of ELAS caused the British High Command to transfer sizable forces to Greece, and even to withdraw a division from the Italian theater, in order to preserve the threatened status quo in Athens and the country at large. The harm this inflicted on the Western Powers was not only appreciable but precisely calculable.

The liberation of Paris provides another example. When the invasion forces broke out of Normandy and began to push for the German frontier, the Allied Supreme Command would have preferred to bypass the city and save precious time, but its Resistance-led insurrection ruled this out. The French capital's victory jamboree cost the Americans four thousand tons of equipment a day, disrupted tactical operations, and delayed the general advance. Furthermore, many of the uncoordinated and random acts of sabotage committed at this period by individual Resistance organizations proved quite as obstructive to advancing Allied troops as they did to the retreating Germans.[29]

But the Allies also suffered badly from the fact that the Resistance movements took time to learn the difficult art of organized conspiracy—a process in which grave mistakes were made and heavy losses incurred. Amateurs and dilettantes were comparatively easy meat for German intelligence agents, who penetrated all the major French Resistance groups with little difficulty. Once on the inside, they not only pried into Resistance plans and operations but discovered where SOE or SIS agents were at work and when and where to expect airdrops of sabotage equipment or SOE-supplied arms.

The Germans kept a careful tally of their successes in this field. During 1942, one French airdrop in every four fell into the hands of their Security Police. By the following year this proportion had risen to over half, or 60 percent.

Airdrops were sometimes allowed to proceed uninterrupted with a view to striking later and more effectively. The Germans pulled off some record hauls in this way. During the summer of 1943 their Security Police raided 32 secret arms and explosives dumps in a single month. There they found 3,239 parachute canisters laden with over 60 tons of arms, explosives, and equipment, including 7,000 hand grenades, 1,600 submachine guns, 3,500 incendiary bombs, and 26 radio sets. In the first seven months of the same year they netted a total of 145 caches of arms and explosives, 64 secret arms dumps accumulated by the disbanded treaty army, no less than 87 radio sets, and all the arms delivered in 43 airdrops.[30] This equipment not only failed to reach the Resistance but was a corresponding drain on Allied resources.

Thanks to sheer inexperience, technical ignorance, or touches of carelessness, many courageous and well-meaning men and women fell prey to the wiles of German Military Intelligence. Particularly in the case of Resistance radio operators, the Germans learned that suitable treatment could—in espionage jargon—"turn" their prisoners. With the aid of these amateur operators, who hoped to save their lives by complying with their captors' outwardly innocuous requests, the German Security Police managed for a while to run eleven French "Resistance" transmitters simultaneously. They even persuaded the Allied Supreme Command to believe in the existence of imaginary Maquis organizations. British intelligence officers who had been counting on the presence in one operationally important coastal area of well-drilled communications centers, Resistance strongpoints, and sabotage teams did not discover until the Normandy landings had taken place that no such facilities existed. Because the Resistance had, so to speak, become a tool of the occupying power in this area,

the Allied forces landing there found themselves in a sinister and dangerous vacuum.[31]

The lengths to which this game could be carried were also demonstrated
in the East. During 1943, "turned" Czech SOE radio operators and parachute agents inserted from the Soviet Union began to fabricate a number
of "Resistance centers" on the instructions and under the control of the
Gestapo. They even invented an illegal "Communist Party of Bohemia and
Moravia" and dispelled any suspicions by radioing Moscow for express
legitimation, which was duly granted. In the winter of 1944–45, representatives of this spurious body met with delegates from genuine Resistance organizations at a Dominican monastery in Prague, where they took
receipt of some "strictly confidential" questionnaires completed by their
unsuspecting victims. Every last one of the genuine Resistance fighters
vanished into Gestapo jails.[32]

How to distinguish the genuine from the fake? Which Resistance organizations were really working for the Gestapo, German Military Intelligence,
or the German Security Police? The true relevance of these questions did
not become clear until the Allies discovered, toward the end of the war,
that the Dutch Resistance and the SOE had been hoodwinked for nearly
two years by "Unternehmen Nordpol" [Operation North Pole].

This celebrated project differed from all the rest in the sophistication of
its methods and the exceptional scale on which it operated. It was made
possible only because some courageous Dutch Resistance fighters, who
had been trained as SOE radio operators and parachute agents in England,
were unlucky enough to be detected by German Intelligence after their
very first parachute landing in Holland. They were then arrested and
"turned."

Under duress, the Dutchmen established contact with SOE headquarters
in London, as arranged, and transmitted messages concocted by their German captors. These contained reports of interest to the British High Command and kept London up to date on the activities of various Dutch Resistance centers. The reports were fictitious: the Resistance centers did not
exist.

More Dutchmen were dispatched by the SOE and likewise fell into the
German trap. And so there arose—at least in the minds of the SOE authorities—a whole network of Resistance groups complete with their own
radio operators. Run by "turned" agents; these phantom networks exchanged information with London via fourteen secret radio links and requested further assistance. The British duly began to supply their Dutch
mirage with arms and reinforce its staff of agents.

One out of every three aircraft approaching the Dutch coast was now
shot down. All the military and sabotage equipment delivered to the spurious Resistance organization by air and sea fell into German hands, includ-

ing fifteen thousand rifles and handguns. Fifty-four SOE men ended up in German prisons, and forty-seven were shot.

Meanwhile, German agents posing as Dutch Resistance fighters organized an "escape network," picked up stranded Allied airmen, took them to "safe houses," treated them hospitably, and radioed their names to London. They even sneaked some of them back to England.

One day, a German freighter laden with aircraft components blew up on the Meuse, right in the middle of Rotterdam. The charges had been laid and detonated by German Military Intelligence agents. Like Third Reich press reports, the encoded radio messages received by London credited this spectacular act of sabotage to one of the fake Resistance centers that were really maintained by "Unternehmen Nordpol."[33]

This large-scale project clearly demonstrates that the Germans were less concerned to combat the Resistance than to employ it as a means of injuring Britain, their principal foe in Western Europe. In exploiting the Resistance, German Intelligence was essentially doing as the Allies did.

A postwar fact-finding committee ruled that the SOE was chiefly to blame for "Unternehmen Nordpol's" almost two-year span of undetected activity. This does not, however, alter the fact that many Resistance organizations were gullible and incautious enough to harm the Allies by allowing German agents to infiltrate their centers and lines of communication. As time went by, their allies in the outside world became more and more uneasy and suspected them, often unfairly, of dangerous incompetence and unreliability.

The reserve and mistrust that reigned in the Allied capitals seemed doubly justified to critics of the Resistance because its weaknesses were compounded by political dissension. Prominent figures like Tito, Bor-Komorowski, and De Gaulle were associated in their minds with a whole host of unpleasant experiences.

Difficult as the great powers must often have seemed to the men and women of the Resistance, the Allies found their partnership just as taxing.

And yet, for all its trials and tribulations, the grand alliance survived.

POSTSCRIPT

Any postscript to this inexhaustible subject must attempt to summarize by briefly reverting to the three basic, closely interwoven factors of provocation, collaboration, and resistance.

Provocation—or what we have here called "the grand challenge"—was discussed in the middle of the war by a senior German official in occupied France. In his experience, the fruits of which he embodied in a report, it was resistance that provoked the occupying power, not vice versa.

In the judgment of the same official, it was a downright perversion of historical fact to assert that the inhabitants of the occupied territories were provoked by the Germans. He claimed that the contrary was true—that the French never rebelled against the occupying power of their own accord, and that resistance was simply "illegal aggression" on the part of outside agents or the long and forever mischief-making arm of revolution.[1]

This viewpoint is interesting because it shows that provocation is not automatically regarded in the same light by all who practice or experience it. The remilitarization of the Rhineland in March 1936 meant very little to the Finns and Portuguese, nor did many Greeks, Irish, or Albanians look upon the invasion of Poland as a directly provocative act. Even in Paris, the capital of an ally committed to Poland by treaty and pledges of mutual assistance, the question of "dying for Danzig" was still under serious debate on the eve of World War II.

On the other hand, repeated provocations of a political, ideological, moral, economic, and military nature combined to create the grand challenge that loomed on the European horizon like a distant thunderhead before impinging on the consciousness of different nations at different stages. For it was not until a country was militarily invaded and subjected to arrogant and inhuman foreign tyranny on its own soil that the grand challenge really declared itself. Becoming steadily more acute as the war progressed, it assumed forms which sooner or later compelled most Europeans to commit themselves one way or the other.

It goes without saying that no aggressor regards his aggression as an affront. To the German official cited above, resistance had no prior history. He saw it as an unexpected, unwarranted—indeed, "illegal"—challenge to the German authorities, who were, from his legalistic viewpoint, entitled by the mere right of conquest to maintain order by any means they chose. To him, a representative of the occupying power, the indelible and intolerable experiences of the defeated French were of no concern.

Thus began a self-perpetuating process characterized by growing ferocity. Originally a reaction, resistance itself became a form of provocation. The occupying power countered with retaliatory measures which in turn provoked the Resistance into hitting back harder. Every act of vengeance was succeeded by retribution, every blow by a riposte, and the end product of this crescendo of violence was a war of terrorism and counterterrorism, or, to resurrect the frightful expression coined by Gottlob Berger, head of the SS Central Office, a war of "clearing murders." The dialectical spiral of mutual provocation and aggravation runs like an unbroken thread, not only through the history of the Resistance, but also—in countries where local militias were active—through that of conditional and unconditional collaboration.

For most of the time, collaboration was what characterized the basic attitude of the majority of the 180 million adult Europeans who were condemned to live with the enemy. Neutral collaborationism, a widespread attitude which eschewed politics as far as possible and construed itself simply as an unavoidable adjustment to adverse circumstances, rendered invaluable service to the German war effort. Not because they were National Socialists, but because they wanted to survive the war or acquire a better standard of living, millions of European workers voluntarily migrated to Germany and worked for Hitler's armaments industry. In the same way, long before they were compelled to do so, businessmen, industrialists, and financiers placed their factories and financial assets—indeed, whole sectors of the national economy—at the Third Reich's disposal. Particularly beneficial to Hitler's war economy was the "qualified collaboration" practiced by men like Marshal Pétain and his government associates, who believed that political commitment would guarantee them a socially stable future and even, if all went well, a lucrative partnership with Hitler's mighty empire.

The occupied countries' economic contribution to the German war machine has been estimated at 104 billion reichsmarks. From this sum, after deducting all expenses, the German war economy derived 60 billions for the purchase and manufacture of arms and military equipment.[2] But for voluntary cooperation on a vast scale, and without the contribution made by voluntary or conscripted labor and by huge consignments of goods and raw materials from the occupied countries, which reached an all-time high in 1944, Europe's industrial output would never have sufficed to do what it did in the final year of the war: despite resistance, sabotage, and devastating strategic bombardment by the Allied air forces, it provided the wherewithal to arm one hundred and thirty German infantry divisions and forty armored divisions—a total of two million men.[3]

It is worth noting that Marshal Pétain's overeager collaboration and his government's extravagant efforts to secure German good will proved utterly abortive. Although France made a bigger industrial contribution to the German war effort than any other country in Europe—42 percent of the total—countless Frenchmen were deported, shot as hostages, or publicly hanged as a deterrent to resistance.[4]

Other occupied countries, too, may in general be said to have plied Germany with more goods than were demanded or expected of them. *Sacro egoismo,* of whatever nationality, was Hitler's most potent ally.

This, however, was only one aspect of collaboration. Tactical collaboration, which proved to be a form of resistance, became almost universally manifest in everyday life wherever resistance was in preparation or in progress. It also played a pre-eminent role in countries where resistance was feasible, as in Denmark during the first three and a half years, only as the basis and underlying theme of a policy that had to maneuver as adroitly as possible between all forms of collaboration and noncollaboration.

Even before the war, the Dutch Government endeavored to define the principles of such a policy and make it incumbent on public servants to observe them in the event of invasion and occupation. The May 1937 directives were based on international law and on the Hague Conventions relating to land warfare, though these were drafted in ignorance of the sort of total war that engulfed Holland in May 1940.

Three years later, in May 1943, the government-in-exile broadcast fresh instructions from London which took account of practical wartime experience and, more especially, of the methods employed by the occupying power. These revised instructions, an excerpt from which can be found on pages 323–25, additionally strove to define the extent and limits of administrative cooperation and the rights and duties of those public servants who were obliged to work with the occupying power. Their most important new feature was a ruling that all public servants were fully and personally accountable to their own government, wherever it might be based, for whatever they did or neglected to do. They would in the future be liable for their actions.

This raised a question transcending the compass of the present book, namely, whether it is possible to organize collaboration and resistance in such a way that they may be classified as measures taken in the overall interests of national defense. Also under this heading comes the concept of unarmed civil resistance.[5]

Finally, where resistance itself is concerned, the sheer abundance of the examples cited here has shown how difficult it is to form a coherent picture. Assessing the value of resistance is just as difficult, if not more so. If its strengths and weaknesses cannot be weighed against each other, where did its value and utility lie?

Certainly not in its military or strategic importance, which is generally exaggerated by its supporters and underrated by many professional military observers. Resistance in Europe may have been far less a military phenomenon than a manifestation of political and human impulses.

When the partisan republic of Ossola fell, J. McCaffery, the SOE chief for northern Italy, wrote a personal letter to Ferruccio Parri, one of the brains and military leaders of the North Italian Liberation Committee, who was soon to become Premier of Italy's first postwar government. This letter illustrates, with exemplary clarity, how the Allies viewed the Resistance and its inflated claims to military importance.

"I have often said," wrote McCaffery, "that many persistent acts of sabotage are the greatest military contribution [you can make] to the Allied cause. Your guerrillas have done good work, we know that, but you wanted armies. Who asked you for them? Not us. Your reasons for that were political. . . .

"None of us will reproach you for this," McCaffery went on, "but please don't reproach our generals, who almost always act in line with military considerations. Above all, don't try to impose your political ideas on us because military considerations don't quite accord with your political concepts."[6]

McCaffery's allusion to ideas in the plural was certainly not fortuitous. The political importance of the Resistance reposed in its plurality, not in its promulgation of a particular idea or political doctrine. It was a reflection of the European spirit which National Socialism wanted to obliterate. It subsisted on utopias, on revolutionary and conservative expectations, on socialist and liberal programs. Its ranks included many distinguished people of all ages and every social and political background. Being a guardian and apostle of European ideas and traditions, it was fundamentally conservative in the broadest sense. Even the Western Communist parties, those instruments of Russian foreign policy, became temporary defenders of the existing order.

After all that has been said, the human aspect of resistance and the Resistance needs no further comment. The unfathomable courage displayed by so many anonymous men and women, and the acts of self-sacrifice that were seldom expected and never demanded of them, speak for themselves.

Even in its organized form, the Resistance was more an attitude of mind and profession of faith than an armed force. As for its historical importance, this is attested by the very legends that surround it to this day.

APPENDIXES

Notes

Full titles of the books and documents mentioned in the following notes, together with their dates and places of publication, are listed in the Bibliography.

N.B. Where the notes refer to English versions of foreign-language books, some excerpts cited in the foregoing text have been freshly translated from the original.

PART ONE—**Hitler's Double Game**

1. A. Spiess and H. Lichtenstein, *Das Unternehmen Tannenberg*, esp. pp. 63, 67 et seq., 76 et seq., 177 et seq. See also ND 2741-PS and W. L. Shirer, *The Rise and Fall of the Third Reich*, p. 595.
2. Spiess/Lichtenstein, op. cit., pp. 156, 162 et seq.
3. E. Klöss (ed.), *Reden des Führers*, p. 22.
4. New York *Times*, September 1, 1939.
5. *IMT Records*, Trial of the Major War Criminals at Nuremberg, Vol. II, p. 451.
6. H. Rauschning, *Hitler Speaks*, p. 123.
7. J.-B. Duroselle, *Histoire diplomatique de 1919 à nos jours*, p. 228; L. Gruchmann, *Der Zweite Weltkrieg*, p. 10.
8. W. Hubatsch (ed.), *Hitlers Weisungen für die Kriegführung*, pp. 19–22.
9. Shirer, op. cit., p. 564.
10. Telegram dated August 29, 1939, reproduced in the *Neue Zürcher Zeitung*, August 30, 1939.
11. K. D. Bracher, "Zusammenbruch des Versailler Systems und Zweiter Weltkrieg," in *Propyläen Weltgeschichte*, ed. by G. Mann and A. Heuss, Vol. IX, p. 431.
12. Hubatsch, op. cit., pp. 23–25.
13. M. Baumont, *Les Origines de la Deuxième Guerre Mondiale*, pp. 179–81, 186. This "peace ballot" was conducted under the presidency of Lord Robert Cecil by the League of Nations Union, which had over a million members. A resolution passed at the Labour Party Conference in Brighton that year took the same line.
14. *Le Temps*, April 12, 1938.
15. Baumont, op. cit., p. 271 et seq.
16. Hubatsch, op. cit., p. 71.

17. F. Halder, *Kriegstagebuch 1939–1942*, Vol. II, p. 32.

18. Ibid., entry for July 13, 1940.

19. Hubatsch, op. cit., p. 97.

20. Ibid., p. 54.

21. Klöss, op. cit., p. 230.

22. Hitler repeatedly assured Belgium and Holland that Germany recognized and guaranteed their territorial inviolability and neutrality, e.g. on January 30, 1937 (Reichstag speech), April 28, 1939 (reply to President Roosevelt), August 26, 1939, and October 6, 1939.

23. Shirer, op. cit., p. 714.

24. Hubatsch, op. cit., p. 39 et seq.

25. Shirer, op. cit., p. 823.

26. W. S. Churchill, *The Second World War*, Vol. III, p. 144 et seq.; Shirer, op. cit., p. 824.

27. Hubatsch, op. cit., pp. 124–26.

28. *IMT*, Vol. XV, p. 424 (testimony of General Alfred Jodl, head of Wehrmacht Operations Staff).

29. W. L. Shirer, *The Challenge of Scandinavia*, pp. 223–25.

30. W. Hubatsch, *Unruhe des Nordens*, p. 191.

31. H. Koht, *Norway, Neutral and Invaded*, p. 65 et seq.

32. Ibid., p. 67.

33. Ibid., p. 197. The opening sentence of the German document ran: "Contrary to the sincere wish of the German people and of their Government to live in peace and friendship with the English and French peoples, and despite the lack of any reasonable ground for a conflict between them, the rulers in London and Paris declared war on the German people." It went on: "With the outbreak of this war of aggression against the existence of the German Reich and of the German people, for which they had long been preparing, England and France began a sea war which was aimed also against the neutral world."

34. Ibid., p. 201. "The German Government therefore expects that the Royal Norwegian Government and [the Norwegian] people will regard the German action with comprehension, and will offer no resistance to it. . . . Any resistance to it would have to be, and would be, broken by the German occupying forces with all the means at their command, and would therefore result only in entirely useless bloodshed. The Royal Norwegian Government is therefore requested to take all measures as rapidly as possible to ensure that the action of the German troops may proceed without friction or difficulty."

35. A. W. Dulles, *Germany's Underground*, p. 58.

36. G. Buchheit, *Der deutsche Geheimdienst*, pp. 298–301.

37. Dulles, op. cit., pp. 58–61.

38. This idea is explicitly contained in the joint German-Soviet declaration of September 28, 1939, which was released on the conclusion of the German-Soviet Boundary and Friendship Treaty of the same date. See W. Hofer (ed.), *Der Nationalsozialismus, Dokumente 1933–1945*, p. 235.

39. Duroselle, op. cit., p. 261 et seq.

40. Halder, op. cit., Vol. I, May 7, 1940; K. Kwiet, *Reichskommissariat Niederlande*, p. 26.

41. Foreign Minister van Kleffens gave a different and, from Zech's point of view, less embarrassing account of the same interview in his book *Der Einfall in die Niederlande*. Where Zech's tears were concerned, his subsequent statements to a Dutch fact-finding committee showed less consideration. See Kwiet, op. cit., p. 29.

42. Churchill, op. cit., Vol. III, p. 320.

43. J. Erickson, *The Soviet High Command*, p. 579; A. Rossi, *Autopsie du Stalinisme*, p. 108. The relevant confirmation may be found in B. S. Telpukhovsky's *Soviet History of the Great Patriotic War*. For a divergent account, see H. Höhne, *Canaris*, pp. 455–56.

44. Rossi, op. cit., esp. pp. 105–10, 208–12.

45. Hubatsch, *Unruhe*, p. 180.

46. ND 2353-PS, quoted in Shirer, *Rise and Fall*, p. 840.

47. Churchill, op. cit., Vol. III, p. 326.

48. Duroselle, op. cit., p. 297.

49. R. Cartier, *Der Zweite Weltkrieg* (German ed.), Vol. I, p. 296.

50. Duroselle, op. cit., p. 298.

51. Rossi, op. cit., p. 109; Shirer, *Rise and Fall*, p. 852 and footnote.

52. C. W. Thayer, *Hands Across the Caviar*, p. 67.

53. A. Ernst, "Die Bereitschaft und Abwehrkraft Norwegens, Dänemarks und der Schweiz," pp. 10, 15. Cf. also p. 12 (aircraft data).

54. Ibid., pp. 24–26.

55. Gruchmann, op. cit., p. 52.

56. J. Haestrup, *Le Mouvement de la Résistance danoise*, p. 4.

57. Germany's big initial successes on the Eastern Front came as a complete surprise to everyone.

58. Rossi, op. cit., p. 32.

59. J. F. Fuller, *The Second World War*, p. 123.

60. Rossi, op. cit., p. 108 (and note 43).

61. E. M. Howell, *The Soviet Partisan Movement*, p. 49; J. A. Armstrong (ed.), *Soviet Partisans in World War II*, p. 14.

62. According to A. Dallin (*German Rule in Russia*), Russian prisoners captured by the end of November 1941 numbered 3,365,000. A report from Dr. Mansfield reproduced by E. L. Homze (*Foreign Labor in Nazi Germany*, p. 80) puts the figure as high as 3,900,000.

PART ONE—**Hitler in the Ascendant**

1. *Hitler's Europe* was the title given by A. J. Toynbee to one volume of his comprehensive *Survey of International Affairs*. The same expression was used by Patricia Harvey in her contribution to that volume ("The Economic Structure of Hitler's Europe"). Subsequently adopted by numerous authorities, it has become a standard term.

2. H. Rauschning, *Hitler Speaks*, p. 16.

3. Hitler's unreported speech to German officer cadets at the Sportpalast on May 30, 1942. The text can be found in *Hitlers Tischgespräche im Führerhauptquartier*, p. 493 (not in English ed.).

4. R. Aron, *Penser la guerre, Clausewitz,* II, "L'Âge planetaire," p. 77.

5. Ibid., p. 91 et seq.

6. A. Hitler, *Mein Kampf,* pp. 258–99; K. Zimmermann, *Die geistigen Grundlagen des Nationalsozialismus,* p. 73 et seq.

7. Karl Clodius's top secret memorandum of May 30, 1940, postulated the eventual incorporation of Denmark, Holland, Belgium, and Luxembourg into a customs and monetary union with the Greater German Reich, together with the creation of a German colonial empire inclusive of the Belgian Congo as well as Germany's own former colonies. The Ritter Memorandum of June 1, 1940, went even further. This envisaged the incorporation of Poland, Bohemia, and Moravia by the Greater German Reich and the formation of a customs and/or monetary union into which—apart from Norway, Denmark, Holland, Belgium, and Luxembourg—the Baltic States, Finland, and Sweden would be integrated, partly "under pressure" and partly "by means of favors." In addition to the territories listed by Clodius, Ritter's new German colonial empire was to take in French Equatorial Africa and British Nigeria. (*Documents on German Foreign Policy,* Series D, Vol. IX, March 18–June 22, 1940, Document No. 354.) These plans remained so nebulous that P. Harvey (in Toynbee, *Survey of International Affairs* [1954]) felt justified in stating that no complete and coherent plan for a European New Order had ever been published. J. Freymond's study of the European New Order (*Le III*ᵉ *Reich et la réorganisation économique de l'Europe 1940–1942: origines et projets,* p. 206 et seq.) draws the following conclusion: "Within the apparently monolithic and hierarchic German political system, which in reality displayed many anarchic features, Hitler's associates—notably his ministers and some leading industrialists—enjoyed a certain amount of latitude for as long as Hitler himself chose not to intervene. But plans and ideas for the European New Order were extraordinarily vague and ill defined. Although numerous plans for a European macroeconomic area were evolved, they carried no political weight."

8. Toynbee, op. cit., Introduction, pp. 3–4.

9. *Hitlers Tischgespräche,* p. 146.

10. Rauschning, op. cit., p. 17.

11. Ibid., p. 46.

12. Ibid., p. 140.

13. Ibid., p. 87.

14. Ibid., p. 90.

15. Ibid., p. 87.

16. From a speech by Goebbels to press representatives on April 5, 1940, cited in H.-A. Jacobsen, *Der Zweite Weltkrieg,* p. 180 et seq.

17. Hitler's address to the generals of all arms of the Wehrmacht on March 30, 1941, and similar pronouncements on June 14, 1941, cited in F. Halder, *Kriegstagebuch 1939–1942,* Vol. II, p. 337. See also Keitel's testimony to the *IMT* on April 4, 1946, and Jacobsen, op. cit., p. 167.

18. One such map, entitled "German Postwar Plans for the East," can be found in A. Dallin, *German Rule in Russia, 1941–1945,* p. 55.

19. C. Child, "The Political Structure of Hitler's Europe," in Toynbee, op. cit., p. 123.

20. Dallin, op. cit., p. 660; *IMT*, Vol. XXXVIII, p. 88.

21. C. Klessmann, *Die Selbstbehauptung einer Nation*, p. 196.

22. S. Lowery, "The Occupied and Satellite Countries in Eastern Europe," in Toynbee, op. cit., p. 556; S. Okecki, "La Résistance et les Alliés," in *European Resistance Movements 1939–1945*, p. 420; *IMT*, Vol. XXIX, p. 444, cited in E. Nolte, *Ebenen des Krieges und Stufen des Widerstandes*, p. 204.

23. Harvey, op. cit., p. 245 et seq.

24. E. L. Homze, *Foreign Labor in Nazi Germany*, p. 153.

25. Ibid., p. 195.

26. Security Service report dated June 12, 1942, on the forcible conscription of labor, cited in E. Hesse, *Der sowjetrussische Partisanenkrieg 1941 bis 1944 im Spiegel deutscher Kampfanweisungen und Befehle*, p. 166.

27. Ibid., report dated July 7, 1942.

28. Harvey, op. cit., p. 245.

29. W. L. Shirer, *The Challenge of Scandinavia*, p. 222.

30. J. Haestrup, "Denmark's Connection with the Allied Powers during the Occupation," in *European Resistance Movements*, p. 284.

31. Ibid., p. 283.

32. E. Thomsen, *Deutsche Besatzungspolitik in Dänemark, 1940–1945*, pp. 129 et seq., 138.

33. Thus the concluding sentence of the German memorandum of April 9, 1940. See W. Hubatsch, *Unruhe des Nordens*, p. 192.

34. Thomsen, op. cit., p. 18.

35. Ibid., p. 15.

36. Ibid., p. 131.

37. R. Albrecht, "La Politique danoise au cours de la première année d'occupation," in *Revue d'Histoire de la Deuxième Guerre Mondiale*, No. 96, p. 119 et seq.

38. H. Boberach (ed.), *Meldungen aus dem Reich*, April 29, 1940, p. 79.

39. W. A. Boelcke (ed.), *Kriegspropaganda 1939–1941*, entry dated January 27, 1940, p. 274.

40. U. von Hassell, *The Von Hassell Diaries, 1938–44*, pp. 76, 90, 96. G. Buchheit, *Der deutsche Geheimdienst*, p. 219 et seq. See also selected letters by Major General Stieff in *Vierteljahreshefte für Zeitgeschichte*, No. 3, 1954.

41. Thomsen, op. cit., p. 8.

42. Ibid., p. 152.

43. Albrecht, op. cit., pp. 119–21. According to a note from General Enno von Rintelen to Ernst von Weizsäcker dated November 17, 1941, Hitler did occasionally share the Foreign Office view that military requirements had to take precedence over "ideological experiments." Thomsen, op. cit., p. 17.

44. W. Best, "Die deutschen Aufsichtsverwaltungen (nur für den Dienstgebrauch)," manuscript, 1941, on which subject see K. Kwiet, *Reichskommissariat Niederlande*, pp. 62, 70.

45. Okecki, loc. cit.

46. Viscount Chilston, "The Occupied Countries in Western Europe," in Toynbee, op. cit., p. 491; Kwiet, op. cit., p. 46.

47. Dallin, op. cit., p. 662.

48. One good example was the military government of Belgium and Northern France, headed by General Alexander von Falkenhausen. All military matters were handled by Falkenhausen's headquarters and his area, district, and local commanders, together with six military courts. In addition, an administrative officer (SS-Brigadeführer Eggert Reeder) was responsible for all spheres of civil administration. He functioned as Belgium's industrial and political chief executive and maintained a separate bureaucracy with representatives in every major industrial concern in the country. Independent of Reeder and his organization, a struggle for power and influence raged between autonomous Foreign Office, Propaganda Ministry, and Gestapo agencies, each with a bureaucracy of its own. In neighboring Holland, a struggle for power went on inside the civil administration itself. Here, four Commissioners General were responsible to the Reich Commissioner (Arthur Seyss-Inquart) for supervising the four most important branches of the indigenous administration. One of this quartet (Hans Fischboeck, Commissioner General for Financial and Economic Affairs) came from the Reich Ministry of Economic Affairs, another (Hanns Albin Rauter) belonged to the SS, and another (Fritz Schmidt, Commissioner General, Special Duties) represented the NSDAP (National Socialist German Labor Party). The Foreign Office was represented by a minister (Otto Bene) who ranked on a par with the four Commissioners General. Over and above this, the Reich Commissioner's Personal Representative was entrusted with on-the-spot supervision of administrative practices in the Dutch provinces. See Chilston, op. cit., p. 479 et seq., and Kwiet, op. cit., p. 79 et seq.

49. Werner Best's notes are dated 1941. Cf. note 44.

PART ONE—**Blood and Tears**

1. Tadeusz Tomaszewski, chief of staff during the defense of Warsaw, states in *Bylem Szefem Sztabu Obrony Warszawy w 1939* (London, 1961) that Warsaw's military activity and strategic importance were almost nil by September 9, 1939, and that the Wehrmacht had no reason to storm the city.

2. U. von Hassell, *The Von Hassell Diaries, 1938–44*, p. 77.

3. According to official Dutch figures (*IMT*, Vol. XXXVI, p. 656). Even if it were true that "the bombardment could not be entirely halted because of inadequate communications" (H.-A. Jacobsen, "Dünkirchen 1940," in *Entscheidungsschlachten des Zweiten Weltkrieges*, p. 27), this would not explain away the basic attitude of the military commanders responsible.

4. H. Rauschning, *Hitler Speaks*, p. 91.

5. W. L. Shirer, *The Rise and Fall of the Third Reich*, p. 824.

6. A. Dragojlović, "Les Attaques aériennes allemandes et la défense de Belgrade pendant la guerre d'avril 1941, Bombardovanje Beograda u drugom svetskom ratu," Historical Archive, Belgrade, 1975, p. 17 et seq.

7. Luftwaffe bombardments and fatal casualties:

CITY	DATE	FATAL CASUALTIES	SOURCE
Warsaw	September 24–27, 1939	Unknown	A. Wolowski states in *La Vie quotidienne à Varsovie,* p. 61, that Polish historians put the number of inhabitants killed during the last week of September 1939 at approximately 27,000.
Rotterdam	May 14, 1940	814	Dutch Government (*IMT,* Vol. XXXVI, p. 656).
London	September 7–8, 1940	842	British Home Office and Air Ministry.
Coventry	November 14, 1940	550 (400)	W. S. Churchill, *The Second World War,* Vol. II, p. 332; R. Cartier, *Der Zweite Weltkrieg* (German ed.), Vol. I, p. 218.
Belgrade	April 6–7, 1941	2,271	Yugoslav Government War Damage Commission; J. Marjanović, "La Courte Guerre d'avril, Bombardovanje Beograda u drugom svetskom ratu (The Bombardment of Belgrade During World War II)," Historical Archive, Belgrade, 1975, pp. 1–5.
London	Entire war	29,890	*Encyclopaedia Britannica* (1951 ed.), Vol. I, p. 459.

The severity with which the Allies hit back, very much later in the war, is evident from the comparative figures given below:

Hamburg	July 26–29, 1943	48,600	R. Cartier, *Der Zweite Weltkrieg* (German ed.), Vol. II, p. 655.
Dresden	February 14–15, 1945	35,000	G. Bergander, *Dresden im Luftkrieg,* pp. 247–74.
Hiroshima	August 6, 1945	78,000	L. Gruchmann, *Der Zweite Weltkrieg,* p. 500.

8. Report dated April 16, 1941, to the Army High Command, Attaché Section. Facsimile reproduced by the Historical Archive, Belgrade, in "Bombardovanje Beograda u drugom svetskom ratu," Belgrade, 1975, p. 46.

9. Ibid., p. 19 of French text.

10. C. Klessmann, *Die Selbstbehauptung einer Nation,* pp. 54–58.

11. E. Wiskemann, "The Occupied and Satellite Countries in Eastern

Europe," in A. J. Toynbee, "Hitler's Europe," *Survey of International Affairs*, pp. 588–89; D. Brandes, *Die Tschechen unter deutschem Protektorat*, Vol. I, p. 92.

12. Viscount Chilston, "The Occupied Countries in Western Europe," in Toynbee, op. cit., p. 486; G. Lovinfosse, "La Résistance belge et les Alliés," in *European Resistance Movements*, p. 280.

13. W. Warmbrunn, *The Dutch under German Occupation*, p. 150.

14. K. Gustmann, *Die schwedische Tagespresse zur Neutralitätsfrage im Zweiten Weltkrieg*, p. 250.

15. In the view of General Thomas, head of the Economics and Armaments Branch, Wehrmacht High Command.

16. A. S. Milward, *The New Order and the French Economy*, p. 80 et seq.

17. Ibid., p. 82.

18. Brandes, op. cit., Vol. I, p. 151.

19. A. Merglen, "Les Chars tchèques dans l'armée d'Hitler," in *Revue Historique de l'Armée*, 1965, No. 2, pp. 151–54.

20. On the effects of this policy in France, where they were universally felt, see also H. Kistenmacher, *Die Auswirkungen der deutschen Besetzung auf die Ernährungswirtschaft Frankreichs während des Zweiten Weltkriegs*.

21. Milward, op. cit., p. 59.

22. Proceedings of the French Delegation to the German Armistice Commission, Vol. I, p. 169.

23. Milward, op. cit., p. 270.

24. P. Harvey, "The Economic Structure of Hitler's Europe," in Toynbee, op. cit., p. 273, citing Davin, *Les Finances de 1939 à 1945*, II, "L'Allemagne," p. 290.

25. Milward, op. cit., p. 287.

26. Ibid., p. 61; also, by the same author, *War, Economy and Society, 1939–1945*, p. 158.

27. Milward, *War, Economy and Society*, pp. 74, 98; Harvey, op. cit., p. 206.

28. Klessmann, op. cit., p. 37.

29. S. Lowery, "The Occupied and Satellite Countries in Eastern Europe," in Toynbee, op. cit., p. 558.

30. Brandes, op. cit., Vol. I, pp. 24, 48, 171, 266, et al.; Chilston, op. cit., pp. 540–45; O. Riste and B. Nøklby, *Norway 1940–1945: The Resistance Movement*, p. 89.

31. All detainees were declared hostages in Belgium on September 19, 1941 (C. J. Child, "The Political Structure of Hitler's Europe," in Toynbee, op. cit., p. 488), and in France on August 22, 1941 (H. Noguères, *Histoire de la Résistance en France*, Vol. II, p. 82). For statistics relating to the Protectorate see Child, op. cit., p. 149, and Brandes, op. cit., Vol. I, p. 48.

32. L. de Jong, "Zwischen Kollaboration und Résistance," in *Probleme des Zweiten Weltkrieges*, p. 250.

33. Noguères, loc. cit.

34. L. de Jong, "Les Pays-Bas dans la Seconde Guerre Mondiale," in *Revue d'Histoire de la Deuxième Guerre Mondiale*, No. 50, p. 25.

35. Riste/Nøklby, op. cit., pp. 54, 70, 89; Chilston, op. cit., p. 545.

36. Brandes, op. cit., Vol. I, pp. 92, 264, 266; H. Luther, *Der französische Widerstand gegen die deutsche Besatzungsmacht und seine Bekämpfung*, p. 126.

37. Luther, op. cit., p. 205.

38. Ibid., p. 216. The threat was not carried out.

39. Ibid., p. 274.

40. Ibid. A reliable account of events at Tulle and similar events at Oradour, together with conflicting reports thereof, may be found in E. Jäckel, *Die deutsche Frankreichpolitik im Zweiten Weltkrieg*, pp. 325–28.

41. C. Falconi, *The Silence of Pius XII*, p. 124.

42. Klessmann, op. cit., pp. 184 et seq., 237.

43. Ibid., p. 184.

44. H. Buchheim et al., *Anatomie des SS-Staates*, p. 113 et seq. (not in English ed.); Luther, op. cit., pp. 131, 137 et seq.

45. E. Thomsen, *Deutsche Besatzungspolitik in Dänemark*, p. 201.

46. Child, op. cit., p. 147.

47. H. Buchheim et al., *The Anatomy of the SS State*, p. 69.

48. Ibid., p. 81.

49. Ibid., p. 77.

50. E. Hesse, *Der sowjetrussische Partisanenkrieg*, p. 35.

51. H. Krausnick, "Die osteuropäische Etappe der Endlösung," in *Probleme des Zweiten Weltkrieges*, p. 215, or Buchheim et al., *The Anatomy*, pp. 81–82.

52. G. Reitlinger, *The Final Solution*, p. 546 (see "Holocaust" table following note 59).

53. The German list of May 1, 1944, can be found in E. L. Homze, *Foreign Labor in Nazi Germany*, p. 83, and A. Dallin, *German Rule in Russia*, p. 427. Cf. also C. Streit, *Keine Kameraden: Die Wehrmacht und die sowjetischen Kriegsgefangenen 1941–1945* (general account).

54. *Ciano's Diplomatic Papers*, p. 264 et seq.; Shirer, op. cit., p. 854 (footnote).

55. To cite only a few examples, national parliaments were dissolved or suspended in Holland during June 1940, in Norway at the end of September 1940, and in Luxembourg at the end of October 1940. All parties except the National Socialists were dissolved or banned in Luxembourg in the fall of 1940, in Norway in September 1940, and in Holland in July 1941. Martial law was proclaimed in Holland during March 1941. In mid-September 1941, Norwegian citizens who contravened German ordinances were made subject to SS jurisdiction, et cetera.

56. Falconi, op. cit., p. 122.

57. Wiskemann, op. cit., p. 589; Brandes, op. cit., Vol. I, p. 164; Chilston, op. cit., p. 513.

58. Falconi, op. cit., p. 115.

59. H. Michel, *Vichy, année 40*, p. 335 et seq.

HOLOCAUST*

JEWS MURDERED 1939–45 Absolute Figures			JEWS MURDERED as a percentage of the Jewish population		
		approx.			approx.
1	Poland	2,400,000	1	Holland	84%
2	U.S.S.R.	700,000	2	Greece	80%
3	Czechoslovakia	218,000	3	Germany	75%
4	Romania	200,000	4	Poland	
5	Hungary	180,000	5	Czechoslovakia	70–75%
6	Germany	160,000	6	Yugoslavia	
7	Holland	104,000	7	Norway	
8	France	63,000	8	Austria	30–35%
9	Greece	60,000	9	Romania	
10	Austria	58,000	10	Belgium	28%
11	Yugoslavia	55,000	11	Hungary	25%
12	Belgium	26,000	12	U.S.S.R.	23%
13	Italy	9,000	13	France	
14	Bulgaria	5,000	14	Italy	20%
15	Norway	700	15	Bulgaria	
16	Denmark	70	16	Denmark	1%
		4,238,770			

* This comparative breakdown uses minimum figures supplied by Gerald Reitlinger and amended in accordance with recent research. They relate to national boundaries as they were before Germany expanded (see note 52).

PART ONE—**The First Confrontation**

1. Apart from Monaco, Gibraltar, and Malta.
2. R. Cartier, *Der Zweite Weltkrieg* (German ed.), Vol. I, p. 143.
3. C. Gutt, *La Belgique au carrefour 1940–1944*, p. 28; Cartier, loc. cit.; W. L. Shirer, *The Rise and Fall of the Third Reich*, p. 729.
4. Gutt, op. cit., p. 45.
5. Cartier, op. cit., Vol. I, p. 144.
6. Gutt, op. cit., p. 56.
7. Ibid., p. 92.
8. Ibid., p. 132.
9. Ibid., p. 130.
10. W. S. Churchill, *The Second World War*, Vol. II, p. 38.
11. P. Baudouin, *Neuf mois au gouvernement*, p. 56; Churchill, op. cit., Vol. II, p. 42.
12. Churchill, loc. cit.
13. R. Griffiths, *Marshal Pétain*, p. 226.
14. Ibid., p. 236.
15. Ibid., p. 241.
16. Ibid.; H. Noguères, *Histoire de la Résistance en France*, Vol. I, p. 30 et seq.

17. Churchill, op. cit., Vol. III, p. 197 et seq.

18. Ibid., pp. 199, 266.

19. K. Kwiet, *Reichskommissariat Niederlande*, p. 40. The heir to the throne, Princess Juliana, had already left for England on May 12.

20. W. L. Shirer, *The Challenge of Scandinavia*, p. 36 et seq.

21. W. Stephenson, *A Man Called Intrepid*, p. 73.

22. Ibid., p. 130.

23. Gutt, op. cit., p. 71.

24. Kwiet, op. cit., p. 41.

25. U. Poch, "Anpassungspolitik ohne Kollaboration," p. 264.

26. O. Riste and B. Nøklby, *Norway 1940–1945: The Resistance Movement*, p. 15; M. Skodvin, "La Presse norvégienne sous l'occupation allemande," in *Revue d'Histoire de la Deuxième Guerre Mondiale*, No. 80, p. 74.

27. R. O. Paxton, *Vichy France*, p. 9.

28. Ibid.

29. Ibid.

30. Ibid., p. 237.

31. Ibid., p. 3.

32. Ibid., p. 13.

33. M. Sperber, *Bis man mir Scherben auf die Augen legt*, p. 253.

34. Paxton, op. cit., p. 17 et seq.

35. D. de Rougemont, *Journal d'une époque*, p. 414.

36. A. Bertelsen, *October '43*, p. 26.

37. A. Gide, *Journal 1939–1942* (July 9, 1940).

38. H. Frenay, *La Nuit finira*, Vol. I, p. 48.

39. Ibid., p. 187.

PART TWO—**Hitler's Europe**

1. S. Okecki, "La Résistance polonaise et les Alliés," in *European Resistance Movements*, p. 422.

2. R. Billiard, *La Contrainte économique sous l'occupation*, p. 240.

PART TWO—**Neutral Collaboration**

1. R. Billiard, *La Contrainte économique sous l'occupation*, p. 105.

2. Ibid., p. 250.

3. K. Kwiet, *Reichskommissariat Niederlande*, p. 70 et seq.

4. W. Warmbrunn, *The Dutch under German Occupation*, p. 92.

5. Kwiet, op. cit., p. 72.

6. Records of the French Delegation to the German Armistice Commission, Vol. II, p. 254.

7. A. S. Milward, *The New Order and the French Economy*, p. 106.

8. Pierre Pucheu, Vichy's Minister of Production from February to July 1941, later testified that his ministry had had to take action against businessmen who were supplying the Germans with more than they asked for. See P. Buttin, *Le Procès Pucheu*, p. 304.

9. P. F. Klemm, "La Production aéronautique française de 1940–1942," in *Revue d'Histoire de la Deuxième Guerre Mondiale*, No. 107, p. 54.

10. Ibid., p. 57.

11. Ibid., p. 56 et seq.

12. Ibid., p. 58, note 2.

13. Ibid., note 4.

14. Milward, op. cit., p. 49.

15. Billiard, op. cit., p. 234.

16. U. Poch, *Der dänische Widerstand in den Jahren 1943–1945*, p. 203. According to a communication dated June 3, 1944, from Svenningsen, head of the Department of External Affairs, to the "Nine-Man Committee," Denmark delivered greater quantities of foodstuffs to Germany than had originally been allocated.

17. E. Thomsen, *Deutsche Besatzungspolitik in Dänemark*, pp. 88–93.

18. Cited from K. Zentner, *Illustrierte Geschichte des Widerstandes in Deutschland und in Europa,* p. 431.

19. *Hitlers Tischgespräche im Führerhauptquartier 1941–1942*, p. 320 (not in English ed.).

20. J. Goebbels, *The Goebbels Diaries*, p. 138.

21. Ibid., p. 75.

22. Ibid., p. 146.

23. Klemm, op. cit., p. 73.

24. W. Bleyer and K. Drobisch, "Fremdarbeiter und Kriegsgefangene als Arbeitskräfte in Deutschland," in *Bulletin des Arbeitskreises "Zweiter Weltkrieg,"* 1970, No. 3, p. 35.

25. Billiard, op. cit., p. 39.

26. E. L. Homze, *Foreign Labor in Nazi Germany*, p. 57.

27. Thomsen, op. cit., p. 56.

28. S. Gudme, *Denmark: Hitler's Model Protectorate*, p. 100.

29. Bleyer/Drobisch, loc. cit. The following figures for voluntary *civilian* workers in Germany at the end of September 1941 are based on German records:

Poles	1,000,000	45.6%*
Italians	272,000	13.0%
Czechs	140,000	6.7%
Belgians	122,000	5.8%
Serbs and Croats	109,000	5.2%
Dutch	93,000	4.4%
Slovaks	80,000	3.8%
French	59,000	2.8%
Hungarians	35,000	1.7%
Others	190,000	9.0%
	2,100,000	100.0%

* Up to the introduction of compulsory labor service in the Government General (October 26, 1939), 110,000 civilian workers had been recruited. Another 1,007,561 workers of both sexes were recruited in eastern Poland between the beginning of the Russian campaign and the introduction of compulsory labor service there (December 19, 1941). Homze, op. cit., p. 65.

30. Ibid.

31. Warmbrunn, op. cit., p. 138 et seq.

32. Ibid., pp. 141 et seq., 144 et seq., 201.

33. Gudme, op. cit., p. 108.

34. Homze, op. cit., p. 36; P. Harvey, "The Economic Structure of Hitler's Europe," in A. J. Toynbee, "Hitler's Europe," *Survey of International Affairs,* p. 245.

35. Harvey, op. cit., p. 244.

36. D. Brandes, *Die Tschechen unter deutschem Protektorat,* Vol. I, p. 154.

37. Ibid., p. 155.

38. Homze, op. cit., pp. 23 et seq., 32, 49.

39. According to a German Foreign Office compilation dated June 6, 1942 (Ha Pol IIa, 1186, NG-109), cited in E. Jäckel, *Die deutsche Frankreichpolitik im Zweiten Weltkrieg,* p. 223 et seq.

40. A. Dallin, *German Rule in Russia,* pp. 536, 551.

41. E. Hesse, *Der sowjetrussische Partisanenkrieg,* p. 124; E. Ziemke, *Soviet Partisans in World War II,* p. 146; Dallin, op. cit., pp. 406, 536.

42. Hesse, op. cit., pp. 124, 192.

43. A. Guérin's *La Résistance,* published in 1976, lists over 1,700 titles for France alone.

44. Generally speaking, these research centers are funded and sponsored at provincial and local levels by Resistance veterans' associations. For example, the smallish and little-known "Istituto Storico della Resistenza" in Cuneo (northern Italy), regularly publishes a journal which lists no less than fifty-two affiliated provincial associations. The number of French and Italian centers devoted exclusively to the history of the national, regional, and local Resistance movements runs into hundreds.

45. The overwhelming majority of Resistance writers concentrate on their own national and regional Resistance movements. Very few historians have so far attempted comprehensive or analytical accounts of the European Resistance, e.g. H. Michel's *Les Mouvements clandestins en Europe* (1974) and *La Guerre de l'ombre* (1970), H. Bernard's *Histoire de la Résistance européenne* (1968), Jørgen Haestrup's *Europe Ablaze* (1978), and M. R. D. Foot's *Resistance* (1977). Also in this category come pictorial accounts such as K. Zentner's *Illustrierte Geschichte des Widerstandes in Deutschland und in Europa* (1966).

Where collaboration as a European phenomenon is concerned, D. Littlejohn's *The Patriotic Traitors* (1972) has the field almost to itself. Like the rest, however, Littlejohn confines himself exclusively to the fascist and National Socialist movements and parties and their leaders—in other words, to a spectacular but unrepresentative aspect of collaboration—and attempts no comparative analysis.

On the other hand, valuable information on the subject has been compiled and analyzed by distinguished historians who treat certain aspects of collaboration as an integral part of national history, e.g. H. Michel, *Vichy, année 40* (1966), E. Jäckel, *Die deutsche Frankreichpolitik im Zweiten Weltkrieg* (1966), D. Wolf, *Die Doriot-Bewegung* (1967), R. O. Paxton, *Vichy France* (1972), C. Lévy, *Les Nouveaux Temps et l'idéologie de la collaboration*

(1974), and others. J.-P. Azéma's *La Collaboration* (1975), P. Ory's *Les Collaborateurs* (1977), and H. Amouroux's books *Le Peuple du désastre* (1977), *Quarante Millions de Pétinistes* (1977), and *Les Beaux Jours des Collabos* (1978), deal exclusively with collaboration in France.

Also worthy of note, though likewise exclusive to France, are three special issues of *Revue d'Histoire de la Deuxième Guerre Mondiale* (Paris)—No. 91 (July 1973), No. 97 (January 1975), and No. 108 (October 1977)—and the fact that a study group of the Paris-based Comité d'Histoire de la Deuxième Guerre Mondiale, headed by R. Rémond, has been applying itself to the subject of collaboration for some years. Although C. Lévy, secretary-general of this research center, noted (in *Revue* No. 108, p. 106) that thirteen doctoral theses on collaboration had been submitted by the fall of 1977, most of these also dealt with regional or local aspects of the subject.

It is difficult to categorize types of collaboration and arrive at a comprehensive definition, as the present book attempts to do in respect of collaboration and resistance alike. J.-P. Azéma, for example, distinguishes between four types of collaboration in France (administrative, governmental, commercial, and ideological), but closer scrutiny shows their scope to be inadequate. S. Hoffmann limits himself to two categories based on motivation: collaboration for reasons of political expediency and for reasons of political affinity to National Socialism. Agreement on this point is rare. As defined by the present study, collaboration signifies conditional or unconditional cooperation with a foreign or forcibly imposed regime, whether approved of, tolerated, or rejected.

46. Cf. Warmbrunn, op. cit., p. 279, and Michel, *Vichy*, p. 272 et seq.
47. W. L. Langer, *Our Vichy Gamble*, p. 168.
48. Ibid.

PART TWO—**Unconditional Collaboration**

1. E. Nolte, *Die faschistischen Bewegungen*, pp. 269–72; D. Littlejohn, *The Patriotic Traitors*, pp. 4–51.
2. M. Boveri, *Treason in the Twentieth Century*, p. 85.
3. Littlejohn, op. cit., p. 9.
4. W. S. Churchill, *The Second World War*, Vol. I, pp. 425, 478–79; W. L. Shirer, *The Rise and Fall of the Third Reich*, pp. 676–78; L. Gruchmann, *Der Zweite Weltkrieg*, p. 49; Boveri, op. cit., pp. 89–90.
5. Shirer, op. cit., p. 704; Gruchmann, op. cit., p. 53.
6. Littlejohn, op. cit., p. 13.
7. P. M. Hayes, "Bref Aperçu de l'histoire de Quisling et du gouvernement de la Norvège de 1940 à 1945," in *Revue d'Histoire de la Deuxième Guerre Mondiale*, No. 66, p. 14 et seq.
8. W. A. Boelcke (ed.), *Kriegspropaganda 1939–1941*, p. 321.
9. Hayes, op. cit., p. 15.
10. C. J. Hambro, *I Saw It Happen in Norway*, p. 49.
11. Hayes, op. cit., p. 12.
12. Boelcke, op. cit., pp. 320, 331.
13. M. Skodvin, "La Presse norvégienne sous l'occupation allemande," in *Revue d'Histoire de la Deuxième Guerre Mondiale*, No. 80, p. 76.

14. Hayes, op. cit., p. 13; Littlejohn, op. cit., p. 19 et seq.

15. H.-D. Loock, "Zur 'Grossgermanischen Politik' des Dritten Reiches," in *Vierteljahreshefte für Zeitgeschichte,* No. 1, 1960, p. 52, note 79.

16. *Hitlers Tischgespräche im Führerhauptquartier,* p. 475 (not in English ed.).

17. J. Goebbels, *The Goebbels Diaries,* p. 46.

18. Boveri, op. cit., p. 88.

19. Littlejohn, op. cit., p. 33 et seq.

20. O. Riste and B. Nøklby, *Norway 1940–1945: The Resistance Movement,* p. 40 et seq.

21. This description of Terboven in U. von Hassell, *The Von Hassell Diaries,* p. 259.

22. Littlejohn, op. cit., pp. 32, 343. It is immaterial that Lie was already a colonel in the Allgemeine SS because his previous rank in that organization had no bearing on his status in the Waffen-SS. Although a mere company commander (an appointment usually held by a captain or lieutenant), Lie was fortunate enough to be given major's rank. He doubtless owed this preferential treatment to his patron, Terboven.

23. Riste/Nøklby, op. cit., p. 72.

24. Hayes, op. cit., p. 35 et seq.

25. Warmbrunn, op. cit., p. 86.

26. K. Kwiet, *Reichskommissariat Niederlande,* p. 112 et seq.

27. Like Quisling's party in Norway, Mussert's based its propaganda on the nationalistic slogan: "Support us, because our party alone can bring about the recovery of freedom and independence." As H.-D. Loock points out, critical remarks about the occupying power, though often uttered for effect, were often genuine. "The Quislings," he writes, "wanted to use the German occupation as a means of gaining power. When they sensed that the Germans were using them merely as a Trojan horse designed to gain power for themselves, they tried to kick against the pricks." (See Loock, op. cit., p. 52.)

28. Kwiet, op. cit., p. 135; Van der Leeuw, "La Presse néerlandaise sous l'occupation allemande," in *Revue d'Histoire de la Deuxième Guerre Mondiale,* No. 80, p. 38 et seq.

29. Ibid., p. 106.

30. In a letter dated November 14, 1942, N. K. C. A. in't Veld, "Cinq lettres de Rauter à Himmler," in *Revue d'Histoire de la Deuxième Guerre Mondiale,* No. 50, p. 51.

31. Kwiet, op. cit., pp. 73, 75.

32. Ibid., p. 106.

33. Ibid., p. 78.

34. A. H. Paape, "Le Mouvement national-socialiste en Hollande," in *Revue d'Histoire de la Deuxième Guerre Mondiale,* No. 66, p. 57.

35. Even the German authorities became faintly uneasy at Rost van Tonningen's all-out collaboration, for instance when he and a group of journalists proceeded to "coordinate" the Dutch press on his personal initiative. They succeeded. Half of Holland's newspapers disappeared, and journalists were coerced into joining a National Socialist Press Guild. In the end, 40 percent of editorial

staffs were headed by NSB members or sympathizers. See Van der Leeuw, op. cit., pp. 29–44.

36. Littlejohn, op. cit.

37. Paape, op. cit., pp. 53, 57.

38. Nolte, op. cit., p. 268; Littlejohn, op. cit., p. 61 et seq.

39. E. Thomsen, *Deutsche Besatzungspolitik in Dänemark*, pp. 70–79, 139.

40. Ibid., p. 63.

41. Despite German victories and massive doses of propaganda, the NSB gained only 50,000 new members by the spring of 1941 and a further 20,000 by the summer of 1943. See Paape, op. cit., pp. 46, 55; Kwiet, op. cit., p. 72 et seq.

42. Kwiet, op. cit., p. 105.

43. Thomsen, op. cit., p. 142.

44. Paape, op. cit., p. 58 et seq.

45. J. Willequet, "Les Fascismes belges et la Seconde Guerre Mondiale," in *Revue d'Histoire de la Deuxième Guerre Mondiale*, No. 66, pp. 85–109; Nolte, op. cit., pp. 272–76; Gruchmann, op. cit., p. 201 et seq.; Littlejohn, op. cit., pp. 135–56.

46. D. Wolf, *Die Doriot-Bewegung*, pp. 27, 30 et seq., 49, 98 et seq., 131, 211, 266; G. Allardyce, "Jacques Doriot et l'esprit fasciste en France," in *Revue d'Histoire de la Deuxième Guerre Mondiale*, No. 97, p. 35.

47. Wolf, op. cit., pp. 177, 209 et seq., 225 et seq., 234 et seq., 236 et seq.

48. Ibid., pp. 246 (giving German source), 266, 269.

49. Ibid., p. 273.

50. An extensive bibliography on Doriot and his movement can be found in Wolf, op. cit.

51. S. Grossmann, "L'Évolution de Marcel Déat," in *Revue d'Histoire de la Deuxième Guerre Mondiale*, No. 97; J. P. Cointet, "Marcel Déat et le parti unique," in *Revue d'Histoire de la Deuxième Guerre Mondiale*, No. 91; Nolte, op. cit., p. 295 et seq.; Littlejohn, op. cit., pp. 214 et seq., 335.

52. A. Merglen, "Soldats français sous uniformes allemands, 1941–1945: LVF et 'Waffen-SS' français," in *Revue d'Histoire de la Deuxième Guerre Mondiale*, No. 108, pp. 71–84; Wolf, op. cit., p. 255.

53. Viscount Chilston, "The Occupied Countries in Western Europe," in A. J. Toynbee, "Hitler's Europe," *Survey of International Affairs*, pp. 513, 516.

54. D. Brandes, *Die Tschechen unter deutschem Protektorat*, Vol. I, p. 25.

55. H. Michel, *La Guerre de l'ombre*, p. 307; A. Dallin, *German Rule in Russia*, p. 14 et seq.

56. H. Teske, *Die Silbernen Spiegel*, p. 80 et seq.

57. J. Thorwald, *Wen sie verderben wollen*, pp. 80 et seq., 317 et seq., 440 et seq.

PART TWO—**Conditional Collaboration**

1. Viscount Chilston, "The Occupied Countries in Western Europe," in A. J. Toynbee, "Hitler's Europe," *Survey of International Affairs*, p. 536; P. M. Hayes, "Quisling et le gouvernement de la Norvège," in *Revue d'Histoire de la Deuxième Guerre Mondiale*, No. 66, pp. 16–19.

2. Chilston, op. cit., p. 510.

3. K. Kwiet, *Reichskommissariat Niederlande*, pp. 97 et seq., 117 et seq.

4. W. Warmbrunn, *The Dutch under German Occupation*, p. 128 et seq.

5. D. Brandes, *Die Tschechen unter deutschem Protektorat*, Vol. I, pp. 41 et seq., 104 et seq. And this happened after attempts had been made, here too, to concretize reservations to such an extent as to render quite feasible the transition from conditional to tactical collaboration (and thus to resistance). Despite its downright National Socialist pronouncements, the party soon began to assist the families of Resistance detainees, gather information for forwarding to London, compile lists of Czechs in custody, and procure detailed plans of various concentration camps. In April 1940 the secretary-general of the National Community, together with several members of its executive and a number of senior officials, was arrested by the Gestapo on suspicion of having supported Czech Resistance organizations. Ibid., pp. 44, 106.

6. H. E. Lichten, *Collaboration, Phantom und Wirklichkeit*, p. 29 et seq.

7. E. Jäckel, *Die deutsche Frankreichpolitik im Zweiten Weltkrieg*, p. 108.

8. W. A. Boelcke (ed.), *Kriegspropaganda 1939–1941*, p. 544.

9. Ibid., pp. 554, 563.

10. Jäckel, op. cit., p. 122 et seq.

11. H. Michel, *Vichy, année 40*, p. 272 et seq.

12. S. Hoffmann, "Aspects du régime de Vichy," in *Revue Française de Science Politique*, Vol. IV, No. 1, 1956, p. 46.

13. Michel, op. cit., p. 147; R. Aron, *Histoire de Vichy, 1940–1944*, pp. 231–37.

14. *Journal de Genève*, cited in *Le Temps*, July 19, 1940. From R. O. Paxton, *Vichy France*, p. 136.

15. H. Noguères, *Histoire de la Résistance en France*, Vol. I, pp. 38, 69; H. Frenay, *La Nuit finira*, I, p. 99 et seq.

16. Noguères, op. cit., Vol. I, p. 72, and Vol. II, p. 692.

17. Ibid., Vol. I, p. 70 et seq., and Vol. II, p. 54.

18. Ibid., Vol. I, p. 65; Frenay, op. cit., Vol. I, p. 99.

19. Noguères, op. cit., Vol. I, p. 282 et seq., and Vol. II, pp. 639, 641.

20. Ibid., Vol. II, p. 692.

21. Ibid., Vol. I, pp. 64, 67.

22. Ibid., p. 65.

23. Ibid., p. 283.

24. Ibid., p. 434 et seq. In *Service secret, 1940–1945* and *Chemins secrets* (an earlier volume of memoirs published under the name "Colonel Groussard"), G. A. Groussard records that General de Gaulle's secret service chief, André Dewavrin ("Passy"), told him that his London trip was known to a number of people in Vichy. Apart from General Huntziger, they included General Lacaille, Dr. Bernard Ménétrel, Marshal Pétain's friend and physician, and Colonel Ronin, head of Air Force Intelligence (*Chemins secrets*, p. 282 et seq.). Groussard informed "Passy" that Huntziger had offered him command of all three Vichy intelligence services if his mission to London succeeded, but that he was acting at his own risk (ibid., p. 284, and *Service secret*, p. 206).

25. Noguères, op. cit., Vol. II, p. 33. It can hardly be doubted that Pétain

and Huntziger were in the picture. Groussard's memoirs reproduce the text of a document drafted and given him by Huntziger. It ran: "I authorize Colonel Groussard to initiate any form of negotiation he deems useful with Free France" (*Chemins secrets*, p. 321, and *Service secret*, p. 232).

26. H. Michel very aptly describes the situation in *Les Courants de pensée de la Résistance*, p. 450.

27. Frenay, op. cit., Vol. I, pp. 235–49.

28. Noguères, op. cit., Vol. II, p. 693.

29. Paxton, op. cit., p. 142 et seq.

30. Ibid., p. 168 et seq.

31. Ibid., p. 182; G. Reitlinger, *The Final Solution*, p. 338.

32. H. Luther, *Der französische Widerstand gegen die deutsche Besatzungsmacht und seine Bekämpfung*, pp. 184, 191; Jäckel, op. cit., p. 192 et seq.; Noguères, op. cit., Vol. II, p. 147 et seq. General Otto von Stülpnagel later opposed further mass executions on grounds of conscience (Luther, op. cit., p. 211 et seq.).

33. Noguères, op. cit., Vol. II, p. 153 et seq.

34. Ibid., p. 150 et seq.

35. R. Griffiths, *Marshal Pétain*, p. 292; Noguères, op. cit., Vol. II, p. 152.

36. Michel, op. cit., p. 265; Paxton, op. cit., pp. 52, 56, 59.

37. Michel, op. cit., p. 266.

38. Ibid., p. 267 et seq.

39. Griffiths, op. cit., p. 243; Jäckel, op. cit., pp. 97, 141.

40. Michel, *Vichy*, pp. 277, 283 et seq.; Paxton, op. cit., p. 60, referring to General Halder's diary entry dated October 10, 1940.

41. Paxton, op. cit., p. 116.

42. Ibid., p. 118, and a good description in Jäckel, op. cit., pp. 157, 179.

43. "Dritter Tätigkeitsbericht der deutschen Waffenstillstandsdelegation für Wirtschaft, 1. 7. bis 31. 12. 1941," ND 1988-PS.

44. Paxton, op. cit., p. 124; Records of the French Delegation to the German Armistice Commission, Vol. IV, p. 396.

45. W. L. Langer, *Our Vichy Gamble*, p. 198 et seq.

46. A. S. Milward, *The New Order and the French Economy*, pp. 119–20.

47. Paxton, op. cit., p. 296.

48. Noguères, op. cit., Vol. II, pp. 635 et seq., 638, 693; D. Cluseau, "L'Arrestation par les Allemands du personnel du 2e Bureau français," in *Revue d'Histoire de la Deuxième Guerre Mondiale*, No. 29, p. 34.

49. Noguères, op. cit., Vol. II, p. 634 et seq.; Luther, op. cit., p. 214. According to Luther, Marshal Pétain welcomed police cooperation.

50. Michel, *Histoire*, p. 104.

51. Cluseau, op. cit., pp. 44–47; Paxton, op. cit., p. 297.

52. Jäckel, op. cit., p. 293 et seq.; Paxton, op. cit., p. 298. In *Monsieur Jean: Die Geheimmission eines Deutschen* (the German in question being Hugo Bleicher, a noncom from the St.-Germain outstation, or Paris headquarters, of German Military Intelligence), E. Borchers describes the brutal methods employed by the Germans' Gallic henchmen: ". . . forced their way into a house, smashed everything that wasn't nailed down, blackjacked men and women who had assembled there for a secret discussion, and stole anything they could lay

hands on. The detainees had watches plucked from their pockets and rings wrenched off their fingers. . . . If the Abwehr [German Military Intelligence] remonstrated with the SD [German Security Service], they were told, 'What are you beefing about? The men do a good job.'" (Borchers, op. cit., p. 41.)

53. A. Dallin, *German Rule in Russia*, p. 566.

54. R. Cartier, *Der Zweite Weltkrieg* (German ed.), Vol. I, pp. 403, 495 et seq.

55. Dallin, op. cit., pp. 554 et seq., 566.

56. Ibid., p. 650.

57. Ibid., pp. 566, 569, 575 et seq., 582 et seq.

58. Ibid., p. 655 et seq.

59. Ibid., pp. 656 et seq., 659; Cartier, op. cit., Vol. II, p. 1030.

PART TWO—**Tactical Collaboration**

1. L. de Jong, "Zwischen Kollaboration und Résistance," in *Probleme des Zweiten Weltkrieges*, p. 252.

2. "Die falsche Alternative" is the title of one of Sperber's essays in *Zur täglichen Weltgeschichte*.

3. S. Gudme, *Denmark: Hitler's Model Protectorate*, p. 87 et seq.; E. Thomsen, *Deutsche Besatzungspolitik in Dänemark*, p. 37 et seq.

4. Thomsen, op. cit., pp. 82–87.

5. Ibid., p. 61 et seq. Of interest in this context is a memorandum dated October 8, 1942, in which Cecil von Renthe-Fink, the German minister and Reich Plenipotentiary, reviewed two and a half years of occupation. He stated, among other things, that although the Danish Government had done all that was specifically demanded of it during his tenure of office, its political measures never went further than was absolutely necessary. Denmark's positive achievements were generally based, not on the wish to contribute to a German victory, but on respect for German strength. "In terms of sentiment, the majority of the Danish people are not—even today—on our side." On the contrary, the bulk of them supported the democratic concept. So did the King. Although he was enough of a realist to refrain from opposing German-Danish cooperation, he was not convinced that Germany would win the war. The Danish Government, people, and King failed to qualify as champions of a New Order. . . . Von Renthe-Fink's verdict on Denmark fairly accurately defines the scope that existed, not only for tactical collaboration, but also for a qualified refusal to collaborate—at least until the political crisis erupted late in August 1943. (Extracts from the memorandum may be found in Thomsen, op. cit., p. 114 et seq.)

6. Diplomatic relations with the Soviet Union had been severed on June 26, 1941. This move, which had no immediate repercussions on Denmark, was made at the Germans' insistence—a concession which the Danish Government was sometimes able to cite when in need of a favor from the occupying power.

7. U. Poch, "Anpassungspolitik ohne Kollaboration," p. 271.

8. Thomsen, op. cit., p. 56 et seq.; Gudme, op. cit., p. 99.

9. R. Eckert, *Die politische Struktur der dänischen Widerstandsbewegung*, p. 26.

10. Thomsen, op. cit., pp. 164–68.

11. D. Brandes, *Die Tschechen unter deutschem Protektorat*, Vol. I, p. 48.

12. Ibid., p. 98 et seq.

13. Ibid., p. 213. See also W. A. Boelcke (ed.), *Kriegspropaganda 1939–1941*, p. 228, record dated November 18, 1939, Point 6.

14. Brandes, op. cit., Vol. I, p. 98.

15. Ibid., p. 49 et seq.

16. Ibid., p. 123 et seq.

17. Ibid., p. 215 et seq.

18. Ibid., pp. 258–61.

19. G. Reitlinger, *The Final Solution*, pp. 66, 265–66; I. Trunk, *Judenrat;* A. S. Hyman, review in the Jerusalem *Post* (international ed.), July 25, 1978.

20. W. Warmbrunn, *The Dutch under German Occupation*, p. 170.

21. Reitlinger, op. cit., p. 57.

22. Warmbrunn, op. cit., p. 170.

23. Ibid., pp. 178, 180 (see illustration on p. 303).

24. Reitlinger, op. cit., p. 60; Trunk, op. cit.

25. L. Baeck, *We Survived*, p. 288.

26. Reitlinger, op. cit., pp. 265–66.

27. Ibid., p. 360; Warmbrunn, op. cit., p. 170 et seq.

28. In December 1947, a Jewish court of honor in Holland came to the conclusion that the Jewish Council's policy of collaboration had been inconsistent with the ethical standards and principles of international law, and morally reprehensible (Warmbrunn, op. cit., p. 184). In *Judenrat*, Trunk published the results of a poll conducted among survivors of the ghetto on their opinion of the Jewish Council and Jewish police. With regard to members of the Jewish Council, 62 percent of those questioned were for them and 14 percent against. As for the Jewish police, their conduct was condemned by 55 percent and approved of by 39 percent.

Die Kontroverse: Hannah Arendt, Eichmann und die Juden presents a compilation of the relevant views and verdicts. Two contributions are of special interest where the present book is concerned, Jacob Robinson's "Jüdische 'Kooperation'" and Manès Sperber's "Churban oder die unfassbare Gewissheit."

* für jüdische

The first issue of the Jewish weekly *Het Joodsche Weekblad* (April 11, 1941), the official organ of the German-appointed Jewish Council of Amsterdam. It represented itself as a trustworthy newspaper whose editorial staff undertook to do everything possible to assist Dutch Jews and benefit their social environment (note 23 refers).

29. A. Dallin, *German Rule in Russia*, p. 530.

30. A. Rossi, *Physiologie du Parti Communiste Français*, p. 1.

31. F. Borkenau, *Der europäische Kommunismus*, p. 279; D. Wolf, *Die Doriot-Bewegung*, p. 243; R. O. Paxton, *Vichy France*, p. 226.

32. A. Rossi, *Les Communistes français pendant la drôle de guerre*, pp. 208 et seq., 218; Borkenau, op. cit., p. 286.

33. *Bulletin d'Information Ouvrière*, No. 3, March 15, 1940, cited in Rossi, *Les Communistes;* excerpt from *Humanité*, ibid., p. 331.

34. *Humanité*, July 4, 1940, cited in Rossi, *Les Communistes*, p. 330.

35. *Humanité*, July 1, 1940, ibid., p. 335.

36. Rossi, *Physiologie*, pp. 15, 395.

37. O. Abetz, *Das offene Problem*, p. 207.

38. Borkenau, op. cit., p. 290; Rossi, *Physiologie*, p. 398.

39. Rossi, *Physiologie*, p. 19, instructions for September–October 1940.

40. Rossi, *Les Communistes*, p. 104.

41. G. Ciano, *Les Archives secrètes du comte Ciano, 1936–1942*, p. 345.

42. Boelcke, op. cit., p. 166.

43. Rossi, *Physiologie*, pp. 404–07, 201; H. Noguères, *Histoire de la Résistance en France*, Vol. I, p. 450.

44. Borkenau, op. cit., p. 240.

45. Thomsen, op. cit., p. 81.

46. Borkenau, op. cit., p. 237 et seq.

47. M. Djilas, *Wartime*, pp. 229–45.

48. R. M. Kennedy, *German Antiguerrilla Operations in the Balcans*, p. 21.

49. H. Luther, *Der französische Widerstand gegen die deutsche Besatzungsmacht und seine Bekämpfung*, p. 48.

50. H. Höhne, *Canaris*, pp. 472–73; *Hitlers Tischgespräche im Führerhauptquartier*, p. 296, note 1 (not in English ed.).

PART THREE—Symbolic Resistance

1. S. Gudme, *Denmark: Hitler's Model Protectorate*, p. 120. Symbolic resistance was also displayed at about the same time (September 1940) by three hundred thousand young people who joined the "Young Denmark to Work" association, their declared aim being to discharge their national responsibilities by promoting Danish intellectual life (ibid., p. 221). In October 1941, a Danish library consultant proceeded to amalgamate the "living-room associations"—a widespread post-invasion phenomenon—into a "Danish Study Circle" whose purpose was to boost public morale and instill faith in Denmark's right of national existence (R. Eckert, *Die politische Struktur der dänischen Widerstandsbewegung*, p. 314 et seq.).

2. D. Brandes, *Die Tschechen unter deutschem Protektorat*, Vol. I, p. 81 et seq.

3. *Lloyd's Register* for 1939, cited in *Whitaker's Almanac* (1957 ed.), p. 614; F. Fjord, *Norwegens totaler Kriegseinsatz*.

4. Fjord, op. cit., p. 202 et seq.

5. K. Zentner, *Illustrierte Geschichte des Widerstandes*, p. 188.

6. Viscount Chilston, "The Occupied Countries of Western Europe," in A. J. Toynbee, "Hitler's Europe," *Survey of International Affairs*, p. 500.

7. O. Riste and B. Nøklby, *Norway 1940–1945: The Resistance Movement*, p. 15.

8. H. Michel, *La Guerre de l'ombre*, p. 92.

9. D. Lampe, *The Savage Canary*, p. 1.

10. K. Kwiet, *Reichskommissariat Niederlande*, p. 43.

11. E. Thomsen, *Deutsche Besatzungspolitik in Dänemark*, p. 155; Michel, op. cit., p. 91 et seq.; H. Michel, *Vichy, année 40*, p. 422 et seq.

12. The title of Henri Michel's book, cited in note 8 above.

13. H. Luther, *Der französische Widerstand gegen die deutsche Besatzungsmacht und seine Bekämpfung*, p. 50.

14. W. Warmbrunn, *The Dutch under German Occupation*, p. 104 et seq.; M. Skodvin, *Gewaltloser Widerstand in Norwegen*, p. 92; Brandes, loc. cit.; U. Poch, "Anpassungspolitik ohne Kollaboration," p. 266 et seq.; Gudme, op. cit., p. 122.

15. Kwiet, op. cit., pp. 122–25.

16. H. Noguères, *Histoire de la Résistance en France*, Vol. I, pp. 171–87.

17. H. Frenay, *La Nuit finira*, Vol. I, p. 183.

18. Warmbrunn, op. cit., p. 153.

19. Ibid., p. 151 et seq.

20. Ibid., p. 136 et seq.; Kwiet, op. cit., pp. 108, 127.

21. Chilston, op. cit., p. 541.

22. Skodvin, op. cit., p. 103; Riste/Nøklby, op. cit., p. 44; P. M. Hayes, "Bref Aperçu de l'histoire de Quisling et du gouvernement de la Norvège," in *Revue d'Histoire de la Deuxième Guerre Mondiale*, No. 66, p. 23 et seq.

23. Chilston, op. cit., p. 514.

24. U. Poch, op. cit., p. 182 et seq.

PART THREE—Polemic Resistance

1. W. Warmbrunn, *The Dutch under German Occupation*, p. 122.

2. E. Thomsen, *Deutsche Besatzungspolitik in Dänemark*, p. 34 et seq.

3. W. L. Shirer, *The Challenge of Scandinavia*, p. 45; Warmbrunn, op. cit., p. 160 et seq.

4. Ibid., p. 161 et seq.

5. O. Riste and B. Nøklby, *Norway 1940–1945: The Resistance Movement*, p. 27 et seq.; M. Skodvin, *Gewaltloser Widerstand in Norwegen*, p. 94 et seq.; P. M. Hayes, "Bref Aperçu de l'histoire de Quisling et du gouvernement de la Norvège," in *Revue d'Histoire de la Deuxième Guerre Mondiale*, No. 66, p. 22 et seq.

6. Riste/Nøklby, op. cit., p. 41 et seq.

7. *Hitlers Tischgespräche im Führerhauptquartier*, p. 315 (not in English ed.).

8. A convincing analysis can be found in Warmbrunn, op. cit., p. 278 et seq.

(FACSIMILE)

The second "edition" of *Geuzenactie*, Holland's first Resistance newspaper, dated May 18, 1940. The first edition, also handwritten, was secretly copied and distributed three days earlier. A hundred and twenty Resistance news sheets had appeared in Holland by the end of 1941. By the end of December 1943, the Underground press had an estimated circulation of 450,000 copies.

9. Ibid., p. 149.

10. Ibid., p. 106 et seq.

11. K. Zentner, *Illustrierte Geschichte des Widerstandes,* p. 200.

12. Warmbrunn, op. cit., p. 148 et seq.

13. U. Poch, "Anpassungspolitik ohne Kollaboration," with special reference to strikes.

14. H. Michel, *La Guerre de l'ombre,* p. 104 et seq.

15. H. Michel, "Rapport Général," in *Résistance Européenne,* p. 16.

16. The total monthly circulation of illegal news sheets and newspapers in France during 1944 has been estimated at 1.5 million copies by Marie Granet, and by Henri Michel at 2 million. Warmbrunn's figure for Holland in 1945 is approximately 2 million, Zentner's for Denmark 2.5 million, and Michel's for Poland 1 million. (M. Granet, "La Presse clandestine en France," a paper presented to the First International Conference on the History of the European Resistance at Liège, in *La Résistance Européenne,* p. 183; see also Michel's "Rapport Général" to the same gathering and his *La Guerre de l'ombre,* p. 104.)

17. Granet, op. cit., pp. 182–91.

18. Warmbrunn, op. cit., p. 222.

19. Ibid., p. 226.

20. Ibid., pp. 228, 245 et seq.

21. H. Noguères, *Histoire de la Résistance en France,* Vol. I, pp. 76, 468–71; D. Brandes, *Die Tschechen unter deutschem Protektorat,* Vol. I, pp. 69 et seq., 294, note 414.

22. On French Resistance literature, see H. Michel, *Les Courants de pensée de la Résistance;* on clandestine literature in Holland, see Warmbrunn, op. cit., p. 257, and, more particularly, D. Dooijes, "Untergrunddrucke in den besetzten Niederlanden 1940 bis 1945," in *Börsenblatt des Deutschen Buchhandels* (Frankfurt ed.), No. 18, March 2, 1979, pp. B3–B21.

23. Michel, *La Guerre de l'ombre,* p. 104.

24. Warmbrunn, op. cit., p. 241 et seq.

25. Ibid., pp. 232, 282.

PART THREE—Defensive Resistance

1. H. Michel, *Vichy, année 40,* p. 421.

2. H. Michel, *Histoire de la Résistance en France,* p. 82.

3. C. Hutton, *Official Secret.* An ingenious expert on escape aids describes the methods he evolved.

4. Michel, *Histoire de la Résistance,* p. 83.

5. *Le Patriote Illustré,* Brussels, No. 42, October 17, 1954.

6. H. Luther, *Der französische Widerstand gegen die deutsche Besatzungsmacht und seine Bekämpfung,* p. 46 et seq.

7. F. La Ruche, *La Neutralité de la Suède,* pp. 104, 154.

8. H. Michel, *La Guerre de l'ombre*, p. 118.

9. W. Warmbrunn, *The Dutch under German Occupation*, pp. 153–56.

10. Viscount Chilston, "The Occupied Countries in Western Europe," in A. J. Toynbee, "Hitler's Europe," *Survey of International Affairs*, p. 486; G. Lovinfosse, "La Résistance belge et les Alliés," in *European Resistance Movements*, p. 280.

11. Warmbrunn, op. cit., p. 152.

12. La Ruche, op. cit., p. 155; A. H. Hicks, "Neutrals and Nonbelligerent Allies," in A. J. Toynbee, "The War and the Neutrals," *Survey of International Affairs*, p. 190 et seq.; K. Gustmann, *Die schwedische Tagespresse zur Neutralitätsfrage*, pp. 250–62.

13. G. Reitlinger, *The Final Solution*, p. 366.

14. K. Kwiet, *Reichskommissariat Niederlande*, p. 151; L. de Jong, *De Bezetting*, Vol. II, p. 49; Warmbrunn, op. cit., pp. 165, 170.

15. Reitlinger, op. cit., pp. 358–89.

16. H. Frenay, *La Nuit finira*, Vol. I, pp. 438, 484; S. Lowery, "The Occupied and Satellite Countries in Eastern Europe," in A. J. Toynbee, "Hitler's Europe," *Survey of International Affairs*, p. 574.

17. Warmbrunn, op. cit., p. 127.

18. E. Thomsen, *Deutsche Besatzungspolitik in Dänemark*, p. 211.

19. L. de Jong stresses this important point in "Anti-Nazi Resistance in the Netherlands," in *Résistance Européenne*, p. 142.

20. Warmbrunn, op. cit., p. 162.

21. Ibid., p. 199 et seq.

22. Ibid., p. 188 et seq.

23. Ibid., p. 193 et seq.

24. Lowery, op. cit., p. 561 et seq.; C. Klessmann, *Die Selbstbehauptung einer Nation*, p. 114.

25. S. Okecki, "La Résistance polonaise et les Alliés," in *European Resistance Movements*, p. 443.

26. Klessmann, op. cit., pp. 126, 132.

27. Ibid., pp. 137, 142, 145; Michel, *La Guerre de l'ombre*, p. 155 et seq.

28. Chilston, op. cit., p. 540.

29. M. Skodvin, *Gewaltloser Widerstand in Norwegen*, p. 93 et seq.; P. M. Hayes, "Bref Aperçu de l'histoire de Quisling et du gouvernement de la Norvège," in *Revue d'Histoire de la Deuxième Guerre Mondiale*, No. 66, p. 22.

30. Chilston, op. cit., p. 487.

31. U. Poch, "Anpassungspolitik ohne Kollaboration."

32. Chilston, op. cit., p. 489.

33. Poch, op. cit.

34. Thomsen, op. cit., p. 178 et seq.

35. Ibid., pp. 179–82.

36. Ibid., pp. 183–90; L. Bindsløv, "La Presse danoise pendant l'occupation," in *Revue d'Histoire de la Deuxième Guerre Mondiale*, No. 80, p. 61 et seq.

37. La Ruche, op. cit., p. 155; H. Hedtoft, foreword to A. Bertelsen, *October '43*.

38. Reitlinger, op. cit., p. 376; La Ruche, loc. cit.

39. Thomsen, op. cit., pp. 180–90.

40. E. Bonjour, *Geschichte der schweizerischen Neutralität*, Vol. IX, p. 581; C. Ludwig, *Die Flüchtlingspolitik der Schweiz*, p. 130; W. Rings, *Schweiz im Krieg*, pp. 322–26.

41. D. Lampe, *The Savage Canary*, pp. 77–83.

42. Reitlinger, op. cit., p. 375.

43. Ibid., p. 184.

44. Ibid., p. 376; Thomsen, op. cit., p. 190.

PART THREE—Offensive Resistance

1. H. Michel, *Les Mouvements clandestins en Europe 1938–1945*, p. 68.

2. J. Haestrup, *Le Mouvement de la Résistance danoise*, pp. 23 et seq., 38; D. Lampe, *The Savage Canary*, p. 114 et seq.

3. D. Brandes, *Die Tschechen unter deutschem Protektorat*, Vol. I, p. 172; H. Michel, *La Guerre de l'ombre*, p. 122.

4. Ibid., p. 123; S. Lowery, "The Occupied and Satellite Countries in Eastern Europe," in A. J. Toynbee, "Hitler's Europe," *Survey of International Affairs*, p. 565; H. Michel, "Les Alliés et la Résistance en Europe," in *European Resistance Movements*, p. 608.

5. A. Guérin, *La Résistance*, pp. 403–06, gives a list of officially recognized intelligence networks together with the dates when they were founded and disbanded and the numbers of their staff and agents.

6. M. Baudot, "La Résistance en France et les Alliés," in *European Resistance Movements*, p. 388.

7. Michel, *La Guerre de l'ombre*, p. 122.

8. E. Hesse, *Der sowjetrussische Partisanenkrieg*, p. 113.

9. D. Bair, *Samuel Beckett: A Biography*, pp. 302–20.

10. E. Thomsen, *Deutsche Besatzungspolitik in Dänemark*, p. 155 et seq.

11. Lampe, op. cit., p. 10.

12. H. Frenay, *La Nuit finira*, Vol. I, p. 292.

13. Baudot, op. cit., p. 389.

14. Haestrup, op. cit., p. 36. Recorded cases of industrial sabotage in Denmark were as follows:

1940	10 cases	1943	969 cases
1941	19 cases	1944	867 cases
1942	122 cases	1945	687 cases

15. O. Riste and B. Nøklby, *Norway 1940–1945: The Resistance Movement*, p. 61.

16. Ibid., p. 59 et seq.; Michel, *La Guerre de l'ombre*, p. 229.

17. C. M. Woodhouse, "The Greek Resistance," in *Résistance Européenne*, pp. 374–90.

18. H. Luther, *Der französische Widerstand gegen die deutsche Besatzungsmacht und seine Bekämpfung*, p. 50.

19. Haestrup, op. cit., p. 36, states that the incidence of railroad sabotage rose from 6 to 328 cases annually between 1942 and 1944.

20. A. H. Hicks, "Neutrals and Nonbelligerent Allies," in A. J. Toynbee, "The War and the Neutrals," *Survey of International Affairs.*

21. Lampe, op. cit., pp. 184–94.

22. Frenay, op. cit., Vol. I, p. 333 et seq., Vol. II, pp. 20, 401, 404.

23. W. Warmbrunn, *The Dutch under German Occupation*, pp. 193–96; N. K. C. A. in't Veld, "Cinq lettres de Rauter à Himmler," in *Revue d'Histoire de la Deuxième Guerre Mondiale*, No. 50, p. 52 et seq.

24. Luther, loc. cit.

25. Thomsen, op. cit., pp. 199–208; L. Bindsløv, "La Presse danoise pendant l'occupation," in *Revue d'Histoire de la Deuxième Guerre Mondiale*, No. 80, p. 65 et seq.; C. J. Child, "The Political Structure of Hitler's Europe," in A. J. Toynbee, "Hitler's Europe," *Survey of International Affairs*, p. 147.

26. Brandes, op. cit., Vol. I, pp. 262–66.

27. F. Fjord, *Norwegens totaler Kriegseinsatz*, p. 64.

28. Riste/Nøklby, op. cit., p. 70.

29. W. Jacobmeyer, *Heimat und Exil: Die Anfänge der polnischen Untergrundbewegung*, p. 236.

30. Ibid., p. 237; Michel, *Les Mouvements*, p. 109.

31. Brandes, op. cit., Vol. I, p. 97.

32. R. Eckert, *Die politische Struktur der dänischen Widerstandsbewegung*, pp. 10, 155.

33. S. Kjelstädli, "The Resistance Movement in Norway and the Allies," in *European Resistance Movements*, pp. 324–39; Michel, *La Guerre de l'ombre*, p. 229.

34. This point is discussed by Henri Bernard in *Histoire de la Résistance* and raised by Henri Michel in *La Guerre de l'ombre*, p. 231.

35. W. S. Churchill, *The Second World War*, Vol. V, p. 466 (Churchill's message to Roosevelt dated May 1, 1944); Kjelstädli, op. cit., p. 333.

36. Churchill, op. cit., Vol. V, pp. 465–68.

37. Kjelstädli, loc. cit.

38. H. Michel, *Les Courants de pensée de la Résistance*, p. 242 et seq.

39. Churchill, op. cit., Vol. V, p. 468.

40. Frenay, op. cit., Vol. II, p. 415.

41. H. Noguères, *Histoire de la Résistance en France*, Vol. II, pp. 158, 373, 524.

42. Ibid., Vol. I, p. 148.

43. Ibid., p. 77.

44. Michel, *Les Mouvements*, p. 60; Kjelstädli, op. cit., pp. 324–39.

45. I. Gérard, "Aperçu sur le rôle de la Résistance militaire en Belgique," in *Résistance Européenne*, pp. 357–73; G. Lovinfosse, "La Résistance belge et les Alliés," in *European Resistance Movements*, pp. 263–97.

46. Frenay, op. cit., Vol. I, p. 476.

47. Ibid., Vol. I, p. 181, Vol. II, p. 206.

48. Ibid., Vol. I, pp. 292, 320.

49. Ibid., p. 260, citing a deliberate show of force.

50. Ibid., p. 337; H. Michel, *Histoire de la Résistance en France*, p. 102.

51. Frenay, op. cit., Vol. I, p. 446.

52. Ibid., p. 358.

53. Gérard, op. cit., p. 365 et seq.

54. H. Amouroux, *La Vie des Français sous l'occupation*, pp. 318–41.

55. Committee for the History of the Resistance of the Czechoslovak People, Prague, "Les Alliés et la Résistance tchécoslovaque," in *European Resistance Movements*, p. 232.

56. Michel, *Histoire de la Résistance*, p. 95.

57. Ibid., p. 99.

58. Amouroux, op. cit., p. 320.

59. A. Guérin, op. cit. (see the map of France on p. 327 below); Luther, op. cit., p. 54; H. Kühnrich, *Der Partisanenkrieg in Europa*, p. 425 et seq.; G. Wright, "Reflections on the French Resistance," in *Political Science Quarterly*, 1962, p. 338; R. Hostache, *Le Conseil de la Résistance*, p. 412.

60. Wright, loc. cit.; Warmbrunn, op. cit., p. 226.

61. E. Boltine, "L'Union soviétique et la Résistance en Europe," in *European Resistance Movements*, p. 39 et seq.

62. Michel, *Les Mouvements*, p. 106.

63. Frenay, op. cit., Vol. II, pp. 421–24.

64. L. de Jong, "Anti-Nazi Resistance in the Netherlands," in *Résistance Européenne*, p. 142 et seq.

65. Warmbrunn, op. cit., p. 196.

66. E.g. Hugo Horwitz and Knud Rassmussen. See Eckert, op. cit., p. 342.

67. K. Zentner, *Illustrierte Geschichte des Widerstandes*, p. 192 et seq.; Haestrup, op. cit., pp. 32, 36; Michel, *Les Mouvements*, p. 58.

68. Riste/Nøklby, op. cit., p. 52; Kjelstädli, op. cit., pp. 324–39.

69. Kjelstädli, loc. cit.

70. Michel, *Les Mouvements*, p. 45; F. W. Deakin, "Great Britain and European Resistance," in *European Resistance Movements*, p. 115 et seq.; F. Parri and F. Venturi, "The Italian Resistance and the Allies," in *European Resistance Movements*, p. xvi.

71. Deakin, loc. cit.

72. Parri/Venturi, loc. cit.

73. Churchill, op. cit., Vol. VI, p. 455.

74. H. Bergwitz, *Die Partisanenrepublik Ossola*, pp. 7, 77, 79 et seq., 119 et seq.

75. N. Kogan, "American Policies Towards European Resistance Movements," in *European Resistance Movements*, p. 87. Cf. the interesting essay on the sociology of the Italian Resistance by M. Legnani, "La Société italienne et la Résistance," in *Revue d'Histoire de la Deuxième Guerre Mondiale*, No. 92, pp. 50–53.

76. Kjelstädli, op. cit., pp. 324–39.

77. Gérard, op. cit., pp. 357–73; Lovinfosse, loc. cit.

78. General Brouhon, "Le Rôle prépondérant de la Résistance dans la libération du port d'Anvers," in *Résistance Européenne*, pp. 257–83.

79. A. Kesselring, *Soldat bis zum letzten Tag*, p. 328 (not in English ed.).

80. Secret report to Allied Headquarters from Colonel Hewitt, the British commander, dated April 1945. Cited in M. G. Vaccarino, "La Résistance au Fascisme en Italie," in *Résistance Européenne*, p. 92 et seq.

81. Parri/Venturi, op. cit., p. xxxix.

82. J.-B. Duroselle, "Les Grands Alliés et la Résistance extérieure française," in *European Resistance Movements*, p. 413.

83. Michel, *Histoire de la Résistance*, p. 108.

84. Ibid., p. 109 et seq.

85. R. Cartier, *Der Zweite Weltkrieg* (German ed.), p. 907.

86. Baudot, op. cit., p. 412 et seq.

87. Michel, *Histoire de la Résistance*, pp. 111, 115–18.

88. Jacobmeyer, op. cit., pp. 24 et seq., 199; Michel, *Les Mouvements*, p. 106.

89. Hesse, op. cit., pp. 39, 42, 53, 55 et seq.

90. A. Fyodorov, *Das Gebietskomitee arbeitet.*

91. Hesse, op. cit., pp. 58–61.

92. J. A. Armstrong (ed.), *Soviet Partisans in World War II*, p. 23 et seq.; E. M. Howell, *The Soviet Partisan Movement*, p. 77; Hesse, op. cit., p. 256; V. Redelis, *Partisanenkrieg: Entstehung und Bekämpfung der Partisanen- und Untergrundbewegung im Mittelabschnitt der Ostfront*, pp. 41, 77.

93. Howell, op. cit., p. 205; Armstrong, op. cit., p. 26 et seq.

94. Armstrong, op. cit., p. 18 et seq.

95. Ibid., p. 35 et seq.; P. Pascal, "Ce que fut en Russie la guerre des partisans," in *Preuves*, No. 50, April 1955, p. 87. (Pascal borrows from D. Karov, *Le Mouvement des partisans dans l'URSS en 1941–1944*, Munich 1944 [in Russian].)

96. Pascal, op. cit., p. 88 et seq.

97. K. M. Dinćić, "Tito et Mihailovitch," in *Revue d'Histoire de la Deuxième Guerre Mondiale*, No. 29, pp. 1–3.

98. Brajusković-Dimitrye, "La Guerre de libération nationale en Yougoslavie," in *Résistance Européenne*, p. 303 et seq.; P. Moraca, *Die Völker Jugoslawiens im Zweiten Weltkrieg*. See H. Kühnrich, *Der Partisanenkrieg in Europa*.

99. Dinćić, op. cit., p. 11 et seq.

100. Ibid., pp. 15–19; R. M. Kennedy, *German Antiguerrilla Operations in the Balcans*, pp. 21 et seq., 37.

101. Kennedy, op. cit., p. 23 et seq.; Dinćić, op. cit., p. 22.

102. Partisan strength at the end of 1943, based on D. Plenca, "Le Mouvement de libération nationale en Yougoslavie et les Alliés," in *European Resistance Movements*; Moraca, op. cit.; and P. Brajović, "Einige militärische Aspekte des Okkupationsregimes in Jugoslawien," 3rd International Congress on the History of the European Resistance at Karlovy Vary, 1963. Losses based on German sources cited in Kennedy, op. cit.

103. F. Mucs, "Quelques aspects de la Résistance armée en Hongrie contre le fascisme," in *European Resistance Movements*, p. 160 et seq.; M. L. Miller, *Bulgaria during the Second World War*, pp. 199–203; Brandes, op. cit., Vol. II, pp. 78, 101, 149 et seq.

PART THREE—**Resistance Enchained**

1. J. Garlinski, *Fighting Auschwitz*, pp. 9–11, 101.
2. Ibid., p. 176.
3. Ibid., p. 177.
4. Ibid., pp. 118, 238, 241 et seq., 285 et seq.
5. Ibid., p. 248 et seq.
6. J.-F. Steiner, *Treblinka: Die Revolte eines Vernichtungslagers*, p. 357.
7. A. Wolowski, *La Vie quotidienne à Varsovie sous l'occupation nazie*, p. 216 (for a report by the officer in charge of resettlement, Warsaw District, January 20, 1941, and for figures kept by the Jewish Council). See also p. 232.
8. Ibid., p. 232 et seq.
9. Ibid., pp. 239–42.
10. Ruth Sakowska, from Wolowski, op. cit., p. 241.
11. Ibid., p. 243; G. Hausner, *Die Vernichtung der Juden*, p. 300.
12. Wolowski, op. cit., p. 235.
13. Ibid., p. 245.
14. Ibid., p. 243 (from M. Edelman, *Le Ghetto en lutte, Varsovie 1945*).
15. Ibid., p. 244.
16. G. Reitlinger, *The Final Solution*, p. 292.
17. Hausner, op. cit., p. 302.
18. Ibid., pp. 302, 304.
19. E. Ringelblum, *Ghetto Warschau: Tagebücher aus dem Chaos*, p. 175.
20. Wolowski, op. cit., p. 247. Ringelblum puts the number of Jews hidden in Warsaw at between two and three thousand (op. cit., p. 243).
21. Hausner, op. cit., pp. 295, 298. The quotations come from Dolek Liebeskind, leader of the Cracow Underground, from a Resistance fighter named Abba Korner, and from Mordechai Tenenbaum-Tamaroff, who led the revolt in the Bialystok ghetto.

PART FOUR—**The Third Front**

1. F. W. Deakin, "Great Britain and European Resistance," in *European Resistance Movements*, pp. 98–119; General R. Barry, "Statement," in *Résistance Européenne*, pp. 349–56; M. R. D. Foot, "L'Aide à la Résistance en Europe," in *Revue d'Histoire de la Deu ème Guerre Mondiale*, No. 90, pp. 39–52.
2. H. Michel, *La Guerre de l'ombre*, pp. 107, 133 et seq.
3. H. Frenay, *La Nuit finira*, Vol. II, p. 6⁻ et seq.
4. Ibid., p. 23.
5. Ibid., p. 27.
6. Ibid., Vol. I, p. 170.
7. Ibid., p. 222.
8. Ibid., p. 303.
9. R. Cartier, *Der Zweite Weltkrieg* (German ed.), Vol. I, p. 185.
10. W. Leahy, *I Was There*, p. 56.

11. P. Smith, *A Desk in Rome*, p. 13 et seq.

12. C. de Gaulle, *L'Appel*, p. 79; H. Michel, *Histoire de la France libre*, p. 81.

13. M. Baudot, "La Résistance en France et les Alliés," in *European Resistance Movements*, p. 403.

14. Ibid., p. 384; H. Michel, *Histoire de la Résistance en France*, p. 24.

15. Thus Walter Lippmann in an address to the Franco-American Club (October 28, 1942). The question, according to Lippmann, was not whether the whole of France stood behind him, but whether he was genuinely and effectively capable of commanding those Frenchmen who were prepared to fight. See W. L. Langer, *Our Vichy Gamble*, p. 298.

16. Deakin, op. cit., pp. 306–09.

17. Baudot, op. cit., p. 384 et seq.; J. Ehrmann, *Grand Strategy*, Vol. V, August 1943–September 1944, p. 324 et seq.

18. Ehrmann, op. cit., p. 327; Michel, *Histoire de la Résistance*, p. 97; Michel, *La Guerre de l'ombre*, p. 345.

19. De Gaulle, op. cit., p. 187.

20. Ibid., p. 186.

21. Ibid., p. 208.

22. J.-B. Duroselle, "Les Grands Alliés et la Résistance extérieure française," in *European Resistance Movements*, p. 406.

23. Ibid., p. 398.

24. Cartier, op. cit., Vol. II, p. 689.

25. Duroselle, op. cit., p. 413.

26. P. Vienot, statements recorded by Jacques Kaiser, *Le Monde*, No. 9141, June 6, 1974.

27. H. Michel, "Les Alliés et la Résistance en Europe," in *European Resistance Movements*, p. 586.

28. H. Stimson and McG. Bundy, *On Active Service in Peace and War*, p. 551.

29. Michel, "Les Alliés et la Résistance," p. 611.

30. Duroselle, op. cit., p. 404.

PART FOUR—**Mutual Aggravation**

1. D. Plenca, "Le Mouvement de la libération nationale en Yougoslavie et les Alliés," in *European Resistance Movements*, pp. 470, 498.

2. Ibid., pp. 468, 497; V. Dedijer, *Tito*, p. 147.

3. K. M. Dincić, "Tito et Michailovitch," in *Revue d'Histoire de la Deuxième Guerre Mondiale*, No. 29, p. 11 et seq.

4. Plenca, op. cit., pp. 473, 499.

5. Dincić, op. cit., p. 20.

6. M. Pijade, *La Fable de l'aide soviétique à l'insurrection nationale yougoslave*, p. 35.

7. Ibid., p. 32.

8. M. Djilas, *Wartime*, pp. 143–44.

9. Pijade, op. cit., p. 47.

10. Ibid., pp. 52, 54 et seq.

11. F. W. Deakin, "Great Britain and European Resistance," in *European Resistance Movements*, p. 111 et seq.

12. Plenca, op. cit., p. 471.

13. F. W. Deakin, *The Embattled Mountain* (see reproduction of a telex transcript).

14. J. Ehrmann, *Grand Strategy*, Vol. V, p. 271 et seq.

15. Djilas, op. cit., p. 474 et seq.; Dedijer, op. cit., p. 206 et seq.

16. H. Michel, "Les Alliés et la Résistance en Europe," in *European Resistance Movements*, p. 600.

17. Ehrmann, op. cit., p. 385 et seq.

18. E. Boltine, "L'Union Soviétique et la Résistance en Europe," in *European Resistance Movements*, p. 34.

19. Ibid.

20. F. Borkenau, *Der europäische Kommunismus*, p. 369.

21. Ehrmann, op. cit., p. 86 et seq.

22. Ibid., p. 61; R. M. Kennedy, *German Antiguerrilla Operations in the Balcans*, p. 61.

23. W. S. Churchill, *The Second World War*, Vol. VI, p. 252.

24. Ibid., p. 198.

25. Borkenau, op. cit., p. 406.

26. Churchill, op. cit., Vol. VI, pp. 267–83; Ehrmann, op. cit., p. 64.

27. Churchill, op. cit., Vol. VI, pp. 255–58.

28. Ibid., p. 261.

29. Ibid., p. 263; Ehrmann, op. cit., p. 61.

30. Borkenau, op. cit., p. 423.

31. A. Wolowski, *La Vie quotidienne à Varsovie*, p. 286.

32. T. Bor-Komorowski, "Le Soulèvement de Varsovie," in *Résistance Européenne*, p. 289.

33. R. Cartier, *Der Zweite Weltkrieg* (German ed.), Vol. II, p. 820 et seq.; H. Michel, *Les Mouvements clandestins en Europe*.

34. *Stalin's Correspondence with Churchill, Attlee, Roosevelt and Truman, 1941–1945*, Vol. II, pp. 248 et seq., 251.

35. Ehrmann, op. cit., p. 372.

36. Ibid., p. 373; *Stalin's Correspondence*, p. 252.

37. Deakin, "Great Britain and European Resistance," p. 114; Michel, *Les Mouvements*, p. 107.

A b s c h r i f t

F e r n s c h r e i b e n

Nach nunmehr erfolgter völliger Schliessung des Kessels
werden Kommunisten zum Teil versuchen, durch die Front durchzu -
brechen.
Befehl: Kein wehrfähiger Mann verlässt den Kessel lebend.
    Frauen untersuchen, ob nicht verkleidete Männer.
                                                        Befh.d.Dt.Tr.i.Kr./Ia
                                                        Nr.2687/43 geh. vom
                                                        29. Mai 1943
Nachrichtlich: 1./ Pz.Jg.Abt. Cajnice
               8./ Art.Rgt. 369 an der Strasse Subsici
               2./ Pi. Btl.369 Gotovusa
               Komp. Sauter Boljanici
               I./Art.Rgt.369 Gotovusa
               Oberleutnant Zimmermann.   Für die Richtigkeit
                                                 der Abschrift:

                                                 Hauptmann.

Transcript of a telex message concerning the treatment of encircled Yugoslav
partisans. The text runs: "Now that the pocket has been completely sealed off,
some of the Communists will attempt to break through our lines. Order: No
able-bodied man to leave the pocket alive. Check women to see if men in disguise" (note 13 refers).

38. *Stalin's Correspondence*, p. 254 et seq.

39. Bor-Komorowski, op. cit., p. 295. According to L. Gruchmann, *Der
Zweite Weltkrieg*, p. 257, 388 out of 1,284 canisters reached their objective.
Ehrmann, op. cit., p. 376, states that the aircraft were able to drop only 30 per-
cent of their payload.

40. Bor-Komorowski, op. cit., p. 294; Gruchmann, loc. cit.

41. Wolowski, op. cit., pp. 359–64.

42. Churchill, op. cit., Vol. VI, p. 123 et seq.

43. In recognizing the Badoglio government (March 13, 1944), Stalin ignored the Allied Consultative Commission, the Italian Communist Party, and
all other political parties and Resistance movements. The statements made by
the General Secretary of the French Communist Party, acting on instructions
from Moscow, called upon local and regional liberation committees not to
usurp the place of government administrators, but to assist them in their efforts
on behalf of public order and safety. The disbanded Resistance groups obediently handed in a large proportion of their arms (see also H. Frenay, *La
Nuit finira*, Vol. II, p. 239 et seq.).

PART FOUR—**Resistance to Resistance**

1. M. Baudot, "La Résistance en France et les Alliés," in *European Resistance Movements*, p. 390.

2. F. W. Deakin, "Great Britain and European Resistance," in *European Resistance Movements*, p. 109.

3. Lieutenant Colonel Rogé, "L'Action militaire de la Résistance française sur la stratégie alliée en 1944," in *Revue de la Défense Nationale*, 1948, No. 52, p. 322 et seq.

4. Report from the senior intelligence officer of Army Group G, Southern France, ND 367, cited in H. Luther, *Der französische Widerstand gegen die deutsche Besatzungsmacht und seine Bekämpfung*, p. 85.

5. B. H. Liddell Hart, *The Defence of the West*, p. 55.

6. Wehrmacht War Diary (Wehrmacht Operations Staff), Vol. IV[1], p. 588.

7. F. Parri and F. Venturi, "The Italian Resistance and the Allies," in *European Resistance Movements*, p. xxxix.

8. S. Kjelstädli, "The Resistance Movement in Norway," in *European Resistance Movements*, p. 79 et seq.

9. S. Okecki, "La Résistance polonaise et les Alliés," in *European Resistance Movements*, pp. 423, 429 et seq.

10. H. Michel, *Les Mouvements clandestins en Europe*, p. 114.

11. T. Bor-Komorowski, "Le Soulèvement de Varsovie," in *Résistance Européenne*, p. 259 et seq.

12. H. Teske, *Die silbernen Spiegel*, p. 206.

13. E. Hesse, *Der sowjetrussische Partisanenkrieg*, p. 256.

14. Ibid., p. 193.

15. J. A. Armstrong (ed.), *Soviet Partisans in World War II*, p. 18.

16. E. M. Howell, *The Soviet Partisan Movement*, p. 73.

17. E. Boltine, "L'Union Soviétique et la Résistance en Europe," in *European Resistance Movements*, p. 47.

18. This volume compiles the results of research conducted by the following historians: John A. Armstrong, Alexander Dallin, Kurt DeWitt, Ralph Mavrogordato, Wilhelm Moll, Eric Waldmann, Gerhard L. Weinberg, and Earl Ziemke. The work of this team was directed by Philip E. Epstein and Alexander Dallin in collaboration with Philip E. Mosely, who then headed the Russian Institute of Columbia University. Subjects discussed include the organization, control, and evolution of the partisan movement; its living conditions and specific group character; its bearing on military operations and psychological warfare; its importance to the Soviet secret service; and the role played by radio- and Soviet Air Force-maintained links with its own general staff in Moscow and with Red Army commanders. About half of this large-format, 800-page volume is devoted to analytical studies and a third to case histories. The rest is reserved for reproductions of documents.

19. Armstrong, op. cit., p. 32.

20. Howell, op. cit., p. 205 et seq.

21. Ibid., p. 210.

22. Armstrong, op. cit., p. 37.

23. H. Michel, "Rapport Général," in *Résistance Européenne*, p. 8; D. Plenca, "Le Mouvement de libération nationale en Yougoslavie et les Alliés," in *European Resistance Movements*, p. 481; R. M. Kennedy, *German Antiguerrilla Operations in the Balcans*, p. 51. Stalin stated at Teheran that only eight Wehrmacht divisions were stationed in Yugoslavia (W. S. Churchill, *The Second World War*, Vol. V, p. 326).

24. Kennedy, op. cit., p. 16.

25. Ibid., p. 13.

26. Ibid., p. 38.

27. Ibid., p. 47 et seq.

28. See table on p. 326.

29. H. Michel, "Les Alliés et la Résistance en Europe," in *European Resistance Movements*, p. 608.

30. H. Luther, *Der französische Widerstand gegen die deutsche Besatzungsmacht und seine Bekämpfung*, p. 47. Luther also cites H. B. Ramcke, *Fallschirmjäger damals*, to the effect that, thanks to radio deception, the seventeen German Security Police commanders in France seized some thirty thousand submachine guns (Ramcke, op. cit., p. 145).

31. Luther, op. cit., p. 83 et seq.

32. D. Brandes, *Die Tschechen unter deutschem Protektorat*, Vol. II, pp. 70, 82.

33. O. Reile, *Geheime Westfront: Die Abwehr 1935–1945*, pp. 356–68; H. Giskes, *Spione überspielen Spione*; J. Schreieder, *Das war das Englandspiel*, München, 1950.

POSTSCRIPT

1. W. Best, "Erinnerungen aus dem besetzten Frankreich, 1940–1942," manuscript. An excerpt appears in H. Luther, *Der französische Widerstand gegen die deutsche Besatzungsmacht und seine Bekämpfung*, p. 88.

2. A. S. Milward, *The New Order and the French Economy*, p. 272.

3. A. Speer, *Inside the Third Reich*, p. 393.

4. Milward, loc. cit.

5. Those currently exploring this problem include the pacifist circle centered on the Berlin quarterly *Gewaltfreie Aktion*, directed by Theodor Ebert.

6. H. Bergwitz, *Die Partisanenrepublik Ossola*, p. 106.

General Documents

Hitler's Europe

The population of the German-occupied territories (260 million) far exceeded the total population of the Soviet Union (then approximately 170 million) and was twice that of the United States (130 million).

Dates of occupation or invasion and surrender, together with approximate populations of the occupied territories of Continental Europe, 1938–1943.

Country	I = Invasion S = Surrender O = Occupation	Approximate population in millions
1 Austria	O – Mar. 12, 1938	6.8 (precisely)
2 Czechoslovakia (Protectorate)	O – Mar. 15, 1939	10
3 Poland	I – Sept. 1, 1939 S – Nov. 6, 1939	35
4 Norway	I – Apr. 9, 1940 S – June 10, 1940	3
5 Denmark	O – Apr. 9, 1940	4
6 Holland	I – May 10, 1940 S – May 15, 1940	9
7 Belgium and Luxembourg	I – May 10, 1940 S – May 28, 1940	9
8 France	I – June 5, 1940 S – June 22, 1940	42 (after complete occupation Nov. 11, 1942)
9 Yugoslavia	I – Apr. 6, 1941 S – Apr. 17, 1941	16
10 Greece	I – Apr. 6, 1941 S – Apr. 23, 1941	8
11 Lithuania	O – June 22, 1941	3
12 Latvia	O – July 2, 1941	2
13 Estonia	O – Aug. 28, 1941	1

14	U.S.S.R. (White Russia and the Ukraine)	I – June 22, 1941	80 (all occupied areas)
15	Italy (in part)	O – Sept. 10, 1943	30 (northern and central Italy)
16	Albania	O – Sept. 10, 1943	1

| | | | 260 |

Hitler's War

The Third Reich

Less than six months after the occupation of Czechoslovakia (March 1939), German forces invade Poland (September 1, 1939).

September 1939

I. THE BLITZKRIEG VICTORIES

Within twenty-seven months, the Wehrmacht conquers and occupies almost the whole of continental Europe: *Poland* (September 1939), *Norway* (April–June 1940), *Holland, Belgium,* and *Luxembourg* (May 1940), half of *France* (June 1940), *Yugoslavia* and *Greece* (April 1941), *White Russia* and the *Ukraine* (June–November 1941). It also occupies *Denmark* (April 1940), *Lithuania* (June 1941), *Latvia* (July 1941), and *Estonia* (August 1941). Total population of the above territories: more than 220 million.

December 1941

II. HIGH-WATER MARK

The capture of *Sebastopol* and the advances to *Stalingrad* and the *Caucasus* mark the farthest limits of German military expansion.

November 1942

III. THE TIDE TURNS

The loss of *Stalingrad* signals a turning point in the war. German forces fall back everywhere: in the East, in North Africa, in Italy (Allies land July 1943). After Italy surrenders (September 1943), the Wehrmacht fights on there and in formerly Italian-occupied territory (Balkans) in the role of a hated and hard-pressed occupying power.

IV. THE FINAL PLUNGE

Hitler's grip on Western Europe is broken by the Allied landing in France (June 1944). Hitler commits suicide and Germany surrenders (May 7, 1945).

Collaboration and Resistance in the West

Hitler's policy of conquest and subjugation, coupled with the economic looting of Europe, disillusions the inhabitants of the occupied territories, most of whom are initially prepared to come to terms and collaborate. Management and labor work in harness for the Third Reich. Millions of workers volunteer for employment in Germany, but displays of *symbolic resistance* are sparked off by the exposure of Hitler's previous duplicity and by Germany's claims to absolute supremacy. Early centers of national resistance take shape. The occupying power reacts sharply, and the first French and Belgian hostages are shot in the summer of 1941.

Polemic and *defensive resistance* are triggered by the economic mobilization of Europe for total war, the universal introduction of forced labor, and coercive attempts at political streamlining. The policy of collaboration fails.

The nationwide fusion of separate Resistance groups and movements in all Western European countries is hastened by the turn of the tide and the increasing brutality of the occupying power. Evaders of forced labor (Maquis) and paramilitary combat units (secret armies) engage in guerrilla warfare against the occupying forces. *Offensive resistance,* notably sabotage and assassination, rapidly intensifies.

Paramilitary Resistance units eventually submit to *unified national control* in all the occupied countries. They disrupt German supply lines and fulfill a strategically useful security and defensive role during the final phase of the war. Like the Russian partisans, they are disbanded when fighting ceases.

Collaboration and Resistance in the East

Thanks to Hitler's war of colonialization and annihilation, as well as his policy of systematic enslavement or deportation and genocide, resistance is very soon organized and placed under unified national command. In *Poland,* a secret army and Underground shadow state come into being during 1939–40; in the *Soviet Union,* concurrently with neutral collaboration on a massive scale (a self-defensive reaction), Communist-organized partisan groups are formed during 1941–42. The Germans take frightful repressive measures. The first 170 Polish hostages are shot in December 1939, and the capture of Kiev is quickly followed by the shooting of 800 Russian hostages in a single day.

In May 1942, a new Moscow-based high command assumes responsibility for equipping Soviet partisan units and directing their operations. In June, Himmler approves a "Master Plan for the East." This provides for the deportation to Siberia of 85 percent of all Poles and 65 percent of all Ukrainians.

Russian partisans, now under centralized command, operate as Red Army auxiliaries behind the German lines, which swiftly move westward as the Wehrmacht falls back. In April 1943, the Warsaw ghetto rises in revolt. In October 1943, the Polish Government-in-exile instructs the Home Army to prosecute its operations against the occupying forces with the utmost vigor.

September 1944: the Red Army drives the last German troops from Soviet soil. The *Warsaw uprising* ends in tragedy. January 1945: Russian forces advance into Silesia. Berlin is encircled by April 24 and occupied by May 2.

Special Cases

PROTECTORATE OF BOHEMIA AND MORAVIA

Encouraged by Germany's interest in Czech arms production and a grant of sham independence from the occupying power, the Czech Government engages in tactical collaboration. This policy breaks down shortly after the outbreak of war and degenerates into total submission. Attempts at organized resistance are quelled.

DENMARK

Occupied without a fight in April 1940. Her government clings to the fiction of neutrality and maintains diplomatic relations with Berlin for three and a half years. This flexible policy of tactical collaboration does not give way to overt and organized resistance until September 1943.

YUGOSLAVIA AND GREECE

After being occupied in April 1941, both countries become the scene of ferocious guerrilla fighting between Communist and non-Communist partisans. *Tito* vainly appeals for Soviet help but is backed by the Western Powers in 1943. In Greece, British forces foil a Communist coup d'état at the end of 1944. Tito's partisans survive World War II to become sole founders of the new Yugoslavia.

ITALY

Surrenders and makes a belated entry into the war against Germany when Hitler's defeat seems probable. She is the only country to generate resistance in the form of a spontaneous anti-Fascist movement which appoints its own national leaders and adapts itself to Allied strategic planning in the latter stages of the war.

Collaboration: The Aftermath

Incomplete official statistics relating to the punishment of collaborators after the war.

In round figures, 170,000 collaborators were jailed, 11,000 sentenced to death, and 2,500 executed in five Western European countries with a combined population amounting to only one quarter of the total for all the occupied territories. These figures refer to cases tried by regular courts. Over 10,000 collaborators are estimated to have been court-martialed and shot in France alone.

	NORWAY	DENMARK	HOLLAND	BELGIUM	FRANCE	TOTAL
Death sentences	30	112	138	4,170	6,471	10,921
Executions	25	46	36	230	2,093[1]	2,430
Jail sentences	18,000[2]	14,495[3]	over 50,000	over 50,000[4]	39,000	171,495
Arrests	?	15,495	120,000	100,000	?	235,495[5]
Trials	?	?	96,044[6]	87,000	?	183,044[7]

[1] Plus approximately 10,000 court-martial sentences carried out by firing squad.
[2] 3,500 sentences of eight years and more.
[3] 3,641 sentences of four years and more.
[4] Including some 16,000 long-term sentences.
[5] This figure covers three countries only.
[6] In France, 3,035 service officers and about 5,000 civil servants were dismissed with ignominy.
[7] This figure relates to Holland and Belgium only.

Legitimate Collaboration

Radio message from the Royal Netherlands Government-in-exile to Dutch public servants working under German occupation (May 1943).

The message referred to a government decree, dated May 1937, in which Dutch administrators were directed how to behave if the country was invaded and occupied by foreign troops. It ran:

1. Military occupation notwithstanding, the state of war continues.
2. Discounting the qualifications embodied in this message, the Royal Government's directives of May 1937 remain legally valid.[1]
3. Pursuant to the Hague Conventions signed by Germany and the provisions relating to the laws and customs of warfare on land, the sovereignty and

[1] Point 9, Paragraph 3, of the 1937 directives stated, inter alia, that the occupying power was not debarred under international law from making a public servant's continuance in office dependent on whether he or she undertook not to deliberately harm the occupying power.

constitution of an occupied country remain inviolate. The Dutch Government may therefore issue instructions to its public servants even when the country itself is under foreign control. Such instructions continue to carry the force of law even when issued and promulgated by radio. All public servants are duty-bound to obey the instructions of their government. Only in exceptional circumstances is it permissible to invoke a state of emergency.

4. The legality of the instructions of 1937 cannot be revoked by any order from the occupying power.

5. Public servants must refrain from doing anything detrimental to Germany's conduct of the war, but they must also refrain from doing anything beneficial to the same. In particular, they must not permit themselves to be harnessed to the German war effort. All such demands must be rejected, for collaboration with the enemy may be undertaken only in the interests of the Dutch people, with a view to mitigating the effects of war and distributing the sacrifices that have to be made as fairly as possible among all sections of the population. The instructions of 1937 are hereby amended in that public servants may not acknowledge or fulfill any unreasonable demand but are not entitled to resign their posts in the event of a dispute unless compelled to do so by the occupying power.[2]

6. In accordance with the requirements of total war, Germany is seeking to mobilize Holland's war potential for her own purposes. All cooperation in this respect is expressly forbidden (the Dutch Premier's broadcast of February 4, 1943, refers).

7. All authorities, especially labor exchanges, are forbidden to assist in the occupying power's "labor deployment" scheme, to divulge personal particulars from the residents' directory, and to notify, assign, or supervise those liable to labor service. Where the procurement of goods and raw materials is concerned, assistance in confiscating them is likewise prohibited except where they are destined solely for the upkeep of occupation personnel. It is also forbidden to assist in the taking of hostages and to undertake military service for the occupying power or recruit others for that purpose.

8. The occupying power is obliged, under international law, to respect the laws in force, in particular the principles relating to the inviolability of personal honor, family life, and religion. The deportation of workers (whether or not as a purely punitive measure), and of Jews and other citizens, is a patent violation of the land warfare Convention. Anti-Jewish measures have no basis in law. All cooperation in this respect is forbidden.

9. During the years of occupation, the insinuation of hostile elements into government and muddled interpretations of the 1937 directives have given rise to a state of affairs which requires that public servants in occupied territory be reminded of their duties.

[2] This rule was designed to guard against the unintentional relinquishment of posts to all-out collaborators who were only too eager to insinuate themselves into positions of administrative power with the help of the German authorities.

10. Full responsibility for complying with these instructions devolves not only on the administration as such, but on the person of each individual public servant.[3]

Partisan Warfare in Yugoslavia

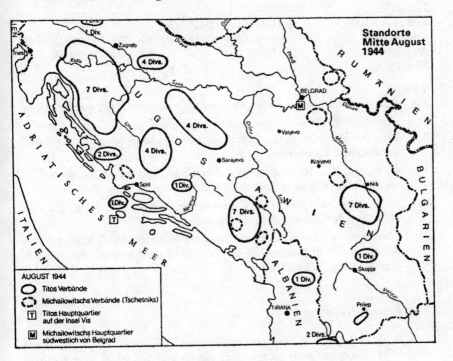

[3] Source: *Enquêtecommissie Regeringsbeleid 1940–1945. Verslag houdende de Uitkomsten van het Onderzoek*, Vol. 7A, The Hague, 1949–56, pp. 38–45.

Tito's partisans: 42 divisions totaling 120,000 men.

Chetniks: Smallish formations totaling 60–70,000 men.

TITO'S PARTISANS	GERMAN ESTIMATES	YUGOSLAV ESTIMATES	EASTERN ESTIMATES
Beginning 1942	–	–	80,000 (M)
End of 1942	–	–	150,000 (K)
Mid-1943	50,000–60,000 (KE)	–	–
End of Sept. 1943	90,000 (KE)	250,000 (B)	–
End of 1943	100,000 (KE)	300,000 (P)	300,000–320,000 (M + K)
Aug. 1944	120,000 (KE)	–	370,000–500,000 (K + M)
Mar. 1945	–	800,000 (B)	–

SOURCES:

KE   German sources cited in R. M. Kennedy, *German Antiguerrilla Operations in the Balcans.*

B   Brajusković-Dimitrye, "La Guerre de libération nationale en Yougoslavie," in *Résistance Européenne.*

P   D. Plenca, "Le Mouvement de la libération nationale en Yougoslavie et les Alliés," in *European Resistance Movements.*

M   P. Moraca, *Die Völker Jugoslawiens im Zweiten Weltkrieg,* cited by H. Kühnrich, *Partisanenkrieg in Europa.*

K   "Les Systèmes d'occupation en Yougoslavie 1941–1945." Report to the 3rd International Congress on the History of the European Resistance at Karlovy Vary, Belgrade 1963.

The French Resistance

Official Allied estimate of "mobilized and armed" Resistance fighters in France on July 11, 1944, and their geographical distribution five weeks after the Normandy landings (M = mobilized, A = armed). Personnel classified as armed possessed weapons of their own in addition to handguns.

Armed:	116,215
Unarmed:	277,255
Total:	393,470

(SOURCE: Supreme Headquarters, Allied Expeditionary Force. Reproduced in A. Guérin, *La Résistance, chronique illustré, 1930–1950.*)

Bibliography

A

Abetz, Otto. *Das offene Problem: Ein Rückblick auf zwei Jahrzehnte deutscher Frankreichpolitik.* Cologne, 1970.

Albrecht, René. "La Politique danoise au cours de la première année d'occupation," in *Revue d'Histoire de la Deuxième Guerre Mondiale,* No. 96. Paris, 1974.

Allardyce, Gilbert. "Jacques Doriot et l'esprit fasciste en France," in *Revue d'Histoire de la Deuxième Guerre Mondiale,* No. 97. Paris, 1975.

Amouroux, H. *La Vie des Français sous l'occupation.* Paris, 1961.

Arendt, Hannah. *Eichmann in Jerusalem.* New York: Viking Press, 1963.

Armstrong, John A., ed. *Soviet Partisans in World War II.* Madison, Wis., 1964.

Aron, Raymond. *Penser la guerre, Clausewitz.* Paris, 1976.

Aron, Robert. *Histoire de Vichy, 1940–1944.* Paris, 1954. *The Vichy Régime, 1941–1944* (abridged English ed.). London, 1958.

Augur (pseudonym). "Die rote Partisanenbewegung," in *Allgemeine Schweizerische Militärzeitung,* Vol. CXV, June–July 1949.

Azéma, Jean-Pierre. *La Collaboration 1940 à 1944.* Paris, 1975.

———. *Les Collaborateurs.* Paris, 1975.

B

Baeck, Leo. *We Survived.* New Haven: Yale University Press, 1949.

Bair, Deirdre. *Samuel Beckett: A Biography.* London: Cape, 1978.

Battaglia, Roberto. *Storia della Resistenza italiana.* Turin, 1953.

Baudot, Marcel. "La Résistance française et les Alliés." See *European Resistance Movements.*

———. "La Résistance française face aux problèmes de répression et d'épuration," in *Revue d'Histoire de la Deuxième Guerre Mondiale,* No. 81. Paris, 1971.

———. "Réseaux d'évasion," in *Revue d'Histoire de la Deuxième Guerre Mondiale,* No. 112. Paris, 1978.

Baudouin, Paul. *Neuf mois au gouvernement.* Paris, 1948.

Bens, Els de. "La Presse au temps de l'occupation de la Belgique (1940–1944)," in *Revue d'Histoire de la Deuxième Guerre Mondiale,* No. 80. Paris, 1970.

Bergander, Götz. "Dresden im Luftkrieg: Vorgeschichte, Zerstörung, Folgen," in *Heyne Geschichte,* Vol. XXVII. Munich, 1979.

Bergwitz, Hubertus. *Die Partisanenrepublik Ossola.* Hanover, 1972.

Bernard, Henri. *Histoire de la Résistance européenne, la "Quatrième Force" de la guerre 1939–1945.* Verviers, 1968.

———. "Les Services de renseignement belges." See *European Resistance Movements.*

Bertelsen, Aage. *October '43*, trans. by Molly Lindholm and Willy Agt. London: Museum Press, 1955.

Beumelberg, Werner. *Jahre ohne Gnade.* Oldenburg, 1952.

Billiard, Robert. *La Contrainte économique sous l'occupation (1940–1944)*. Brussels, 1946.

Billig, Joseph. *Le Commissariat français aux questions juives* (3 vols.). Paris, 1955–60.

Bindsløv, L. "La Presse danoise pendant l'occupation (1940–1945)," in *Revue d'Histoire de la Deuxième Guerre Mondiale*, No. 80. Paris, 1970.

Bleyer, W.; and Drobisch, K. "Fremdarbeiter und Kriegsgefangene als Arbeitskräfte in Deutschland," in *Bulletin des Arbeitskreises "Zweiter Weltkrieg."* East Berlin, 1970.

Bloch, Marc. *L'Étrange Défaite.* Paris, 1957.

Boberach, Heinz, ed. *Kriegspropaganda 1939–1944.* Neuwied, 1965.

Boelcke, Willi A., ed. *Kriegspropaganda 1939–1941* (secret ministerial conferences at the Reich Propaganda Ministry). Stuttgart, 1966.

Böhme, H. *Der deutsch-französische Waffenstillstand im Zweiten Weltkrieg: Entstehung und Grundlagen des Waffenstillstandes von 1940.* Stuttgart, 1966.

Boltine, E. "L'Union Soviétique et la Résistance en Europe." See *European Resistance Movements.*

Bonjour, Edgar. *Geschichte der schweizerischen Neutralität*, Vol. IX (documents). Basel, 1976.

Borchers, Jean. *Monsieur Jean: Die Geheimmission eines Deutschen.* Hanover, 1951.

Borkenau, Franz. *Der europäische Kommunismus.* Bern, 1952.

Bor-Komorowski, T. "Le Soulèvement de Varsovie." See *Résistance Européenne.*

Bouhon, General. "Le Rôle prépondérant de la Résistance dans la libération du port d'Anvers." See *Résistance Européenne.*

Bourderon, Roger. "Le Régime de Vichy était-il fasciste? Essai d'approche de la question," in *Revue d'Histoire de la Deuxième Guerre Mondiale*, No. 91. Paris, 1973.

Boveri, Margret. *Treason in the Twentieth Century*, trans. by Jonathan Steinberg. London: Macdonald & Co., 1961.

Bracher, Karl Dietrich. *The German Dictatorship: The Origins, Structure, and Effects of National Socialism*, trans. by Jean Steinberg. New York: Praeger, 1970.

———. "Zusammenbruch des Versailler Systems und Zweiter Weltkrieg," in *Propyläen Weltgeschichte*, Vol. IX, ed. by Golo Mann. Frankfurt: Alfred Heuss, 1976.

Brajusković-Dimitrye. "La Guerre de libération nationale en Yougoslavie (1941–1945)." See *Résistance Européenne.*

Brandes, Detlef. *Die Tschechen unter deutschem Protektorat.* Vol. I: *1939–1942;* Vol. II: *1942–1945.* Munich, 1969 and 1975.

Brandt, Willy. *Krieg in Norwegen.* Zurich, 1942.

Broszat, Martin. "Faschismus und Kollaboration in Ostmitteleuropa," in *Vierteljahreshefte für Zeitgeschichte*, No. 14. Stuttgart, 1966.

——. "Nationalsozialistische Konzentrationslager 1933–1945." See Buchheim et al.

Buchheim, Hans; Broszat, Martin; Krausnick, Helmut; and Jacobsen, Hans-Adolf. *Anatomie des SS-Staates*. Freiburg, 1965. *The Anatomy of the SS State*, trans. by R. H. Barry, Marian Jackson, and Dorothy Long. London: Collins, 1968.

Buchheit, Gert. *Der deutsche Geheimdienst*. Munich, 1966.

Bullock, Alan. *Hitler: A Study in Tyranny* (rev. ed.). New York: Harper & Row, 1962.

Burckhardt, Carl J. *Meine Danziger Mission 1937–1939*. Munich, 1962.

Büttin, Paul. *Le Procès Pucheu*. Paris, 1948.

Byrnes, James F. *Speaking Frankly*. New York, 1947.

C

Cadorna, Raffaele. *La Riscossa dal 25 Luglio alla Liberazione*. Milan, 1946.

Cartier, Raymond. *La Seconde Guerre Mondiale* (2 vols.). Paris, 1965. *Der Zweite Weltkrieg* (German ed.). Munich, 1967.

Céré, Roger; and Rousseau, Charles. *Chronologie du conflit mondial (1939–1945)*. Paris, 1945.

Child, Clifton J. "The Political Structure of Hitler's Europe." See Toynbee (1954).

Chilston, Viscount. "The Occupied Countries in Western Europe." See Toynbee (1954).

Christensen, Synnøve. *Ich bin eine norwegische Frau*. Zurich, 1943.

Churchill, Winston S. *The Second World War* (6 vols.). London: Cassell, 1948–54.

Ciano, Galeazzo. *Ciano's Diplomatic Papers*. London, 1948.

——. *Les Archives secrètes du comte Ciano*. Paris, 1949.

——. *The Ciano Diaries, 1939–1943*, ed. by Hugh Gibson. New York and Toronto, 1946; London, 1947.

Cluseau, D. "L'Arrestation par les Allemands du personnel du 2ᵉ Bureau français," in *Revue d'Histoire de la Deuxième Guerre Mondiale*, No. 29. Paris, 1958.

Cointet, J.-P. "Marcel Déat et le parti unique," in *Revue d'Histoire de la Deuxième Guerre Mondiale*, No. 91. Paris, 1973.

Conti, Laura. *La Resistenza in Italia 1943–1945*. Milan, 1961.

D

Dallin, Alexander. *German Rule in Russia, 1941–1945*. London and New York: Macmillan, 1957.

Dank, Milton. *The French against the French: Collaboration and Resistance*. Philadelphia and New York, 1974.

Deakin, F. W. *The Embattled Mountain*. London: Weidenfeld & Nicolson, 1971.

——. "Great Britain and European Resistance." See *European Resistance Movements*.

Dedijer, Vladimir. *Tito*. Berlin, 1953.

de Gaulle, Charles. *Mémoires de Guerre* (3 vols.). Paris, 1954 and 1959.

Delvaux, Franz. *Luxemburg im Zweiten Weltkrieg*. Luxembourg, 1946.

Dinćić, K. M. "Tito et Mihailovitch, leur conflit et ses suites," in *Revue d'Histoire de la Deuxième Guerre Mondiale*, No. 29. Paris, 1958.

Djilas, Milovan. *Wartime*, trans. by Michael B. Petrovich. London: Secker & Warburg, 1977.

Documents concerning German-Polish relations, presented by the Secretary of State for Foreign Affairs to Parliament. London, 1939.

Documents on German Foreign Policy, 1918–45, Series D, Vol. IX (March 19–June 22, 1940).

Dooijes, Dick. "Untergrunddrucke in den besetzten Niederlanden 1940 bis 1945," in *Börsenblatt des Deutschen Buchhandels* (Frankfurt ed.), No. 18, March 2, 1979.

Drobisch, Klaus (ed.). *Juden unterm Hakenkreuz: Verfolgung und Ausrottung der deutschen Juden 1933–1945*. Frankfurt, 1973.

Duff, Katherine. "Economic Relations between Germany and Italy." See Toynbee (1954).

Dulles, Allen Welsh. *Germany's Underground*. London and New York: Macmillan, 1947.

Duroselle, J.-B. *Histoire diplomatique de 1919 à nos jours*. Paris, 1974.

————. "Les Grands Alliés et la Résistance extérieure française." See *European Resistance Movements*.

E

Eckert, Rüdiger. *Die politische Struktur der dänischen Widerstandsbewegung im Zweiten Weltkrieg: Eine Untersuchung über die Bedeutung der illegalen Presse und einiger repräsentativen Vertreter der Widerstandsgruppen*. Hamburg, 1969.

Ehrmann, John. *Grand Strategy*. Vol. V: *Relations with Russia;* Vol. VI: *October 1944–August 1945*. London: HMSO, 1956.

Erickson, John. *The Soviet High Command: A Political-Military History, 1918–1941*. New York: St. Martin's Press, 1962.

Ernst, Alfred. "Die Bereitschaft und Abwehrkraft Norwegens, Dänemarks und der Schweiz in deutscher Sicht: Neutrale Kleinstaaten im Zweiten Weltkrieg," in *Schriften der Schweizerischen Vereinigung für Militärgeschichte und Militärwissenschaften*, Vol. I. Münsingen, 1973.

European Resistance Movements, 1939–45. Conference Proceedings of the Second International Conference on the History of the Resistance Movements. Oxford: Pergamon Press, 1964.

F

Falconi, Carlo. *The Silence of Pius XII*, trans. by Bernard Wall. London: Faber & Faber, 1970.

Feis, Herbert. *The Spanish Story*. New York, 1948.

Fest, Joachim. *Hitler*, trans. by Richard and Clara Winston. London: Weidenfeld & Nicolson, 1974.

Fjord, Fridtjof. *Norwegens totaler Kriegseinsatz: Vier Jahre Okkupation*. Zurich, 1944.

Foot, M. R. D. *Resistance: An Analysis of European Resistance to Nazism, 1940–1945*. London: Eyre Methuen, 1977.

————. *Six Faces of Courage*. London: Paladin, 1978.

——. *SOE in France: An Account of the Work of the British Special Operations Executive in France, 1940–1944.* London, 1966.

Fox (Baker), Annette. "The Power of Small States," in *Diplomacy in World War II.* Chicago, 1959.

Frenay, Henri. *La Nuit finira: Mémoires de Résistance 1940–1943.* Paris, 1973.

Freymond, Jean. *Le IIIᵉ Reich et la réorganisation économique de l'Europe 1940–1942: origines et projets.* Geneva, 1974.

Friedländer, Saul. *Pius XII und das Dritte Reich.* Hamburg, 1965.

Friedman, Philip. "Jewish Resistance to Nazism: Its Various Forms and Aspects." See *Résistance Européenne.*

Fuller, J. F. *The Second World War.* London: Eyre and Spottiswoode, 1948.

Funk, A. *Charles de Gaulle: The Crucial Years.* Norman: University of Oklahoma Press, 1959.

Fyodorov, A. *Das Gebietskomitee arbeitet.* Berlin, 1959.

G

Garlinski, Józef. *Fighting Auschwitz. The Resistance Movement in the Concentration Camp.* London: Julian Friedmann, 1975.

Georges, Colonel (Robert Noireau). *Le Temps des partisans.* Paris, 1978.

Gérard, Ivan. "Aperçu sur le rôle de la Résistance militaire en Belgique." See *Résistance Européenne.*

Gide, André. *Journal 1939–1942.* Paris, 1946.

Gisevius, Hans Bernd. *Adolf Hitler.* Droemer Knaur, 1967.

Giskes, Hermann. *Spione überspielen Spione.* Hamburg, 1959.

Goebbels, J. *The Goebbels Diaries,* trans. and ed. by Louis P. Lochner. London: Hamish Hamilton, 1948.

Goldberger, N. "La Résistance en Roumanie et les Alliés." See *European Resistance Movements.*

——. "Les Alliés et la Résistance tchécoslovaque." See *European Resistance Movements.*

Gordon, Bertram. "Un Soldat du fascisme: l'évolution politique de Joseph Darnand," in *Revue d'Histoire de la Deuxième Guerre Mondiale,* No. 108. Paris, 1977.

Gosztony, Peter. "Der 9. September 1944: Eine Studie zur Frage der Neutralität und Wehrbereitschaft am Beispiel der Septemberereignisse 1944 in Bulgarien," in *Schriften der Schweizerischen Vereinigung für Militärgeschichte und Militärwissenschaften,* No. 1. Münsingen, 1973.

Graml, Hermann. "Europa zwischen den Kriegen," in *Weltgeschichte des 20. Jahrhunderts.* Munich: Deutscher Taschenbuchverlag, 1969.

Granet, Marie. "La Presse clandestine en France." See *Résistance Européenne.*

Griffiths, Richard. *Marshal Pétain.* London: Constable, 1970.

Grossman, S. "L'Évolution de Marcel Déat," in *Revue d'Histoire de la Deuxième Guerre Mondiale,* No. 97. Paris, 1975.

Groussard, Colonel. *Chemins secrets.* Paris, 1948.

Groussard, Georges A. *Service secret, 1940–1945.* Paris, 1964.

Gruchmann, Lothar. *Der Zweite Weltkrieg.* Munich: Deutscher Taschenbuchverlag, 1975.

Gudme, Sten. *Denmark: Hitler's Model Protectorate.* London, 1942.

Guérin, Alain. *La Résistance, chronique illustré, 1930–1950*. Paris, 1976.

Gustmann, Kurt. *Die schwedische Tagespresse zur Neutralitätsfrage im Zweiten Weltkrieg*. Münster, 1958.

Gutt, Camille. *La Belgique au carrefour 1940–1944*. Paris, 1971.

H

Haestrup, Jørgen. "Denmark's Connection with the Allied Powers during the Occupation." See *European Resistance Movements*.

——. *Europe Ablaze. An Analysis of the History of the European Resistance Movements, 1939–1945*. Odense University Press, 1978.

——. *Le Mouvement de la Résistance danoise, 1940–1945*. Copenhagen, 1970.

Haffner, Sebastian. *Anmerkungen zu Hitler*. Munich, 1978.

Hagglöf, Gunnar. *Diplomat: Memoirs of a Swedish Envoy*. London: Bodley Head, 1972.

Halder, Franz. *Kriegstagebuch 1939–1942* (3 vols.), ed. by H.-A. Jacobsen. Stuttgart, 1962–64.

Hambro, Carl J. *I Saw It Happen in Norway*. London, 1940.

Harris, C. R. S. *The Allied Military Administration of Italy, 1943–1945*. London: HMSO, 1958.

Hart, B. H. Liddell. *The Defense of the West*. London, 1950.

Harvey, Patricia. "The Economic Structure of Hitler's Europe." See Toynbee (1954).

Hassell, Ulrich von. *The Von Hassell Diaries, 1938–44*. London, 1948.

Hausner, Gideon. *Die Vernichtung der Juden: Das grösste Verbrechen der Geschichte*. Munich, 1979.

Hawes, Stephen; and White, Ralph (eds.) *Resistance in Europe 1939–1945*. London: Penguin Books.

Hayes, Paul M. *Quisling: The Career and Political Ideas of Vidkun Quisling, 1887–1945*. Newton Abbot: David and Charles, 1971.

Hedtoft, Hans. Foreword to Bertelsen, Aage, *October '43* (q.v.).

Heiber, Helmut (ed.). *Lagebesprechungen im Führerhauptquartier* (records of Hitler's military conferences, 1942–45). Munich: Deutscher Taschenbuchverlag, 1963.

Henderson, Sir Nevile. *Failure of a Mission: Berlin 1937–1939*. London and New York, 1940.

Herdeg, W. *Grundzüge der Besatzungsverwaltung in den west- und nordeuropäischen Ländern*. Tübingen, 1953.

Hesse, Erich. *Der sowjetrussische Partisanenkrieg 1941–1944*. Göttingen, 1969.

Hicks, Agnes H. "Neutrals and Nonbelligerent Allies." See Toynbee (1956).

Hillgruber, Andreas (ed.). *Staatsmänner und Diplomaten bei Hitler* (confidential notes on discussions with foreign representatives, 1939–41). Munich: Deutscher Taschenbuchverlag, 1969.

Hitler, Adolf. *Hitler's Mein Kampf*, trans. by Ralph Manheim. London: Hutchinson, 1969.

Hitlers Tischgespräche im Führerhauptquartier 1941–1942. Stuttgart, 1965. *Hitler's Table Talk* (2nd ed.), trans. by Norman Cameron and R. H. Stevens, introduced and with a new preface by H. R. Trevor-Roper. London: Weidenfeld and Nicolson, 1973.

Hofer, Walther (ed.). *Der Nationalsozialismus: Dokumente 1933 bis 1945.* Frankfurt, 1957.

Hoffmann, Stanley. "Aspects du régime de Vichy," in *Revue Française de Science Politique,* Vol. VI, No. 1. Paris, 1956.

——. "Vichy devant l'histoire: collaborateurs et 'collaborationnistes,'" in *Preuves,* No. 220. Paris, 1967.

Höhne, Heinz. *Canaris,* trans. by J. Maxwell Brownjohn. London: Secker & Warburg; Garden City, N.Y.: Doubleday, 1979.

Homze, Edward L. *Foreign Labor in Nazi Germany.* Princeton, 1967.

Hoop, Jean-Marie d'. "La Main-d'oeuvre française au service de l'Allemagne," in *Revue d'Histoire de la Deuxième Guerre Mondiale,* No. 81. Paris, 1971.

Höss, Rudolf. *Kommandant in Auschwitz,* ed. by Martin Broszat. Stuttgart, 1958. *Commandant of Auschwitz.* London, 1959; New York, 1960.

Hostache, René. *Le Conseil national de la Résistance.* Paris, 1958.

Howell, Edgar M. *The Soviet Partisan Movement, 1941–1944.* Department of the Army Pamphlet 20–244. Washington, 1956.

Hubatsch, Walther (ed.). *Hitlers Weisungen für die Kriegführung.* Munich: Deutscher Taschenbuchverlag, 1965.

——. *Unruhe im Norden: Studien zur deutsch-skandinavischen Geschichte.* Göttingen, 1956.

Hutton, Clayton. *Official Secret.* London, 1960.

I

Italiaander, Rolf (ed.). *Diktatoren im Nacken.* Munich, 1971.

J

Jäckel, Eberhard. *Die deutsche Frankreichpolitik im Zweiten Weltkrieg.* Stuttgart, 1966.

Jacobmeyer, Wolfgang. *Heimat und Exil: Die Anfänge der polnischen Untergrundbewegung im Zweiten Weltkrieg.* Hamburg, 1973.

Jacobsen, Hans-Adolf. "Nationalsozialistische Konzentrationslager 1933–1945." See Buchheim et al.

——; and Rohwer, Jürgen (eds.). *Entscheidungsschlachten des Zweiten Weltkrieges.* Frankfurt, 1960.

Jacomet, A. "Les Chefs du francisme: Marcel Bucard et Paul Guiraud," in *Revue d'Histoire de la Deuxième Guerre Mondiale,* No. 97. Paris, 1975.

Jong, Louis de. "Anti-Nazi Resistance in the Netherlands." See *Résistance Européenne.*

——. "Les Pays-Bas dans la seconde guerre mondiale," in *Revue d'Histoire de la Deuxième Guerre Mondiale,* No. 50. Paris, 1963.

——. "The Dutch Resistance Movement and the Allies (1940–1945)." See *European Resistance Movements.*

——. "Zwischen Kollaboration und Résistance," in Hillgruber (ed.), *Probleme des Zweiten Weltkrieges.* Cologne, 1967.

K

Karol, K. S. *Polen zwischen Ost und West.* Hamburg, 1962.

Kennedy, Robert M. *German Antiguerrilla Operations in the Balcans.* Washington, 1954.

Kesselring, Albert. *Soldat bis zum letzten Tag.* Bonn, 1953. *The Memoirs of Field Marshal Kesselring,* trans. by Lynton Hudson. London: William Kimber, 1953 (repr. 1974).

Kistenmacher, H. *Die Auswirkungen der deutschen Besetzung auf die Ernährungswirtschaft Frankreichs während des Zweiten Weltkrieges.* Tübingen, 1959.

Kjelstädli, S. "The Resistance Movement in Norway and the Allies, 1940–1945." See *European Resistance Movements.*

Kleffens, E. N. van. *Der Einfall in die Niederlande.* Zurich, 1941.

Klemm, Peter F. "La Production aéronautique française de 1940 à 1942," in *Revue d'Histoire de la Deuxième Guerre Mondiale,* No. 107. Paris, 1977.

Klessmann, Christoph. *Die Selbstbehauptung einer Nation: NS-Kulturpolitik und polnische Widerstandsbewegung.* Düsseldorf, 1971.

Klöss, Erhard (ed.). *Reden des Führers: Politik und Propaganda Adolf Hitlers, 1922–1945.* Munich: Deutscher Taschenbuchverlag, 1967.

Koch, Henri. *Sie boten Trotz, 1939–1945: Luxemburger im Freiheitskampf.* Luxembourg, 1974.

Kock, Erich. *Unterdrückung und Widerstand: 5 Jahre deutscher Besetzung in den Niederlanden 1940–1945.* Dortmund, 1960.

Kogan, Norman. "American Policies Towards European Resistance Movements." See *European Resistance Movements.*
———. *Italy and the Allies.* Cambridge, 1956.

Kogon, Eugen. *Der SS-Staat: Das System der deutschen Konzentrationslager.* Munich, 1974. *The Theory and Practice of Hell,* trans. by Heinz Norden. London: Secker & Warburg, 1950.

Koht, Halvdan. *Norway, Neutral and Invaded.* London: Hutchinson, 1941.

Kordt, Erich. *Nicht aus den Akten.* Stuttgart, 1950.

Kraus, Ota; and Kulka, Erich. *The Death Factory.* Oxford: Pergamon Press, 1966.

Kühnrich, Heinz. *Der Partisanenkrieg in Europa.* Berlin, 1965.

Kwiet, Konrad. *Reichskommissariat Niederlande.* Stuttgart, 1968.
———. "Zur Geschichte der Mussertbewegung," in *Vierteljahreshefte für Zeitgeschichte,* April 1970.

L

Lampe, David. *The Savage Canary: The Story of Resistance in Denmark.* London: Cassell, 1957; Corgi, 1976.

Langer, William L. *Our Vichy Gamble.* New York, 1947; Hamden, Conn.: Archon, 1965.

La Ruche, François. *La Neutralité de la Suède: dix années d'un politique, 1939–1949.* Paris, 1953.

Laval, Pierre. *Laval parle: notes et mémoires.* Geneva, 1947.

Leahy, William. *I Was There.* London: Gollancz, 1950.

Leeuw, Van der, "La Presse néerlandaise sous l'occupation allemande," in *Revue d'Histoire de la Deuxième Guerre Mondiale,* No. 80. Paris, 1970.

Legnani, Massimo. "La Société italienne et la Résistance," in *Revue d'Histoire de la Deuxième Guerre Mondiale,* No. 92. Paris, 1973.

Lettres secrètes échangées de janvier 1940 à mai 1943 par Hitler et Mussolini. Paris, 1946.

Lévy, Claude. "La Presse de collaboration en France occupée: conditions d'existence," in *Revue d'Histoire de la Deuxième Guerre Mondiale,* No. 80. Paris, 1970.

——. *Les Nouveaux Temps et l'idéologie de la collaboration.* Paris, 1974.

Lichten, H. E. (alias Riesser, Hans). *Collaboration, Phantom und Wirklichkeit.* Zurich, 1948.

Lichtenstein, Heiner; and Spiess, Alfred. *Das Unternehmen Tannenberg: Der Anlass zum Zweiten Weltkrieg.* Wiesbaden and Munich, 1979.

Littlejohn, David. *The Patriotic Traitors. A History of Collaboration in German-Occupied Europe, 1940–1945.* London, 1972.

Loock, Hans-Dietrich. "Zur 'Grossgermanischen Politik' des Dritten Reiches," in *Vierteljahreshefte für Zeitgeschichte,* No. 1, 1960.

Lovinfosse, Georges. "La Résistance belge et les Alliés." See *European Resistance Movements.*

Lowery, Sidney. "The Occupied and Satellite Countries in Eastern Europe." See Toynbee (1954).

Ludwig, Carl. *Die Flüchtlingspolitik der Schweiz seit 1933 bis zur Gegenwart (1957).* Bern, 1966.

Luther, Hans. *Der französische Widerstand gegen die deutsche Besatzungsmacht und seine Bekämpfung.* Tübingen, 1957.

Lüthy, Herbert. *Bis zur Neige: Epilog des Zweiten Weltkrieges 1944/45.* St. Gallen, 1945.

——. "De Gaulle–Frankreich persönlich?" in *Der Monat,* No. 98. Berlin, 1956.

——. *Frankreichs Uhren gehen anders.* Zurich, 1954.

——. *Fünf Minuten vor 12: Feldzüge und Konferenzen von Stalingrad bis Teheran.* St. Gallen, 1944.

——. *Nach dem Untergang des Abendlandes. Zeitkritische Essays.* Cologne, 1965.

M

Macksey, Kenneth. *The Partisans of Europe in World War II.* London: Hart-Davis MacGibbon, 1975.

Marjanović, Jovan. *La Courte Guerre d'avril, Bombardovanje Beograda u drugom svetskom ratu* (The Bombardment of Belgrade in World War II). Belgrade, 1975.

Medlicott, W. N. "De Munich à Prague," in *Revue d'Histoire de la Deuxième Guerre Mondiale,* No. 13. Paris, 1954.

——. *The Economic Blockade* (2 vols.). London: HMSO, 1952 and 1959.

Merglen, Albert. "Les Chars tchèques dans l'armée d'Hitler," in *Revue Historique de l'Armée,* No. 2. Paris, 1965.

——. "Soldats français sous uniformes allemands, 1941–1945: LVF et 'Waffen-SS' français," in *Revue d'Histoire de la Deuxième Guerre Mondiale,* No. 108. Paris, 1977.

Mez, Lutz. "Der Widerstand gegen die Zwangsmobilisierung in Norwegen

1943/44," in *Gewaltfreie Aktion, Vierteljahreshefte für Frieden und Gerechtigkeit,* Yr. 3, Nos. 9–10. Berlin, 1971.

Michel, Henri. *Histoire de la France libre.* Paris, 1972.

——. *Histoire de la Résistance en France, 1940–1944.* Paris, 1975.

——. *La Guerre de l'ombre: La Résistance en Europe.* Paris, 1970.

——. "La Révolution nationale. Latitude d'action du gouvernement de Vichy," in *Revue d'Histoire de la Deuxième Guerre Mondiale,* No. 81. Paris, 1971.

——. "Les Alliés et la Résistance en Europe." See *European Resistance Movements.*

——. *Les Courants de pensée de la Résistance.* Paris, 1962.

——. *Les Mouvements clandestins en Europe 1938–1945.* Paris, 1974.

——. "Rapport Générale à la Première Conférence Internationale sur l'Histoire de la Résistance à Liège." See *Résistance Européenne.*

——. *Vichy, année 1940.* Paris, 1966.

Miller, Marshall Lee. *Bulgaria during the Second World War.* Stanford, 1975.

Milward, Alan S. "Hitlers Konzept des Blitzkrieges," in Hillgruber (ed.), *Probleme des Zweiten Weltkrieges.* Cologne, 1967.

——. *The German Economy at War.* London, 1965.

——. *The New Order and the French Economy.* Oxford: Clarendon Press, 1970.

——. *War, Economy and Society, 1939–1945.* London: Allen Lane, 1977.

Mosse, Georg. *Internationaler Faschismus 1920–1945.* Munich, 1966.

Mucs, Ferencs. "Quelques aspects de la Résistance armée en Hongrie contre le fascisme." See *European Resistance Movements.*

Müller, Hans (ed.). *Katholische Kirche und Nationalsozialismus.* Munich: Deutscher Taschenbuchverlag, 1965.

N

Neubacher, H. *Sonderauftrag Südost 1940–1945: Bericht eines fliegenden Diplomaten.* Göttingen, 1956.

Noguères, Henri. *Histoire de la Résistance en France de 1940 à 1945* (4 vols.). Paris, 1967–73.

Nolte, Ernst. *Der Faschismus in seiner Epoche.* Munich, 1963.

——. *Die faschistischen Bewegungen: Die Krise des liberalen Systems und die Entwicklung der Faschismen.* Munich: Deutscher Taschenbuchverlag, 1966.

——. "Ebenen des Krieges und Stufen des Widerstandes," in Hillgruber (ed.), *Probleme des Zweiten Weltkrieges.* Cologne, 1967.

O

Okecki, S. "La Résistance polonaise et les Alliés." See *European Resistance Movements.*

Ory, Pascal. *Les Collaborateurs.* Paris, 1977.

P

Paape, A. H. "Le Mouvement national-socialiste en Hollande," in *Revue d'Histoire de la Deuxième Guerre Mondiale,* No. 66. Paris, 1967.

Parri, F.; and Venturi, F. "The Italian Resistance and the Allies." See *European Resistance Movements.*

Pascal, Pierre. "Ce que fut en Russie la guerre des partisans," in *Preuves,* No. 50. Paris, 1955.

Passerin D'Entreves, Alessandro and Ettore. "Federico Chabod e la Valle d'Aosta," in *Rivista Storica Italiana*, Vol. LXXII, No. IV.

Paxton, Robert. *Vichy France: Old Guard and New Order*. London: Barrie & Jenkins, 1972.

Pijade, Moša. *La Fable de l'aide soviétique à l'insurrection nationale yougoslave*. Paris, 1950.

Pinér, I. "Le Rôle joué par les Communistes dans le mouvement hongrois de Résistance." See *European Resistance Movements*.

Plenca, Dušan. "Le Mouvement de libération nationale en Yougoslavie et les Alliés." See *European Resistance Movements*.

Poch, Ulrich. "Anpassungspolitik ohne Kollaboration. Der dänische Widerstand von 1940 bis 1943," in *Ziviler Widerstand, Fallstudien aus der innenpolitischen Friedens- und Konfliktforschung*, ed. by Theodor Ebert. Düsseldorf, 1970.

Pyromaglou, C. "La Résistance grecque et les Alliés." See *European Resistance Movements*.

R

Ramcke, H. B. *Fallschirmjäger damals*. Frankfurt, 1951.

Rauschning, Hermann. *Die Revolution des Nihilismus: Kulisse und Wirklichkeit im Dritten Reich*. Zurich, 1938. *The Revolution of Nihilism*. London and New York, 1939 (U.K. title: *Germany's Revolution of Destruction*).

———. *Hitler Speaks*. London: Thornton Butterworth, 1939 (U.S. title: *Voice of Destruction*).

Redelis, Valdis. *Partisanenkrieg: Entstehung und Bekämpfung der Partisanen- und Untergrundbewegung im Mittelabschnitt der Ostfront, 1941–1943*. Heidelberg, 1958.

Reich, Wilhelm. *Die Massenpsychologie des Faschismus*. Cologne and Zurich, 1971.

Reile, Oscar. *Geheime Westfront: Die Abwehr 1935–1945*. Munich, 1962.

Reitlinger, Gerald. *The Final Solution*. London: Vallentine, Mitchell, 1953; Sphere Books, 1971.

Renzo, Felice de. *Le Interpretazioni del fascismo*. Bari, 1974.

Résistance Européenne, La. Proceedings of the First International Conference on the History of the Resistance Movements: European Resistance Movements, 1939–1945. Oxford: Pergamon Press, 1960.

Richard, Lionel. "Drieu La Rochelle et la Nouvelle Revue Française des années noires," in *Revue d'Histoire de la Deuxième Guerre Mondiale*, No. 97. Paris, 1975.

Riesser, Hans (alias Lichten, H. E.). *Collaboration, Phantom und Wirklichkeit*. Zurich, 1948.

Ringelblum, Emanuel. *Ghetto Warschau: Tagebücher aus dem Chaos*. Stuttgart, 1967.

Rings, Werner. *Advokaten des Feindes: Das Abenteuer der politischen Neutralität*. Vienna and Düsseldorf, 1966.

———. *Schweiz im Krieg 1933–1945*. Zurich, 1974.

Riste, Olav; and Nøklby, Berit. *Norway 1940–1945: The Resistance Movement*. Oslo, 1970.

Robinson, Jacob. "Jüdische 'Kooperation,'" in *Die Kontroverse: Hannah Arendt, Eichmann und die Juden*. Munich, 1964.

Roos, Hans. "Deutschland, Polen und die Sowjetunion im Zweiten Weltkrieg," in Hillgruber (ed.), *Probleme des Zweiten Weltkrieges*. Cologne, 1967.

Rossi, Angelo. *Autopsie du Stalinisme* (avec le texte intégral du Rapport Krouchtchev). Paris, 1957.

——. *Les Communistes français pendant la drôle de guerre*. Paris, 1951.

——. *Physiologie du parti communiste français*. Paris, 1948.

Rougemont, Denis de. *Journal d'un époque (1926–1946)*. Paris, 1968.

Rustow, Dankwart A. *The Politics of Compromise*. Princeton, 1955.

Rutkowski, Adam (ed.). *Lutte des juifs en France à l'époque de l'occupation (1940–1944)*. Paris, 1975.

S

Salis, J. R. von. *Weltgeschichte der neuesten Zeit*. Vol. III: *Von Versailles bis Hiroshima, 1919–1945*. Zurich, 1962.

Schmidt, Paul. *Als Statist auf diplomatischer Bühne*. Bonn, 1949. *Hitler's Interpreter*. New York and London, 1951.

Schramm, Percy E. *Hitler als militärischer Führer*. Frankfurt, 1962.

Schreieder, Josef. *Das war das Englandspiel*. Munich, 1950.

Schroers, Rolf. *Der Partisan: Ein Beitrag zur politischen Anthropologie*. Cologne and Berlin, 1961.

Secchia, Pietro; and Frassati, Filippo. *La Resistenza e gli Alleati*. Milan, 1962.

Seidmann, Peter. *Der Mensch im Widerstand: Studien zur anthropologischen Psychologie*. Bern, 1974.

Sérant, Paul. *Les Vaincus de la libération: l'épuration en Europe occidentale à la fin de la Seconde Guerre Mondiale*. Paris, 1964.

Seraphim, Hans-Günther (ed.). *Das politische Tagebuch Alfred Rosenbergs aus den Jahren 1934–35 und 1939–40*. Munich: Deutscher Taschenbuchverlag, 1964.

Serrigny, General. *Trente ans avec Pétain*. Paris, 1959.

Sharp, Gene. "Die Technik der gewaltlosen Aktion," in *Gewaltloser Widerstand gegen Aggressoren: Probleme, Beispiele, Strategien*, ed. by Adam Roberts. Göttingen, 1971.

Shirer, William L. *The Challenge of Scandinavia*. London: Robert Hale, 1956.

——. *The Rise and Fall of the Third Reich*. London: Secker & Warburg, 1960.

Sicard, M. Y. *Histoire de la collaboration*. Paris, 1964.

Skodvin, M. "La Presse norvégienne sous l'occupation allemande," in *Revue d'Histoire de la Deuxième Guerre Mondiale*, No. 80. Paris, 1970.

Skottsberg Ahman, Brita. *Scandinavian Foreign Policy, Past and Present*. Ithaca and New York, 1950.

Smith, Patrick. *A Desk in Rome*. London: Collins, 1974.

Soucy, R. "Le Fascisme de Drieu La Rochelle," in *Revue d'Histoire de la Deuxième Guerre Mondiale*, No. 66. Paris, 1967.

Spaak, Paul-Henri. *The Continuing Battle: Memoirs of a European*. London: Weidenfeld and Nicolson, 1971.

Speer, Albert. *Inside the Third Reich*, trans. by Richard and Clara Winston. London: Weidenfeld and Nicolson, 1970.

Sperber, Manès. *Bis man mir Scherben auf die Augen legt: All das vergangene . . .* Vienna, 1977.

——. "Churban oder die unfassbare Gewissheit," in *Die Kontroverse: Hannah Arendt, Eichmann und die Juden.* Munich, 1964.

——. *Zur täglichen Weltgeschichte* (essays). Cologne, 1967.

Stalin's Correspondence with Churchill, Attlee, Roosevelt and Truman. London, 1958.

Staub, Hans. *De Gaulle.* Lucerne, 1966.

Steiner, Jean-François. *Treblinka: Die Revolte eines Vernichtungslagers.* Geneva.

Stettinius, Edward R. *Yalta, Roosevelt and the Russians.* Garden City, N.Y.: Doubleday, 1949.

Stevenson, William. *A Man Called Intrepid: The Secret War, 1939–1945.* London and New York: Macmillan, 1976.

Stimson, Henry L.; and Bundy, McGeorge. *On Active Service in Peace and War.* London and New York: Hutchinson, 1947.

Streit, Christian. *Keine Kameraden: Die Wehrmacht und die sowjetischen Kriegsgefangenen, 1941–1945.* Stuttgart, 1978.

——. "Sur la Résistance non communiste en Slovaquie: compte rendu," in *Revue d'Histoire de la Deuxième Guerre Mondiale,* No. 88. Paris, 1972.

T

Teske, Hermann. *Die silbernen Spiegel: Generalstabsdienst unter der Lupe.* Heidelberg, 1952.

Thayer, C. W. *Hands across the Caviar.* Philadelphia, 1952.

Thomsen, Erich. *Deutsche Besatzungspolitik in Dänemark, 1940–1945.* Düsseldorf, 1971.

Thorwald, Jürgen. *Wen sie verderben wollen.* Stuttgart, 1952.

Toynbee, Arnold J.; and Toynbee, Veronica M. (eds.). "Hitler's Europe," *Survey of International Affairs.* London, 1954.

——. "The War and the Neutrals," *Survey of International Affairs.* London, 1956.

Treue, Wilhelm. "Hitlers Denkschrift zum Vierjahresplan 1936," in *Vierteljahreshefte für Zeitgeschichte,* No. 3. Stuttgart, 1955.

Trunk, Isaiah. *Judenrat.* New York, 1978.

U

Ulshöfer, O. *Einflussnahme auf Wirtschaftsunternehmen in den besetzten west- und südosteuropäischen Ländern.* Tübingen, 1958.

V

Vaccarino, M. G. "La Résistance au fascisme en Italie de 1923 à 1945." See *Résistance Européenne.*

Valiani, Leo. *Dall' antifascismo alla resistenza.* Milan, 1959.

Veld, N. K. C. A. in't. "Cinq lettres de Rauter à Himmler," in *Revue d'Histoire de la Deuxième Guerre Mondiale,* No. 50. Paris, 1963.

Vienot, Pierre. Remarks recorded by Jacques Kaiser, *Le Monde,* No. 9141, June 6, 1974.

Vigneras, Marcel. *Rearming the French.* Washington, 1957.

W

Warlimont, Walter. *Im Hauptquartier der deutschen Wehrmacht 1939–1945.* Frankfurt, 1962. *Inside Hitler's Headquarters, 1939–45,* trans. by R. H. Barry. London: Weidenfeld and Nicolson, 1964.

Warmbrunn, Werner. *The Dutch under German Occupation 1940–1945.* Stanford and Oxford, 1963.

Willequet, Jacques. "Les Fascismes belges et la Seconde Guerre Mondiale," in *Revue d'Histoire de la Deuxième Guerre Mondiale,* No. 66. Paris, 1967.

Wiskemann, Elizabeth. *The Europe I Saw.* London: Collins, 1968.

———. "The Italian Resistance Movement." See Toynbee (1954).

Wolf, Dieter. *Die Doriot-Bewegung: Ein Beitrag zur Geschichte des französischen Faschismus.* Ştuttgart, 1967.

Wolfers, Arnold. *Britain and France Between Two Wars: Conflicting Strategies of Peace since Versailles.* New York, 1940.

Wolowski, Alexandre. *La Vie quotidienne à Varsovie sous l'occupation nazie.* Paris, 1977.

Woodhouse, C. M. *Apple of Discord.* London, 1948.

———. "The Greek Resistance." See *Résistance Européenne.*

Wright, Gordon. "Reflections on the French Resistance," in *Political Science Quarterly,* No. 3, 1962.

Wulf, Joseph. *Presse und Funk im Dritten Reich.* Rororo, 1966.

Z

Zentner, Kurt. *Illustrierte Geschichte des Widerstandes in Deutschland und in Europa, 1933–1945.* Munich, 1966.

Ziemke, Earl. *Soviet Partisans in World War II.* Madison, Wis., 1964.

Zimmermann, Karl. *Die geistigen Grundlagen des Nationalsozialismus.* Leipzig, 1933.

Index of Place Names

Index of Personal Names